The Psychology of Ethnic and Cultural Conflict

The Psychology of Ethnic and Cultural Conflict

Edited by Yueh-Ting Lee, Clark McCauley,
Fathali Moghaddam, and Stephen Worchel

Psychological Dimensions to War and Peace
Harvey Langholtz, Series Editor

Westport, Connecticut
London

MT

Library of Congress Cataloging-in-Publication Data

The psychology of ethnic and cultural conflict / edited by Yueh-Ting Lee . . . [et al.].
    p. cm.—(Psychological dimensions to war and peace, ISSN 1540–5265)
Includes bibliographical references and index.
    ISBN 0–275–97983–0 (alk. paper)
    1. Ethnopsychology. 2. Ethnic conflict. 3. Culture conflict. 4. Violence. I. Lee,
Yueh-Ting. II. Series.
GN502.P79   2004
155.88—dc21   2003044225

British Library Cataloguing in Publication Data is available.

Library of Congress Catalog Card Number: 2003044225
ISBN: 0–275–97983–0
ISSN: 1540–5265

First published in 2004

Praeger Publishers, 88 Post Road West, Westport, CT 06881
An imprint of Greenwood Publishing Group, Inc.
www.praeger.com

Printed in the United States of America

The paper used in this book complies with the
Permanent Paper Standard issued by the National
Information Standards Organization (Z39.48–1984).

10 9 8 7 6 5 4 3 2 1

6/11/04

Contents

Series Foreword

With the close of the cold war and the turning of the millennium a decade later, it seemed humanity could hope for an end to the frequency and level of conflict as it existed during the bloodiest century in history. Superpower rivalry was over and it appeared the powerful civilized nations had found ways to settled their differences without making war on each other. Globalization, cable television, the Internet, and ease of travel showed us that cultural and ethnic diversity were things of beauty and richness to be respected and enjoyed.

But on the morning of September 11, 2001, it suddenly became starkly clear that although the nations of the world might not be in conflict with each other, some of the peoples of the world were. The decision to attack the United States was not made by a head of state and was not carried out by an army of an enemy nation. This was a conflict that was defined not along traditional lines of international borders, politics, and alliances, but along ethnic, cultural, religious, and ideological lines. The world was a battlefield, we lived on it, and there would be no protection offered to innocent civilian life.

Perhaps it was naïve of us to have ignored the evidence that there had been conflicts going on all around us that had not been defined by national borders. The 1990s had seen ethnically based genocide in Rwanda, ethnic cleansing and the violent division of the former Yugoslavia along religious and ethnic lines, the bombing of U.S. embassies in Kenya and Tanzania, the U.S.S. *Cole*, Oklahoma City, the gas attack on the Tokyo subway, and of course the first attack on the World Trade Center in 1993. The Catholic-Protestant conflict in Northern Ireland seemed to be slowly moving toward peace but the hopes for any resolution of the Israeli-Palestinian conflict would prove to be elusive. Of grave concern was the nuclear standoff between predominantly Hindu India and predominantly Moslem Pakistan. These conflicts and incidents were all rooted in what were fundamentally ethnic and cultural clashes.

So it is certainly timely that Lee, McCauley, Moghaddam, Worchel, and 23 other contributing authors representing seven nations should now explore the topic through *The Psychology of Ethnic and Cultural Conflict*. In the 16 chapters that follow, these psychologists, anthropologists, sociologists, educators, political scientists, practitioners, and specialists in ethnic studies have examined culture and ethnicity as a basis for conflict. This book constitutes neither a condemnation nor a defense of any ethnic or cultural group. Rather, it is an objective and scientific examination of the topic. The reader will see where some differing ethnic and cultural groups live together in harmony, whereas others live in seemingly perpetual conflict. Through examples from Bulgaria, China, Estonia, Hawaii, India, Iran, Israel, Latvia, Lithuania, New Zealand, Northern Ireland, Oklahoma, Pakistan, Palestine, Russia, Rwanda, South Africa, and Texas, the authors will seek to uncover some of the differentiating features and characteristics that will lead to these varying outcomes. Through both original empirical research and the comparison of the writings as different as those of Freud, Hardin, Sherif, Stalin, Tversky, and Kahneman, the authors provide a thorough and fair view of the topic.

Is there some hope that the contact hypothesis may be valid in its prediction that through contact and interpersonal exposure, people of differing ethnic and cultural groups may come to know, appreciate, and respect each other? Or will we eventually come to accept Worchel's assertion in chapter 15 that "The seeds of ethnic conflict are always present in the soil of the human landscape"? The authors of this book have explored these questions. Perhaps as history continues to reveal itself over the next few years, we may begin to better understand the psychology of ethnic and cultural conflict.

Harvey Langholtz
Williamsburg, Virginia

Preface

Today there are over six billion people in the world. They have different physical appearances, ethnic and cultural beliefs, values, and behavioral patterns. It does not matter whether we are black, white, yellow, brown, or red. Neither does it matter whether we are American, Mexican, Brazilian, French, Irish, Israeli, Croatian, African, Indian, or Chinese. Neither does it matter whether we are Christian, Jewish, Muslim, Buddhist, or atheist. After all, we are human beings. Our human nature is pretty much the same. As Confucius put it, "People are similar by nature, but through habituation become quite different from each other." Whether we are peaceful or violent toward each other depends in large part on whether we can understand and appreciate cultural and ethnic differences.

Thus our book is a response to the enormous challenge of managing ethnic diversity in the twenty-first century. Increased international trade, migration, and travel have dramatically altered patterns of ethnic contact around the world. People of different ethnicities now routinely come into contact with one another in work, social, and other settings, and the amount of interethnic contact promises to increase in the future. In particular, this book attempts to address how ethnic contact is related to identity and conflict. Interethnic contact involves people who often look different, and have different cultural and ethnic beliefs, values, and behavioral patterns. In many cases, such differences are exaggerated to solidify ethnic boundaries and serve ethnic solidarity, to build up walls around groups rather than to celebrate cultural diversity.

Events over the last few decades—including 9–11 and violent conflict in Rwanda, Israel, Yugoslavia, Afghanistan, the Indian subcontinent, and dozens of other "hot spots"—suggest that we are not moving in the right direction. This book aims to be both conceptual and practical in addressing ethnic violence and cultural conflict with a global perspective. Thus, our goal is not only a scientific update, but also a practical guide for those who interact with people from different ethnic and cultural groups both at home and abroad.

As editors, we appreciate four institutions (Minnesota State University at Mankato, Bryn Mawr College, Georgetown University, University of Hawaii at Hilo) for their direct and indirect support of this book project. The Dean's office at the College of Social and Behavioral Sciences and Academic Vice President's office at Minnesota State University provided grants for Yueh-Ting Lee while he was working on this project.

We want to thank the following individuals for assisting us in reviewing manuscripts and providing insightful comments and constructive criticisms: Marilynn Brewer (Ohio State University), Chao Chen and Lee Jussim (Rutgers University), Rong Ma (Beijing University, China), Kimberly O'Farrell (Minnesota State University at Mankato), Carey Ryan (University of Nebraska at Omaha), Frederick Slocum (Minnesota State University at Mankato), and Donald Taylor (McGill University). Thanks are also extended to Timothy Gardner and Abdulkadir Alasow, two graduate students (Minnesota State University at Mankato), for helping us with indexing the book and other matters. Finally we want to express sincere appreciation for the support provided by Ms. Debora Carvalko and her colleagues from the Greenwood Publishing Group as well as the team at Impressions Book and Journal Services.

YTL
CRM
FMM
SW

PART I

Introduction

CHAPTER 1

The Global Challenge of Ethnic and Cultural Conflict

Yueh-Ting Lee, Fathali Moghaddam, Clark McCauley,
and Stephen Worchel

The tragedy of 9–11 has forced the world, and particularly the United States, to confront what seems to be a harsher set of circumstances in the post–cold war era. Many people had hoped that the end of the cold war would lead to real international peace and a decline in political conflict in both higher-income and lower-income societies around the globe. This hope has been dashed by a series of devastating events since the early 1990s. First, war in the former communist states of Eastern Europe swept aside the dream that transition from dictatorship to democracy would be peaceful in areas such as Bosnia. Second, increased conflicts in the Near and Middle East, as well as in the Indian subcontinent, have posed serious threats to world peace. The cold war is over, but peace seems no closer.

The unexpected rise in conflict during the post–cold war era is coupled with an unexpected basis for group formation. Classic accounts of modernization, particularly those influenced by Marx, predicted that the old basis for divisions, such as tribe and religion, would be swept aside. As hundreds of millions of people poured from rural to urban areas worldwide during the nineteenth and twentieth centuries, it was expected that new alliances would be formed, based on social class in particular. This prediction has not proved correct, and ancient alliances continue to form the basis of conflict in the twenty-first century.

The focus of this volume is on conflict between ethnic and cultural groups, both of which are associated with the ancient ties and alliances people feel, rather than with modern alliances such as social class or labor or professional association. An *ethnic group* consists of people who perceive themselves as having a common descent. This perception is often associated with land, leadership, shared language, religion, and lifestyle. A *cultural group* consists of people who share enough to define a distinct meaning system, a worldview that leads them to evaluate people and events in a distinct way. It is politically important to the extent that the shared meaning system is not only shared but also perceived as shared, and becomes especially important if the meaning system is seen as threatened (also see Campbell, 1967; Hall, 1975). In other words, ethnicity is often but not necessarily part of the shared perspective that defines a cultural group as a group entity (see Campbell, 1958). Simply put, culture is embedded in "variable systems of meaning" (Rohner, 1984) or "human-made part of the environment" (Herkovits, 1948; see also H. Triandis, 1994) and "is learned and shared by members of a society" (Lee, McCauley, & Draguns, 1999, p. 5). Based on the Greek concept of *ethnos*, ethnicity refers to the people of a nation or tribe (often with languages; land or territory; leadership; and lifestyle, or religious, or other beliefs and behaviors). Although it is associated with culture and is often used interchangeably with culture as well as with race, ethnicity focuses on "groups that are characterized in terms of a common nationality, culture, or language" (Betancourt & Lopez, 1993, p. 631). Cultural background can be a determinant of ethnic identity or affiliation, but being part of an ethnic group can also determine culture. For example, as members of an ethnic group interact with each other, ethnicity becomes a means by which culture is transmitted (see Betancourt & Lopez).

The relation between ethnicity and culture is intimate because it is only through culture that individuals come to recognize ethnic markers, to give particular values to different ethnic groups, and to identify with the ethnic in-group. The subtle relationship between culture and ethnicity becomes clearer when we look, as outsiders, at the ways in which people very different from us categorize the social world into ethnic groups. For example, consider this tale, part of the oral tradition of Easter Islanders, about conflict between two ethnic groups who were their ancestors:

Once upon a time there were Long-ears and Short-ears. The Long-ears came from the east first, the Short-ears from the west later. The first were industrious and in charge of monuments and the great works. The Short-ears patiently toiled for two hundred years with the monuments in honor of the Long-ears; then they conspired and made revolt. They pushed the Long-ears down into their own burning pyre and ruled the island alone thereafter. (Heyerdahl, 1989, p. 239)

The meaning of "Long-ear" and "Short-ear" was clear to the ancient Easter Islanders, because their culture informed them how to interpret and give meaning to ear length as a basis for ethnic categorization. But in contemporary Western societies, we do not use length of ear as a basis for ethnic groupings. Instead, our culture informs us about other markers (e.g., skin color, eye shape). It is only through archeological and anthropological studies that we can come to understand the basis of ethnic conflict in the culture of the ancient Easter Island. Thus, one reason for coupling ethnicity and culture is that ethnicity only becomes visible and meaningful through culture. In some cases, ethnic or group conflict endures because "the settlers have either not attempted to or have been unsuccessful in exterminating the native or population as occurred in the Americas, Australia, and the Western Cape of South Africa" (Mitchell, 2000, p. 1). In other words, ethnic and cultural conflict occurred when the short ears (e.g., Europeans) did not always drive away the long ears (natives).

A second important reason for focusing on both ethnic conflict and cultural conflict is that both play a fundamental role in intergroup relations in the twenty-first century. This is to some degree reflected in psychological research on ethnicity over the last few decades (e.g., Boucher, Landis, & Clark, 1987; Chirot & Seligman, 2001) and in the cultural turn in psychology since the early 1980s (Moghaddam, 2002). The importance of culture has been heightened by recent events, and some insightful observers have noted that there is an ongoing clash of cultures and civilizations internationally (Huntington, 1993, 1996, 2000). Huntington (2000, p. 609) argues that "culture and cultural identities, which at the broadest level are civilizational identities, are shaping the patterns of cohesion, disintegration, and conflict in the post-Cold War world". Huntington's one major theme in this conflict appears to be "authentic" Islamic culture (particularly as represented by the Islamic states, such as Iran, Pakistan, Iraq, and other Islamic states vs. modern Christian culture as represented by the United States, and other Western societies).

Such conflicts are fundamentally cultural, in the sense that they are based on competition between meaning systems. For example, as a religion (which is part of culture), radical Islamic movements in the Near and Middle East, in North Africa, and in the Indian subcontinent are in large part a reaction against West-leaning repressive Arab governments (Huntington, 1993, 1996, 2000). Radical Muslims attempt to make the role of ethnicity secondary in this conflict. Soon after coming to power in Iran in 1979, Ayatollah Ruhollah Khomeini sent this message to the millions of Muslims who had come from different parts of the world to participate in the Hajj to Mecca that year:

Dear sisters and brothers, in whatever country you may live . . . Defend fearlessly and unhesitatingly the peoples and countries of Islam against their enemies. . . . loudly proclaim the crimes of the enemies of Islam. (Khomeini, 1981, p. 276)

However, such attempts to unite all Muslims under one banner have not been successful, in part because ethnic differences resurface and conflicts erupt between groups of Muslims, such as the eight-year war between Iran and Iraq, the former being predominantly Persian in population and the latter mainly Arab.

The focus on both ethnic and cultural conflict reflects the dynamic and complex nature of national and international conflict in the twenty-first century. The traditional static approach to such conflict is not viable, in part because the interactive, fluid, and changing nature of cultures around the world is also changing the meaning and significance of ethnic markers and ethnic identity more rapidly. Similar dramatic shifts are taking place within nations. For example, in the United States the ethnic landscape has dramatically changed in the last few decades, in part because Hispanic/Latino Americans have risen in number at such a fast pace that they have caught up with—and are quickly overtaking—the number of African Americans. Hispanics/Latinos already are the majority group in some regions of the country (e.g., Miami, Florida). This rapid increase in numbers has been associated with major cultural changes within the United States, through which Hispanic ethnicity is defined and evaluated. As the title of a recent book suggests, "American skin" is changing both in color and meaning, and within this context the meaning of Hispanic is also changing (Wynter, 2002).

TOWARD A MULTIDISCIPLINARY ACCOUNT OF ETHNIC AND CULTURAL CONFLICT

As social scientists, we are keenly aware that ethnic and cultural conflicts have not received adequate research attention in our disciplines, despite early evidence of the importance of ethnic and cultural groups (Allport, 1937; Benedict, 1934; Kluckhohn & Murray, 1953, 1965; Mead, 1956). Psychologically, the decline of interest in global ethnic and cultural issues after World War II may be partly attributed to biases in traditional psychology, reflecting (1) individuocentrism or individual-orientedness, (2) experimentalism, and (3) psychological reductionism or psychologism (Bond, 1988; Lee, 1994; Lee et al., 1999; Lee, Jussim, & McCauley, 1995; Lee & Ottai, 1995; Pepitone, 1989). Another factor has been the dominant ideology in the cold war period, according to which global ethnic and cultural conflict was secondary to the communist-capitalist (or democratic) demarcation (e.g., Gurr, 2000; Mays, Bullock, Rosenzweig, & Wessells, 1998; Moghaddam, 1998; Sadowski, 1998; Worchel, 1999).

Mays and her colleagues (1998) noted four primary reasons for why psychologists and other social scientists have failed to adequately meet the challenge of global ethnic and cultural conflict. First, there is a shortage of well-trained psychologists or social scientists in many war-torn countries. Second, traditional social and cross-cultural research focuses on individual and small-group processes, and is ill suited for addressing the communal and societal problems produced by war or conflict. Third, the linkage between conflict theory and practice is relatively weak and a unifying conflict-resolution theory is lacking. Even domain-specific theories of ethnic conflict are underdeveloped. Finally, traditional Western, and particularly North American, social scientists and their research continue to be ethnocentric (or Euro-centric or Westo-centric), which makes it difficult to apply their research to many contexts around the world, including some in North America itself.

Despite these weaknesses, however, there are several bodies of psychological research that can serve toward better understanding ethnic and cultural conflict. First, there is a solid body of North American research on minority-majority relations (e.g., Aguirre & Turner, 1998; Brewer, 1979; Dovidio & Gaertner, 2000; Hacker, 1995). Second, two groups of researchers have explored the relationship between culture and behavior. The first group, best represented by the *Journal of Cross-Cultural Psychology*, has adopted traditional causal models and traditional methodology, typically incorporating culture as an independent variable in research studies (e.g., Berry, Poortinga, & Pandey, 1997; Bond, 1996; Brislin, 2000; Hofstede, 1991, 2001; Landis & Bhagat, 1996; Lee & Ottati, 1993; Lonner & Malpass, 1994; H. Triandis, 1994, 1996; H. Trandis, 1989, 1995). The second group, best represented by the newer journal *Culture & Psychology*, has adopted a normative model of behavior and has preferred qualitative methods shared with the "new social psychologies" of Europe (Cole, 1996; Harré, 2002; Stigler, Shweder, & Herdt, 1990). This diversity of approaches is a sign of the vibrancy and good health of cultural research (see Moghaddam & Harré, 1995), although there is need for greater communication between groups of researchers.

There is also a need for psychologists to communicate and collaborate more effectively with scholars from other disciplines, because ethnic and cultural conflict can be best understood through broader perspectives. With a few exceptions (e.g., Horowitz, 1985, 2001), the more constructive publications in this domain have involved collaborations of researchers from within and outside the discipline of psychology. For example, in 1998, a group of sociologists, psychologists, and other social scientists authored a series of timely papers on ethnic conflict from international perspectives in *American Psychologist* (Mays et al., 1998). This issue includes ethnic and cultural problems in Rwanda (D. N. Smith, 1998); Northern Ireland (Cairns & Darby, 1998); Israel and Palestine (Rouhana & Bar-Tal, 1998); Sri Lanka (Rogers, Spencer, & Uyangoda, 1998); and Guatemala, Peru, and Puerto Rico (Comas-Diaz, Lyke, & Alarcon, 1998). This landmark event underlined the point that ethnic conflict and cultural problems are not only unique to the United States, but are also common to many other countries and regions, including Bosnia, Rwanda, Brazil,

Puerto Rico, Canada, Ireland, Sri Lanka, Indonesia, and certainly Israel and Palestine.

Mays and her colleagues have argued that "Because many ethnic conflicts are rooted in political, economic and social histories, including colonialism, and are fueled by interacting historic, political, economic and social influences, psychological analysis of the causes of ethnic conflict cannot be conducted reasonably in a stand-alone manner. Rather ethnic conflict resolution must be embedded in a multidisciplinary framework" (Mays et al., 1998, p. 738). We agree with this argument and have invited sociologists, political scientists, anthropologists, and historians, in addition to psychologists, to contribute to the discussion.

Thus, this volume is in line with efforts to adopt a more dynamic, multidisciplinary approach to conflict in the twenty-first century. First, ethnicity is not treated as a static phenomenon, with fixed boundaries and meanings. Rather, the markers and meanings of ethnicity change with the changes in culture. Second, cultural systems can form the basis of intragroup and intergroup conflict, but ethnicity can also play a role in such conflicts as a marker of cultural difference. The dynamic approach to conflict becomes even more important at a time when advanced transportation and communications systems have impacted the intergroup contact and group identity.

CONTACT AND IDENTITY

Advanced communications, transportation, and technology have made the global village a reality. The contemporary world is characterized by increased contact between people from different parts of the globe, who now find themselves interacting with numerous out-groups. Associated with these trends have been conflicts, wars, and riots within societies (see Gurr, 2000; Morris-Hale, 1996). Examples include suicidal bombings and military killings in Israel, war in Bosnia, and genocide in Rwanda. Second, increased contact sometimes means increased conflicts between cultural systems, such as Islamic fundamentalists versus Western secular culture. Underlying such conflicts at the national and international levels is deep concern for cultural identity (e.g., LeVine & Campbell, 1972; McCauley, 2000; Tajfel, 1981; Tajfel & Turner, 1986; Taylor & Moghaddam, 1994).

If interethnic and intercultural contact is unavoidable in the global village, in what conditions does contact help to foster intergroup peace, rather than create conflict? The existing literature on contact is relevant to this question (Allport, 1954; Amir, 1969, 1976; Cook, 1962; Horowitz, 1985; LeVine & Campbell, 1972; Miller & Brewer, 1984; see review by Forbes, 1997). We are aware that other theories—for example, social identity theory and realistic conflict theory, relative deprivation theory, cost and benefit theory, equity theory (see Tajfel, 1981; Tajfel & Turner, 1986; see also

Forbes, 1997; Horowitz, 1985; LeVine & Campbell, 1972; McCauley, 2000; Worchel, 1999), sociobiological theory (e.g., Brown, 1991; Dennen, 1995; Wilson, 1975), five-stage theory (Taylor & Moghaddam, 1994), and social dominance theory (Sidanius & Pratto, 1999)—may also be important in interpreting ethnic and cultural conflict. However, contact seems to be most fundamental or primitive. After an extensive review of the major intergroup theories, Taylor and Moghaddam concluded, "Contact between groups is an implicit theme underlying most theories of intergroup relations" (p. 197). As Bramel's research (Bramel, this volume) suggests, contact is the first step in intergroup relations. But without understanding and appreciating differences between groups, contact facilitates intergroup conflict.

A major reason for a focus on contact is that in the twenty-first century, interethnic and intercultural contact is increasing and is likely to become an even more important feature of human life. Thus, we believe that theory and research on contact need to be enriched and expanded. The existing literature is limited in several ways. First, the main focus of contact research has been Black-White relations in the United States in the 1960s and 1970s. Will contact research in the past be applicable to specific ethnic and cultural conflicts in the international context? Second, the approach to ethnicity has been static rather than dynamic. This is rather similar to what Lake and Rothchild (1998, pp. 5–7) call the *primordialist approach* to the study of ethnic conflict: the idea that ethnicity is a fixed characteristic of individuals and communities (Connor, 1994; Issacs, 1975; Kaplan, 1993; A. D. Smith, 1986; van den Berghe, 1981). For example, contact research typically begins from an assumption that actors can be categorized neatly as Serbs, Dakotans, Zulu, or Chechens. The problem with this approach is too much emphasis on fixed identity and its failure to account for variation in the level of ethnic conflict over time and place.

We propose a move toward a more dynamic approach, one that emphasizes how changing cultural conditions are associated with changes in intergroup contact. This is more in line with some aspects of two other political science approaches to the study of ethnic conflict. The *instrumentalist approach* focuses on identity as a tool used by individuals, groups, or elites to obtain some larger, typically material end (e.g., Brass, 1985; Lake & Rothchild, 1998). Ethnicity is mainly a label or set of symbolic ties that is used for the political agenda of certain individuals or groups. This approach has the advantage of incorporating change and of viewing people as intentional and active agents. This is the approach we endorse. But we are not in agreement with the assumption, underlying this approach, that ethnicity is something that can be manipulated at will, like political party affiliation. We view ethnicity as embedded within and influenced by the larger sociohistorical context, to be understood within a relational framework (Esman, 1994; Lake & Rothchild, p. 6).

This view is in some ways similar to a *constructionist perspective* found among political scientists studying ethnic conflict. Constructionists emphasize the social origin and nature of ethnicity (Brubaker, 1995; Young, 1993). According to this approach, ethnicity is neither immutable nor completely open. Instead, ethnicity is constructed from dense webs of social interaction; it is not an individual attribute, but a social phenomenon. An individual, for example, usually has little choice in his or her ethnic identity. As social interactions change, one's ethnic identity evolves. Our emphasis on the role of (changing) culture in defining the markers and meaning of ethnicity is in harmony with this approach. The collapse of the previous Soviet Union and East Europe led to interaction changes that generated ethnic conflict in Chechnya, and in Bosnia, Serbia, and Croatia (which used to be part of Yugoslavia).

But our view also has elements in common with the instrumental approach in that we recognize that ethnic conflict can be stimulated by elites who use ethnicity for their own narrow interests (Lake & Rothchild, 1998, p. 6). For example, Shui-Bian Chen in Taiwan is a radical member of the Democratic Progressive Party that strongly supports Taiwan's independence from Mainland China. By stressing Taiwan's identity, Chen was elected president in Taiwan in what might be considered an instrumental play on ethnicity. However, Taiwan's situation is the outcome of colonialism and World War II. Without Japanese and American intervention and involvement, Taiwan would have been part of China with no conflict between mainlanders and native Taiwanese. This is a more constructionist interpretation.

Thus, two conceptual themes running through most of the discussions in this volume are contact and identity. Although our intention is not to test specific aspects of the contact hypothesis or social identity theory, our discussions are intended to expand our understanding of the nature of contact and identity at the international level.

CONTACT, IDENTITY, AND POLICIES FOR MANAGING DIVERSITY

Immigrant-receiving societies, such as the United States, Canada, Australia, and New Zealand, have historically faced the challenge of managing diversity, as millions of immigrants poured in from different parts of the world. Increased intergroup contact has created new international conditions in the twenty-first century, so that people in most parts of the world are now facing this same challenge. Even in countries with supposedly homogenous cultures, the recent movements of populations have brought about the challenge of managing diversity. For example, the arrival of millions of Turks in Germany, North Africans in France, South Asians in England, and East Europeans in Austria, Switzerland, and Belgium has presented new challenges to formerly homogeneous societies. How should diversity be managed?

The traditional policies for managing diversity can be conceptualized as lying on a continuum, with complete assimilation at one extreme and total retention of differences at the other extreme (see Moghaddam, 1998, chap. 14; see also O'Leary, 2001). Similar to such formulas as "$A + B + C = A$" (where A is a dominant group, and B and C are different minority groups; see Fong & Shinagawa, 2000, p. 4), assimilation involves the abandonment of ethnic minority differences in conformity to the dominant white Anglo group. Minority groups (e.g., B and C) lose their cultural traits to become part of the dominant group. If early history in the United States primarily focused on assimilation, the United States is also cited as an example of the melting-pot model. Amalgamation, or the melting-pot model, pertains to the process by which diverse racial and ethnic groups are blended together to form a new society that incorporates the special contributions of each group, as can be seen in the formula $A + B + C = D$, where A, B, and C are distinct groups who come together to form D as a unique society (Fong & Shinagawa, p. 4). Finally, cultural pluralism can be stated as $A + B + C = A + B + C$. But this is a double-edged sword. In its negative extreme, segregation occurs that is "the social and geographic separation within a society of people based on race and/or ethnicity, class, religion, or other social characteristic" (Fong & Shinagawa, p. 4). On its positive side, people tend to accept and understand differences. Various groups retain their culture and their cultural identities, and they have the opportunities to exist on their own terms while interacting with each other (Gordon, 1964; Lee et al., 1995).

Focusing on the positive side, "$A + B + C = A + B + C$" philosophically requires openness to, or tolerance of, differences. According to Daoism (or Taoism) by Laozi, the natural world and human beings are so diverse and complicated that we must be open to the differences and tolerant of those differences (Lee, 1996, 2003). The *Tao-Te Ching (Dao-De Jing)* says, "The one with great De (or humanistic virtue) tends to be tolerant and open to everything because the one must follow *the Dao*" (Laozi, chap. 21, cited from Wing, 1986). In other words, openness and tolerance are the essential and fundamental ways (Dao or Tao) for human beings. Without openness and tolerance, it is very difficult for human beings to be in harmony with nature and other human beings.

Diversity retention involves policies to support group differences, as represented by the Canadian policy of "multiculturalism within a bilingual framework." But both assimilation and diversity retention are being practiced simultaneously in nearly every country. The clash of these policies is often associated with major conflicts, such as the continuing struggles between globalization and its enemies, be they radical Muslims or

Green Party supporters or defenders of local tribal ways of life in South America and elsewhere.

The struggle between assimilation and diversity retention is not taking place in a historical vacuum: the past has a strong and direct impact on this struggle, in part because some groups attempt to retain aspects of the past and prevent change. For example, in the U.S. context it has been claimed that "Americans remain committed to common values and are still exposed to common cultural experiences" (Wuthnow, 1999, p. 19). But critics point out that if there are common values, they tend to be European-centric or Western (Smelster & Alexander, 1999).

Aguirre and Turner (1998) have identified five types of discrimination: genocide, expulsion, exclusion, segregation, and selective inclusion. Unfortunately, major examples of each of these types of discrimination is reflected in the U.S. treatment of minorities: (1) genocide against Native Americans (Stannard, 1992); (2) expulsion of Mexicans when the Treaty of Guadalupe Hidalgo was signed in 1848 as well as during the Great Depression; (3) exclusion through the Chinese Exclusion Act in 1882; (4) segregation according to the "separate but equal" doctrine in 1896 after the U.S. Supreme court's decision on the *Plessy v. Ferguson* case, which upheld segregation between whites and the colored; and (5) selective inclusion through symbolic tokenism today (see also Brislin, 2000, pp. 214–220; Dinnerstein, Nichols, & Reimers, 1996). Perhaps failure to understand and appreciate ethnic group differences is psychologically the core of these five types of discrimination.

Each major immigrant group may have experienced discrimination in ways that are to some extent distinct, for example, as reflected by the history of U.S. immigration policy (Cao & Novas, 1996; Takaki, 1989). Personal accounts of their experiences by Chinese immigrants, for example, give witness to their special experiences (Rico & Mano, 2001). The first anti-immigration law in the history of the United States was the Chinese Exclusion Act, which was issued in 1882 (Cao & Novas; Takaki). However, a common theme to many intergroup relationships in the United States, as well in many other parts of the world, seems to be the native/nonnative distinction or the conflict between newcomers and natives (see Mitchell, 2000).

In conclusion, the modern world is characterized by increased intergroup contact, and a major challenge confronting modern states is to develop effective policies for managing diversity. This challenge traditionally confronted immigrant-receiving societies, as reflected by ongoing debates about varieties of assimilation and multiculturalism (Taylor & Moghaddam, 1994), but is now present in Japan and in European countries that have previously been thought of as relatively homogenous. The present volume contributes to the debate about diversity management policies by exploring issues of intergroup contact and identity.

PLAN OF THE BOOK

Between the introductory and concluding chapters of this volume, the 14 contributed chapters are organized in three main parts. The three main parts are respectively concerned with broad historical and conceptual issues, clashes of cultural beliefs, and more applied issues dealing with specific types of intergroup conflict. All of the chapters deal in various ways, directly or indirectly, with contact and identity.

Four chapters are included in Part 2, with a focus on the broad conceptual background to the issues of contact and identity. Contributors address these issues from anthropological, psychological, political, and sociological perspectives. Following Hardin's tragedy of the commons (Chapter 2), Allen and Chagnon address the importance of small-scale (e.g., kinship) cooperative communities that mimic those of our hunter-gatherer evolutionary past. Their chapter suggests restructuring home, school, neighborhood, and international environments where small, cohesive communities had a vested interest in sustainably cooperating and maintaining the resources embodied in their neighborhoods and locales. Bramel (Chapter 3) examines the history of the contact hypothesis, arguing that the contact hypothesis has been based on untested assumptions about intergroup similarities. He urges psychologists to rethink the contact hypothesis and to move their research more in line with the multicultural realities of modern societies. In Chapter 4, Forbes investigates contact hypotheses and finds that more contact means more conflicts of interest. In Chapter 5, Yang, Power, Takaku, and Posas review ethnic issues of immigration and conflict both in North America and around the world.

Part 3 consists of six chapters that deal with cultural and ethnic conflict in the context of Iran (Moghaddam, Chapter 6), Israel (Oren, Bar-Tal, & David, Chapter 7), South Africa and New Zealand (Duckitt, Chapter 8), the Baltic States (Draguns, Chapter 9), China (Bilik, Lee, Shi, & Phan, Chapter 10) and the 9-11 event in the United States (Lee, Takaku, Ottati, & Yan, Chapter 11). An overarching theme in these chapters is change, and intergroup contact under changing local and international conditions. Each discussion highlights the tensions and conflicts arising out of contact between groups with widely different, and in some ways conflicting, cultural systems: fundamentalist Islam in contact with the secular West (Moghaddam), Arabs in contact with Israelis (Oren, Bar-Tal, & David), White Afrikaners and European-Pakeha New Zealanders in contact with natives in their respective societies (Duckitt), contact between Estonians, Latvians, and Lithuanians, and between this "Baltic group" and various out-groups (Draguns). In Draguns's chapter, for instance, more Russian influence on those Baltic group (e.g., more and more Russians who used to migrate to Latvia, Estonia, and Lithuania) made those groups claim their independent ethnic identity and exercised their reversal discrimination against

Russian in their territories. Perhaps part of the challenge faced by groups coming into contact with out-groups that have fundamentally different cultural systems is that at least some aspects of their own identity are changed, or at least challenged. In Chapter 10, Bilik and his colleagues address Chinese ethnic and cultural issues from a historical and psychological perspective, including how contact between different ethnic Chinese affects ethnic change processes and recategorization. Chapter 11 (Lee, Takaku, Ottati, & Yan) reports on how three cultures (Christian American, Chinese, and Muslim Pakistan) reacted to the 9-11 event and why they responded in a different way. Apparently, global contact may lead to global conflict when people fail to understand and appreciate their differences.

Whereas Part 3 focuses mainly on groups with different cultural systems (including religious differences), in Part 4 the focus is more on the practical management and prevention of cultural conflict and ethnic violence. Part 4 includes four chapters that more directly either address how cultural conflict may be managed in business as can be seen in Chapter 12 (Brislin & Liu) or address how deadline ethnic violence or conflict may be prevented and handled as can be seen in Chapter 13 (Levin & Rabrenovic), in Chapter 14 (McCauley & Bock), as well as in Chapter 15 (Worchel). The major goal in Part 4 is to move toward a better understanding of communications and a better management of breakdowns, conflicts, direct aggression, and other negative experiences that often arise out of intergroup contact. No doubt, each case is in some ways unique, but there are also some important similarities across cases. Our hope is that by examining detailed case studies in an international context, we can arrive at broader lessons for better handling and preventing intergroup conflict.

CONCLUSION

The geopolitical situation in today's world is a conundrum for the social scientist interested in intergroup relations. On one hand, contact between ethnic and cultural groups is greater (and easier) than at any time in human history. One can eat breakfast with Germans in Munich, board an airplane (albeit a supersonic one) and lunch with Arabs in Cairo, have dinner with Indians in Bombay, and bed down with the Tamil in Sri Lanka. Members of the most distant ethnic group are only a phone call away. Television programs compete to dissect the most intimate habits of the remotest tribal groups. All of these factors tend to fuse people into forming a global community.

On the other hand, there is a growing tide toward dividing the world into homogeneous ethnic and cultural subgroups. The map of Europe is being redrawn around ethnic groups. Yugoslavia has fragmented into a half dozen ethnic communities, the Soviet Union is no longer a union, and

Czechoslovakia has experienced a velvet revolution separating Czech and Slovaks into separate countries. The Basques are stepping up their demands for a distinct state. On the other hand, East and West Germany have merged into a single German republic, and this magnet is attracting ethnic Germans from Russia and Poland. In Asia, North and South Korea seem to be attempting to erase the national line that divides Koreans. China continues to bridge the national divide with Taiwan, and Timor has split from Indonesia. Ethnicity is becoming a common denominator that brings some people together, but resists the blending implied by a global community.

Indeed these are interesting times. All and all, the forces set into motion by the human tide give added urgency to developing an understanding of intergroup relations. Whether the press is toward unification and contact or toward separation and isolation, insight into the relationship between groups is critical. Our aim in this book is to provide perspectives from several fields into the dynamic of this relationship. Our hope is that an examination of the various contributions will give the reader a greater appreciation of the complexity and intriguing nature of the issues that face our world in this domain.

REFERENCES

Aguirre, A., & Turner, J. (1998). *American ethnicity: The dynamics and consequence of discrimination*. New York: McGraw-Hill.

Allport, G. W. (1937). *Personality: A psychological interpretation*. New York: Henry Holt and Co.

Allport, G. W. (1954). *The nature of prejudice*. Reading, MA: Addison-Wesley.

Amir, Y. (1969). The role of intergroup contact in ethnic relations. *Psychological Bulletin, 71*, 319–342.

Amir, Y. (1976). The role of intergroup contact in change of prejudice and ethnic relations. In P. A. Katz (Ed.), *Towards the elimination of racism* (pp. 245–308). New York: Pergamon.

Benedict, R. (1934). *Patterns of culture*. Boston: Houghton Mifflin.

Berry, J., Poortinga, Y., & Pandey, J. (Eds.). (1997). *Handbook of cross-cultural psychology: Theory and method* (2nd ed., Vol. 1). Boston: Allyn & Bacon.

Betancourt, H., & Lopez, S. R. (1993). The study of culture, ethnicity and race in American Psychology. *American Psychologist, 48*(6), 629–637.

Bond, M. (1988). *Cross-cultural challenge to social psychology*. Newbury, CA: Sage.

Bond, M. (1996). *Handbook of Chinese psychology*. Hong Kong: Oxford University Press.

Boucher, J., Landis, D., & Clark, K. A. (1987). *Ethnic conflict: International perspectives.* Newbury Park, CA: Sage.

Brass, P. (1985). *Ethnic groups and the state.* London: Croom-Helm.

Brewer, M. B. (1979). Ingroup bias in the minimal intergroup situation: A cognitive-motivational analysis. *Psychological Bulletin, 86,* 307–324.

Brislin, R. (2000). *Understanding culture's influence's on behavior.* Philadelphia: Harcourt.

Brown, D. E. (1991). *Human universals.* New York: McGraw-Hill.

Brubaker, R. (1995, Spring). National minorities, nationalizing states, and external national homeland in the new Europe. *Daedalus,* 107–132.

Cairns, E., & Darby, J. (1998). The conflict in Northern Ireland: Causes, consequences, and control. *American Psychologist, 53*(7), 754–760.

Cao, L., & Novas, H. (1996). *Everything you need to know about Asian American history.* New York: Plume.

Campbell, D. T. (1958). Common fate, similarities, and other indices of the status of aggregates of persons as social entities. *Behavioral Science, 3,* 14–25.

Campbell, D. T. (1967). Stereotypes and perceptions of group differences. *American Psychologist, 22,* 817–829.

Chirot, D., & Seligman, M. E. P. (2001). *Ethnopolitical warfare: Causes, consequences, and possible solutions.* Washington, DC: American Psychological Association.

Cole, M. (1996). *Cultural psychology: A once and future discipline.* Cambridge, MA: Harvard University Press.

Comas-Diaz, L., Lykes, M. B., & Alarcon, R. D. (1998). Ethnic conflict and the psychology of the liberation in Guatemala, Peru, and Puerto Rico. *American Psychologist, 53*(7), 777–792.

Connor, W. (1994). *Ethnonationalism: The quest for understanding.* Princeton, NJ: Princeton University Press.

Cook, S. W. (1962). The systematic analysis of socially significant events: A strategy for social research. *Journal of Social Issues, 18*(2), 66–84.

Dennen, J. van der (1995). *The origin of war: The evolution of a male-coalitional reproductive strategy.* Groningen, the Netherlands: The Origin Press.

Dinnerstein, L., Nichols, R. L., & Reimers, D. M. (1996). *Natives and strangers: A multicultural history of Americans.* New York: Oxford University Press.

Dovidio, J. F., & Gaertner, S. L. (2000). Aversive racism and selection decisions: 1989 and 1999. *Psychological Science, 11,* 315–319.

Esman, M. J. (1994). *Ethnic politics.* Ithaca: Cornell University Press.

Fong, T. P., & Shinagawa, L. H. (2000). *Asian Americans: Experiences and perspectives.* Upper Saddle River, NJ: Prentice Hall.

Forbes, H. D. (1997). *Ethnic conflict: Commerce, culture, and the contact hypothesis.* New Haven, CT: Yale University Press.

Gordon, M. (1964). *Assimilation in American life: The role of race, religion, and national origins.* New York: Oxford University Press.

Gurr, T. R. (2000). *Peoples vs. states: Ethnopolitical conflict and accommodation at the end of the 20th century.* Washington, DC: US Institute of Peace.

Hacker, A. (1995). *Two nations: Black and white, separate, hostile and unequal.* New York: Ballantine Books (Random House).

Hall, E. T. (1975). *Beyond culture.* Garden City, NY: Anchor Press.

Harré, R. (2002). *Cognitive science.* London: Sage.

Herkovits, M. (1948). *Man and his works.* New York: Knopf.

Heyerdahl, T. (1989). *Easter Island: The mystery solved.* New York: Random House.

Hofstede, G. (1991). *Cultures and organizations: Software of the mind.* London: McGraw-Hill.

Hofstede, G. (2001). *Culture's consequences: Comparing values, behaviors, institutions and organizations across nations.* Thousand Oaks, CA: Sage.

Horowitz, D. L. (1985). *Ethnic groups in conflict.* Berkeley, CA: University of California Press.

Horowitz, D. L. (2001). *The deadly ethnic riot.* Berkeley, CA: University of California Press.

Huntington, S. P. (1993). The clash of civilizations? *Foreign Affairs, 72*(3), 22–49.

Huntington, S. P. (1996). *The clash of civilizations and the remaking of world order.* New York: Simon & Schuster.

Huntington, S. P. (2000). Try again: A reply to Russett, Oneal & Cox. *Journal of Peace Research, 37*(5), 609–610.

Issacs, H. (1975). *Idols of the tribe: Group identity and political change.* New York: Harper & Row.

Kaplan, R. D. (1993). *Balkan ghosts: A journey through history.* New York: St. Martin's Press.

Khomeini, R. (1981). *Islam and revolution: Writings and declarations of Imam Khomeini* (H. Algar, Trans.). Berkeley, CA.: Mizan Press.

Kluckhohn, C., & Murray, H. (1953). *Personality in nature, society and culture.* New York: Alfred A. Knopf.

Kluckhohn, C., & Murray, H. (1965). *Personality in nature, society and culture.* New York: Alfred A. Knopf.

Lake, D. A., & Rothchild, D. (1998). *The international spread of ethnic conflict: Fear, diffusion, and escalation.* Princeton, NJ: Princeton University Press.

Landis, D., & Bhagat, R. (1996). *Handbook of intercultural training* (2nd ed.). Thousands Oaks, CA: Sage.

LeVine, R. A., & Campbell, D. T. (1972). *Ethnocentrism: Theories of conflict, ethnic attitudes and group behavior.* New York: Wiley.

Lee, Y.-T. (1994). Why does psychology have cultural limitations? *American Psychologist, 49,* 524–525.

Lee, Y.-T. (1996). It is difference, not prejudice, that engenders intergroup tension: Revisiting Ichheiserian research. *American Psychologist* 51(3), 267–268.

Lee, Y.-T. (2003). Daoistic humanism in ancient China: Broadening personality and counseling theories in the 21st century. *Journal of Humanistic Psychology, 43*, 64–85.

Lee, Y.-T., Jussim, L., & McCauley, C. (Eds.). (1995). *Stereotype accuracy: Toward appreciating group differences.* Washington, DC: The American psychological Association.

Lee, Y.-T., McCauley, C. R., & Draguns, J. (Eds.). (1999). *Personality and personality perception across cultures.* Mahwah, NJ: Lawrence Erlbaum Associates.

Lee, Y.-T., & Ottati, V. (1993). Determinants of ingroup and outgroup perception of heterogeneity: An investigation of Chinese-American stereotypes. *Journal of Cross-Cultural Psychology, 24,* 298–318.

Lee, Y.-T., & Ottati, V. (1995). Perceived group homogeneity as a function of group membership salience and stereotype threats. *Personality and Social Psychology Bulletin 21*(6), 612–621.

Lonner, W. J., & Malpass, R. (1994). *Psychology and culture.* Boston: Allyn & Bacon.

Mays, V. M., Bullock, M., Rosenzweig, M. R., & Wessells, M. (1998). Ethnic conflict: Global challenges and psychological perspectives. *American Psychologist, 53*(7), 737–742.

McCauley, C. (2000). How President Bush moved the U.S. into the Gulf War: Three theories of group conflict and the construction of moral violation. *Journal for the Study of Peace and Conflict, 2000–2001* (Annual ed.), 32–42.

Mead, M. (1956). The cross-cultural approach to the study of personality. In J. L. McCary (Ed.), *Psychology of personality* (pp. 201–252). New York: Grove Press.

Miller, N., & Brewer, M. B. (1984). *Groups in contact: The psychology of desegregation.* New York: Academic.

Mitchell, T. G. (2000). *Native vs. settler: Ethnic conflict in Israel/Palestine, Northern Ireland, and South Africa.* Westport, CT: Greenwood Press.

Moghaddam, F. M. (1998). *Social psychology: Exploring universals in social behavior.* New York: Freeman.

Moghaddam, F. M. (2002). *The individual and society: A cultural integration.* New York: Freeman/Worth.

Moghaddam, F. M., & Harré, R. (1995). But is it science? Traditional and alternative approaches to the study of social behavior. *World Psychology, 1,* 47–78.

Morris-Hale, W. (1996). *Conflict and harmony in multi-ethnic societies: An international perspective.* New York: Peter Lang.

O'Leary, B. (2001). Nationalism and ethnicity: Research agendas on theories of the sources and their regulation. In D. Chirot & M. Seligman (Eds.), *Ethnopolitical warfare: Causes, consequences and possible solutions* (pp. 37–48). Washington, DC: APA Books.

Pepitone, A. (1989). Toward a cultural social psychology. *Psychology and Developing Societies, 1,* 5–19.

Rico, R. B., & Mano, S. (2001). *American Mosaic.* Boston: Houghton Mifflin.

Rogers, J. D., Spencer, J., & Uyangoda, J. (1998). Sri Lanka: Political violence and ethnic conflict. *American Psychologist, 53*(7), 770–777.

Rohner, R. (1984). Towards a conception of culture for cross-cultural psychology. *Journal of Cross-Cultural Psychology, 15,* 111–138.

Rouhana, N. N., & Bar-Tal, D. (1998). Psychological dynamics of intractable ethnonational conflict: The Israeli-Palestinian case. *American Psychologist, 53*(7), 761–770.

Sadowski, Y. (1998). *The myth of global chaos.* Washington, DC: Brookings.

Sidanius, J., & Pratto, F. (1999). *Social dominance: An intergroup theory of social hierarchy and oppression.* New York: Cambridge University Press.

Smelster, N. J., & Alexander, J. C. (1999). *Diversity and its discontents: Cultural conflict and common ground in contemporary American society.* Princeton, NJ: Princeton University Press.

Stannard, D. E. (1992). *American holocaust: Columbus and the conquest of the New World.* New York: Oxford University Press.

Stigler, R. A., Shweder, R., & Herdt, G. (Eds.). (1990). *Cultural psychology.* New York: Cambridge University Press.

Smith, A. D. (1986). *The ethnic origins of nations.* New York: Basil Blackwell.

Smith, D. N. (1998). The psychocultural roots of genocide: Legitimacy and crisis in Rwanda. *American Psychologist, 53*(7), 743–753.

Tajfel, H. (1981). *Human groups and social categories.* Cambridge, UK: Cambridge University Press.

Tajfel, H., & Turner, J. C. (1986). The social identity theory of intergroup behavior. In S. Worchel & W. G. Austin (Eds.), *Psychology of intergroup relations* (pp. 7–24). Chicago: Nelson-Hall.

Takaki, R. (1989). *Strangers from a different shore: A history of Asian Americans.* Boston: Little Brown.

Taylor, D. M., & Moghaddam, F. M. (1994). Theories of intergroup relations: International social psychological perspectives (2nd ed.). Westport, CT: Praeger.

Triandis, H. (1994). *Culture and social behavior.* New York: McGraw-Hill.

Triandis, H. (1996). The psychological measurement of cultural syndromes. *American Psychologist, 51,* 407–415.

Triandis, H. C. (1989). The self and social behavior in differing cultural contexts. *Psychological Review, 96,* 506–520.

Triandis, H. C. (1995). *Individualism and collectivism.* Boulder, CO: Westview Press.

van den Berghe, P. (1981). *The ethnic phenomenon*. New York: Elsevier.

Wilson, E. O. (1975). *Sociobiology: The new synthesis*. Cambridge, MA: Harvard University Press.

Wing, R. L. (1986). *The Tao (Dao) of Power: A translation of Tao Te Ching (or Dao De Jing) by Lao Tzu (or Laozi)*. Garden City, NY: Dolphin Book/Doubleday & Co.

Worchel, S. (1999). *Written in blood: Ethnic identity and the struggle for human harmony*. New York: Worth.

Wuthnow, R. (1999). The culture of discontent. In N. J. Smelster & J. C. Alexander (Eds.), *Diversity and its discontents: Cultural conflict and commons ground in contemporary American society* (pp. 19–35). Princeton, NJ: Princeton University Press.

Wynter, L. E. (2002). *American skin: Pop culture, big business and the end of White America*. New York: Crown.

Young, M. C. (1993). *The rising tide of cultural pluralism: The nation-state at bay?* Madison, WI: University of Wisconsin Press.

PART II

Conceptual Issues in Contact between Ethnic and Cultural Groups

The Tragedy of the Commons Revisited: The Role of Kinship and Coresidence in the Establishment and Maintenance of Corporate In-Group Boundaries in Commons Dilemmas

Wayne E. Allen and Napoleon A. Chagnon

The fundamental ethical problem of the industrial age is to find a solution to the tragedy of the commons.
—Pierre L. van den Berghe, *The Ethnic Phenomenon*

INTRODUCTION

The problem of the *tragedy of the commons* can provide useful insight into the distinctions between physical group formation processes and symbolic, or categorical, affiliation in establishing attachments and bonds, and therefore in-group identities and membership. These distinctions take on great relevance when individuals are confronted with the conflicts engendered by commons dilemmas in the real world. At issue are the evolutionary role of inclusive fitness (kin selection) and coresidential proximity in facilitating kin recognition and reciprocity. Long-term physical association and familiarity are essential features of social group formation processes that lead to the establishment of strong in-group bonds and attachments (Bowlby, 1969; Chisholm, 1996; Freeman, 1973). And it is now well known that bonds and attachments promote in-group solidarity, which ameliorates the levels of competition and violence in intragroup conflicts (Eibl-Eibesfeldt, 1998; Johnson, 2001; Meyer, 2002). But at the same time, the creation of bonds and maintenance of bounded in-group identities can exacerbate intergroup differences when members of differing social groups are confronted with limiting resources in commons dilemmas (Brewer, 1986; Brewer & Silver, 2000; Kramer & Brewer, 1984). Explicating and understanding this process has become especially relevant since the events of 9/11 and the accelerating juggernaut of escalating ethnic, religious, and cultural conflict associated with the last of the world's oil resources (Ahmed, 2002; Klare, 2001; Korten, 2001).

Central to understanding this problem are the empirical distinctions between *social groups* and *social categories.* Social groups are populations of individuals who interact in space and time. Social categories are classificatory sets of individuals. Arbitrary symbolic characteristics (or sets of characteristics) define membership in the category. Incipient human social groups were coresidential kin groups—that is, spatially, biologically, and socially bounded populations. Incipient social categories were likely kinship terms, lineal descent categories, and common interest associations (Allen, 1998; Keesing, 1975; Palmer, Fredrickson, & Tilley, 1997). Most contemporary social scientists regularly conflate and confuse these significant empirical distinctions when discussing ethnic, racial, or cultural "groups," which in reality are not groups at all, but categories.

When one examines conflicts that are engendered over essential limiting resources that occur in commons contexts, one can see that Hardin's original formulation of the tragedy of the commons was profound but incomplete. It envisioned each actor as an unaffiliated ego with no group membership and therefore distinctive, ego-based, selfish economic interests. And this characterization was assumed to be so even if the actors had an implied categorical affiliation such as membership in the same society or "culture," or even the same ethnicity, nationality, or race. This, not so surprisingly, is in keeping with characterizations in formal microeconomic theory in which individuals are posited to be self-interested and self-aggrandizing, and therefore implicitly unaffiliated.

Darwinian evolutionary theory and ethnographic studies of tribal peoples, however, reveal that for the vast majority of human evolution, the actors coming to commons scenarios had embedded and bounded in-group identities. Identities were a product of strong affective bonds and attachments established during an individual's lifetime through the mechanisms of biological relatedness, coresidence, and cooperation in small, kin-based corporate groups (Eibl-Eibesfeldt, 1998; Johnson, 2001; Meyer, 2002). Corporateness was established among kin groups by long-term coresidence and cooperation around limiting somatic and reproductive resources. Coresidential affiliation and cooperation established boundaries around in-group identity, which could be extended through categorical affiliations such as marriage, kinship, or trade alliances. But coresidence—that is, long-term physical association and familiarity—and cooperation among close kin and reciprocators were always the empirical linchpins that reified categorical affiliation into group membership in our evolutionary past.

In-group membership has played a significant role throughout human history in ameliorating intragroup conflict when confronted with commons dilemmas. In-group identity facilitates solidarity and cooperation among individuals within territories held and defended by small, localized, coresiding corporate descent groups (Eibl-Eibesfeldt, 1998; Johnson, 2001; Meyer, 2002; Sanderson, 2001). Coresidence functioned to physically reify and actualize in-group identities. An aspect of that identity has always been abstract, symbolic, or categorical. Categorical affiliation, however, does not function in modern nontribal societies like group affiliation did in tribal societies. Categories do not mitigate self-aggrandizement like group solidarity does when confronted with conflicts engendered by commons dilemmas. This can be seen in the fact that categorical affiliation alone, such as ethnicity, religion, or nationality, requires the establishment and implementation of some sort of formal coercive regime such as treaties, laws, contracts, and private or state property tenure to mitigate conflicts between individuals and groups over resources in perceived commons (Carneiro, 1968; Hardin, 1968; Olson, 1971; Ostrom, 1990).

At the same time, however, membership in small, localized band and tribal groups exacerbated intergroup conflicts in our past by establishing, maintaining, and defending group boundaries when confronted with limiting resources in commons scenarios (Eibl-Eibesfeldt & Salter, 1998; James & Goetze, 2001). With the advent of states and colonialism, a situation has developed in the world in which resource pools like frontiers and "free" markets are perceived as commons for which competing groups or members of differing socially constructed categories vie (Ahmed, 2002; Eibl-Eibesfeldt & Salter, 1998; James and Goetze, 2001; Klare, 2001; Korten, 2001). A key to understanding potential intergroup and intercategorical conflicts associated with commons dilemmas, then, lies in the distinctions between the strength of the affiliative bonds engendered by physical propinquity processes in small-scale societies, and the weak bonds engendered by categorical affiliation in large, modern societies (Eibl-Eibesfeldt & Salter, 1998).

HARDIN'S TRAGEDY OF THE COMMONS

In 1968, Garrett Hardin published a work whose impact on scientific thought would be profound. "The Tragedy of the Commons" (Hardin, 1968) was a seemingly insoluble problem that was immediately recognized by ecologists and other scientists as an elegant, simple, and useful model regarding the conflicts involved in the exploitation of common-property resources. It was easily integrated into academic curricula and has become part of the intellectual paradigm in disciplines like political science, economics, behavioral ecology, anthropology, environmental sciences, and resource science and policy (see www.indiana.edu/~work shop/wsl/tragedy.htm for a comprehensive commons bibliography). Scholars in these fields found it a powerful heuristic model that explains and predicts the differences between idealized representations of collective interests and the actual strategies employed by individuals when they exploit common-property resources in the environment.

Hardin's tragedy of the commons is premised on formal microeconomic assumptions about the nature of individuals. This is to say, it implies that individuals are self-interested and self-aggrandizing rational calculators who pursue the maximization of *satisfactions* or *utility*. Hardin's characterization assumes that where there is a common-property resource with open access, each individual will calculate his self-interest in relationship to that of other individuals who have access to the resource. Each actor coming to the commons will perform such a calculation and will attempt to maximize the utility of the resource(s) for himself. Benefits accrue to each individual actor when there is open access to the commons because the short-term costs associated with exploiting it are minimal.

Hardin postulated that the actors behave this way because they have no prior investment of time or energy in the commons, and therefore no individual ownership interest. Individual ownership, according to Hardin (1968), leads to territorial defense and *prudent predation*—that is, harvesting restraint and resource conservation—of the resources present in the commons. Because there is no prior ownership investment in the form of territorial defense, the commons is perceived as a free utility available to all actors who have access to it. According to Hardin (ibid.), it is a process in which each actor engages in self-interested strategizing and exploitation that gradually, yet ultimately, leads to collective overexploitation and the eventual degradation of the resource(s) in question. One is left with a sobering conclusion derived from Hardin's formulation: Unless a socially constructed and territorially bounded form of *competitive exclusion* (den Boer, 1986; Hardin, 1960) is instituted to coerce cooperation from individuals, such as private property or state property tenure, common-pool resources are inevitably doomed to overexploitation and extinction (Fig. 2.1).

Hardin and others, though, have failed to ask significant theoretical questions informed by Darwinian evolutionary biology: What if all the actors coming to the commons were kin with overlapping inclusive fitness interests (Hamilton, 1964; Maynard-Smith, 1964)? What if they grew up, resided, and associated together in localized groups, and were therefore familiar and cooperated in most instances? Long-term membership in affectively bonded coresidential corporate kin groups meant in-group affil-

Figure 2.1
Garrett Hardin's Open-Access and Unmanaged Commons.
"The Tragedy of the Commons": In Hardin's classic characterization of the commons, each actor is assumed to be an unaffiliated ego with individual economic interests, a supposition consistent with formal microeconomic theory. Implicit but unstated in Hardin's original formulation is the presumption that each actor also has individual genetic interests—i.e., a coefficient of relatedness of 1.0 to self and 0.0 to other actors in the scenario—as well as a distinct ontogeny or developmental life history. Each individual actor is therefore predisposed to pursue selfish genetic and economic interests.

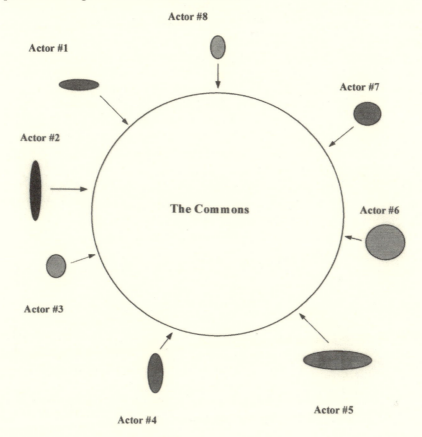

Source: Adapted from Allen, 1998.

iation mechanisms were more than just symbolic during our evolutionary past.

In the tribal world where we spent the vast majority of our evolutionary history, biological kinship predicts nepotistic restraint, solicitude, and co-operation. It also predicts bounded coresidence and local in-group membership. And most important, it predicts rights and obligations, along with a sense of in-group solidarity, ethnocentrism, and corporateness among local group members. In-group solidarity, though, is accompanied by chronic xenophobia toward and aggressive conflict with out-group members. Anthropologists have long been well aware of the ubiquitous fact that overlapping kinship interests in the tribal world translate into overlapping economic interests, cooperation, coresidence, and group solidarity (Sahlins, 1972). During the Pleistocene, the hominid actors who formed the localized cohorts coming to commons scenarios would have been either highly related kin and therefore long-term coresiders and co-operators, or unrelated "strangers," and therefore competitors. On average, individuals would *not* have been selected to degrade a commons if the commons were part of a larger territorial estate that was held, defended, and shared in common—that is, a kin-based *corporate* estate (Fig. 2.2 below, adapted from Allen, 1998). Collective overexploitation of the type Hardin described would have only obtained where distantly related or unrelated strangers with no long-term vested interests in one another, and therefore no physical affiliation, either biological or coresidential, came together in commons scenarios (Fig. 2.1).

KINSHIP AND CORESIDENCE: AMELIORATING IN-GROUP CONFLICT AND COMPETITION

Most applications of Hardin's model to commons-dilemma scenarios have consistently ignored the findings of evolutionary biologists and behavioral ecologists concerning kin recognition and nepotistic solicitude and restraint, as well as the ethnographic data on hunter-gatherers (H-Gs) and tribal peoples that demonstrate the role of kin relatedness in biasing resource use and economic exchanges (Daly & Wilson, 1983; Krebs & Davies, 1987; Sahlins, 1972). Few researchers have taken into account the high coefficients of relatedness among members of localized H-G or tribal groups (for exceptions, see Chagnon, 1996; Ziker, 2002; and for a theoretical overview, see E. A. Smith, 1997). The high coefficient of kin relatedness among members of localized groups in bands and tribes is the genealogical (biological and physical) reality of kinship, and it has consistently been ignored by most contemporary social scientists even though anthropologists have long been aware of the presence of kin-directed altruism among members of such groups (Firth, 1936; Fortes, 1969; Sahlins, 1972).

Figure 2.2
Kin-Based Corporate Commons.
Each actor is assumed to have had a life history of genetic, spatial, and social affiliation with the other actors coming to the commons. They are members of a corporate kin group and a coresidential cohort. Recognized membership is calibrated by sociospatial proximity during ontogenetic development. Corporate parameters are synonymous with kinship, coresidence, territoriality, and in-group boundaries and identities. The actors coming to the commons have overlapping genetic and economic interests with the other actors using the commons. The commons is part of a corporately held "estate," where in-group membership confers rights of open access as well as obligations for defense, prudent predation, and sharing and pooling of resources with other in-group members.

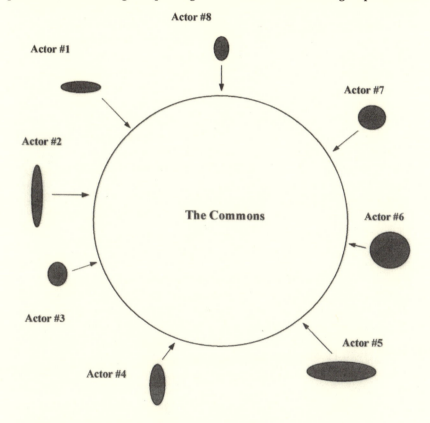

Biophobia is rampant in the social sciences, accompanied by an overemphasis on symbols, symbolizing behaviors, and symbolic designations and meanings. The potential role in human evolution of what Hamilton (1964) identified as *inclusive fitness* is never even considered when examining the physical establishment of in-groups and group identity in commons scenarios (see Baden, 1977; Harden & Baden, 1977; Ostrom, 1990).

Most ecological studies that focus on commons issues conspicuously ignore Darwinian evolutionary theory, behavioral ecology, coefficients of relatedness, and kin selection. Nor is there a consideration of the implications of coresidence mechanisms like physical proximity, association, and familiarity in the acquisition and establishment of affective bonds, attachments, kin recognition, and collective territorial behavior among potential cooperators or competitors. A significant part of the problem is that social scientists regularly conflate social groups with social categories. Social groups are on-the-ground, empirically observable populations interacting in space and time, whereas social categories are abstractions that consist of either internally generated or externally projected classificatory stereotypes (i.e., generalizations).

Hardin's characterization of the commons dilemma is not flawed on this account, however. Rather, the model does not distinguish between assumptions about the nature of individuals in resource-use settings where the majority of the actors coming to the commons are strangers, such as occurs in contemporary commons scenarios, and those where the majority of the actors coming to commons scenarios are recognized as kin, coresiders, and cooperators, and therefore members of corporate in-groups. For over 99.9 percent of our evolutionary history, the actors coming to the commons would have been members of localized foraging groups who coresided, cooperated, and recognized one another de facto as close kin, and therefore as in-group members and potential reciprocators (Allman, 1994; Daly & Wilson, 1983).

Contemporary H-G bands and horticulturalist and pastoralist tribal communities are kin based, their members share and pool their efforts, and they cooperate with members of the coresidential in-group most of the time. But they also live in a world where ethnocentrism, xenophobia, and chronic violent conflict with perceived outsiders characterize intergroup competition. *Outsider* in the tribal world usually means any stranger from outside the local group, or in rare instances from outside the regional polity. But people in this category are also potential (or actual) in-laws or reciprocators who are ambivalently perceived as both potential competitors and cooperators. In the tribal world, in-group and out-group members often share a categorical-yet-distant, and therefore very weak, symbolic (i.e., "ethnic") affiliation with one another. Interactions at this level are precarious and often erupt in violence. It is an affiliative continuum going from group to category, in-group to out-group, kin to reciprocator to stranger, close to distant, and strong bonds to weak or nonexistent attachments. This has profound implications for understanding the ambivalence associated with, as well as the strengths and weaknesses of, attachments formed by categorical bonds alone.

Derek Freeman (1973) points out the biological significance of physical attachments in establishing what Meyer Fortes (1969) characterized as

"Kinship [that] is binding: it creates inescapable claims and obligations" (ibid., p. 242). Fortes (1969) claimed "the axiom of amity" is a "rule of prescriptive altruism." Freeman (ibid.) insightfully recognized that it is physical attachments formed by proximity during ontogeny that facilitate "the axiom of amity." Psychological mechanisms for forming attachments were selected in our evolutionary past to promote kin recognition, nepotistic solicitude, and prudent predation—for example, sharing and pooling—within an in-group's bounded territorial estate (ibid., Bowlby, 1969; Petrovich & Gewirtz, 1985; Reite & Field, 1985; Taylor, 1988; Tuan, 1990).

Kin-based cooperation is not unique to symbol and language-using humans either, for it is ubiquitous among social animals in nature, as are territoriality and occasional conflicts with unrecognized or "strange" competitors. In their introductory text to behavioral ecology, Krebs and Davies (1987) state:

it will be obvious to any naturalist that animals do not behave selfishly all the time. (p. 243)

There is now a rapidly growing body of evidence that individuals can indeed recognize kin and even distinguish close kin from distant kin. (p. 253)

Concerning humans, Daly and Wilson, in *Sex, Evolution, and Behavior* (1983), say:

Kinship is a basic organizing principle of every human society . . . People everywhere understand the concept of a **dimension from close to distant kin.** (p. 321)

Kinship mitigates conflict; the risk of homicide, for example, is much greater between nonrelatives living together (and between in-laws) than between blood kin. The other side of the coin is that blood relationship is highly predictive of the frequency of cooperative interaction. . . . Napoleon Chagnon has shown, for example, that blood relationship is a better predictor of solidarity in conflicts among the Yanomamö Indians than is terminological kinship. (pp. 322–23)

And finally, Eric Alden Smith (1997), in his evolutionary analysis of models applicable in studying H-G foraging group size and composition, says:

the artificial notion of individuals pursuing their own best interests in blissful isolation from others, akin to the "Robinson Crusoe" fiction of classical economics, can be replaced by a socially dynamic view of adaptation, wherein the best strategy to pursue depends on what other actors are doing, and on their relatedness to each other. (p. 51)

Although Hardin's model is incomplete, it unintentionally reveals that understanding the physical mechanics of nascent group formation is essential. The physical process of developmental calibration within a small group leads to in-group cooperation and out-group competition in commons dilemmas. Individuals are social beings and do not exist in the unaffiliated ether of theoretical models. Hardin's model is normative and presumes individuals are selfish in all settings, when in fact they are designed by evolution to behave so only when dealing with in-group cheaters and out-group members who are distant, unrelated strangers. Hardin's model does not take into account the evolutionary role of kin relatedness in establishing socially embedded identities. The ontogenetic role of spatial proximity—that is, coresidence, physical association, and familiarity—in predicting cooperative behavior in commons scenarios is thus ignored.

Is there a difference in the strength of bonds and attachments established in the distinctive processes of group affiliation versus categorical (or terminological) affiliation? Group affiliation is a spatial and temporal bonding process that results from developmental imprinting within a social cohort. It is neurobiological and neurohormonal in its proximate emotional functioning, and therefore a physical process and phenomenon. Thus, it is a sociobiological construct. Categorical affiliation, on the other hand, can reinforce group formation processes, or even countermand them in some instances. It represents a communication mechanism on the continuum of group formation processes. It is a symbolic process ancillary to and embedded in group formation processes. Therefore, the bonds established in this process are inherently tied to those established through physical group formation processes. They are ancillary to group formation processes and through repeated exposure have a sort of imprinting, and therefore affective, component in their construction as well. But symbol acquisition is tied to in-group badging and marking—that is, social communication—and although oftentimes an unconscious process, it is more facultative and ambivalent than group identity acquisition alone. This is why one sees group identity acquisition all across the animal kingdom that is reinforced by categorical designations like boundary marking and ritualized displays. But in social animals other than humans, one never sees categories or boundaries without groups. It is only among humans that one sees individuals attempting to surrogate symbolic affiliation for group affiliation. We would caution that this is somewhat deceptive, however, for if one were to examine this phenomenon more closely, one would see that categorical affiliation is in fact always physically facilitated and reinforced "on the ground" through interactions within a localized population or cohort—that is, a social group.

Most contemporary researchers focus on symbols and meanings and thereby miss the importance of biological kinship and physical association in establishing territorial affiliation, nepotistic bonds, cooperation and restraint, and corporate coalitions when confronted with commons dilemmas (for the pioneering exception, see Chagnon, 1996). One simply must take into account human evolution and the potential role of kin related-ness and inclusive fitness (Hamilton, 1964), as well as kin recognition that is calibrated by coresidence in small social groups during development (Bateson, 1981; Hepper, 1991) when discussing the in-group/out-group dynamics involved in cooperation and conflicts over resources.

One should not underestimate the significance of Hardin's contribution to a scientific analysis of these and related questions. The tragedy of the commons is one of the most significant intellectual contributions in the latter half of the twentieth century. One can see his predictions played out daily in the modern world wherever people, albeit *strangers*, are compet-ing for open-access, common-property resources. What is at issue, then, is a precise explication of when and where Hardin's model will be an accurate predictor of collective human behavior and in what instances it might not.

SOCIAL GROUPS VERSUS SOCIAL CATEGORIES— A KEY DISTINCTION

In small-scale foraging societies, the kinship system is predicated on bilateral descent. Local residential groups known as bands or camps con-sist of bilaterally organized consanguineal and affinal kin. In tribal soci-eties, kinship is predicated on unilineal descent and local residential groups usually consist of members from a minimum of at least two line-ages or clans (Chagnon, 1996). Lineages and clans are both unilineal de-scent groups, but lineages trace their ancestry to a known ancestor and clans trace their ancestry to a totemic or symbolic ancestor. Both represent social categories, but clans extend their categorical affiliation further through a common totemic symbol. There is always an element of sym-bolic classification and categorization in unilineal descent systems, but it is the conjoining of the material realities of biological descent and spatial coresidence, along with manipulation of the classificatory kinship system by individuals who are pursuing their self-interests that crystallizes the classificatory or categorical structure into a physical group reality.

Anthropologists have often confused and conflated the idealized kin-ship system and prescribed residence pattern—that is, abstracted cate-gories of sociospatial organization—with the one that actually exists empirically (Keesing 1975; Palmer et al., 1997). The physical factors of biological descent, spatial coresidence, and access to land or resources—somatic or reproductive—are what reify such categorical representations into real and meaningful units of group affiliation. The material reality, where individual actors share coresidence and access to somatic or repro-ductive resources, functions to crystallize cultural or social categories into social groups (ibid.). Social categories do play a role in the construction of identities, the demarcation of social and spatial boundaries, and the allocation of resources in the objective world (Lee 1976). According to Richard Lee (ibid., p. 75), though, a great deal of confusion has arisen due to a confounding of "the *behavior* of groups in their space and the *conceptions* or *folk view* of the people about themselves and their land. The latter type of data, though important, is at best an imperfect reflection of the actual arrangements of persons on the ground."

In-group membership, then, is a classificatory status—an abstract reality—that is reified through an actor's socioecological role—an objective reality. Individual actors' socioecological roles are determined by ascribed kinship statuses, along with usufructory and tenured associations within a residential group or locale, or in association with a limiting material resource. For example, high-status individuals in localized H-G groups are the recognized *egos* in bilateral "nodal" kindreds, and therefore the recognized "owners" of limiting material resources (Helm, 1965, 1968). It is a process that results in the physical incorporation of local H-G in-groups into what Allen (1998) called "residential kindreds."

Are local bilateral kindreds that form H-G residential groups *corporate* in nature? The evidence is that they are (Allen, 1998; Brown, 1974, 1991; Goodenough, 1955, 1970; Lewis, 1991; Panitch, 1980). The question has saliency for discussions concerning the permeability or impermeability of sociospatial boundaries in H-G residential groupings. Previously, local residential groups among H-Gs were characterized by anthropologists as being relatively impermeable patrilineal corporate entities based on three organizing principles: (1) band exogamy; (2) patrilocal postmarital residence; and (3) band territoriality. Recently, however, many anthropologists have found local residential group membership is fluid, and therefore seemingly *noncorporate* (Helm, 1965, 1968; Lee, 1976). Thus, there has been a decreased emphasis on corporate groups and an increasing emphasis on categorical affiliation and negotiated meanings and identities in H-G studies. What is often overlooked, though, is the fact that this debate is premised on a false dichotomy that confuses and often conflates spatial membership—a physical social group—with social membership—an abstract social category. A social category only has salience when the human actors involved coalesce into a social group in real space and time for a concerted purpose, such as coresidence, subsistence, production, warfare, trade, ceremonies, or consumption (ibid., Lee, 1976).

An H-G or tribal coresidential cohort is made up of bilaterally close kin and affines (in-laws) who are members of a larger regional polity that is based on symbolic kinship writ large—an incipient ethnic "group." This is a linguistically and spatially defined *corporate category*, oftentimes referred to as a *regional band* (Helm, 1965, 1968), a *tribe* (Chagnon, 1996), or an incipient *ethny* (van den Berghe, 1987, 1990). Membership in these larger social categories, which is based on shared geographical region and shared customs, language, and common descent, allows somewhat fluid membership between localized groupings. But group transfer only occurs after following recognized permission-seeking protocols that are implicitly based on invoking some form of kinship proximity, real or fictive, to the recognized egos that control access to limiting material resources held on behalf of their localized corporate (k)in-group.

The corporateness of local residential groups among H-Gs and tribal peoples is predicated on the identity of high-status individuals who are the living embodiment of the corporate kin group's spatial and social—that is, their material—interests. These individuals are the *ego nodes* of kindreds in bands and *heads* of lineages or clans in tribes. They are the recognized owners of localized home ranges or herds. They control rights of access to and obligations surrounding valuable limiting resources that are the physical nexus of a residential group's identity. Among H-Gs, these recognized owners are most often same-sex siblings or parallel cousins (who are classificatory siblings) who resided and grew up together in close spatial proximity for most of their lives. These "owners" thus constitute the physical nexus of the bilateral nodal kindreds mentioned earlier (Goodenough, 1970; Murdock, 1968).

Kin groups and coresidential cohorts in traditional societies have a graded in-group, or *ethnic,* identity (van den Berghe, 1987). It is reified through usufruct of a material resource or a locale and physical proximity to conspecifics more effectively than through symbolic association alone. Corporate kin groups are graded along a categorical continuum from *ego* to *relative* to *ally* to *stranger.* Although these categories are often expressed as symbolic or classificatory constructs, they are not merely symbolic, but instead represent a physical reality. That reality consists of graduated degrees of consanguinity, affinity, residential proximity, reciprocity, or affiliation extending out in social, temporal, and three-dimensional space from ego (Tuan 1990).

Membership in the larger social category of regional band or tribe is always somehow physically marked and bounded, usually by dialect, dress, adornment, or common customs (van den Berghe, 1987). Categorical membership in the larger polity confers rights to seek access, as well as obligations to share, that are physically actualized through coresidence and cooperation within a localized in-group. People must follow a permission-seeking protocol for accessing another local group's corporately owned territory. The local group's spatial boundaries correlate strongly at any given time with the social boundaries of the residential group (Jochim, 1983; Taylor, 1988; van den Berghe, 1987, 1990). Physical membership in local residential groupings is somewhat fluid for peripheral members who have an ascribed "in-group" status due to categorical membership in a larger regional polity. But this is only so for those who are categorically defined as *kin.* Everyone must have a place in the kinship network or they are not human because they then do not have a place in the system of rights and obligations, which defines where, when, and with whom they may reside and interact, as well as what resources they may use. Those who do not have a recognized status or role in the system are strangers and therefore potential enemies.

It must be understood that social and spatial boundaries are always symbolic to some degree, even among the most rudimentary social life forms. For example, boundaries in the animal world may be based on pheromones, ritualizations, or displays. These ubiquitous behaviors in social animals create incipient symbols, such as pheromones in urine or ritualized displays, whose intrinsic meaning is used to represent an extrinsic proprietary claim associated with a somatic or reproductive resource. These symbolic markers or behaviors, which humans have evolved and elaborated more than any other species, represent a behavioral capacity to exploit and convey information about spatial or social territoriality and affiliation (d'Aquili, Laughlin, & McManus, 1979).

The corporate estate, then, should be viewed as common property that can be real estate—that is, physical property—or simply ownership of the rights of access and obligations to share and cooperate that are associated with an in-group's identity (Axelrod, 1984; Chagnon, 1996; Goodenough, 1955, 1970; Keesing, 1975; Taylor, 1988; van den Berghe, 1987, 1990). Categorical identity must always be actualized in the real world through the physical means of establishing membership in a local group. Access to the corporate estate is obtained through permission to coreside or work with a group and exploit resources. Along with *rights* of access come reciprocal *obligations* (J. G. E. Smith, 1976, 1978). Spatial coresidence among H-Gs is ascribed by categorical membership conferred through birth, or through social alliance institutions such as kinship, marriage, trading, spouse-sharing partnerships, and adoption. In all instances, however, categorical membership is physically reified through group membership.

"Ethnic" (or tribal) markers are symbolic signifiers of categorical kinship employed in large-scale societies to convey in-group identity, which confers rights of access to corporate commons. The incipient ethnic in-group in human prehistory was defined by H-G camps or bands and the regional polity of which they were a part (Keesing, 1975). Categorical kin among H-Gs could be symbolically extended as widely as the *regional band* or *tribe*, depending on the political need. It was the incipient ethnic polity categorically writ large (Jochim, 1983; Taylor, 1988; van den Berghe, 1987, 1990). The regional band or the tribe therefore became, for all intents and purposes, symbolically represented as an extended kin group—the incipient *ethny* (van den Berghe, 1987).

Modern ethnic "groups" are simply kin groups categorically extended and projected onto a larger polity that holds defining symbols in common, most often a language, folk attire and accouterments, a common history, and a shared territory (ibid.). This symbolic identity is often conveyed in narratives about "shared blood," history, and a homeland where common ethnicity and language sanction and promote in-group identity and solidarity. But in modern world reality, if two members of a common ethnic group, which is in fact an ethnic category and not a group, are strangers, then there is a real potential for a defection in exchanges. Simply stated, strangers whose only affinity is categorical lack a prior history of the spatial and temporal—that is, physical—association and familiarity that predicts cooperation in exchanges. Individuals will defect more often when the unifying factor of an in-group is merely a symbol—for example, an ethnic marker or a formal, contractual agreement—than they will when the unifying factor is long-term association in the form of biological, social, spatial, and temporal propinquity.

In the modern world, strange actors make defecting exchange partners but "necessary bedfellows," so to speak. Most exchanges occur between strangers who have some categorical affiliation but who lack the strong emotional attachments and exchange reputations that are formed and acquired during mutual life histories of living in small groups. Therefore, the actors have little basis other than symbolic markers, categorical affiliations, social constructs, and contractual arrangements for judging the exchange reputations of one another (Frey, 1998). Formal social contracts based on symbolic values can easily be counterfeited, and thereby promote cheating and defection, much more so than informal exchange arrangements based on reputations established by living in small coresidential groups.

At issue, then, are several major areas of theoretical concern in the social sciences: (1) the evolved nature of human beings and their cooperative in-group behavior and competitive out-group behavior; (2) the appropriate level of analysis for studying human nature and group behavior; (3) social group versus social category assumptions and explanatory models in the social sciences; (4) whether and in what social contexts humans have evolved to pursue strategies for exploiting the commons through either rate maximizing or risk minimizing; and finally, (5) whether or not Darwinian theory can provide the foundation for an integrated analysis whose methods are applicable on differing social levels, including the level of individuals, local groups, and larger sociopolitical categorical designations, where macrolevel analyses of cooperation and competition, such as political ecology and world systems theory, obtain (Bryant, 1992; Wolf, 1982).

Human behavioral ecology (Borgerhoff Mulder, 1991; Cronk, 1991) posits that individual organisms are not designed to pursue proximate goals such as the maximization of reproductive success, or foraging outcomes, or any other satisfaction or utility, per se. Human behavioral ecologists contend that coevolution, through the mechanism of kin selection, has designed individuals who reside in local kin-based cohorts to exercise nepotistic restraint and cooperate in the majority of instances, thereby optimizing their inclusive fitness through risk-reduction strategies (Salter et al., 2002). To observe this phenomenon, though, one must study humans in contemporary environments that most closely replicate past evolutionary environments (Chagnon, 1975, 1979, 1981, 1996); otherwise, one may simply be observing proximate adaptiveness to evolutionarily novel environments rather than ultimate adaptations to past evolutionary environments (Symons, 1990).

One might only observe a preponderance of competitive, self-aggrandizing, maximizing behaviors among humans in statistically unique—that is, evolutionarily novel—modern contexts. These could be called *novel environments of ontogeny* (NEO). Increasing dependencies on specialized trade between strangers have characterized the modern urban market economies that have obtained for the past 5,000 years or so of human history. Population increase, sedentary changes in settlement pattern, and increasing emphasis on categorical designations like social ranking, ethnicity, religion, nationality, and so forth have accompanied the agricultural revolution and increasing stratification and complexity. This has led to an increase in exchanges between individuals who are categorical in-group members but not members of the same physically localized group.

Actors in the modern world unconsciously perceive one another as nonkin and therefore potential defectors when encountered in exchanges. Most exchanges in the modern world occur between strangers whose only affiliation might be symbolic. Actors tend to have short-term histories of common-interest association and therefore uncertain exchange reputations. Strangers form opportunistic coalitions and they can easily defect if the costs become too high (Axelrod, 1984). The modern urbane world has become so novel and exotic relative to our design features that people are becoming more and more like Collin Turnbull's (1972) *Ik*, a group of mountain people in Africa who experienced severe colonial disruption and as a result have become the epitome of selfishness and self-aggrandizement in the ethnographic record. Population increase and the urban demographic transition have led to the swamping of relatively stable traditional social patterns.

Past environments that selected human behaviors would have been characterized by exchanges between both kin and nonkin. A simple evolutionary rule would have been, *When close cooperate and when distant defect*. It just seems that self-aggrandizing, competitive behaviors are so universal today because there are now so many competitive interactions between strangers and subsequent defections that they bias studies of exchange behavior in commons scenarios. They then take on an exaggerated preponderance in the literature. Social scientists have missed the point because they mistakenly focus on symbols, conveyed meaning, and categorical affiliation.

Cross-cultural ethnographic data demonstrate that there is a social spectrum in which kin recognition and nepotistic biasing, accompanied by cooperation in land tenure, harvesting strategies, and sharing practices, obtain when communities are small and cohesive, one end of the social spectrum. But aggression, aversions, and competition toward perceived outsiders obtain when communities become so large that most exchanges occur between strangers (Chagnon 1996). Communities then exceed the capacity for physical association and familiarity to calibrate kin recognition and kin selection mechanisms that mediate and mitigate self-aggrandizing social exchanges. The majority of exchanges occur between categorically affiliated strangers. Exchanges are then mediated by contracts and coercion to prevent self-aggrandizing cheating and defections, the other end of the social spectrum (Carneiro, 1968).

CONCLUSION

Let us return to Pierre van den Berghe's fundamental problem, stated at the beginning of this essay—finding a solution to the tragedy of the commons as an ethical challenge. Let us put his question into a broader context and relate it to some of the history of recent questions in anthropology.

Garrett Hardin drew attention to what, in a strict sense, is a dilemma of our own making, perhaps the logical result of a post-market economy— what the first author has characterized as the tragedy of the moderns.

In a wonderful essay written nearly 50 years ago, economic historian Karl Polanyi drew attention to the historical novelty of the *market* as a distinct economic form in an essay entitled "Aristotle Discovers the Economy" (Polanyi, 1957). Pre-market economies are embedded in kinship or kinship-like institutions and are the types of provisioning systems (economic systems) that have been historically studied by anthropologists. The tragedy of the commons is part of a broader economic question in anthropology and has to do with human economic systems—how humans provision themselves. In turn, this raises the question of what lies behind decisions made by individuals and whether human nature and evolved human behavior has anything to do with it.

By the time of Aristotle, the market economy and the political state had been around for over a millennium. Yet, even in the twentieth century, anthropologists were rather slow to recognize that the tribal economies they were studying were not only different in *quality* from market economies, but they were different in *kind* as well. Indeed, as recently as the 1960s and 1970s, anthropologists were debating whether or not the assumptions lying behind formal economic theory—individuals maximizing profit, commodity value being largely determined by scarcity, Adam Smith's "Invisible Hand" guided economic decisions, etc. (Dalton, G. 1961; Sahlins, M. 1968, 1972; Fried, M. 1967)—and what, if anything, these issues had to do with the evolution of political systems and the development of complex (state organized) societies.

It was not until William D. Hamilton, Robert Trivers, and other theoretical biologists developed powerful new insights into the behavior and ultimate objectives of organisms that an understanding of kinship in a profoundly new way, a genetic and biological way, emerged. To biologists, *kinship* has to do with demonstrable pedigrees and genetics. To anthropologists, kinship more often means "symbolic constructs" and most of them go out of their way to deny that kinship has anything to do with genetic relatedness.

These new biological views were made dramatically popular by E. O. Wilson (1975), R. D. Alexander (somewhat later with large amounts of additional data [1979]), and R. Dawkins (in an easily readable but sophisticated popular book [1976]). The new biological theory persuasively argued that all social interactions had potential reproductive consequences, not just economic or other purely social consequences. Favoring and disfavoring neighbors in social interactions had reproductive implications because it could potentially be a way to spread your own genes, a radical new twist to Darwinian theory. These arguments flew in the face of standard anthropological theory (Tooby and Cosmides, 1992), a theme that has more recently been developed by Steven Pinker in a critique of general social science assumption and theory (Pinker, 2002). Chagnon, with William Irons, drew attention to these issues as early as 1979 (Chagnon and Irons, 1979), and many others have done so as well.

Unfortunately, because of the long history of biophobia in anthropology, this theoretical implication not only fell on deaf ears but was immediately and vigorously repudiated by most cultural anthropologists. A stunning example of this is the somewhat preposterous condemnation of sociobiology by Marshall Sahlins (1976). His arguments were so outrageous that Richard Dawkins named a biological fallacy in his honor: the Sahlins Fallacy. An example of his claims would be that rocks cannot fall down because they are incapable of calculating their own mass. Sahlins argued that tribesmen could not behave according to predictions from inclusive fitness theory, because their languages do not have words for fractions or decimals. He then proclaimed (from his accumulated anthropological wisdom) that this theory could not apply to humans—just as gravity does not apply to rocks or Newton's apple. According to the logic of Sahlins, rocks and apples would have to fall up.

Post-Hamiltonian developments in Darwinian theory added an entirely new dimension to Hardin's tragedy of the commons conundrum because it raised the possibility that there might have been circumstances in the past when people—our own remote tribal ancestors and contemporary unacculturated tribesmen—did not degrade their environments like we are inclined to do. According to these developments, nepotism, the "prescriptive altruism" of kinship relatedness, as well as cooperation based on common genetic interests, thwarted these tendencies.

However, in scientific inquiry, hope and faith are poor guides for research and the pursuit of truth. As advocates of evolutionary theory, we would like to believe (perhaps at the bottom of our hearts and secretly) that there might be a magnificent, dignified exception to Hardin's tragedy of the commons, a solution that might even make us feel good about humans and what it is in their nature to do.

The stark reality is that despite our own efforts to find an empirically convincing exception to the tragedy of the commons through our own long-term field studies, the known facts still tend to support Hardin's argument. Although it is possible, on the other hand, that the relevance of inclusive fitness theory to the tragedy of the commons dilemma, especially our own field research attempts, might have been methodologically flawed or inadequate in other ways. Perhaps others might produce more convincing challenges to the astonishing problem that Hardin laid bare to all of us in the social and biological sciences.

Hardin's argument was presented to academic contemporaries who live in market-dominated economies and who generally assume them to be the natural state of economic things. His arguments and logic are relevant in this environment.

Let's take a more penetrating look at what we and other anthropologists must consider. First, evidence that humans are ecologically prudent and have a natural conservation ethic has little empirical support from both archaeological and anthropological field studies. The idea of an *ecologically Noble Savage* has next to no empirical support (see Krech, 1999).

Second, the conditions under which a commons tragedy could be avoided in a pristine tribal environment or under conditions obtaining in the distant historical human past—the EEA environments—would have to be very special. There would have to be long periods of homeostasis which means all social and ecological conditions would remain in balance and without change. There would need to be zero population growth (ZPG) and no ability to change carrying capacity by, for example, adding new (lower valued) food items that were previously unused. If even a small population growth rate occurred, the assumptions of inclusive fitness theory might not restrain the degradation of habitat due to population growth and more frequent interactions among increasingly distant individuals. This is both a theoretical and an empirical question that is testable in fieldwork settings among tribal people.

Unless these conditions are met, one predictable consequence would be that individuals would have to become more discriminating in favoring neighbors perceived as kin and disfavoring neighbors as more distant. All tribesmen (the kin-defined in-group members) would shift to a more restricted in-group, as in "only my clan members." As population grew and pressure on resources increased, even more restricted kin-defined in-groups would take form—"only my brothers and sisters and their families." As conditions worsened, the in-group, as predicted by inclusive fitness theory, would become even yet smaller with "my immediate family and one or two of my most trustworthy genetic brothers."

This would eventually lead to something like the aforementioned example of the Ik people described by anthropologist Colin Turnbull, where the Ik were eventually taking the food out of the mouths of their dying kinsmen and neighbors just to survive another day.

Meanwhile, and very important in the logic of the tragedy of the commons argument, former friends and remotely related kinsmen would now be members of the out-group, coveting your resources and willing to take them by force if necessary. Ironically, the arguments about kin altruism and sharing, are the same arguments required to explain the limits of kin altruism and the beginning boundaries of xenophobia: non-kin and distantly related kin are potential enemies and predators, and their activities most certainly would not fit into the parameters of Hardin's theory.

One should end chapters like this with an expression of hope in the concluding statement. Let us attempt to conclude with that tone. We continue to believe that it would be useful and theoretically productive to look for those possible instances, archaeologically and ethnographically, where humans violated the conditions assumed in Hardin's formulation of the tragedy of the commons dilemma—that groups of humans did not degrade the commons because they were cooperative and kin-selected altruists. These kinds of studies might lead to a promising set of insights into why nepotism and kinship ultimately, perhaps even necessarily, disappeared as the exclusive organizing principles of human societies and why larger groups such as states, empires, and nations were able to form. These large, complex conglomerations were based on a different kind of trust and cooperation: altruism founded on reciprocity among non-related neighbors. These also probably contributed to, and accelerated, a necessary new way to detect social cheaters, defectors, and otherwise unreliable neighbors. As anthropologist Meyer Fortes characterized it, kinship amity is based on prescriptive altruism. It was the social matrix that got us through most of our history, but it was also a persistent and pervasive condition that we had to overcome to build cities, empires, and nations. If you think that life is pleasant and idyllic in a small, kin-dominated and kin-organized group, go live in one for a couple of years before you proclaim this. The people Chagnon studied—the Yanomamö of Venezuela—complained most about having to live with people they didn't like, who happened to be their relatives. It was only the fear of being decimated by their neighbors that they did so.

Hardin's tragedy of the commons is about this recent period of time in our history . . . before Aristotle noticed that economic things had changed. Both of the authors of this essay knew Garrett Hardin, took theoretical inspiration from him, and enjoyed lively discussions with him. He was a mentor to Wayne Allen, a University colleague to Napolean Chagnon. Both of us were deeply saddened to learn of the deaths of Professor Hardin and his wife in September 2003, and his life and achievements will be forever remembered.

REFERENCES

Ahmed, N. M. (2002). *The war on freedom: How and why America was attacked September 11, 2001.* Joshua Tree, CA: Tree of Life Publications.

Alexander, R. (1979). *Darwinism and human affairs.* London: Pitman Publishing, Ltd.

Allen, W. E. (1998). *Sustainable resource economies versus extractive surplus economies in the Canadian subarctic: A reassessment of Hardin's "Tragedy of the Commons."* Ph.D. dissertation in anthropology, University of California at Santa Barbara.

Allman, W. F. (1994). *The stone age present: How evolution has shaped modern life—From sex, violence, and language to emotions, morals, and communities.* New York: Simon & Schuster.

Axelrod, R. (1984). *The evolution of cooperation.* New York: Basic Books.

Baden, J. (1977). A primer for the management of common pool resources. In G. Hardin & J. Baden (Eds.), *Managing the commons.* San Francisco: W. H. Freeman and Co.

Bateson, P. P. G. (1981). Ontogeny of behavior. *British Medical Bulletin,* 37(2): 159–64.

Borgerhoff Mulder, M. (1991). Human behavioral ecology. In J. R. Krebs & N. B. Davies (Eds.), *Behavioral ecology: An evolutionary approach* (3rd ed., pp. 69–98). Oxford: Blackwell Scientific Publications.

Bowlby, J. (1969). *Attachment.* New York: Basic Books.

Brewer, M. B. (1986). The role of ethnocentrism in intergroup conflict. In S. Worchel & W. Austin (Eds.), *Psychology and intergroup relations.* Chicago: Nelson Hall.

Brewer, M. B., & Silver, M. D. (2000). Group distinctiveness, social identification, and collective mobilization. In Sheldon Stryker & Timothy J. Owens (Eds.), *Self, identity, and social movements: Social movements, protest, and contention.* Minneapolis, MN: University of Minnesota Press.

Brown, D. E. (1974). Corporations and social classification. *Current Anthropology 15,* 29–52.

Brown, D. E. (1991). *Human universals*. New York: McGraw-Hill.

Bryant, R. L. (1992). Political ecology: An emerging research agenda in Third-World studies. *Geography 11*(1), 12–36.

Carneiro, R. L. (1968). A theory of the origin of the state. *Science, 169*(3947), 733–738.

Chagnon, N. A. (1975). Genealogy, solidarity and relatedness: Limits to local group size and patterns of fissioning in an expanding population. *Yearbook of Physical Anthropology, 19*, 95–110.

Chagnon, N. A. (1979). Mate competition, favoring close kin and village fissioning among the Yanomamö Indians. In N. A. Chagnon & W. Irons (Eds.), *Evolutionary biology and human social behavior*. North Scituate, MA: Duxberry Press.

Chagnon, N. A. (1981). Terminological kinship, genealogical relatedness and village fissioning among the Yanomamö Indians. In R. Alexander & D. Tinkle (Eds.), *Natural selection and social behavior: Recent research and new theory* (pp. 490–508). New York: Chiron Press.

Chagnon, N. A. (1996). *Yanomamö* (5th ed. with accompanying *Ax Fight* CD-ROM). San Diego, CA: Harcourt Brace Jovanovich College.

Chisholm, J. (1996). The evolutionary ecology of attachment organization. *Human Nature 7*(1), 1–38.

Cronk, L. (1991). Human behavioral ecology. *Annual Review of Anthropology 20*, 25–53.

Dalton, G. (1961). Economic theory and anthropology. *American Anthropologist 63*, 1–25.

Daly, M., & Wilson, M. (1983). *Sex, evolution, and behavior*. Belmont, CA: Wadsworth.

d'Aquili, E. G., Laughlin, C. D., Jr., & McManus, J. (1979). *The spectrum of ritual: A biogenetic structural analysis*. New York: Columbia University Press.

Dawkins, R. (1976). *The selfish gene*. Oxford: Oxford University Press.

den Boer, P. J. (1986). The present status of the competitive exclusion principle. *Trends in Ecology and Evolution 1*, 25–28.

Eibl-Eibesfeldt, I. (1998). Us and others: The familial roots of ethnonationalism. In Irenäus Eibl-Eibesfeldt & Frank K. Salter (Eds.), *Ethnic conflict and indoctrination: Altruism and identity in evolutionary perspective*. New York: Berghahn Books.

Eibl-Eibesfeldt, I., & Salter, F. K. (Eds.). (1998). *Ethnic conflict and indoctrination: Altruism and identity in evolutionary perspective*. New York: Berghahn Books.

Firth, R. (1936). *We, the Tikopia: Kinship in primitive Polynesia* (1963 ed.). Boston: Beacon Press.

Fortes, M. (1969). *Kinship and the social order: The legacy of Lewis Henry Morgan*. Chicago: Aldine.

Freeman, D. (1973). Kinship, attachment behaviour and the primary bond.

In J. Goody (Ed.), *The character of kinship.* Cambridge: Cambridge University Press.

Frey, S. (1998). Prejudice and inferential communication: A new look at an old problem. In I. Eibl-Eibesfeldt & F. K. Salter (Eds.), *Ethnic conflict and indoctrination: Altruism and identity in evolutionary perspective.* New York: Berghahn Books.

Fried, M. (1967). *The evolution of political society.* New York: Random House.

Goodenough, W. H. (1955). A problem in Malayo-Polynesian social organization. *American Anthropologist, 57,* 71–83.

Goodenough, W. H. (1970). *Description and comparison in cultural anthropology.* Chicago: University of Chicago Press.

Hamilton, W. D. (1964). The genetical evolution of social behavior. I and II. *Journal of Theoretical Biology, 7,* 1–52.

Hardin, G. (1960). The competitive exclusion principle. *Science, 131,* 1292–1297.

Hardin, G. (1968). The tragedy of the commons. *Science, 162,* 1243–1248.

Hardin, G., & Baden, J. (Eds.). (1977). *Managing the commons.* New York: W. H. Freeman & Co.

Helm, J. (1965). Bilaterality in the socio-territorial organization of the Arctic Drainage Dene. *Ethnology* 4(4), 361–385.

Helm, J. (1968). The nature of Dogrib socio-territorial groups. In R. B. Lee & I. Devore (Eds.), *Man the hunter* (pp. 118–125). Chicago: Aldine.

Hepper, P. G. (Ed.). (1991). *Kin recognition.* Cambridge: Cambridge University Press.

James, P., & Goetze, D. (Eds.). (2001). *Evolutionary theory and ethnic conflict.* Westport, CT: Praeger.

Jochim, M. A. (1983). *Strategies for survival: Cultural behavior in an ecological context.* New York: Academic Press.

Johnson, G. (2001). The roots of ethnic conflict: An evolutionary perspective. In Patrick James & David Goetze (Eds.), *Evolutionary theory and ethnic conflict.* Westport, CT: Praeger.

Keeley, L. H. (1996). *War before civilization: The myth of the peaceful savage.* New York: Oxford University Press.

Keesing, R. M. (1975). *Kin groups and social structure.* New York: Holt, Rinehart & Winston.

Klare, M. T. (2001). *Resource wars: The new landscape of global conflict.* New York: Henry Holt and Co.

Korten, D. C. (2001). *When corporations rule the world.* San Francisco: Kumarian Press & Berrett-Koehler.

Kramer, R., & Brewer, M. B. (1984). Effects of group identity on resource use in a simulated commons dilemma. *Journal of Personality and Social Psychology 46,* 1044–1057.

Krebs, J. R., & Davies, N. B. (1987). *An introduction to behavioral ecology.* Oxford: Blackwell Scientific Publications.

Krech III, S. (1999). *The ecological Indian: Myth and history*. New York: W. W. Norton & Co.

Lee, R. B. (1976). !Kung spatial organization: An ecological and historical perspective. In R. B. Lee & I. DeVore (Eds.), *Kalahari hunter-gatherers: Studies of the !Kung San and their neighbors*. Cambridge: Harvard University Press.

Lewis, H. T. (1991). *Ilocano irrigation: The corporate resolution*. University of Hawaii Press.

Maynard Smith, J. (1964). Group selection and kin selection. *Nature, 201*, 1145–1147.

Meyer, Peter. (2002). Ethnic solidarity as risk avoidance: An evolutionary view. In Frank K. Salter (Ed.), *Risky transactions: Trust, kinship, and ethnicity*. New York: Berghahn Books.

Murdock, G. P. (1968). Cognatic forms of social organization. In P. Bohannan & J. Middleton (Eds.), *Kinship and social organization*. New York: The Natural History Press.

Olson, M. (1971). *The logic of collective action: Public goods and the theory of groups*. Cambridge: Harvard University Press.

Ostrom, E. (1990). *Governing the commons: The evolution of institutions for collective action*. Cambridge: Cambridge University Press.

Palmer, C. T., Fredrickson, B. E., & Tilley, C. F. (1997). Categories and gatherings: Group selection and the mythology of cultural anthropology. *Evolution and Human Behavior, 18*(5), 291–308.

Panitch, L. (1980). Recent theorizations of corporatism. *British Journal of Sociology, 31*, 159–187.

Petrovich, S. B. & J. L. Gewirtz. (1985). The attachment learning process and its relation to cultural and biological evolution: Proximate and ultimate considerations. In M. Reite & T. Fields, (Eds.), *The psychology of attachment and separation*. New York: Academic Press.

Sahlins, M. (1972). *Stone age economics*. London: Tavistock.

Sahlins, M. (1976). *The use and abuse of biology: An anthropological critique of sociobiology*. Ann Arbor: The University of Michigan Press.

Salter, F. K. (Ed.). (2002). *Risky transactions: Trust, kinship, and ethnicity*. New York: Berghahn Books.

Sanderson, S. K. (2001). *The evolution of human sociality: A Darwinian conflict perspective*. New York: Rowman & Littlefield.

Smith, E. A. (1988). Risk and uncertainty in the "original affluent society": Evolutionary ecology of resource-sharing and land tenure. In T. Ingold, D. Riches, & J. Woodburn (Eds.), *Hunters and gatherers: Vol. 1. History, evolution and social change*. Oxford: Berg.

Smith, E. A. (1997). Inuit foraging groups: Some simple models incorporating conflicts of interest, relatedness, and central place sharing. In L. Betzig (Ed.), *Human nature: A critical reader*. Oxford: Oxford University Press.

Smith, J. G. E. (1976). Local band organization of the Caribou-Eater Chipewayan in the 18th and early 19th centuries. *Western Canadian Journal of Anthropology* 6(1), 72–90.

Smith, J. G. E. (1978). Economic uncertainty in an "original affluent society": Caribou and Caribou-Eater Chipewayan adaptive strategies. *Arctic Anthropology* 15(1), 68–88.

Symons, D. (1990). Adaptiveness and adaptation. *Ethology and Sociobiology* 11, 4/5.

Taylor, R. (1988). *Human territorial functioning: An empirical, evolutionary perspective on individual and small group territorial cognitions, behaviors, and consequences.* Cambridge: Cambridge University Press.

Tooby, J. and L. Cosmides. (1992). The psychological foundations of culture. In J. Barkow, L. Cosmides, and J. Tooby, (Eds.), *The adapted mind.* Oxford: Oxford University Press.

Tuan, Y.-F. (1990). *Topophilia: A study of environmental perception, attitudes, and values.* New York: Columbia University Press.

Turnbull, C. M. (1972). *The mountain people.* New York: Simon & Schuster.

van den Berghe, P. L. (1987). *The ethnic phenomenon.* New York: Praeger.

van den Berghe, P. L. (1990). *Human family systems: An evolutionary view.* Prospect Heights, IL: Waveland Press.

Wilson, E. (1975). *Sociobiology: The new synthesis.* Cambridge, MA: Harvard University Press.

Wolf, E. (1982). *Europe and the people without history.* Berkeley, CA: University of California Press.

Wrangham, R., & Peterson, D. (1996). *Demonic males: Apes and the origins of human violence.* Boston: Houghton Mifflin.

Ziker, John P. (2002). *Peoples of the Tundra: Northern Siberians in the postcommunist transition.* Prospect Heights, IL: Waveland Press.

CHAPTER 3

The Strange Career of the Contact Hypothesis

Dana Bramel

In a world in which groups in contact seem so often at each other's throat, it may appear surprising that the "contact hypothesis" (G. W. Allport, 1954) remains, according to the authoritative *Handbook of Social Psychology,* "one of the most long-lived and successful ideas in the history of social psychology" (Brewer and Brown, 1998). I shall argue that this idea that contact would reduce prejudice arose in a specific historical period (World War II) and had the unexamined underlying assumption that most ethnic/national/racial groups within American society were more culturally similar to each other than their members imagined. This assumption of basic similarity had developed rather recently in social psychology (1930s), in part as a reaction against the prevalent "scientific" racism (Gould, 1981) in psychology in general—according to which fundamental differences (e.g., I.Q., criminality) among groups were considered proven. With the rise of racist and aggressive Nazism, and then the need for societal unity during the war, social psychologists found themselves emphasizing the common humanity of all people and denouncing vigorously racist and ethnocentric stereotypes that asserted differences. In this context of assumed similarity, optimism about the effects of intergroup contacts would seem justifiable.

A careless reading of Gordon Allport's (1954) careful definition of "prejudice" could also be seen as encouraging this tendency to minimize the role of group differences in causing antagonism: "clashes of interests and values do occur," but "these conflicts are not in themselves instances of prejudice" (p. 88). That is, he restricted the term "prejudice" to those cases in which there was no reality basis for intergroup hostility (Forbes, 1997).

Technically, then—a point that most readers of Allport seem to have missed (e.g., I. Katz, 1991)—prejudice is not caused by real behavioral/ cultural differences or competition between groups. A group toward which you are prejudiced, for Allport, is one that does not actually possess the unpleasant characteristics you attribute to it. In regard to such prejudices, then, contact would be most likely to reveal a similarity that could only work to undermine the negative stereotypes associated with that type of (irrational, unprovoked) hostility. From Allport's definition, therefore—though he didn't actually state this—the contact hypothesis reduces almost to a truism in regard to prejudice, but certainly not in regard to antagonisms, which are anchored in real conflict (whether material or cultural). Unfortunately, he was one of the few in the field (along with Krech and Crutchfield [1948], Asch [1952], and Campbell [1967]; see also Ichheiser, 1946) in that period to take realistic conflict and real intergroup behavioral differences (G. W. Allport, 1954, pp. 85–162) seriously. His insistence that we treat prejudice and real conflict differently was generally ignored. It went against the social psychological orthodoxy that had emerged in the World War II period.

The core assumption—that contact would, by revealing an essential similarity, undermine hostile intergroup attitudes and beliefs—apparently persisted in American social psychology even into and through the period (1960s to the 1990s, at least) of the rediscovery of group identities (i.e., cultural differences, typically), praise of diversity and multiculturalism, identity politics, and religious fundamentalism. True, the contact hypothesis accumulated over these years endless amendments, called "conditions" ("equal status" was one of the first), aimed at keeping it afloat (yet making it heavier, unwieldy, unconvincing). But what seems to have escaped general notice in our field is the major cultural shift in modern societies (at least until very recently?) toward a questioning of that assumption of homogeneity, and the reemergence of strongly felt and often socially approved assertions of group differences. Shouldn't this lead us to a reexamination of the heretofore unrecognized assumption of "no difference" that made the contact hypothesis probably too plausible to our classic thinkers of the 1940s to 1960s? It might also suggest that we take a second look at the idea that people are fated to react negatively to the different and are capable of appreciating, as if narcissistically, only those others who seem identical to the self.

This is not the place for a thorough reevaluation of the venerable contact hypothesis, a task that Forbes (1997), for example, has admirably undertaken. My purpose, instead, is to show the evolution of the underlying assumption of intergroup similarities, and then to demonstrate how this ideologically driven a priori led to some distorted thinking in selected classic studies by Deutsch and Collins (1951) and Cook (1978). Although we admire the commitment of these researchers to universalistic principles about a common humanity, and applaud their idealism and optimism about the possibilities of intergroup harmony (especially in regard to blacks and whites in the United States), it may be useful to point out that their implicit assumptions tended to obscure and prettify a much more conflict-ridden social reality—one that we are now, perhaps, more willing to recognize. I say "perhaps" because it is also possible that the return to the psychology of a nation under siege could reverse the trend toward a relaxed and open orientation toward internal diversity and conflict.

FLOYD ALLPORT: ASK NOT IF GROUPS ARE DIFFERENT; ASK FIRST WHETHER THEY EVEN EXIST

Gordon Allport's older brother, considered a founder of experimental social psychology, took a radically individualist view of social phenomena, denying any reality to groups as such (other than as a statistical conglomerate of individuals). He was important in turning the field away from a study of groups in relation to each other. However, he made at least one exception to this rule, and attempted to account for the ostracism of blacks by whites. Accepting the scientific dogma of the time about blacks' inferior intelligence, he argued (F. H. Allport, 1924, p. 386) that this difference is not sufficient to explain the ostracism, and that one would have to look for additional characteristics of black people in order to do so. Thus, the cause is some undesirable trait of black people, not some psychological dynamic in the ostracizers themselves. In a discussion of the lynching of black people, he asserted that these murders could be justified on the grounds that blacks were "too poorly socialized to be controlled by any power less than fear of immediate death" (p. 397). I cite this shocking sympathy for lynch mobs in order to show how striking is the change from 1924 to, say, 1939, in the way that social psychologists (including Floyd Allport himself) talked about intergroup hostilities. In the latter period, all focus was on the irrationality of the haters, and the characteristics of the targeted group became largely irrelevant in an explanation of the content of stereotypes.

In 1931, Allport took the anti-group battle directly to the enemy—sociology (see Ross, 1991)—engaging in a debate with University of Chicago sociologist Louis Wirth, who argued that young, second-generation hyphenated Americans were torn among three cultures (parents, White Anglo-Saxon Protestants [WASP], gang of peers), and that law-breaking behavior often emerged from this "culture conflict." Allport's rejoinder:

If cultural conflict exists only in so far as the individual behaves as though it exists, then a good way to abolish it would be to get the individual to behave as though it did not exist. Dr. Wirth would do this by getting him to envisage the ideals or culture of a larger and a more inclusive group. I would proceed in the opposite manner by getting him to react for the time as though he were not a member of, that is not constrained by, any group at all. . . . Why not abolish the consciousness of membership? (F. H. Allport, 1931, p. 494)

Thus the solution to the conflict of cultures begins with a recognition that such "fictions" exist only in the minds of people, and to abandon such imaginings could only be a blessing. Recognizing economic conflict (among individuals, of course), Allport asserted that "the opponents merely seize upon conspicuous cultural difference as tools or as rationalizations" (p. 497).

In the classic stereotype study that Daniel Katz published with Kenneth Braly (1933), the Allport doctrine of group "fictions" was firmly in place: "almost any characteristic can become attached to any race and stick there without scarcely any factual basis" (p. 289). The stereotyping process "can arise only so long as individuals accept consciously or unconsciously the group fallacy attitude toward place of birth and skin color. To the realist there are no racial or national groups which exist as entities and which determine the characteristics of the group members" (ibid.). In coining the term "stereotype," Lippmann (1922) had expressed the highly educated person's contempt for the simple-minded masses; taking this a step further, Katz and Braly were suggesting that even Princeton students' views of nationality groups, often consensual and confidently expressed, had very little relation to reality. The perfectly valid psychological point that beliefs about others are influenced by emotional factors seems to have led to a denial of any role at all for real world group differences. At the same time, a modest advance had been made: by 1933, Katz had discreetly separated himself from the Floyd Allport (1924) view that antiblack racism is justified. That racism had now become an irrational "race-name prejudice" just like any other.

Paradoxically, the abandonment by psychologists of beliefs in major group differences came in large part through the influence of anthropologists—the very people who specialized precisely in describing the great variety of human cultures. Franz Boas and his students were among the staunchest critics of the intelligence testers and their doctrines of inborn differences, contributing to the shift around 1930 in psychology away from the prevalent scientific racism (Stocking, 1968). Their voices joined with those of a small minority within psychology (e.g., Bond, 1924) to argue that IQ differences could readily be explained by social, cultural, and educational factors. One of Boas's students was Canadian social psychologist Otto Klineberg, who published in 1935 a powerful demonstration of the impact of the low educational quality of their schools on the test scores of many American blacks.

But how about the cultural differences between groups within America?

Wouldn't the Boasian message about the power of culture result in a more "culturalist" social psychology of intergroup relations, one more sensitive to the ways in which groups of varying national and ethnic origins might enter into friction and conflict with each other? No, this did not happen (Matthews, 1970). Although Boas devoted much of his work to combatting racism, he seems not to have put much emphasis on the cultural aspects of intergroup relations in America, probably believing that differences were destined to disappear via assimilation (intermarriage, etc.). His cultural relativism—which involved a strong plea for tolerance and respect for differences—could certainly be read as containing an implicit message that such differences were a cause of frictions. But his student Otto Klineberg apparently consistently minimized this factor in intergroup relations. Defining prejudice as "not based upon actual experience," he continued, "in some cases a difference in folkways and in values may create certain misunderstandings that contribute to hostility" (1954, p. 514). The use of the term "misunderstanding" indicates how little the actual differences counted for him; he cited the extreme prejudice against the Jews in 1930s Germany as an example of a highly assimilated (i.e., similar) group nevertheless being viciously attacked.

PSYCHOLOGISTS' REACTION TO NAZISM: PREJUDICE AS ENTIRELY IRRATIONAL, BASE, AND BASELESS

The horrors of Nazism sounded the death toll for theories of race differences in U.S. social psychology and no doubt also inhibited explorations of intrasocietal cultural differences as potential causes of antagonism. The Society for the Psychological Study of Social Issues (SPSSI; founded in 1935) presented a statement at the 1938 convention of the American Psychological Association denouncing the "current emphasis on 'racial differences'" in Germany and Italy, and warning that these may be on the increase in the United States as well. Arguing that research has found no "inherent psychological differences" among "so-called 'races,'" the document draws the logical conclusion that such (nonexistent) differences cannot, therefore, be "the explanation of current racial hatred and persecution."

The question of other kinds of differences (e.g., culture, class), which could arise from variations in the conditions of living of social groups over time, is not broached directly in the SPSSI statement (signed, by the way, by both Floyd and Gordon Allport). But there is an implication that, in America, such differences are not of great importance: "Here in America we have clear indications of the manner in which members of different racial and national groups have combined to create a common culture."

A significant number of Jewish researchers had by the mid-1930s partially succeeded in overcoming anti-Semitic barriers in American academia, and begun contributing to the study of prejudice (e.g., Katz, Klineberg, Horowitz/Hartley). Anti-Semitism may have seemed to them, as well as to others in that period, a model for prejudice in general (Higham, 1984; Samelson, 1978), and its glaring irrationality was certainly its most salient characteristic. At about the same time, Sherif (1936) produced his brilliant demonstration of how social norms can develop in a group concerning the degree of movement of a perfectly stationary point of light in a darkened room. The stage was set for a strengthening of the view that beliefs and attitudes were anything but a reflection of intergroup realities.

The influential studies by Eugene Horowitz (1936; and Hartley, 1946, based on 1938 data and funded in part by the Conference on Jewish Relations) give the tone. The intergroup attitudes did not seem to respond to any direct experiences with members of the out-group. In the 1936 study of boys' interracial attitudes, exposure to a vague Sherif-like norm inculcated by adults emerged as the only important factor (other than age), that might explain the general tendency to reject the anonymous black boys (photographs). In the 1938 study, college students judged various social groups, including nonexistent ones with imaginary names (e.g., Pireneans). The results indicated to Hartley that students apparently had a global attitude of liking/disliking toward out-groups, which applied across the board and without much of any connection to real group characteristics or relationships.

Another major blow to the idea that intergroup attitudes reflect real differences and conflicts between groups came in the work of psychoanalyst/sociologist John Dollard and his associates (Dollard, Doob, Miller, Mowrer, & Sears, 1939). Dollard had an intimate understanding of black-white relations in the U.S. South (*Caste and Class in a Southern Town*, 1937), and his analysis often spoke of conflict in this context. In regard to white racism, he wrote that it is "a defensive attitude intended to preserve white prerogatives in the caste situation and aggressively to resist any pressure from the Negro side to change his inferior position" (p. 441). But in the next pages, this rather sociological insight receded in the face of the irrationalist one. He spoke of "daily life" frustrations, the buildup of a "generalized hostility," and of how the Negro serves as a convenient socially designated target onto which "this irrational affect is drained off," finally citing Horowitz (1936) approvingly for showing that prejudice comes not from "actual contact, i.e., real reason for hating the Negro," but rather from "contact with the tradition of race prejudice" (p. 444).

In the influential book *Frustration and Aggression* (Dollard et al., 1939), there is, as in his earlier book, considerable attention given to real conflicts between groups (e.g., in "race riots") and to material factors affecting intergroup relations (e.g., the price of cotton affecting lynching). But the part of the message retained by students of prejudice has been the irrationalist one—the displacement of aggression onto completely innocent, weak, and often already denigrated out-groups, as we have already seen in Dollard's (1937) concluding pages. The fascinating question became the following: How is the target selected? The case of the Jews in Germany is discussed at length. But in that debate, the relation of the target to the prejudiced group (e.g., its cultural similarity, economic rivalries) was unimportant; the interesting question was, rather, the relation between the displacement target (scapegoat) and the *frustrater* (e.g., in terms of stimulus generalization, in the behaviorist paradigm). Displacement of aggression onto innocent targets became one of the standard accounts of prejudice in American social psychology (cf., e.g., Berkowitz, 1962).

To summarize the dominant American social psychological view of the causes of prejudice, as of 1940, we have seen that negative attitudes toward out-groups are generally not a response to something the out-group is or has done. Cultural differences and intergroup rivalries may have been common currency in sociology (e.g., at the University of Chicago around Robert E. Park), but psychologists clearly preferred more autistic, solipsistic, Freudian-derived accounts of prejudice. It was recognized, on some level, that to talk about differences was to risk giving ammunition to the racists, at a time when Adolph Hitler's policies were becoming more widely known, and national unity an ever more important goal. Melville Herskovits, for example—an important student of anthropologist Franz Boas—found himself intellectually isolated when he investigated the survival of African cultural elements in blacks in the Americas, and he was aware that his work could be taken by racists to mean that African Americans were only partly "civilized" (Herskovits, 1941; Szwed, 1972). In a later period, Ryan (1971) brilliantly showed how the "differences" of an alleged "culture of poverty" could be instrumentalized in racist ways, "blaming the victim."

The Katz and Braly (1935–36) statement about alleged characteristics attributed to out-groups can be taken as representative of social psychology's public stance (it was heartily seconded in G. W. Allport's *The Nature of Prejudice*, 1954): "We are probably dealing here with the rationalizations rather than the causes of prejudice." Not only are these attributions rationalizations (justifications for emotionally derived attitudes), but they are typically counterfactual.

As to the probable effect of contact with members of the out-group, Katz and Braly were skeptical, arguing that black people were quite familiar to whites in the South, but prejudice toward them certainly no less. In fact, given social psychology's penchant in this period for the irrational, it was not at all clear how contact with a disliked group—even one not significantly different culturally!—could reduce prejudices rooted in emotions (rather than cognitions). In their survey of recent work on reducing prejudice, Kurt Lewin's associates, Lippitt and Radke (1946), listed as their "point #1" that prejudice has no relation to "actual experiences of the individual," and is unaffected by contact. Only later would Muzafer Sherif and his colleagues (1961, cooperation to reach "superordinate goals," related perhaps to Lewin's [1939] stress on "interdependence" and "common fate" as unifiers) successfully test some effective solutions, dealing with antagonisms between rigorously similar groups of boys in summer camps.

DEUTSCH AND COLLINS (1951) ON INTERRACIAL HOUSING: A STRANGE TREATMENT OF SURPRISING RESULTS

Given the theoretical context described earlier, what might psychologists expect if black and white families were thrown together in newly constructed public housing apartment buildings? The orthodox prediction would have to be rather pessimistic concerning a reduction in prejudice. True, there should not be a big problem of cultural differences between the two populations—as we have seen, such differences played no major role in the orthodox view. But social psychologists were skeptical that contact could overcome emotionally rooted, deeply irrational attitudes. It was clear that simply providing the facts about the out-group would be far from sufficient.

As a psychologist in the Lewinian tradition, in which similarity (which could, one might argue, be revealed via contact) was explicitly denied an important role in constituting a sense of groupness (Lewin, 1939), Morton Deutsch probably had reason to fear that this "natural experiment" might fail. The fact that it did not fail, and the manner in which the surprising results were presented, constituted important steps in establishing the contact hypothesis as an idea to be taken seriously. This important and ambitious study contrasting integrated and segregated housing projects in New York and New Jersey was carried out under the direction of Deutsch and Mary Evans Collins and published in 1951 as *Interracial Housing: A Psychological Evaluation of a Social Experiment.*

Although the empirical study of interracial attitudes and perceptions is an excellent one and its reputation largely deserved—it is still frequently cited in social psychology textbooks and handbooks—there are a number of very curious problems and inconsistencies between theory and data that have never to my knowledge been discussed in print. These contradictions are particularly illuminating for the issue that interests us here—the covert assumption that cultural and behavioral differences between groups (here, blacks and whites) in the United States are unimportant insofar as hostilities and stereotypes are concerned.

The theoretical background to the study is presented in appendix A of the Deutsch & Collins study (1951, pp. 132–149). It draws from historical and sociological knowledge and theory to explain the origin, maintenance, and enduring strength of American race prejudice. In fact, it portrays the situation so bleakly that the reader must wonder whether the rather superficial social contact of much apartment living could have a major impact on it. "Powerful political and economic groups" benefit from the exploitation of black people and from the "prejudices which prevent the development of feelings of solidarity between Negro and white workers." As for the psychological benefits: "For the less powerful . . . which no longer have (or never had) an economic or political stake in prejudice, prejudices serve the less 'rational' functions of preserving or enhancing ego and social status" (1951, p. 134). Although prejudice has its origins in an upper-class ideology justifying the superexploitation of black people, it eventually gathers a "momentum" of its own and becomes "independent of the initial political and economic functions." Thus, a Marxist explanation, based on the work of Oliver Cox (1948), is used to account for the origin of the ideology of black natural inferiority, whereas a more psychological analysis is used to explain how these prejudices satisfy certain "less rational" needs among lower-class white people. This brief overview of the bases of prejudice constitutes an impressive and plausible integration of sociological and psychological insights available at the time.

The authors imply that historical changes in intergroup relationships lead to some changes in the dynamic of prejudice, as direct superexploitation of blacks (as in slavery) declines. In addition to the momentum of its own, prejudice is then maintained by a dynamic whose description is drawn from the work of Swedish economist Gunnar Myrdal (*An American Dilemma*, 1944). The existence of the "American Creed" of equality forces whites who are hostile and discriminatory toward blacks to find elaborate justifications for this un-American behavior, to ward off feelings of guilt or shame. This process strengthens most of the existing derogatory stereotypes of blacks.

Also taken from Myrdal is the concept of the "vicious circle," whereby race discrimination forces black people to be—relative to whites—poorer, more badly housed, less educated/skilled, less clean/well-dressed, and even to be different in "culture and personality" (Myrdal, 1944, p. 956 ff).[1] Here is how Deutsch and Collins put the issue of cultural differences: "The environment shapes the culture of the Negroes, determines their values, and influences their behavior. Since this environment is different from that which the average white person experiences, he is estranged by the Negro culture and Negro behavior" (1951, p. 140). The effect of the system of exploitation and discrimination is, they argued, to make most black people different in very distinctive and visible ways from the majority of more prosperous whites. The return effect of this on whites is to reinforce prejudices toward blacks. The prejudiced white rarely meets a black person whose behavior and demeanor would "destroy his prejudice." Even if the black person happens to be of "equal status," the white person would most likely avoid interaction and resist perceiving the equality between self and other.

The reader of this historical and theoretical overview senses considerable pessimism about the eventual effects of black-white contact. To make matters even worse, not only would an "equal status" black person be ecologically rare, avoided, and misperceived, but also a rise in the status of blacks, if noticed, would be experienced as a threat to the white person's status. As long as blacks remain "subservient," this "relatively enhances the status of the whites." Further, in some sense, prejudiced whites are comfortable with the "difference" of blacks in America, and the black person will be more "liked" if he ceases "trying to become like the rest of society and remains contentedly in an inferior position" (p. 133; how far we've come, in the twenty-first century, from the time when a black person would be ridiculed and attacked by whites for "acting white!")

Up to about page 145 in this appendix (which extends to p. 149), white race prejudice in America appears overwhelmingly buttressed by a myriad of powerful sociological and psychological factors, including a huge dose of historically precipitated differences of many kinds between the two groups. This theory seems worlds apart from the social psychological conventional wisdom I have described earlier. There is practically no hint, up to this point in the theoretical overview of black-white relations, that interracial contact in a housing project could overcome these solidly overdetermined, materially based attitudes and stereotypes. The reader gets the impression that white neighbors of blacks would be caught in a hopeless conflict between refusing even to see the equality of the blacks and then being disturbed and threatened by any interracial similarity that did penetrate their cognitive defenses. In neither case do the predicted dynamics—which are not, in fact, presented in the form of specific research hypotheses to be tested—lead to a decrease in hostility or stereotyping.

At this point in their presentation, the authors reintroduce the empirical results of their study (p. 146), which have, of course, already been fully presented in the body of the text. These show rather convincingly that the attitudes and stereotypes held by white housewives living in integrated projects had become, on average, more positive (relative to those in segregated living conditions) toward the black residents of the same projects. Asked directly about common stereotypes of black people in general (not just in the project), specifically "lazy and ignorant," "can't be trusted," and "different and strange," only 22 percent of integrated occupants agreed with the entire set, whereas 41 percent of the segregated whites did so. Summarizing, Deutsch and Collins write that the results of their study show that "intimate, equal-status contact with Negroes (who, of course, do not conform to the stereotypes)" disrupts "the rationales for prejudiced sentiments." Somehow, the bleak theory drawn from history, Marxism, psychoanalysis, and sociology (social status hierarchies, and what Blumer [1958] later called threats to "group position") goes up into thin air in the face of what the tables and statistical analyses reveal.

I say "into thin air" because no mention is made of the stark incompatibility between the theory and the empirical findings, as if the two parts of the scientific tapestry interweave perfectly. There are no seams showing. The black residents "of course" do not conform to the stereotypes (is this because the contact is asserted, without proof, to be "equal status," and people of equal status would necessarily be similar?). Further, judging from the remarkably positive data on traits attributed and liking for blacks, any such freshly discovered similarity and equality does not seem to have been particularly threatening to the white residents.

If the non-Lewinian reasoning about whites discovering that blacks are similar to themselves (or are truly human beings sharing "la condition humaine") had been a core idea in developing the housing study, we would expect to find a detailed exposition of the methodology for measuring the degree of actual similarity. We do not; nor is much space devoted to showing that "status" or "social class" was similar.[2]

The authors don't raise the issue of objective similarities, contenting themselves with showing that residents of the integrated and segregated units differed in their perceptions of similarity to black residents in general. On the "pretty much the same . . . or different?" question, 80 percent of the integrated chose "same," compared with 58 percent of the segregated. We are given no data on the self-descriptions of whites, which would enable us to see whether these in fact corresponded to the traits attributed to black residents. Nor are we given any assurance that these attributions of similarity preceded the changed attitude (there were no precontact measures), rather than serving simply as rationalizations for such a change. The authors conclude, as if confirming the social psychological (no differences) orthodoxy that their pessimistic theory had never embraced, "the housewives in the integrated projects have had more opportunity to perceive the essential similarity" (p. 82).

Thus, the contact hypothesis was forcefully launched by researchers who, judging from their theoretical framework (appendix A), apparently hadn't believed in it, and who had expressed their skepticism about black-white behavioral similarity and equality of class or status. They made the best of the apparent failure (not admitted in the book) of their historical/sociological framework, and did a respectable job of trying to account for the encouraging integration-friendly results. Although their theory had not prepared them for the striking results, it was in fact not abandoned, as can be seen in the last pages of the appendix. The authors were aware that much more than simple contact was happening in these government-built and administered housing projects.

What seems to have happened in this landmark book is the following: beginning with a pessimistic theory about the deep roots of white racism in America, the authors had an opportunity to study a situation that brought together a host of ecologically very unlikely circumstances of equality and cooperation, as if experimentally designed to undo (by affirmative government action accompanied by an explicitly antiracist educational effort [Deutsch & Collins, p. 142]) the heavy legacy of a strife-torn interracial past. The integrated housing was the kind of dramatic intervention (preceded by some government-initiated integration in the U.S. armed forces during World War II) that could possibly break the "vicious circle" for blacks and quiet the frustrations and status anxieties of whites. But this integration goes well beyond mere contact between members of the two groups, and the authors list (1951, p. 144) major social and economic changes they deem necessary. These include raising the socioeconomic status of blacks and eliminating the discrimination that puts them at a disadvantage and reinforces prejudice. Once government has put its authority behind a major integration project, and the project administration establishes an antiracist norm, the social psychological microprocesses can take effect. This seems to be the reasoning of Deutsch and Collins, which allows them to argue that "stateways" can overcome the racist "folkways." What was missing from their pessimistic theory of racism's endurance, they implied, was a new element in history—aggressive government action (as in the recent successful war against racist fascism) to undo those poisonous intergroup differences.

CAN CONTACT CHANGE STEREOTYPES WHEN THERE ARE NO GROUP DIFFERENCES AT ALL? THE HERCULEAN EFFORTS OF STUART COOK

Associated with Deutsch and Collins in researching housing integration effects, Stuart Cook later put the contact hypothesis to test in a monumental series of experiments that M. Brewster Smith (1994) called "the most laborious and realistic laboratory study of attitude change ever attempted." The flavor of Cook's approach can be sensed from the opening of his 1978 paper summarizing the research program he had pursued since the mid-1940s: "One of our most persistent faiths has been that if members of hostile groups came to know each other through personal contact, the development of mutual understanding and liking would follow and would neutralize the negative relationships that formerly existed" (p. 97). Although rarely explicitly argued, it is clear from reading Cook's papers in this period that he clung to the social psychological orthodoxy of no fundamental cultural differences between American blacks and whites. Starting with this implicit assumption, he could permit himself to arrange highly sanitized two-person interactions lasting a total of 40 hours each between white college students and black persons selected and scripted to be "black" in skin color only. He apparently went to considerable lengths to construct personas for his black experimental confederates that would be as similar as possible to the profile of the typical white participant whose attitudes were being studied. If contact led—as seemed eminently reasonable to Cook—to the discovery of this similarity that had been meticulously supervised by the experimenter, and then the changed attitude generalized to blacks as a group, the contact hypothesis would be supported.

For Cook, an essential condition for the success of the contact situation was that "the attributes of the disliked group members with whom the contact occurs are such as to disconfirm the prevailing stereotyped beliefs about them" (1978, p. 97). This does not mean that he viewed prejudice as based in a reaction to real group differences; the reader looks in vain for any statement to that effect in his various publications. In that respect, he was very much in the orthodox tradition. But he did believe that the discovery of nondifference was important in reducing prejudice.

That he considered black-white intergroup differences as relatively unimportant in the United States is suggested by the fact that he never presented the "selection" of a stereotype-disconfirming black confederate as a problem (Cook, 1969, 1978). One finds no mention in his writings of the technical dilemma that this person might in fact (it's an empirical question) be very unrepresentative of black people in general—not possessing the commonly attributed traits, being similar to the white participant in "background, education, and interests," and, to top it off, having a "pleasant personality" (friendly, unaggressive, undefensive, "able, ambitious, and self-respecting"). The very use of the term "stereotype-disconfirming" (Cook, 1978, p. 97) is indicative here: because for psychologists stereotypes are, technically, inaccurate perceptions, most black persons would, in an interpersonal interaction, therefore behave in unique ways that would necessarily contradict them. If Cook believed this, then, indeed, the representativeness of the black confederate might appear relatively unproblematic to him. Describing lunch break conversations programmed over each of the 20 days of interaction, Cook (1969, p. 193) tells us that the "Negro confederates" brought in "facts about themselves"—all kinds of "personal feelings" and "information"—but neglects to specify whether these were scripted or real, as if this question were not very important.

Results consistent with the contact hypothesis in such an unrepresentative situation might help to bolster Cook's "faith," but should not overcome our skepticism about the ability of such an experiment to tell us something about actual interactions between persons living in the race-divided world described by Myrdal and by Deutsch and Collins in their social-historical overview. What is particularly poignant about Cook's ambitious study, however, is that even under these ideal conditions of imposed and probably unrealistic similarity, he detected only minimal improvement in white attitudes toward blacks as a group (Cook, 1978, p. 101).

With Stuart Cook, the list of conditions necessary to make contact work gets longer and longer, to the point where the theory boils down to this: favorable attitude change will occur when everything that happens is "intimate," "friendly," "equal," "cooperative," and so forth. In short, harmony will result when everything that happens is harmonious. Have the independent and dependent variables in the experiment been confounded here? Friendliness and favorable beliefs/attitudes are supposed to be the dependent variables. But, instead, we find that the causal factors being studied as possible explanations of later positive attitudes are themselves perilously close to those very same kinds of positive attitudes (consider "pleasant personality," for example, which would seem to foreclose any negative reaction to such a person).[3] With this kind of reasoning and its experimental incarnation, it is virtually impossible, one would think, to fail to get the desired positive results. If one sets up an experimental situation in which people can only experience harmonious relations, won't they end up tending to say they can get along? Surely, we can accept this rather obvious point.

But, of course, the interesting question for Cook was whether this positive experience would produce a change in white participants' views of black people in general. I think that a disinterested and careful reader of his results, as summarized in his 1978 paper, would have to conclude that very little positive change occurred (statistically significant in only one of the two substantial replications of the experiment), as, indeed, was the case in a number of field studies he had carried out (Cook, 1978). When one takes into account all the "positives" injected into the laboratory interaction, one is disappointed by how little effect all of this had on white students' attitudes toward blacks. Although Cook tried to accent the positive in his various findings (partly by minimizing, implicitly, the real differences in America between blacks and whites), there is something poignant in this meager scientific harvest from the long research career of a social psychologist who contributed importantly, in other ways, to the struggle for racial integration in the *United States* (e.g., see Kluger, 1975).

His own disappointment emerged in public in his important overview of school integration research, entitled, "Did We Mislead the Supreme Court?" (Cook, 1979). His answer to the question was that social scientists were not guilty. If intergroup attitudes had not much improved in integrated schools, it was largely because the host of necessary conditions for contact to work were typically absent. Among these was "equal status": "due to racial differentials in socio-economic status and initial achievement levels, equivalence of positions and functions among students has been only partially achieved" (p. 431). Indeed, this would be much more difficult to achieve than had been the case in his own highly artificial laboratory experiment. In the real world, black-white differences (and not solely those of mainly socioeconomic origin—the only ones Cook mentioned, characteristically) were interfering seriously (on cultural differences, see, e.g., Schofield, 1989, and Fordham, 1996). The civil rights and black liberation movements were injecting new forms of "difference," as "acting white" ceased for many young black people to be a positive value.

Jones (1998) helps us to summarize the problem that this new positive self-evaluation of formerly stigmatized group identities poses for the contact hypothesis: "The underlying premise for this approach was the general idea that except for skin color, we are all essentially the same. Equality rested ultimately on presumed similarity. But the decade of the civil rights movement had consequences that challenged assumptions about the core problem. Blacks began to reject the similarity assumption and proclaimed their differences as defining, and their stigmatized skin color as a mark of honor, not oppression. Difference, not similarity, carried psychological force and promoted subjective well-being" (p. 643).

CONCLUSION: HAS SOCIAL PSYCHOLOGY BEEN TRIPPED UP IN THE SHIFT FROM NATIONAL UNITY TO MULTICULTURALISM AND IDENTITY POLITICS?

Focusing on case studies of two classic research projects concerning intergroup contact, I have attempted to show that they are plagued by hidden and untested assumptions about a homogeneous American culture. Among the sources for these assumptions in the 1940s was the necessary mobilization of the society (including its social scientists) around the goal of defeating a dangerous enemy that proclaimed its superiority and advanced aggressively in the name of irreducible differences among ethnic and "racial" groups. There followed a cold war period in which the United States itself was accused of racism, and some social scientists (e.g., Kluckhohn, 1949) rushed, perhaps too eagerly, once again, to deny any material basis for such internal divisions—this in a period when racial segregation was solidly in place in many spheres of American life.

Psychologists can perhaps be excused for having incorporated that patriotic anti-Nazi effort into the very center of their science, but should we let those extra-scientific considerations permanently distort our understanding of intergroup relations? Such an understanding should, surely, include a clear view of the nature of the differences that may divide us. If the study of such differences is more the province of sociologists, anthropologists, or economists, then should we perhaps listen to them?

For most recent historians, in any case, the presentation of intergroup cultural differences has changed considerably since the 1940s and 1950s (Hollinger, 1995; Svonkin, 1997). Hollinger, for example, writes that "a chorus of voices" now accuse those earlier observers of "ignoring difference and emphasizing sameness" (p. 10). Back then, for psychologists, to assert that the Other (e.g., blacks, Jews) was different was, essentially, to be "prejudiced"; more recently, it appears that, for many people, to refuse to recognize the Other's proudly proclaimed difference is to be "racist," "anti-Semitic," and so forth. It's not clear to me that social psychologists studying prejudice and stereotypes in recent years have examined all of the relevant implications of this for their definitions, theory, and research.

Much as it has been scorned by some in the last 10 years (Lind, 1996, and Malik, 1996, provide intelligent critiques), identity politics and multiculturalism—or at least the multiplicity of subcultures in the United States—are phenomena whose consequences the social psychology of prejudice and racism has been slow to recognize. The theoretical underpinnings (especially the assumption of similarity) of the venerable contact hypothesis should probably be high on the list for a thorough reevaluation.

NOTES

1. Note how this description—by an economist, not a psychologist—deviates from the standard "no difference" account in what one might call the "politically correct" dominant social psychology of the World War II period.

2. True, measures of objective (in relation to perceived) characteristics of out-groups have rarely been undertaken by social psychologists, as G. W. Allport (1954), Brigham (1971), and Lee et al. (1994) have pointed out. LaPiere's (1936) study of actual police records of criminal convictions, to check on the stereotype of Armenians in California, was the work of a sociologist. See the illuminating discussion of these accuracy issues in Mackie (1973).

3. An even more serious breech of rigorous methodology in the experimental condition (i.e., where there was protracted contact with the black confederate) was the following: at one point in the series of sessions, a "respected" white confederate engaged in a scripted interaction with the prejudiced white participant, which forcefully encouraged her to "share disapproval" of and condemn segregation and discrimination against black people (Cook, 1969, p. 193). Control participants, of course, were spared this questionable manipulation. The dependent measures of attitude change included, as it happened, a questionnaire about desegregation. Clearly, Cook's experiment manipulated, as he occasionally admitted, much more than merely cooperative contact.

REFERENCES

Allport, F. H. (1924). *Social psychology*. Boston: Houghton Mifflin.

Allport, F. H. (1931). Culture conflict versus the individual as factors in delinquency. *Social Forces, 9*, 493–497.

Allport, G. W. (1954). *The nature of prejudice*. Cambridge, MA: Addison-Wesley.

Asch, S. (1952). *Social psychology*. Englewood Cliffs, NJ: Prentice-Hall.

Berkowitz, L. (1962). *Aggression: A social psychological analysis*. New York: McGraw-Hill.

Blumer, H. (1958). Race prejudice as a sense of group position. *Pacific Sociological Review, 1*, 3–7.

Bond, H. M. (1924, July). What the army "intelligence" tests measured. *Opportunity*, 197–202.

Brewer, M. B., & Brown, R. J. (1998). Intergroup relations. In D. T. Gilbert, S. T. Fiske, & G. Lindzey (Eds.), *Handbook of social psychology* (Vol. 2). Boston: McGraw-Hill.

Brigham, J. V. (1971). Ethnic stereotypes. *Psychological Bulletin, 76*, 15–38.

Campbell, D. T. (1967). Stereotypes and the perception of group differences. *American Psychologist, 22*, 817–829.

Cook, S. (1969). Motives in a conceptual analysis of attitude-related behavior. In *Nebraska Symposium on Motivation*: Vol. 17 (pp. 179–231). Lincoln: University of Nebraska Press.

Cook, S. W. (1978). Interpersonal and attitudinal outcomes in cooperating interracial groups. *Journal of Research and Development in Education, 12*, 97–113.

Cook, S. W. (1979). Social science and school desegregation: Did we mislead the Supreme Court? *Personality and Social Psychology Bulletin, 5*, 420–437.

Cox, O. C. (1948). *Caste, class, and race*. New York: Doubleday.

Deutsch, M., & Collins, M. E. (1951). *Interracial housing: A psychological evaluation of a social experiment*. Minneapolis, MN: University of Minnesota.

Dollard, J. (1937). *Caste and class in a southern town*. New York: Doubleday.

Dollard, J., Doob, L., Miller, N. E., Mowrer, O. H., & Sears, R. R. (1939). *Frustration and aggression*. New Haven, CT: Yale.

Forbes, D. (1997). *Ethnic conflict: Commerce, culture, and the contact hypothesis*. New Haven, CT: Yale University.

Fordham, S. (1996). *Blacked out: Dilemmas of race, identity, and success at Capital High*. Chicago: University of Chicago.

Gould, S. J. (1981). *The mismeasure of man*. New York: Norton.

Hartley, E. (1946). *Problems in prejudice*. New York: King's Crown.

Herskovits, M. J. (1941). *The myth of the Negro past*. New York: Harper & Brothers.

Higham, J. (1984). *Send these to me: Immigrants in urban America*. Baltimore: Johns Hopkins.

Hollinger, D. A. (1995). *Postethnic America*. New York: Basic Books.

Horowitz, E. L. (1936). The development of attitude toward the Negro. *Archives of Psychology*, (94).

Ichheiser, G. (1946). The Jews and anti-Semitism. *Sociometry, 9*, 92–108.

Jones, J. M. (1998). Psychological knowledge and the new American dilemma of race. *Journal of Social Issues, 54*, 641–662.

Katz, D., & Braly, K. (1933). Racial stereotypes of one hundred college students. *Journal of Abnormal and Social Psychology, 28*, 280–290.

Katz, D., & Braly, K. (1935–1936). Racial prejudice and racial stereotypes. *Journal of Abnormal and Social Psychology, 30*, 175–193.

Katz, I. (1991). Gordon Allport's "The nature of prejudice." *Political Psychology, 12*, 125–157.

Klineberg, O. (1954). *Social psychology*. New York: Holt.

Kluckhohn, C. (1949). *Mirror for man*. New York: Whittlesey House.

Kluger, R. (1975). *Simple justice: The history of Brown v. Board of Education and black America's struggle for equality*. New York: Vintage.

Krech, D., & Crutchfield, R. S. (1948). *Theory and problems of social psychology*. New York: McGraw-Hill.

LaPiere, R. (1936). Type-rationalizations of group antipathy. *Social Forces, 15*, 232–237.

Lee, Y.-T., Jussim, L. J., & McCauley, C. R. (1995). *Stereotype accuracy: Toward appreciating group differences*. Washington, DC: American Psychological Association.

Lewin, K. (1939). Field theory and experiment in social psychology. In K. Lewin, *Field theory in social science*. New York: Harper & Brothers. (1951)

Lind, M. (1996). *The next American nation: The new nationalism and the fourth American revolution*. New York: Free Press.

Lippitt, R., & Radke, M. (1946). New trends in the investigation of prejudice. *The Annals, 244*, 167–176.

Lippmann, W. (1922). *Public opinion*. New York: Macmillan.

Mackie, M. (1973). Arriving at "truth" by definition: The case of stereotype inaccuracy. *Social Problems, 20*, 431–447.

Malik, K. (1996). *The meaning of race*. New York: New York University.

Matthews, F. H. (1970). The revolt against Americanism: Cultural pluralism and cultural relativism as an ideology of liberation. *Canadian Review of American Studies, 1*, 3–31.

Myrdal, G. (1944). *An American dilemma. The Negro problem and modern democracy*. New York: Harper & Brothers.

Ross, D. (1991). *The origins of American social science*. New York: Cambridge University Press.

Ryan, W. (1971). *Blaming the victim*. New York: Pantheon.

Samelson, F. (1978). From "race psychology" to "studies in prejudice." *Journal of the History of Behavioral Science, 14,* 265–278.

Schofield, J. W. (1989). *Black and white in school: Trust, tension, or tolerance.* New York: Teachers College.

Sherif, M. (1936). *The psychology of social norms.* New York: Harper and Row.

Sherif, M., Harvey, O. J., Hood, W. R., & Sherif, C. (1961). *Intergroup conflict and cooperation.* Norman, OK: University of Oklahoma Book Exchange.

Smith, M. B. (1994). Stuart Cook. *American Psychologist, 49,* 521–522.

Stocking, G. W. (1968). *Race, culture, and evolution: Essays in the history of anthropology.* New York: Free Press.

Svonkin, S. (1997). *Jews against prejudice.* New York: Columbia University.

Szwed, J. (1972). An American anthropological dilemma: The politics of Afro-American culture. In D. Hymes (Ed.), *Reinventing anthropology.* New York: Pantheon.

CHAPTER 4

Ethnic Conflict and the Contact Hypothesis

H. D. Forbes

Ethnic conflict has complex causes and diverse effects, ranging from petty slights to murderous violence. Some light can be thrown on its causes by focussing on the two correlations commonly found in situations of ethnic contact and conflict. On the one hand, there is the easily observed *negative* correlation that supports the familiar "contact hypothesis": the more personal contact, the less conflict (prejudice, discrimination, hostility, etc.). On the other hand, there is the *positive* correlation suggested by many historical and sociological studies of contact situations. As a leading authority on intergroup attitudes has recently observed, "The world is experiencing two major intergroup trends—massive migration and increased group conflict" (Pettigrew, 1998b, 77). In other words, more contact and more conflict. But how is this possible? How can higher levels of contact be associated with both increases and decreases in the indicators of ethnic antagonism? The theory associated with the contact hypothesis— "contact theory"—provides a possible answer to this question, but one, I shall argue, that obscures more than it illuminates and that has more political than scientific appeal. First, however, the basic problem of two correlations will be clarified by reviewing some findings from an early study of the contact hypothesis.

TWO CORRELATIONS

The contact hypothesis is a broad generalization about the effects of personal contact between the members of different ethnic or racial groups on their prejudiced opinions and discriminatory behavior. The basic idea is that more contact between individuals belonging to antagonistic social groups (defined by culture, language, beliefs, skin color, nationality, etc.) tends to undermine the negative stereotypes they have of each other and to reduce their mutual antipathies, thus improving intergroup relations by making people more willing to deal with each other as equals. In short, more contact means less ethnic or cultural conflict, other things being equal.

This is a familiar, even a banal idea. It has been a staple of social scientists' accounts of prejudice and discrimination for a long time. In recent decades, it has generally been treated as an empirical hypothesis, tested in a variety of ways, and frequently vindicated, despite the apparently contrary trends—more contact and more conflict—just noted. (For recent discussions of the research literature, see Brewer and Gaertner, 2001; Miller, 2002; Pettigrew, 1998a; and Pettigrew and Tropp, 2000.)

To understand the difficulty here, it will be helpful to consider some results from a study done in the 1950s by sociologist Robin Williams, who conducted surveys of social contacts and ethnic attitudes in four cities in different regions of the United States (Williams, 1964). Table 4.1 shows four tabulations drawn from this study to illustrate the kinds of statistical relations routinely observed when personal contact and prejudiced attitudes are correlated. In all four tables—all four cities—greater reported contact between members of the White majority and one or more relevant minorities is clearly associated with lower levels of prejudice against those minorities. This negative correlation is stronger, it seems, in Valley City (with respect to Mexican Americans) than in Hometown (with respect to minorities generally) or in Southport (with respect to African Americans), but in all four cities the individuals who reported having personal relations with one or more members of one or more racial or ethnic minorities were less likely to express prejudiced opinions than were those who had no such contacts.

These results suggest that prejudice can be reduced and intergroup relations improved by encouraging more contact across group boundaries. Admittedly, this conclusion requires a jump from correlation to causation. It is thus vulnerable to a variety of objections having to do with the interpretation of the variables involved, the strength of the relationships shown, the direction of causation, the role of third variables, and the difference between attitudes and behavior. In addition, the conclusion must confront the basic objection suggested earlier. Aren't high levels of contact often associated with high levels of prejudice and discrimination in the parts of the world where different racial and ethnic groups live in close proximity and come into contact most frequently?

If the simplest reading of Williams's tables were true—if more contact always reduced average levels of intergroup antipathy—then one would expect proximity to encourage personal contact and this in turn to produce

Table 4.1
Contact and Prejudice at the Individual Level

| | Hometown (Elmira, NY) | | | | Valley City (Bakersfield, CA) | | |
	No Contact	Contact	Total		No Contact	Contact	Total
High Prejudice	56%	38%	**49%**		64%	28%	**57%**
Low Prejudice	44	62	51		36	72	43
(N =)	(261)	(161)	(422)		(140)	(32)	(172)

| | Steelville (Steubenville, OH) | | | | Southport (Savannah, GA) | | |
	No Contact	Contact	Total		No Contact	Contact	Total
High Prejudice	82%	55%	**63%**		73%	53%	**70%**
Low Prejudice	18	45	37		27	47	30
(N =)	(60)	(135)	(195)		(175)	(32)	(207)

Note: The tabulation (Table 7.19) from which these figures are calculated includes breakdowns for opportunities for interaction as well as actual interaction (or contact). Differences in opportunities have been disregarded in creating the four simple tables shown. The measures of prejudice are different in the different cities. For Hometown, it is an index of general prejudice; for Valley City, a single question about liking or disliking Mexican Americans; for Southport, a similar question about Negroes; and for Steelville, an open-ended question about liking of minority groups.

Source: Robin M. Williams, Jr., *Strangers Next Door: Ethnic Relations in American Communities* (Englewood Cliffs, NJ: Prentice-Hall, 1964), pp. 170–71.

low levels of prejudice and discrimination, generally speaking. One would not expect high levels of conflict, often erupting into violence, in those parts of the world where different racial and ethnic groups are in the most frequent contact. Yet this seems to be what we observe. For example, there seems to have been more racial prejudice, discrimination, violence, and oppression, generally speaking, at least in the past, in the southern United States and less in the North or the West. Similarly, the tensions between the different nationalities in the Balkans seem to have grown worse during the past century, despite the increasing opportunities they have had to meet and to form close personal relations. More generally, neighboring peoples—the French and the Germans, for example, or the Indians and the Pakistanis—seem to have the greatest trouble getting along, not those who live farther apart, such as the Peruvians and the Palestinians or the Tamils and the Turks. The more contact, it seems, the more trouble.

Before considering the standard response to these somewhat naive observations, let me clarify the problem I am pointing to by presenting more figures extracted from the text and tables of Williams (1964).

As indicated earlier, the four cities involved in this study were chosen to represent different regions of the United States. In all of the regions, in the 1950s, there were significant numbers of African Americans, and in all of the surveys, the White respondents were asked about their attitudes toward Negroes. In the different cities (and regions), however, the relative numbers of Blacks varied greatly, being lowest in the West and highest in the South. It is possible, therefore, to relate the overall levels of prejudice against Blacks in these four cities to the Black proportions of their populations. Of course, to have a valid measure of differences in average attitudes, one must use the same measure of prejudice in all of the cities. One cannot, as was done in constructing Table 4.1, use different measures in different cities.

Table 4.2 shows (a) the Black proportions of the populations of the four cities, (b) the proportions of the White populations of two of the cities that reported opportunities for contact with Blacks and actual personal relations with one or more Blacks, and (c) the responses of the Whites in all four cities to a common measure of prejudice, a question about Blacks demanding too much. In brief, Table 4.2 suggests that the opportunities for contact and actual contact with a minority increase as the minority proportion of an urban population increases, but so does the prejudice expressed against it—and this despite the fact, as we have already seen, that greater contact goes with less prejudice for the individuals reporting the contact.

Tables 4.1 and 4.2 clearly illustrate two apparently contradictory relationships, but they cannot, of course, establish that two such correlations between contact and conflict exist universally. A thousand respondents chosen from four cities in one country at one period in its history are obviously not a sufficient basis for such a broad generalization. But the pattern shown is suggestive nonetheless. There seem to be different relations between contact and conflict at different levels of analysis. This possibility, although it was recognized from the beginning of empirical research on the contact hypothesis more than 50 years ago, has been ob-

Table 4.2
Aggregate Contact Variables and Prejudice

City	Blacks as a Percentage of the Total Population	Whites Reporting an Opportunity for Contact	Whites Reporting Contact	Percentage of Whites Showing Prejudice toward Blacks
Elmira, NY	3%			22%
Bakersfield, CA	8%	41%	3%	39%
Steubenville, OH	10%			41%
Savannah, GA	40%	70%	11%	58%

Note: The percentages reporting an opportunity for contact and actual social interaction are calculated from the marginal frequencies shown for Valley City (Bakersfield) and Southport (Savannah) in Tables 7.9 and 7.19. Prejudice was measured by means of a question about whether Blacks were demanding more than they had a right to.

Source: Williams, *Strangers Next Door*, pp. 51, 158, 170–71, 226, 228, 230, and 232.

scured by the theory associated with the hypothesis, which attempts to explain different correlations between contact and conflict without distinguishing different levels of analysis.

CONTACT THEORY

Proponents of the contact hypothesis usually think of intergroup contact as having an effect on prejudiced attitudes and discriminatory behavior because of its effects on stereotyping. To simplify, they think that hostile stereotypes are born of social isolation and broken by personal acquaintance (e.g., Allport, 1954, chap. 16). They recognize, of course, that the cognitive and emotional mechanisms involved in the development and modification of intergroup attitudes are very complex: they can be affected by many variables. In principle, therefore, it should be possible to explain and predict different relations between contact and conflict (prejudice, discrimination, stereotyping, hostility, etc.) by taking these conditioning variables into account. It should be possible to specify the kinds and situations of contact that will have desirable effects and those that will have negative effects. When contact is the right kind of contact, in a favorable setting, it should tend to reduce prejudice and discrimination. Otherwise, contact may have no effects or even bad effects. Rather than breaking hostile stereotypes, it may just foster their growth.

This response—this introduction of additional variables having to do with different kinds or situations of contact—is what I mean by contact theory. By putting some qualifications on the simplest contact hypothesis, it seems to overcome the most damaging objections to it, but without abandoning its underlying ideas or its most important practical implications. The practical problem becomes how to foster the right kind of contact, in the right situations—or more practically, how to ensure that the situations in which contact naturally occurs will have the desirable characteristics that yield positive effects of contact.

Different authors have focussed on different variables and so have developed different versions of contact theory. More than 50 different mediating variables have been suggested by different contact theorists to specify the conditions for positive effects of contact. But three major variables have been repeatedly cited as crucial determinants of its effects:

1. The equality or inequality of status of the different groups in contact;
2. Their cooperative or competitive interdependence in the pursuit of common goals; and
3. The presence or absence of social norms supporting intergroup contact.

Depending on the values of these variables in different situations, the reasoning is, greater contact will either exacerbate or relieve intergroup hostility. As a leading exponent of the theory put it a generation ago, increasing interaction just intensifies whatever processes of separation or accommodation are already underway. "More interracial contact can lead either to greater prejudice and rejection or to greater respect and acceptance, depending upon the situation in which it occurs. The basic issue, then, concerns the types of situations in which contact leads to distrust and those in which it leads to trust" (Pettigrew, 1971, p. 275). Thus, in the situations mentioned earlier, such as race relations in the southern states, there may have been a lot of contact, but there has also been a lot of prejudice and discrimination because the contact has been casual contact in a situation of inequality, without cooperative interdependence in the pursuit of common goals, and contrary to law and convention. Therefore, the contact just reinforced the preexisting prejudices and deepened the intergroup conflict. Only if the situations had been different—if they had been situations of equality and cooperation in which contact across group boundaries could lead to true acquaintance because it had the support of those in authority—would it have had the good effects anticipated in the contact hypothesis.

Is this the right way to think about the puzzling correlations we observe between contact and conflict? There is no denying, of course, that different measures of hostile attitudes, in different situations, with different people, involved in different kinds of contact, will have somewhat different relations to quantitative measures of contact. The negative correlations will vary, and this variation may well be explained in part by the variables featured in contact theory. Nonetheless, the more closely the theory is examined, the less satisfactory it seems to be as a response to the major objection outlined earlier. It does not explain why there is often a positive correlation between contact and conflict when comparing different situations of personal contact. In theory it could do so, and the earliest contact theorists seem to have thought that it would.[1] But in fact it does not.

In fact, we do not observe essentially different correlations—differing in sign—between personal contact and hostile attitudes in different social and demographic situations. Rather, we observe roughly similar correlations in all of the relevant situations, despite whatever effects the variables highlighted in contact theory may have. The point is nicely illustrated by the four cross-tabulations in Table 4.1. As already noted, they show different degrees of statistical association between contact and prejudice: the relationship is strongest in Valley City and weakest, it seems, in Hometown. But everywhere the association is roughly the same. Everywhere it is a moderately strong negative correlation: the more contact, the less prejudice. It is not, as contact theory would require, negative in some situations and positive in others. Everywhere it is *negative*.

This crucial point is clearly stated and strongly emphasized in the book from which these figures have been taken. "Out of hundreds of tabulations, there emerges the major finding that *in all the surveys in all communities and for all groups, majority and minorities, the greater the frequency of interaction, the lower the prevalence of ethnic prejudice*" (Williams, 1964, pp. 167–68). The last part of this statement is set in italic type by its author to emphasize its importance. Everywhere, in all situations, with all possible combinations of groups, a simple negative correlation between contact and prejudice was found. This was indeed an important finding. But what the study did *not* find is equally important: it did not find essentially different correlations in the different cities representing different situations of contact. In short, Williams provided some impressive evidence to support the simplest contact hypothesis, but also some impressive evidence against the reasoning that I am calling contact theory—as a theory about how to reconcile the truth of the simplest hypothesis with the historical and sociological facts about ethnic mixing and ethnic conflict (cf. Pettigrew, 1959, 1998a; Pettigrew and Tropp, 2000).

LEVELS OF ANALYSIS

A more satisfactory approach to the two-correlations problem—the problem of understanding how our indicators of ethnic conflict can vary directly with the numerical density of minority groups, despite the apparent truth of the simplest, most basic contact hypothesis—depends on making a clear distinction between individual-level and aggregate-level relationships. Because the relevant individual-aggregate distinction is easily misunderstood, I will begin by presenting a simplified example in detail, to show more clearly than do the incomplete data from *Strangers Next Door* what exactly I mean by distinguishing the individual level from the aggregate level.

Table 4.3 is a simplified or idealized version of Table 4.2. Imagine four towns, A, B, C, and D, with different percentages of some unspecified minority, as shown in the first column. Imagine that the rates of contact between majority and minority individuals in these towns are simply a function of their relative numbers in each town. Let the rates of contact of the majority with the minority be the chance that two individuals chosen at random from each town's population will be from different groups. The result will be the rates shown in the second column (e.g., [.1 × .9] + [.9 × .1] = .18). Finally, assume that the level of prejudice among the majority in each town—their proportion scoring high on some measure of prejudice—is simply a function of the town's minority percentage, as shown in the third column. Then we have a table that shows strongly positive correlations between minority density, frequency of contact across the group boundary, and prejudice among the majority. The variables involved in these correlations describe aggregates—the towns—not individuals, even though the data are in a sense data about individuals. It is the towns that are being compared in Table 4.3, not their individual citizens. Disregard for the moment why there may be the aggregate-level correlations shown in the table: just assume they exist.

Next, use the percentages in contact and the percentages prejudiced from Table 4.3 to determine the marginal frequencies for four new tables

Table 4.3
Hypothetical Relations between Minority Density, Contact, and Prejudice

Towns	Minority Percentage	Percentage of Majority in Contact	Percentage of Majority Prejudiced
A (Amityville)	10%	18%	15%
B (Beaconsville)	20%	32%	20%
C (Centerville)	30%	42%	25%
D (Downsville)	40%	48%	30%

Note: Prejudiced % = 10 + 1/2 (Minority %) r = 1.0

that could arise from comparing the individual citizens of these towns on a town-by-town basis. Table 4.4 shows one possible set of tables of this kind—tables showing individual-level correlations between contact and prejudice. The marginal frequencies of these tables correspond to the percentages shown in Table 4.3.

Now the crucial thing to appreciate about the four subtables of Table 4.4 is that their marginal frequencies do *not* completely determine their internal frequencies and therefore do not determine the individual-level correlations between contact and prejudice. In the lingo of statisticians, one degree of freedom remains in each of these subtables. In other words, given the marginals, we can choose the internal frequencies of our imaginary cross-tabulations to show a positive correlation (more contact, more prejudice), a negative one (more contact, less prejudice), or no correlation

Table 4.4
Hypothetical Relations between Contact and Prejudice at the Individual Level

	Amityville					Beaconsville		
	No Contact	Contact				No Contact	Contact	
High P	15 (18%)	(0%)	15	High P		18 (26%)	2 (6%)	20
Low P	67	18	85	Low P		50	30	80
	82	18	100%			68	32	100%

	Centerville					Downsville		
	No Contact	Contact				No Contact	Contact	
High P	19 (33%)	6 (14%)	25	High P		21 (40%)	9 (19%)	30
Low P	39	36	75	Low P		31	39	70
	58	42	100%			52	48	100%

at all. I have chosen them so that the correlations all correspond, more or less, to the correlations shown earlier in Table 4.1, that is, so that the difference in prejudice in each town between the contact and no contact conditions is about 20 percentage points (compare the italicized percentages).

These are imaginary towns and imaginary statistical relations. But they show what it means here to distinguish between individual-level and aggregate-level relationships, and they demonstrate that the correlations between the same two variables, contact and prejudice, having to do ultimately with the same individuals, *can* be (not *must* be) radically different—different in sign as well as in magnitude—at different levels of analysis.

This is not an easy fact to see clearly, but it is a fact, as these tables show. And empirical research on contact and conflict shows that it is a relevant fact for understanding ethnic conflict. In a book published five years ago (Forbes, 1997), I reviewed about 250 studies of intergroup contact and its correlates. A simple overall pattern emerged from my review. In brief, it is the pattern suggested by *Strangers Next Door* and by my imaginary example: significant negative correlations, almost without exception, at the individual level; a mix of weak positive and negative correlations at very low levels of aggregation; and stronger correlations, usually positive, at higher levels of aggregation.

The individual-aggregate distinction thus provides a simple solution, up to a point, of the problem that we started with, the puzzling contrast between the statistical relationship that supports the contact hypothesis (a negative correlation) and the strikingly high levels of negative attitudes we often observe in situations of close contact between different groups (that is, a positive correlation between contact and prejudice at the aggregate level). This limited solution consists in saying that the individual-level relationship is simply not the same as the aggregate-level one, even though they involve the same variables and the same individuals. One is negative, the other positive.

This is a satisfying solution only up to a point, however, for nothing has been said as yet about why two such different statistical relationships might exist. I have shown how it is possible that they can coexist, and suggested that both relationships are in fact commonly observed, but I have said nothing about why this is so. To understand why, we need to consider an alternative to contact theory, which I shall call, for lack of a better term, "ethnic conflict theory."

ETHNIC CONFLICT THEORY

Contact may have an effect on the conflict variables (prejudice, discrimination, hostility, etc.) because of its effect on cultural differences, rather than on stereotyping, and it may be a cause of antagonistic relationships more often than a cure for them, because, given cultural differences between groups, contact sets up conflicts of interest regarding how exactly the groups are to converge on a common culture or common norms in their dealings with each other. To see more clearly what relationships are now being postulated, it will be best to focus, for the time being, on language and linguistic differences.

Consider two individuals who have grown up speaking different languages and who now, as adults, have some reason to associate with one another. There may be economic reasons for their association, having to do with trading or employment; or they may fall in love with each other and want to live together; or more fancifully, they may be two lonely survivors on a tropical island after a shipwreck. Whatever the reasons, let us simply assume that each finds some important rewards contingent on association and cooperation with the other. For the moment, it is the consequences of their association, not its causes, that concern us. What are these consequences likely to be?

At first there is bound to be some misunderstanding, frustration, and mutual irritation. But after a time, and assuming that the reasons for association persist, each of them is likely to learn more effective ways of communicating with the other. They may learn each other's languages, or adopt one of them, or converge on a mélange of the two to facilitate their cooperation.

If more than a handful of individuals from two linguistic groups frequently find themselves in the situation just described, then we say that there is contact between these two groups. The more the groups become interdependent in ways that require or encourage frequent communication across the linguistic boundary, the more contact there is between them. If large numbers of their members have strong incentives to associate frequently with members of the other group, there will be a lot of contact between the groups.

The incentives for contact or association that we have postulated are at the same time incentives for linguistic assimilation or linguistic homogenization. Different languages impede easy cooperation. To secure the benefits of association, those in contact must, generally speaking, be able to communicate easily with each other, that is to say, they must share a common language.

Because contact is potentially a cause of assimilation, it is also a cause of conflict. In situations of the kind we are considering, it often does not matter, in the end, which group adopts which language, or how the two languages mix, so long as the net effect is greater similarity between the groups. It does not matter, in other words, whether the languages of the different groups "melt" to form some new alloy or whether one group simply adopts the language of the other, and if so, which one. The long-term benefits of change are contingent only upon increasing mutual intelligibility and do not depend on how this is achieved.

The situation is of course quite different in the short run from the perspective of either one of the groups, because most adults have difficulty learning a new language. Thus it makes a great deal of difference to each individual in the situation of contact whether he (or she) or someone else is required to learn a new language. While the process of homogenization is taking place, the net advantage to any group of greater mutual intelligibility will partly depend upon whether they are making the necessary adaptations or whether the other group is bearing these costs. Because of the costs of change, each of the groups will benefit if it can somehow induce members of the other group to adopt its language while at the same time preventing its own members from learning the alien language. Each group will want to stiffen the resistance of its own members to assimilation, because each "defection" adds to the pressure on the remaining "loyalists" to defect. Conversely, the stiffer the group's resistance, the better the chances that it will succeed in making the other group bear the costs of assimilation (Deutsch, 1953; Laitin, 1988, 1998; Laponce, 1987; Lieberson, 1970).

This conflict of interest created by contact and differences is expressed in what can be called "lingocentrism"—short for linguistic ethnocentrism. Lingocentrism is a handy term for efforts to isolate and subordinate linguistic out-groups (or for demands for such isolation and subordination) in order to reduce the incentives and opportunities for the wrong kind of assimilation (of the members of one's own group) and to increase the pressures for the right kind of assimilation (of the others, toward one's own language). Lingocentrism can also embrace the various ways that resistance to assimilation is strengthened among linguistic compatriots, such as by cultivating hatred of linguistic rivals (as domineering brutes or natural slaves or crafty swindlers) and contempt for their languages (as an ugly babble, lacking clarity, precision, humor, depth, authenticity, and the other virtues that good languages have). Finally, it is a broad enough term to cover even the efforts that can be made to purify a language by finding native terms to replace foreign borrowings.

Now if we compare individuals in the situation we are imagining, lingocentric beliefs, demands, and actions will presumably be less common or less intense, on the average, among those who have established contact with the linguistic outsiders and who have already learned to deal with them in an amicable way, and they will be more commonly found and more intense among those who have remained relatively isolated from the outsiders. As shown earlier, this negative individual-level relationship can coexist with a positive correlation between contact and lingocentrism at the aggregate level, over time or when comparing whole communities.

Returning to this aggregate level, lingocentrism (that is, the various expressions of the underlying conflict of interest between the groups in contact) will tend to react back, as it were, on its causes. It will tend to reduce the contact between the groups and to reinforce their linguistic differences. Lingocentric individuals will be reluctant to associate with their linguistic rivals, particularly when family and friends condemn such association. After all, who really wants to learn another language, particularly if it's the language of servants or of the oppressors of one's people?

There is only an apparent contradiction here between saying, on the one hand, that contact tends to reduce the differences between the groups in question through assimilation and blending and, on the other hand, that it also generates efforts to protect or even to increase these differences. Between any two variables there can be more than one causal relationship. The analysis so far has involved three principal variables or dimensions of change, and although it is obviously a simplification of some very complicated and obscure processes, it is perhaps complex enough at this point that a picture may now be worth more than a thousand more words.

Figure 4.1 provides a simple diagram using causal arrows of different kinds to represent the relationships I have been describing between three key variables. The heavy black arrows represent the interaction between contact (C) and cultural differences (D) that I am assuming causes ethnocentrism (E)—the postulated relationship that is stated more formally in the first point above the diagram. The lighter unbroken arrow from E to C represents the tendency of the ethnocentrisms generated by contact to reduce that contact, as stated in point 2. Finally, the broken arrows represent the dependence, over a longer period of time, of cultural differences on contact and ethnocentrism (point 3). X, Y, and Z stand for unknown exogenous variables, or outside influences, that affect the three mutually interdependent variables of the model.

In presenting this model I have slipped, without any explanation, from talking about linguistic differences and lingocentrism to talking about ethnic differences generally and ethnocentrism. This shift, and my use of language as a surrogate for culture, requires much more justification than I can provide here. Similarly, I will pass over the difficulties of moving from my simplified world of only two groups to the real world of many groups. But let me make two claims on behalf of the simplified model I have outlined.

First, it provides a possible explanation for the two apparently contradictory, but really compatible, correlations between contact and prejudice noted earlier, that is, the negative correlations that are almost always found at the individual level and the positive correlations generally observed at the aggregate level. In the light of the model, this dual pattern ceases to be just a brute fact and becomes something that we have a reason to expect.

Figure 4.1
A Three-Variable Model of Ethnic Conflict
1. Ethnocentrism (E) depends upon, and increases with, the amount of contact (C) between any two groups and the magnitude of the cultural differences (D) that distinguish them. These two factors interact to determine each group's level of ethnocentrism. A group will show no ethnocentrism with regard to another group if either (a) its members have no contacts with that other group, or (b) there are no differences in the customs and values of the two groups.
2. The amount of contact between any two groups depends upon their proximity and the incentives for contact between their members (because of factors such as technology or the state of development of the forces of production and hence the possibilities that exist for profitable specialization and trade) and upon the levels of ethnocentrism of the two groups. Higher levels of ethnocentrism, other things remaining the same, tend to reduce the contact between the groups or to slow down its increase.
3. The cultural differences between any two groups will be influenced by the contact between them and the mutual repulsions resulting from this contact. An increase in contact, other things remaining the same, will speed up cultural assimilation or, equivalently, reduce the growth of cultural differences caused by other factors. Conversely, an increase in ethnocentrism will reduce the rate of assimilation or increase the rate at which cultural differences develop—again assuming that all other things remain unchanged. The adjustment of cultural differences to changes in the levels of contact and ethnocentrism takes a relatively long time to work itself out.

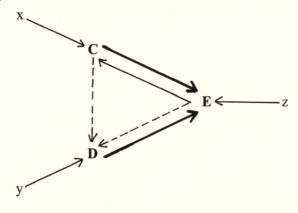

Second, by explaining this pattern, the model suggests that contact theory may be seriously misleading. If our goal were only to change the attitudes of particular individuals, the theory might serve us well, even without the complicated qualifications added by recent theorists, but as a guide to improving the relations between groups, it may be prescribing exactly the wrong medicine. To reduce the conflict of interest between ethnic groups, and the manifestations of this conflict in ethnocentric attitudes and behavior, the model I have outlined suggests that we should reduce contact, not increase it in the hope of breaking more stereotypes. When thinking about the larger problem of intergroup relations, it suggests, we should not let ourselves be distracted by whatever good effects of personal contact (and assimilation) we see at the individual level. As managers of ethnic contact and conflict, we should try to keep our eyes on the ball.

POLITICS AND SOCIAL SCIENCE

A method for reducing the prejudices of particular individuals would be of little interest if it were clear that its indirect effects added more to the stock of prejudice than its immediate, direct effects subtracted from it. Such a method would be like a homeopathic drug that somehow cured a few patients of some minor ailments but whose ill effects were felt by a lot of bystanders. Is contact such a cure for prejudice?

There are reasons to think that it is. There has never been as much contact between people of different races, religions, and nationalities as there is today. Yet never before, it seems, has there been so much hatred and violence associated with ethnic differences. No one will presumably deny the overall increase in contact across ethnic boundaries because of changes in modes of transportation and communication, the growth of cities, the development of a global economy, and the great migrations of the past several centuries. Sweeping generalizations about trends in prejudice and discrimination are more easily disputed, but it may be safe to say, nonetheless, that ethnic rivalry remains, even where it is safely under control (for example, in great cosmopolitan cities such as London, Toronto, and New York), at least as large and menacing a problem today as it was a century or two ago. In short, recent experience seems to belie the optimistic theories that were seriously entertained as recently as a generation ago—that growing contact across ethnic boundaries would soon dissolve ancient ethnic loyalties and antipathies and produce a pacified world, or at least the one orthodox Marxists expected, where rational class conflict would no longer be buried under irrational racial and religious antagonisms.

The alternative to contact theory I have outlined—the model of contact as a cause of conflicts of interest due to the fear of assimilation—may have some merit, then, as a corrective to these earlier views, but can one reasonably claim that it is simply true? The problem is not any lack of striking anecdotal evidence for the relationships shown in the arrow diagram earlier, if each is considered separately. For example, as already explained, we know that high levels of contact often coexist with high levels of ethnic antagonism, and it is easy to see that this may be due to a simple causal connection. (Allport was willing to call the relationship in question a law.) It may be harder to see that intense hostility could, simultaneously, reduce contact, but the idea is certainly plausible, and the evidence commonly presented for the standard contact hypothesis can serve equally well as evidence for this contrary idea (e.g., Table 4.1 earlier, treating prejudice as the independent variable). Similarly, each of the other links can easily be illustrated, taking them one at a time. The real problems begin when we put all these links together and consider the result to be a basic explanation for what we call prejudice and discrimination. Is the resulting model, as a basis for thinking about ethnic conflict in all its forms, sound or misleading? Would it make sense to try to test such a model, which is obviously much more complicated than any simple empirical proposition? Might it not be more sensible to ask, not whether the model is true or false, but where it may be true, or in what sense it may be true?

Nothing much can be said here about the difficulties that stand in the way of clear answers to these difficult questions. They go beyond the standard topics in social science methodology.[2] But one can observe that contact theory has long been favored—and alternatives to it have long been neglected—without any serious attempt to assess the relevant evidence. To understand why, it may help to consider the political context of what may seem, at first glance, to be a strictly scientific question.

Contact theory and the standard contact hypothesis start from a familiar assumption about the customary practices and beliefs that distinguish one ethnic group from another, namely, that these differences may provide pretexts or rationalizations for prejudice and discrimination, but they are not to be counted among their real causes (cf. Allport, 1954, chap. 1). Like theological puzzles or a preference for pasta or pierogies, such differences belong to the private sphere of life. They raise no legitimate questions of public policy and cannot, therefore, be the source of any realistic conflicts of interest. It follows that personal contacts should generally improve intergroup relations. If people mix with each other, they will eventually see how similar they are at bottom, how misleading their old stereotypes were, how much they can all benefit from peaceful exchange, and even how amusing and enjoyable their little differences can be. This reasoning can be supported by empirical studies that compare individuals with and without personal relations outside their own groups. The positive effects of contact shown in such studies are the only effects that really need to be taken into account, according to the theory. If a situation of frequent contact happens to be a situation of intense conflict—even if there seems to be a lawful relationship between the overall amount of contact and the amount of conflict—this can be attributed to the contact, contact theorists say, only if it has been the wrong kind of contact, in unfavorable circumstances. The right kind of contact, in favorable circumstances, could only alleviate the conflicts in question, not aggravate them. Moreover, the empirical research shows that virtually all of the ordinary situations of contact are ones in which personal contact has positive effects. To maximize these positive effects, it seems, individuals should come into contact as equals, cooperating in the pursuit of common goals (such as victory in an athletic contest or a war), with the support of their superiors.

The model of ethnic conflict outlined earlier challenges this way of thinking about prejudice and discrimination. Without dismissing personal contact as unimportant, it shifts attention from the quirks of individual psychology to social processes and noneconomic conflicts of interest (cf. Varshney, 2001). Despite the plausibility of the model's assumptions, however, and despite its success in resolving some empirical puzzles, as I have tried to show, it remains vulnerable to an essentially practical objection—that it gives far too much attention to cultural differences as a cause of conflict.

Like any theory or model of social interactions, a model of ethnic conflict, if it is thought to be true, is likely to be the basis for practical attempts to deal with the processes it describes. Description is implicitly prescription. But would it really be wise to try to reduce ethnic conflict by reducing contact across ethnocultural boundaries, as the model earlier suggests, or by trying to force the pace of assimilation? In the past, the basic ideas of the model have been used to justify attempts, for example, to restrict contact between racial and ethnic groups by "nationalistic" policies of segregation, political independence, and economic autarky. But what have been the results of such attempts, one may ask. Given the long-term and apparently inexorable upward trend in contact, and given its powerful economic and technological causes, such policies may well be condemned as costly, unjust, and ultimately futile. Rather than trying to reduce conflict by reducing contact, the better practical alternative, it may seem clear, is to minimize the tensions that contact produces by suppressing its worst manifestations while quietly promoting cultural harmonization or homogenization.

Contact theory can thus provide an appealing rationale for what common sense may suggest the political authorities must do. It construes policies of enforced equality and cooperation, not as the authoritative imposition of new cultural norms, but as the creation of conditions for the breaking of misleading stereotypes and the attainment of greater rationality. It puts the most benign possible interpretation on policies that minimize violence in the short run and erase differences in the long run.

This political usefulness of conventional contact theory, rather than its strictly scientific merits, may provide the best explanation of its popularity and resilience. It provides a reassuring response to the uneasiness associated with some long-term trends and the public policies associated with them. It encourages the belief that more contact will mean, not more latent tensions, tighter restrictions, and less diversity, but fewer foolish prejudices, a more practical, less superstitious approach to life, and ultimately, a freer and more peaceful society.

To be sure, speculation about the politics of an empirical theory can easily degenerate into bitter, fruitless argument. Nonetheless, in this case it may suggest some good reasons for thinking that more must be taken into account, in order to understand the survival of contact theory, than just the hard evidence supporting its claims.

Fifty years ago, Gordon Allport tried to deal with the most obvious objections to "the method of contact" by making a distinction between casual contact and true acquaintance—as if one could promote true acquaintance without increasing casual contacts and as if the independent variables in simple empirical studies of the contact hypothesis had generally been measures of the former, not the latter. Neither of these suppositions was true, and the theory that Allport proposed, to the extent that it could be tested, was soon falsified. This has been reasonably well known for at least a generation. Nonetheless, variations on the basic themes of the theory continue to be put forward, even if the main difficulty it was meant to overcome is no longer clearly explained. Indeed, the greater the contrary evidence, the greater the ingenuity contact theorists have shown in developing new versions of the theory. Like the old defenders of Ptolemaic astronomy, who added epicycles to their epicycles, contact theorists have complicated and refined their theory rather than giving any serious consideration to the most important alternatives to it (e.g., Pettigrew, 1998a).

The theory may be vulnerable, however, to a change in political climate. As liberal societies become more and more multicultural, it becomes harder and harder to think of their problems of ethnic conflict in the old liberal way—as problems of the relations between individuals rooted in their irrational prejudices and thus amenable to resolution through the promotion of friendly personal contacts. It becomes more and more necessary to see them as problems of the relationships between groups rooted in their cultural differences and conflicting demands for recognition (cf. Tajfel, 1982). If this less individualistic view were ever to take hold, the contact hypothesis and contact theory might quietly fade from view, replaced by some other theory, more closely related to the one I have outlined earlier, which would deal more openly with questions about cultural differences and the threat of assimilation.

NOTES

1. Thus Gordon Allport's classic statement of the contact hypothesis (Allport, 1954, p. 281) was preceded by a lengthy discussion of ten "sociocultural laws of prejudice" relating differences in prejudiced attitudes to differences in social and cultural conditions. According to two of these laws, prejudice increases with (a) ethnic heterogeneity, and (b) the sizes and rates of increase of minority groups (pp. 221–222 and 227–229). In

other words, not all contact *dispels* prejudice; some must actually *increase* it. As Allport says later, "Prejudice varies with the numerical density of a minority group. . . . The more contact the more trouble" (p. 263; also p. 488). It is much too simple, therefore, he says, to think that merely by bringing people together without regard to ethnicity, race, religion, or national origin, we can easily destroy stereotypes and develop friendly attitudes. Rather, we must assume that there are different kinds of contact, in different situations, with different effects on prejudice. More specifically, we must distinguish "casual contacts," which tend to increase prejudice, from "true acquaintance," which lessens it. To clarify this distinction, Allport offered a lengthy (30-item) list of variables that he thought deserved investigation as possible determinants of the positive or negative effects of contact. The most important of these variables, having to do with equal status, common goals, and institutional supports, were incorporated in his final, frequently quoted statement of the contact hypothesis (p. 281). Allport's reasoning is reproduced in Pettigrew (1971), pp. 274–278, and Pettigrew (1998a), pp. 67–68, but without any reference to "sociocultural laws."

2. They are discussed at length in Forbes (1997), chaps. 6 and 7. For an interesting recent attempt to deal with some of the difficulties, see Ihlanfeldt and Scafidi (2002), which analyses the mutually interdependent effects of contact on prejudice and prejudice on contact, using data from three American cities at a low level of aggregation (census blocks). The most interesting conclusion that emerges from the rather tortuous statistics of the study is that "neighbourhood contact affects the preferences of Whites only if this contact is with Blacks of about the same or higher social status, as measured by educational achievement" (p. 633).

REFERENCES

Allport, G. W. (1954). *The nature of prejudice*. Reading, MA: Addison-Wesley.

Brewer, M. B., & Gaertner, S. L. (2001). Toward reduction of prejudice: Intergroup contact and social categorization. In A. Tesser, et al. (Eds.), *Blackwell handbook of social psychology: Vol. 3. Intergroup processes* (pp. 451–472). Oxford: Basil Blackwell.

Deutsch, K. W. (1953). *Nationalism and social communication: An inquiry into the foundations of nationality*. Cambridge, MA: MIT Press.

Forbes, H. D. (1997). *Ethnic conflict: Commerce, culture, and the contact hypothesis*. New Haven, CT: Yale University Press.

Ihlanfeldt, K. R., & Scafidi, B. P. (2002). The neighbourhood contact hypothesis: Evidence from the Multicity Study of Urban Inequality. *Urban Studies, 39*, 619–641.

Laitin, D. D. (1988). Language games. *Comparative Politics, 20*, 289–302.

Laitin, D. D. (1998). *Identity in formation: The Russian-speaking populations in the near abroad*. Ithaca, NY: Cornell University Press.

Laponce, J. A. (1987). *Languages and their territories* (A. Martin-Sperry, Trans.). Toronto: University of Toronto Press.

Lieberson, S. (1970). *Language and ethnic relations in Canada*. New York: John Wiley.

Miller, N. (2002). Personalization and the promise of contact theory. *Journal of Social Issues, 58*(2), 387–410.

Pettigrew, T. F. (1959). Regional differences in anti-Negro prejudice. *Journal of Abnormal and Social Psychology, 59*, 28–36.

Pettigrew, T. F. (1971). *Racially separate or together?* New York: McGraw-Hill.

Pettigrew, T. F. (1998a). Intergroup contact theory. *Annual Review of Psychology, 49*, 65–85.

Pettigrew, T. F. (1998b). Reactions toward the new minorities of western Europe. *Annual Review of Sociology, 24*, 77–103.

Pettigrew, T. F., & Tropp, L. R. (2000). Does intergroup contact reduce prejudice? Recent meta-analytic findings. In S. Oskamp (Ed.), *Reducing prejudice and discrimination: Social psychological perspectives* (pp. 93–114). Mahwah, NJ: Lawrence Erlbaum.

Tajfel, H. (1982). Social psychology of intergroup relations. *Annual Review of Psychology, 33*, 1–29.

Varshney, A. (2001). Ethnic conflict and civil society: India and beyond. *World Politics, 53*, 362–398.

Williams, R. M. (1964). *Strangers next door: Ethnic relations in American communities*. Englewood Cliffs, NJ: Prentice-Hall.

CHAPTER 5

Immigration and Ethnic Conflict in Comparative Perspective

Philip Q. Yang, Stephanie Power,
Seiji Takaku, and Luis Posas

There appears to be a growing recognition that ethnic conflict will remain a common phenomenon in the contemporary world (Horowitz, 1985; Khinduka, 1995). The prediction of waning importance of ethnicity and decreasing ethnic conflict by Marxist and modernization theories has met with an overwhelming rejection. In almost every society with two or more ethnic groups, we are left with some form of conflict (Prentice & Miller, 1999). Evidence on the ubiquity of ethnic conflict abounds (e.g., Gurr, 1993; Gurr & Harff, 1994; Khinduka, 1995; United Nations, 1993). Immigration is often assumed to be a key condition leading to ethnic conflict. However, how immigration is related to ethnic conflict is not very well understood. In both immigration studies and ethnic studies, there is an inadequate theorization about the relationship between immigration and ethnic conflict, and there is little systematic cross-national comparative evidence on this relationship. This chapter is a step toward filling these gaps in the literature. Rather than hypothesis testing, our main purpose is to generate hypotheses for further testing using cross-national data. The narratives of the experiences of selected immigration countries serve as an empirical basis of our hypotheses.

CONCEPTUALIZING IMMIGRATION AND ETHNIC CONFLICT

Following Yang's (2000) definition, we define ethnic conflict as any expressed sentiments or actions between ethnic groups that are hostile or antagonistic, which include nonviolent confrontation, violent confrontation, and expressed hostile sentiments through verbal, written, or symbolic forms. Immigration refers to permanent population movement into a country from another country. In this article, we focus on whether and how immigration influences ethnic conflict. Our main research questions are as follows: Does immigration cause ethnic conflict? If so, how does immigration lead to ethnic conflict? If not, why doesn't immigration have an impact on ethnic conflict?

A widely held belief is that immigration inevitably causes ethnic conflict because group contact naturally leads to intergroup competition and strife. We label this the "inevitable hypothesis." Robert Park's (1950) well-known Race Relations Cycle sowed the seeds of this hypothesis. According to Park, the Race Relations Cycle contains four stages: (1) *contact* between groups through migration or exploration; (2) *competition* between groups for scarce resources, which often leads to conflict; (3) *accommodation*, including the establishment of laws, customs, and rules to regulate intergroup conflict and relations; and (4) *assimilation* of smaller and weaker groups into a larger or dominant one. He asserted that this cycle is universally applicable and the sequence is "apparently progressive and irreversible." Apparently, the first two stages address the relationship between migration and ethnic conflict, and the last two deal with conflict resolution and outcome. The gist of Park's theory is that migration brings different ethnic groups into contact, which inevitably brings about intergroup competition and conflict. Competition and conflict will diminish as a result of accommodation, and the final outcome is assimilation into the dominant culture and the creation of a new equilibrium. In contemporary time, the inevitable hypothesis does not lack supporters. Ordinary people often tie immigration with ethnic tensions and clashes. In particular, opponents of immigration frequently make immigration a culprit of ethnic conflict.

We propose an alternative argument called the "conditional hypothesis." We argue that immigration does not always or inevitably cause ethnic (including cultural) conflict, and it induces ethnic strife only under certain conditions. Immigration is a primary way to bring different ethnic groups into contact, which establishes a precondition for potential ethnic conflict. However, group contact is only a necessary condition, but not a sufficient one, for ethnic conflict.[1] Whether group contact and competition develop into conflict depends on specific situations. Then, the crucial question becomes, under what conditions does immigration cause ethnic conflict? The literature suggests the following important factors.

First, direct competition between groups for scarce resources is a major source of ethnic conflict. Barth (1956, 1969) proposed the concept of "niche overlap"—the exploitation and occupation of the same resources desired by other competitors. To him, niche overlap is a key mechanism through which competition turns into conflict. Olzak (1992) further elaborated how niche overlap induces ethnic conflict. The essence of this so-called competition theory lies in direct competition for limited resources. If different ethnic groups do not occupy an overlapping environment, ethnic conflict is not likely to occur. This perspective is very similar to the argument of realistic group conflict theory developed by psychologists, which assumes that sources of conflict such as incompatible goals and competition for scarce resources are realistic (Sherif, 1966; Sherif, Harvey, White, Hood, & Sherif, 1961).

Second, an unequal distribution of resources and power by government promotes antagonism between groups, especially between dominant and subordinate groups (Tajfel & Turner, 1986). The state is seldom an impartial arbiter of ethnic interests. As Omi and Winant (1994, p. 82) pointed out, "the state *is* inherently racial. Far from *intervening* in racial conflicts, the state is itself increasingly the preeminent site of racial conflict." The state often represents the interest of the dominant group. The dominant group uses the authority of government to implement its wills, retain its position of advantages, and discriminate against scapegoat minorities. Favoritism toward some ethnic groups and discrimination against other groups are a common characteristic of many contemporary states (Rupesinghe, 1989). Ethnic tensions and conflicts are instigated or fanned by the inequitable allocation of resources and power. On the other hand, a fair treatment of different ethnic groups can reduce conflict and advance ethnic harmony. "There will be no racial (or ethnic) peace without racial (or ethnic) justice" (Stone, 1985).

Third, how to cope with cultural differences in language, religion, custom, and so forth can induce or defuse ethnic conflict. When new groups migrate to a society, they bring with them their distinct cultural traditions. The transplanted culture and the host culture are not always in consonance. In conjunction with competition for limited resources, cultural differences often arouse the phobias of cultural invasion, loss of national identity, and relative decline of dominant culture and group (Huntington, 1996). Massive phobias will then engender negative public opinions and campaigns against the new groups. A government policy based on the assumption of cultural superiority or inferiority and the institutional suppression of one culture in favor of another often leads to clashes. In contrast, a deliberate multicultural policy facilitates intergroup integration and harmony.

Fourth, a perceived threat of a large new immigrant group to older groups often causes individual and/or institutional discrimination against the new group and therefore the antagonism. This means that size of immigrant group matters. Existing groups, especially the dominant group, fear the economic, political, and cultural competition of a large new immigrant group. As a result, they launch social movements, institute state policies, or take individual discriminatory actions against the large new group. As shown following, ample evidence documents that large new groups are often targets of ethnic antagonism, whereas a small group is spared. Some evidence also suggests that size of minority population is a predictor of racial riots in American cities in the 1960s (e.g., Spilerman, 1970, 1971).

Finally, a perceived threat of a lower-status immigrant group can induce ethnic conflict. Split labor market theory contends that as unskilled workers precipitate competition, ethnic antagonism arises (Bonacich, 1972). An increase in the supply of unskilled laborers constitutes a major threat to native workers because immigrant workers who are willing to work at any price can undercut existing wages (Shanahan & Olzak, 1999). Hence, the overall class ranking of the immigrant group is negatively associated with the likelihood of ethnic conflict. Similarly, some psychologists (e.g., Tajfel & Turner, 1986) also recognized that a low status should intensify intergroup hostility.

The remainder of this chapter narrates the historical and contemporary experiences of selected major immigration countries to shed light on the foregoing two competing hypotheses. Space constraint precludes the selection of all major immigration countries. The United States, Canada, Australia, Germany, and Japan are chosen either because of their large immigration flows and/or because of their distinct experiences of immigration and ethnic conflict, which can facilitate cross-national comparison.

UNITED STATES OF AMERICA

The United States is a nation of immigrants and remains the largest immigrant-receiving country in the world today. A glance of the history of immigration and ethnic conflict in America can help us understand the relationship between the two. Prior to the arrival of Christopher Columbus in the New World in 1492, between 7.5 million and 18 million Indians resided in North America, including the United States and Canada (Dobyns, 1983, pp. 42, 298; Stannard, 1992, p. 268; Thornton, 1987, p. 32). The permanent settlement of European migrants did not bring about immediate clash with the Indians. There was a short period of peaceful coexistence and cooperation. The Indians and European settlers engaged in fur trade. In Massachusetts, the Indians assisted the Puritans to overcome their hardship in their first year, and they celebrated harvest together by sharing turkeys, potatoes, and so on: thus the origin of Thanksgiving. However, peaceful coexistence did not last for very long. Soon, fighting between the Indians and the Europeans erupted, leading to the conquest of Indians. The primary cause of this conflict was the direct competition between the two groups for resources, especially for land. As a result of disease, starvation, and violence, the Indian population in North America had decreased to about 250,000 by 1890.

During the founding of the 13 English colonies, although the bulk of settlers came from England, significant numbers also hailed from the Netherlands, Sweden, Ireland, and German states. Conflicts occurred between European settlers of various origins over the control of territories. For example, the Dutch arrived in 1623 and established their colony called the New Netherlands in New Amsterdam at the southern tip of the Manhattan Island in 1624. Later the English fought with the Dutch over the control of the New Netherlands in 1632. The defeat of the Dutch led to the English takeover and renaming of the New Netherlands to New York (Olson, 1994).

The gold rush lured tens of thousands of Chinese to America beginning in 1848 (Takaki, 1989). Significant Chinese-white conflict did not begin until 1849 when a significant number of Chinese immigrants arrived. The fears of their large number, "strange" physical appearance, distinct cultural traditions, and willingness to accept low-paying jobs, as well as racism led to the anti-Chinese movement. Numerous anti-Chinese attacks and riots occurred (Chen, 1980). Representing the interest of the white majority, the governments at the various levels in California passed many discriminatory laws against the Chinese. The institutional discrimination also incited actions against the Chinese. The Chinese problem and conflict were resolved with the passage of the Chinese Exclusion Act of 1882 by Congress (Chen, 1980; Takaki, 1989). The Chinese became the first group to be excluded from immigration in the history of the United States. Later, the Japanese problem and the Filipino problem were resolved with the Gentlemen's Agreement of 1907–08 and the Tydings-McDuffie Act of 1934, respectively, which amounted to Japanese and Filipino exclusions from immigration.

During the period of "old immigration" from western and northern Europe, the immigration of the predominantly Catholic Irish in the mid-nineteenth century often engendered tensions with the established Protestant groups. Anti-Catholicism was widespread. Besides their religious difference, the low-class background and large size of Irish immigrants were key factors leading to the conflict. In contrast, French immigrants, with a much smaller size and middle-class background, did not encounter many problems with the Protestant groups, although they were also largely Catholic. During the period of "new immigration" from eastern and southern Europe at the turn of the nineteenth and twentieth centuries, the settlement of southern and eastern Europeans into the cities of the east resulted in ethnic conflict because of the fears of the working-class segments of the Anglo population that newcomers would take their jobs. In particular, Italian immigrants encountered similar problems facing the Irish immigrants early on because of their peasant or unskilled working-class background and large size in addition to their Catholicism. The conditions of the eastern and southern European migrants changed only when the economy of the country began to grow as a result of the demands of the incipient industrial growth and a new threat represented by the exodus of African Americas from the south to the north (Schaefer, 2000).

In the post-1965 period, the level of immigration has continued to increase and the sources of immigration have shifted from Europe to Asia and Latin America (Yang, 1995). The large immigration of minority immigrants has transformed America's racial and ethnic landscape, resulting in the so-called browning of America (Johnson, Farrell, & Guinn, 1997). Concomitant with ethnic transformation come ethnic conflicts. In particular, adding to a less well documented dimension of ethnic conflicts, recent studies (Johnson et al.; Johnson & Oliver, 1989; Min, 1996) show that conflicts often occur between minorities. Johnson et al. grouped these conflicts into five types: (1) conflict caused by residential transition from black to brown, or resident-transition-induced conflict (e.g., black-Latino conflict); (2) conflict induced by business succession, or entrepreneurially induced conflict (e.g., Korean-black conflicts); (3) conflict induced by employer's preference in hiring immigrants over native workers (employer-induced conflict); (4) conflict caused by advantage of being bilingual versus being monolingual in employment opportunity (linguistic-induced conflict); and (5) Proposition 187-induced conflict. All of these conflicts are associated with direct competitions between groups for residential neighborhood, business, job opportunities, and power. Group size and class composition also matter.

Reports about conflicts between whites and minority immigrants also abound. For example, recent immigrants from Latin America have experienced ethnic conflict sometimes long after the period of settlement often associated with fluctuations in the global and local economy. Mahler (1995) reported that Salvadoran immigrants who settled in Long Island developed a pattern of relations characterized by mutual assistance with the broader Anglo population, although this balance was altered by a downturn in the local economy, which was responding to the restructuring of the global economy. Mahler reported that the dominant group feared that the presence of immigrants would affect property values and put a strain on community resources. As a result, the dominant group began to pressure city hall to pass city ordinances as mechanisms to exclude immigrants from attaining housing and to make decisions at the school board level to keep immigrant children from entering schools.

The foregoing review of historical and contemporary evidence on immigration and ethnic conflict in the United States indicates that factors suggested by the conditional hypothesis contribute greatly to ethnic conflicts associated with immigration. For example, competitions between Indians and whites for land, between the English and the Dutch for control of territories, between the Chinese and whites for jobs, between blacks and Latinos for residential neighborhood and political power, and between blacks and Koreans for businesses and resources gave rise to various forms of violent or nonviolent antagonisms; institutional discriminations against minority groups (e.g., Asians) in the form of laws and policies exasperated ethnic relations between Asians and whites; cultural (including religious) divides and racism aroused strife between Protestant groups and Catholic groups and between whites and the Chinese; and large and low-status immigrant groups (e.g., Irish, Italians, Chinese, Mexicans) often became targets of attacks.

CANADA

Very similar to the United States, Canada is also a nation of immigrants and one of a few major immigration countries today. Unlike the United States that was founded primarily by Anglo-Saxon Protestants from England, however, "Canada was founded as a nation on two cultures and two languages—two nations in one sovereign state" (Riseborough, 1975, p. 1). This helps explain why the conflict between English Canadians and French Canadians has been most salient. In 1533, a French explorer named Jacques Cartier traveled along the St. Lawrence River and claimed the territories for France. In 1605, French migrants established a colony called New France. Also in the early seventeenth century, British settlers established colonies in Canada. At the beginning, there were virtually two nations. Migration only brought the two groups into contact. It was the direct competition for control over the new territories that initiated their centuries-old conflicts until this date. The British-French competition for dominance in North America led to a war. In 1759, the British forces defeated the French in Quebec City and ended French colonialism. As a result, New France became part of the British colonial empire. During the American Revolution, about 50,000 English loyalists in the 13 colonies migrated to Nova Scotia and Quebec. They soon clashed with the French majority over economic and political issues. The English gradually dominated the economy of Quebec because the French business elite left after the English conquest. In order to separate the two groups, Canada established Upper Canada and Lower Canada. The former consisted of a mostly English-speaking population and later became Ontario, and the latter consisted of a mostly French-speaking population and later became Quebec. The British North America Act of 1867 united all provinces of Canada into the Dominion of Canada.

Nevertheless, the founding of a unified colony under English domination did not end the tensions and conflicts between English-speaking Canadians (anglophones) and French-speaking Canadians (francophones). English domination continued to engender conflict. "[F]or the minority, French Speaking Canadians it has been a ceaseless struggle to retain their separate culture, and they have never felt they have received the complete cultural, political or economic equality of English speaking Canadians" (Riseborough, 1975, p. 1). Especially in Quebec, francophones faced a variety of disadvantages. Businesses were largely controlled by anglophones. Francophones got the least-skilled and lowest-ranking jobs. They held very few governmental positions. Their needs for preserving their cultural tradition such as French schools and other institutions were ignored. Anglophones in Quebec often held negative attitudes toward francophones. The unfair treatment led to the resistance and the Quebec independence movement. This Quebec separation movement, dubbed the "Quite Revolution," started in the 1960s. In 1968, the Parti Québécois led by René Lévesque was formed. The goal of the party was to seek the liberation of the French community and to establish a sovereignty association (i.e., political sovereignty and economic ties) between Canada and Quebec. The Parti Québécois was defeated in the early 1970s by the Liberal Party, but it was gaining influence. In 1976, the Parti Québécois won the election as the government of Quebec. In 1980, a referendum on sovereignty association was taken in Quebec. The idea of sovereignty association was rejected by a 3–2 margin. In 1987, Quebec and the Canadian federal government reached the so-called Meech Lake Accord, which would give the province broad independent powers. Quebec would be recognized as a "distinct society." The agreement was approved by Quebec but rejected by other provinces. In 1995, Quebecers were asked again to go to the polls to decide a referendum on Quebec's sovereignty. The result of the vote almost made independence a reality, with 50.5 percent nays and 49.5 percent yeas. The separatists vowed to continue and call for another referendum in the future.

In addition to economic inequality and imbalance in political power, the English-French conflict can be attributed to cultural divide over language. French was adopted as an official language of Quebec in the 1960s as a result of the bilingualism movement in Canada. In 1974, the Liberal Quebec government enacted Bill 22, making French the official language of Quebec. Immigrant children must pass a language test to determine if they had a right to English schooling. The Bill was vehemently opposed by anglophones for being too restrictive and was opposed by francophones for not going far enough in the promotion of French. In 1977, the Quebec government adopted Bill 101, the Chapter of the French Language, which made French the official language of Quebec society. Namely, it was the prime language not only in official matters, but also in schools, businesses, and all spheres of life. In 1988, the Canada Supreme Court struck down part of the Quebec Language Law (Bill 101) that requires all commercial signs only in French, but Quebec Premier Bourassa invoked a special clause of the Canadian constitution to override the court's ruling and thus maintain the law. As of today, language continues to be a defining issue dividing francophones and anglophones and to be a fuse of their conflict.

The migration of European settlers also brought them into contact with Native Peoples (aboriginal Canadians) including various tribes of North American Indians, Inuit, and Métis. The experience of Canadian aboriginals was similar to that of American Indians, but it was not as violent as in the United States. European settlers conquered the aboriginals. The aboriginal people were also driven from their lands to reserves (similar to reservations in the United States). They also experienced forced assimilation. They were devalued in Canadian history. Today, the first "Canadians" on the land have remained segregated largely from the rest of the Canadian population and remain the most disadvantaged group in Canada, especially in terms of income (Stelcner, 2000). They have the highest rates of mortality, morbidity, alcoholism, suicide, unemployment, poverty, and poor housing among all segments of the population. In recent years, the aboriginal demands for correcting the historical wrongs (e.g., land claims, fishing rights) increased. In 1999, Canada created a new territory (called Nunavut) dominated by Inuit, which recognizes the territorial rights of the Inuit. Today, the relationship between the aboriginals and the rest of the Canadian population is still very much one of conflict. The aboriginals are adamant in maintaining their own culture while resisting the values of this country because they had their own culture before Canada came into being. Among the rest of Canadians, this appears to be problematic because there is a desire that everyone should live under the same rules and embrace this new culture of Canada, as well as their original culture. This is still a major source of conflict within Canada to this day.

In contemporary time, Canada has continued to absorb immigrants from all over the world. Recent years saw a large influx of immigrants from Asia, the Pacific, Latin America, and the Caribbean. However, "immigration into Canada has not generated major sources of conflict," although ethnic prejudice and racist attitudes as well as potential sources of conflict do exist (Richmond, 1988). This may be in part attributed to the multiculturalism policy adopted by the Canadian government in 1971. The policy supports the activities of "non-official language" ethnic groups in such spheres as ethnic press, ethnic cultural events, assisted programs of language instruction, and ethnic towns. People of different ethnic backgrounds are allowed to maintain their cultures and identities. This policy appears to smooth ethnic relations and reduce potential ethnic tensions and conflicts. Additionally, plenty of land and resources available to all immigrants may lessen competition and therefore contribute to a low level of ethnic conflict in Canada (Herman, 1999).

The story of immigration and ethnic conflict in Canada also appears to be supportive of the conditional hypothesis. Ethnic conflict does not arise in all contexts of immigration. The English-French conflict commenced as a result of their competition for territorial control in North America and has continued, especially in Quebec, because of the economic and political inequality and language divide of the two groups. The aboriginal-white hostility originated from the historical conquest of the natives and has persisted owing to the continuous unequal distribution of resources. Relatively less tension between the new immigrant groups and the established ones may be credited to the multiculturalism policy of the Canadian government. The experience of the French in Canada illustrates that a large group with a significant lower-class segment often becomes the target of discrimination and attack because it is more likely to be perceived as a threat to the dominant group.

AUSTRALIA

Australia is a young country created by immigration. Prior to the arrival of British settlers in 1788, an estimated 500,000 Aborigines and Torres Strait Islanders—the indigenous—inhabited this land. At the time of industrialization, Australia became a destination to which Britain transferred some of its surplus population, first criminals and soldiers and later free settlers. Beginning in 1788, mainly British migrants plus a minority of Irish built the Australian colonies. The indigenous population resisted the colonization of the more powerful migrant population. The natives were massacred, dislodged, and socially marginalized. By the late nineteenth century, their number had dwindled to about 50,000. Without doubt, the competition for land and control led to this genocide.

In addition to the British and Irish, relatively smaller numbers of Germans, Italians, and other Europeans also arrived. These groups often encountered hostility and discrimination. However, racism against non-European groups was strongest (Castles & Vasta, 2000). In particular, the Chinese who arrived during the gold rushes in the 1850s and the South Pacific Islanders who were recruited as cheap plantation laborers in the late nineteenth century endured the hardest hit. Accusing the Chinese of unfair competition and fearing their large number, white miners undertook violent acts against them on the goldfields. The trade unions boycotted goods made by Chinese workers.

From 1890 to 1945, the level of immigration was relatively low because of economic conditions. Nevertheless, some Italians, as well as Greeks and other southern Europeans, entered as sugarcane workers to replace Pacific Islanders sent away after 1901. They experienced a lot of discrimination. They were barred from buying land or entering certain occupations. In 1934, the "anti-Dago riots" in Western Australia killed several people.

The initial victories of Japan in World War II made it clear that Britain could no longer protect Australia and that a larger population and a stronger manufacturing sector were important for Australia's national security. However, British immigration was not sufficient to meet Australia's population needs. Hence, over time Australia gradually relaxed its White Australia Policy introduced since the time of federation in 1901 to include immigrants from various sources. First accepted between 1947 and 1951 were refugees from Baltic and Slavonic countries who were both "racially acceptable" and anticommunist. In the 1950s and 1960s, southern Europeans who were initially deemed racially unacceptable and politically suspect because of strong communist parties in Italy and Greece were admitted in significant numbers. Later, a further liberalization of family reunification led to the recruitment of immigrants from Yugoslavia and Latin America and of educated and professional Asians. As a result of changes in immigration policy, Australia has witnessed rapid population growth and increasing ethnic diversity. From the end of World War II to the early 1990s, the population of Australia more than doubled, largely because of immigration (Foster & Stockley, 1990). The sources of immigration also diversified to include immigrants from all over Europe and Asia. In the 1970s, the White Australia Policy was eventually revoked because of the shortage of workers and the loss of migrants to other countries. Thus, a point system was introduced to entice skilled workers to Australia.

In terms of ethnic policy, Australia has largely defined itself as a nation with a common heritage and a common culture. Assimilation, or Anglo-Australization, was the goal in the post–World War II period, and ethnic groups were expected to become assimilated into the culture of Australia (Richmond, 1988). It would seem to outside observers that assimilation had worked relatively well (Foster & Stockley, 1990). By 1965, however, the government became aware of the fact that many migrants were opting to leave Australia because of the economic hardships and discrimination they experienced. Not wanting to lose migrants, the government designed a series of policy changes to improve the social integration of immigrants and their children. It started to pay attention to the needs of these immigrants and to recognize their cultural backgrounds. By the 1970s, a new approach known as multiculturalism began to emerge as a way of maintaining social cohesion in an ethnically diverse society. In 1977, the Australian Ethnic Affairs Council suggested the following principles for a successful multicultural society: "social cohesion," "cultural identity," and "equal opportunity and access." Later, the principle of "equal responsibility for, commitment to and participation in society" was added (Australian Council on Population and Ethnic Affairs, 1982). The government developed new programs to cater to the needs of ethnic communities and promoted cultural understanding. In the period of 1987–1996, multiculturalism became institutionalized as many multicultural agencies were founded.

One of the most disadvantaged groups in Australia is the indigenous people. "Indigenous people of Australia are both less likely to be employed and more likely to be out of the labor force than are nonindigenous people" (Myers, 2000, p. 365). Up until very recently, the Aborigines in Australia were essentially invisible to the rest of the population. As a result of a growing ethnic mobilization and demands, the Australian government has shown a commitment to correcting the historical wrongs by compensating the Aborigines for the past unjust treatments and through the embracing of multiculturalism.

Despite these problems between the various ethnic groups, there has rarely been open conflict as a result of contemporary immigration. The reason is that the Australian government has done a good job in reducing ethnic conflicts before they become too dangerous. Its relative success in this regard may be due to several factors:

- The good economy and plenty of jobs lessened competition between immigrants and the natives. There was not much concern about immigrants stealing jobs away from native citizens.
- New immigrants were thought to be permanent settlers and full citizens and hence were more accepted by the rest of the population.
- The government moved away from assimilationist ideals to multicultural ideals, and the social environment became much more tolerant and accepting of those who were different, despite racist ideas that had prevailed in the past. (Castles & Vasta, 2000)

However, in 1996, a conservative government came to power. Since then, we saw a speedy move away from multiculturalism back to assimilation. Policies that began to benefit ethnic minorities were slowly stripped away. Immigration policies were tightened, and benefits for immigrants were reduced. In 1999, Australia reevaluated its immigration policy to insure that it would be able to compete in the global market. Despite previous discriminatory practices in immigration and in the treatment of migrants, the government has become committed to "nondiscriminatory immigration policies which do not take into account characteristics such as race, religion or ethnic origin" (Australian Chamber of Commerce and Industry, 1999). The goal is to increase the number of migrants entering the country and to essentially counterbalance those emigrating from Australia.[2] This goal then is driven by the economy in the hopes of being more competitive in the global immigration market. For now, Australians appear to show an increased interest in not only increasing immigration but also insuring that these migrants are happy to live in their new harmonious land.

Australia's experience is consistent with the conditional hypothesis as well. Historically, competitions for land and job and racism against new groups resulted in conflicts between the British and Aborigines, European groups and non-European groups, and older European groups and newer European groups. The Chinese and other new European groups became targets of whites or older European groups partly because of their group sizes and status. In contemporary time, the abolition of the White Australia Policy and the adoption of a multiculturalism policy appear to reduce ethnic antagonism.

GERMANY

In a strictly demographic sense, Germany has not been a country of immigration because government-sanctioned permanent settlement of immigrants has been very limited. One of the goals of Germany's immigration policy is to reduce immigration from the non-European community. As recently as 1997, the German government attempted to force the unemployed German citizens to work in the fields rather than allowing Polish and French workers to come and do the work. This illustrates how serious Germany has been in resisting immigration in the past (Holk, 2000). Traditionally, Germany has seen itself as a nation of ethnic homogeneity, and the restrictionist immigration policy is in part a reflection of its desire to maintain this ethnic homogeneity. This homogeneity also seems to suggest a lack of ethnic conflict as one would expect.

However, on closer look it is not difficult to find that as an officially nonimmigrant country Germany does have many migrants. Most migrants admitted are "guestworkers" (Koopmans, 1999). The guestworkers program started in the mid-1950s and 1960s in an effort to attract foreign workers to meet the labor needs of the nation. These workers were expected to leave when the job was completed. Of course not all migrants obliged. For instance, between 1950 and 1995, an estimated twenty-eight million guestworkers came to Germany, and about twenty million returned (Martin, 1994). Significant numbers of them stayed. Some of them have resided in Germany for most of their life. Although they are eligible for full economic and social benefits enjoyed by German citizens, they cannot become German citizens. Even their German-born children are denied rights to German citizenship. They become temporary sojourners for life. These guestworkers are truly the "perpetual foreigners."

The presence of guestworkers and their descendants suggests that Germany is not as homogeneous as one would like to believe. In the year 2000, there were 7.3 million non-Germans who lived in Germany, including 5.8 million immigrants and 1.5 million non-Germans born in Germany. Approximately one-quarter of the populations in Frankfurt and Munich and about 10–20 percent of the populations in Stuttgart, Cologne, and Berlin were foreign-born (Martin, 1994). Over one million Muslims live in

Germany. Multi-ethnicity has become a permanent characteristic of modern Germany.

Germany's restrictionist immigration policy and exclusionist ethnic policy have consequences. The variety of discrimination experienced by various groups of "permanent sojourners" appears to yield a great deal of ethnic conflicts. The most publicized and long-lasting conflict is the one between Turks and Germans. The Turks are the largest migrant group in Germany with a total of 1.7 million (Gurr & Harff, 1994). Most are long-time residents who make a major contribution to the German economy. The presence of Turkish guestworkers in Germany began in 1961 as a result of a bilateral agreement between West Germany and Turkey following West Germany's initial recruitment of some workers from Italy, Greece, and Yugoslavia. The number of Turks in Germany had rapidly increased to 650,000 by 1976, many of whom were members of Turkey's Kurdish minority. Initially, the Turks encountered informal discrimination in access to better-paying jobs and good housing. By the 1990s, their economic position had substantially improved. By law, their economic and social rights are guaranteed to the same extent as those of German citizens. However, their political rights are still limited. Initially, the Turks were deprived of citizenship rights. They could not vote or run for political office. The lack of citizenship excluded Turks from the German community and provided an implicit license for subtle yet persistent and widespread discrimination. On the other hand, according to Article 116 of the German Basic Law and Germany's 1913 naturalization law, any immigrant who can demonstrate his or her German descent will be granted German citizenship. Some progress in citizenship rights has been made over time. The new citizenship law, effective at the beginning of 1993, allowed foreigners who have lived in Germany for 15 years (or 8 years if under age 23) to apply for citizenship. Nevertheless, the ban of dual citizenship and an increase in citizenship application fee to $300 discouraged application. Moreover, most applications reportedly were rejected by police investigators for minor tax or traffic offenses and sometimes for reasons authorities would not reveal. Opinion polls have shown high proportions of nativism and xenophobia (Gurr & Harff, 1994). Many Germans consider Turks as the "most difficult foreigners" to integrate into German society because of their relatively low levels of education and occupational skills, the importance of Islam in their daily lives, and the political division within the Turkish communities in Turkey and Germany (Martin, 1994, p. 207). After the reunification of Germany, attacks on Turks by neo-Nazi skinheads escalated. From mid-1991 to 1993, more than 4,500 publicized attacks on foreigners and citizens who were thought to be foreigners occurred in reunited Germany. These attacks were based on the belief that the foreigners were taking jobs, apartments, and government assistance from the natives. These events led to a marked increase in Turk-

ish active participation in large nationwide demonstrations that were organized by Germans opposing racism and neo-Nazism. In 1993, clashes
occurred between stone-throwing, club-wielding Turkish demonstrators
and police in Salingen and other cities, and four teenage Turks were arrested for trying to set fire to the office of a conservative political party in
Bavaria. These events and statements of militant Turks signaled a potential rise in future ethnic violence. It appears that discriminatory treatment
of Turks and other minorities played a key role in ethnic conflict in Germany. The large number of Turks in Germany may have increased the
perceived threat to Germans and therefore contributed to the extent of
ethnic conflict between the Germans and Turks.

In recent years, attempts have been made to change immigration and
ethnic policies, much as we saw in Canada and Australia. In March 2002,
Germany enacted a new immigration law, and President Johannes Rau of
Germany signed it into law in June 2002, to take effect January 1, 2003.
The new immigration policy aims at moving Germany toward "a country
of immigration" and pressing newcomers to integrate. In particular, it
includes the so-called German "Green Card" program in order to attract
skilled labor, particularly in the high-tech industries.[3] One of the reasons
that prompted the change in immigration policy is labor shortage due to
the declining birth rate, which could lead to disastrous effects on the economy. An adequate supply of labor through immigration will insure the
competitiveness of Germany in the global economy. Another consideration is to reduce ethnic conflicts. The new law has met challenges from
the conservatives and created controversies (Graham, 2002).

In addition to change in immigration policy, change in ethnic policy
will also have an impact on reducing ethnic conflict. Integrating immigrants into German society is the key to resolving ethnic conflict. Whereas
in the past immigrants were thought to be temporary residents and essentially excluded from German society, now the goal is to make them a
part of society. Since 1998, there has been a movement toward this ethnic
acceptance. The new immigration law requires immigrants to integrate
by studying the German language, culture, laws, and history. This approach seems to be in line with assimilation rather than multiculturalism
observed in Canada, Australia, and the United States. Whether this approach will work in Germany remains to be seen. If Germany truly wants
to be able to attract new migrants, it will have to insure that the policies
are welcoming and friendly toward new immigrants.

In sum, Germany is a nonimmigration country with a large number of
immigrants, especially Turks. The German-Turk antagonism stems from
economic competition between them, political exclusion of Turks and
other immigrants, and racism against immigrants. The large Turkish immigrant community and its relatively lower status render Turks the bear-
ers of the brunt of attacks, whereas few conflicts between Germans and

other smaller immigrant groups have been reported. Hence, the German experience appears to lend support to the conditional hypothesis.

JAPAN

Historically, Japan has been considered a homogeneous society, a society with only one race. However, this dominant view has been challenged by a number of recent studies conducted within Japan (e.g., Shimada, 1994; Yoshino, 1992) as well as from the outside (e.g., Hicks, 1998; Sellek, 1994; Weiner, 1997). These studies have sought to reveal that Japan is indeed a home to people of diverse racial backgrounds and to uncover many problems (economical, political, and social) that have been faced by those "hidden minorities." But, who are those hidden minorities in Japan? Where do they come from and why? Do they suffer from relative economic, political, and social deprivations (or other forms of racism) as those experienced by minorities in other societies in the world? If so, are those problems causing inter-ethnic strife between the minority communities and the majority Japanese community? These are the key questions being addressed in this section to examine whether the inevitable hypothesis or the conditional hypothesis is more plausible.

It is true that Japan is relatively homogeneous in comparison to other industrialized countries in the world. However, a significant proportion (over six million) of 125 million people residing in Japan are believed to be minorities (Hicks, 1998). Among these minorities, the Burakumin, or a caste of "untouchables" used to be known as the Eta (meaning "those full of filth"), are the only indigenous minority from the Tokugawa feudalism period. The other oldest minorities are the Ainu (or the indigenous people of Hokkaido) and the Ryukyuan/Okinawan populations. Both of these minority populations were incorporated into Japanese society during the late nineteenth century when Japan defined its borders against China in the south and imperial Russia in the north as feudalism ended (Weiner, 1997). The minority population further increased when many Chinese and Koreans immigrated into Japan as a direct consequence of Japanese imperialism between the early and the middle twentieth century. Now their descendants are believed to comprise about 1 percent of the total Japanese population (Sellek, 1994). The most recent influx of immigrants came from Latin American countries, mainly Brazil, Peru, Argentina, Bolivia, and Paraguay. These Latin American immigrants of Japanese descent are known as *Nikkeijin*. Consequently, their racial background makes them "preferred" immigrants over others. According to the 1990 Japan census, other foreign minorities in Japan also included 43,000 Filipinos, 36,000 Americans, 97,000 British, 6,300 Thai, and 68,800 others (Hicks, 1998). In light of these facts, Japan is, in reality, not as homogeneous as its people and the world claim.

Japan is one of only a few industrialized countries that have achieved high economic growth without depending extensively on the use of immigrant workers. Nonetheless, since the mid-to-late 1980s when Japan's economy began to grow rapidly, the immigration of foreign workers into the Japanese workforce has begun to increase rapidly as well (Shimada, 1994). Although there are various reasons for why these foreign workers have entered Japanese industries, Sellek (1994) argued that at least two factors have contributed greatly to this migration. First, one of the main attractions of Japan for those migrant workers is the fact that Japan's economic power has pushed its median income level far above that of neighboring countries. According to the *1990 World Development Report* by World Bank, in 1988 the per capita income of Japan was 123 times that of Bangladesh, 64 times that of China, 60 times that of Pakistan, and 33 times that of the Philippines. Since then, the gaps in income between Japan and these countries have narrowed but remain substantial (see Soubbotina & Sheram, 2000). Second, along with its rapid economic growth in the 1980s, many Japanese industries started suffering from a severe shortage of Japanese workers who were willing to do necessary menial or unskilled jobs. Faced with a potential employment crisis, these companies started hiring cheap foreign laborers.

Although, on the surface, it seems that both the foreign workers and Japanese industries are benefiting from the recent influx of the foreign workers, a serious problem has developed in recent years—a majority of those foreign workers are illegal. Many attribute this problem to defects in the current legislation pertaining to foreign workers. Specifically, the current Immigration Control and Refugee Recognition Act (ICRRA) permits legal residency of those foreign workers with special skills or knowledge that cannot be substituted by Japanese nationals. The problem arises because the majority of the foreign workers are hired for their menial labor, which does not require any special skills or knowledge, and as a result, they are not granted their legal employment status. Shimada (1994, p. 5) succinctly describes and predicts more serious problems in the near future if nothing is done to properly remedy this situation.

Since illegal workers are relegated to an underground existence because of their illegal status, no one has any grasp of the real situation. Hence, there is no guarantee that employers will respect their basic human rights as workers, and this dangerous state of affairs could lead to deteriorating health, the formation of ghettoes, various social problems including crime, and the creation of a permanent underclass in society. Dependence on cheap foreign labor also threatens the working conditions of Japanese marginal workers and could impede efforts to modernize industry.

In recent years, several organized demonstrations were held in Tokyo to protest against the presence of illegal foreigners. In one such instance, a neo-Nazi group called The League of State Socialists began a campaign in April 1993 to drive illegal foreigners, especially those from Iran, out of Yoyogi Park in Tokyo, where many of them tend to gather. This group put up signboards with swastikas and banners with headings such as "drive out illegal migrant workers" or "recover Yoyogi Park for the Japanese" (McCarthy, 1993).

However, this type of blatant interethnic conflict is very rare in Japan for a couple of reasons. First, for interethnic conflict to occur, immigration problems must be perceived as threats to Japanese natives. According to realistic group conflict theory (Le Vine and Campbell, 1972; Sherif, 1966; Sherif et al., 1961), when two groups are in competition for scarce resources, they often relegate and threaten each other. This creates hostility between them, which naturally produces prejudice and discrimination, the foundations for intergroup conflicts. In the case of Japan, the existence of a very strict immigration policy (i.e., ICRRA) makes it difficult for foreign workers to compete with Japanese natives for scarce job opportunities, thereby reducing the possibility of interethnic conflicts. Specifically, because of strict guidelines of the ICRRA, there are only a few legal foreign workers who are capable of competing against Japanese natives for scarce job markets. And, even if these legal immigrants do land a job, many of them cannot hold it for a long time because the Japanese government's immigration policy does not grant permanent residency or citizenship to those legal temporary foreign workers (Sellek, 1994; Shimada, 1994).

Second, the selective nature of the ICRRA also softens the impact of immigration, which in turn prevents interethnic conflicts. Specifically, although the current immigration laws have been designed to prevent the entry of foreign workers without special skills or knowledge, the *Nikkeijin* are exempt from these laws. In fact, because of this special treatment, the number of legal *Nikkeijin* workers increased 17-fold in just three years, from 8,400 in 1988 to 148,000 in 1991, making them the majority of legal immigrant workers in Japan (Shimada, 1994, p. 23). This means that, for *Nikkeijin* workers, race or ethnicity cannot be used as a dividing line that often triggers interethnic conflicts simply because *Nikkeijin* are Japanese by race and they are a part of the in-group in Japanese society because of their similar appearance (Sellek, 1994; Shimada, 1994; Tajfel & Turner, 1986; Weiner, 1997). And, even if conflicts do occur between the Japanese natives and the Nikkeijin workers, such conflicts cannot be considered interethnic by definition because of their race being Japanese.

Even though these factors collectively contribute to the small number of interethnic conflicts actually reported in Japan, the number of instances of conflicts is potentially much higher. This is because there exists a more serious problem in Japan that may be preventing interethnic problems from surfacing. For such instances of interethnic conflicts to be documented, incidents of various forms of discrimination must first be made public. However, even though many illegal aliens indeed suffer from various forms of discrimination at work (e.g., work without pay, forced hard labor, dismissal without proper explanations), there is not much they can do to challenge these problems. Specifically, if these illegal foreign workers who suffer violations of human rights were to seek protection under the labor laws, they would have to reveal their illegal status, in which case they may be faced with deportation, a risky consequence that only few are willing to take. Consequently, few cases are ever reported.

Taking the various factors covered in this section together, one thing becomes clear: In Japan, mere immigration does not inevitably lead to interethnic conflicts. A lack of ethnic conflict in Japan appears to be associated with the Japanese government's policy of recruiting *Nikkeijin* and the exclusion of other ethnic groups from immigration, and with a lack of direct competition for resources. However, there exists a far worse problem hidden beneath the rare occurrence of such conflicts.

SUMMARY AND CONCLUSION

Ethnic conflict is a global phenomenon (Horowitz, 1985), which is pervasive in multi-ethnic societies (Khinduka, 1995). In the dawn of the twenty-first century, we have seen no sign of decreasing ethnic conflicts; rather, there are indications of increasing conflicts. Migration is one of the basic modes that brings different ethnic groups into contact. Psychologists (Allport, 1954; Pettigrew, 1998) have long argued that under certain conditions, contact facilitates intergroup relations. We turn to the obverse of the contact hypothesis. We contend that under certain conditions, contact brought about by migration can also cause intergroup conflict. However, we should emphasize that migration and the resulting contact do not intrinsically beget ethnic conflict. Only under certain conditions will migration and contact generate conflict between groups. These conditions include, but are not limited to, direct group competition for scarce resources; unequal allocation of socioeconomic resources and political power; ethnic and cultural policy based on ethnic or cultural superiority or inferiority; and perceived threats from other groups, especially those with a large size and lower-class backgrounds. We label this perspective the "conditional hypothesis," in contrast to the "inevitable hypothesis" that assumes ethnic conflict as a natural outcome of immigration.

The historical and contemporary evidence of selected major immigration countries reviewed in this chapter seems to give little credence to the inevitable hypothesis, but lends substantial support to our conditional hypothesis. Table 5.1 summarizes the association between each of the five highlighted conditions and ethnic conflict for each of the five selected immigration countries. It is evident that when these conditions are pres-

Table 5.1
Conditions that Played a Role in the Presence of Ethnic Conflicts in Selected Immigration Countries

Conditions	USA	Canada	Australia	Germany	Japan
Direct competition for scarce resources	•	•	•	•	
Unequal distribution of resources and power by government	•	•	•	•	
Ethnic policy based on cultural superiority or inferiority	•	•	•	•	
Perceived threat of a large immigrant group	•	•	•	•	
Perceived threat of lower-status immigrant group	•	•	•	•	

Note: • Presence of condition and ethnic conflict.

ent, so is ethnic conflict. This is particularly true in the United States, Canada, Australia, and Germany. In contrast, in Japan none of these conditions is present, and hence we see little conflict along ethnic lines. In tandem, the contact hypothesis and the conditional hypothesis offer a more complete picture of the role of migration and contact in relation to ethnic conflict.

NOTES

1. Some social psychologists (Allport, 1954; Pettigrew, 1998) have suggested that contact between members of different groups can improve intergroup relations under the right conditions (e.g., equal group status, cooperation for common goals, support by authority figures, opportunities to interact with out-group members, behavior change, and in-group reappraisal).

2. For every four migrants arriving in Australia, one person departs permanently.

3. The German "Green Card" program is much more similar to the H1-B visa program in the United States than to the permanent Green Card program. Because of the popularity of the U.S. Green Card in Germany, the government chose to name the program after the better-known U.S. Green Card in order to increase its appeal.

REFERENCES

Allport, Gordon. (1954). *The nature of prejudice*. Cambridge, MA: Addison-Wesley.

Australian Chamber of Commerce and Industry. 1999. *Immigration*. [Online]. http://www.acci.asn.au/index_policypapers.htm

Australian Council on Population and Ethnic Affairs. (1982). *Multicultur- alism for all Australians: Our developing nationhood.* Canberra: Austra- lian Government Publishing Service.

Barth, Frederick. (1956). Ecological relationships of ethnic groups in Swat, North Pakistan. *American Anthropologist, 58,* 1079–1089.

Barth, Frederick. (1969). *Ethnic groups and boundaries.* Boston: Little, Brown.

Bonacich, Edna. (1972). A theory of ethnic antagonism: The split labor market. *American Sociological Review, 37,* 547–559.

Castles, S., & Vasta, E. (2000). Ethnicity in Australian society. In J. Najman & J. Western (Eds.), *A sociology of Australian society* (3rd ed.). South Melbourne: Macmillan Co. of Australia.

Chen, Jack. (1980). *The Chinese of America.* San Francisco: Harper.

Dobyns, Henry. (1983). *Their number become thinned: Native American popu- lation dynamics in eastern North America.* Knoxville, TN: University of Tennessee Press.

Foster, L., & Stockley, D. (1990). The politics of ethnicity: Multicultural policy in Australia. *International Journal of Group Tensions, 20*(2), 145–166.

Graham, Stephen. (2002, July 15). With elections ahead, German conser- vatives seek to overturn new immigration law in supreme court. *The Associated Press.*

Gurr, Ted. (1993). *Minorities at risk: A global view of ethnic conflicts.* Wash- ington, DC: United States Institute of Peace.

Gurr, Ted, & Harff, Barbara. (1994). *Ethnic conflict in world politics.* Boulder, CO: Westview Press.

Herman, H. V. (1999). *Ethnic conflicts in Canada and the former Yugoslavia.* [On-line]. www3.sympatico.ca/harryvh/ethconflict/canyug.html

Hicks, G. (1998). *Japan's hidden apartheid: The Korean minority and the Japa- nese.* Brookfield, VT: Ashgate.

Holk, S. (2000). Undocumented migration in the USA and Germany: An analysis of the German case with cross-references to the U.S. situ- ation. [On-line]. www.ccis-ucsd.org

Horowitz, D. (1985). *Ethnic groups in conflict.* Berkeley, CA: University of California Press.

Huntington, Samuel. (1996). *The clash of civilizations and the remaking of world order.* New York: Simon and Schuster.

Johnson, James, Farrell, Walter, & Guinn, Chandra. (1997). Immigration reform and the browning of America: Tensions, conflicts and com- munity instability in metropolitan Los Angeles. *International Migra- tion Review, 31*(4), 1055–1095.

Johnson, James, & Oliver, Melvin. (1989). Interethnic minority conflict in urban America: The effects of economic and social dislocations. *Ur- ban Geography, 10,* 449–463.

Khinduka, S. K. (1995). Ethnic conflicts: Can anything be done? *Social Development Issues, 17*(1), 1–17.

Koopmans, R. (1999). Germany and its immigrants: An ambivalent relationship. *Journal of Ethnic and Migration Studies, 25*(4), 627–647.

Le Vine, R. A., & Campbell, D. T. (1972). *Ethnocentrism: Theories of conflict, ethnic attitudes, and group behavior.* New York: Wiley.

Mahler, Sarah. (1995). *Salvadorans in suburbia: Symbiosis and conflict.* Boston: Allyn and Bacon.

Martin, Philip. (1994). Germany: Reluctant land of immigration. In Wayne Cornelius, Philip Martin, & James Hollifield (Eds.), *Controlling immigration: A global perspective* (pp. 189–231). Stanford, CA: Stanford University Press.

McCarthy, T. (1993, April 12). Racists cast a shadow on the rising sun. *The Independent.*

Min, Pyong Gap. (1996). *Caught in the middle: Korean communities in New York and Los Angeles.* Berkeley, CA: University of California Press.

Myers, S. L. (2000). If not reconciliation, then what? *Review of Social Economy, 58*(3), 361–381.

Olson, James. (1994). *The ethnic dimension in American history.* New York: St. Martin's Press.

Olzak, Susan. (1992). *The dynamics of ethnic competition and conflict.* Stanford, CA: Stanford University Press.

Omi, Michael, & Winant, Howard. (1994). *Racial formation in the United States from the 1960s to the 1990s* (2nd ed.). New York: Routledge.

Park, Robert. (1950). *Race and Culture, Vol. 1.* Glencoe, Illinois: Free Press.

Pettigrew, T. F. (1998). Intergroup contact theory. *Annual Review of Psychology, 49,* 65–85.

Prentice, D. A., & Miller, D. T. (1999). *Cultural divides.* New York: Russell Sage Foundation.

Richmond, Anthony. (1988). *Immigration and ethnic conflict.* New York: St. Martin's Press.

Riseborough, D. J. (1975). *Canada and the French.* New York: Facts on File.

Rupesinghe, K. (1989). *Conflict resolution in Uganda.* Athens, OH: Ohio University Press.

Schaefer, Richard. (2000). *Racial and ethnic groups* (8th ed.). Upper Saddle River, NJ: Prentice Hall.

Sellek, Y. (1994). Illegal foreign migrant workers in Japan: Change and challenge in Japanese society. In J. M. Brown & R. Foot (Eds.), *Migration: The Asian experience* (pp. 169–201). New York: St. Martin's Press.

Shanahan, Suzanne, & Olzak, Susan. (1999). The effects of immigrant diversity and ethnic composition on collective conflict in urban America: An assessment of two moments of mass migration, 1869–1924 and 1963–1993. *Journal of American Ethnic History, 18*(3), 40–64.

Sherif, Muzafer. (1966). *Group conflict and cooperation.* London: Routledge & Kegan Paul.

Sherif, M., Harvey, O. J., White, B. J., Hood, W. R., & Sherif, C. W. (1961). *Robbers cave experiment: Group conflict and cooperation.* Norman, OK: Oklahoma University Press.

Shimada, H. (1994). *Japan's "guest workers."* Tokyo: University of Tokyo Press.

Soubbotina, T. P., & Sheram, K. (2000). *Beyond economic growth: Meeting the challenges of global development.* Washington, DC: World Bank.

Spilerman, S. (1970). The causes of racial disturbances: A comparison of alternative explanations. *American Sociological Review, 35,* 627–649.

Spilerman, S. (1971). The causes of racial disturbances: Test of an explanation. *American Sociological Review, 36,* 427–442.

Stannard, David. (1992). *American holocaust: Columbia and the conquest of the new world.* Oxford: Oxford University Press.

Stelcner, M. (2000). Earning differentials among ethnic groups in Canada: A review of the research. *Review of the Social Economy, 58*(3), 295–316.

Stone, J. (1985). *Racial conflict in contemporary society.* Cambridge, MA: Harvard University Press.

Tajfel, H., & Turner, J. (1986). The social identity theory of intergroup behavior. In S. Worchel & W. G. Austin (Eds.), *Psychology of intergroup relations* (pp. 7–24). Chicago: Nelson-Hall.

Takaki, Ronald. 1989. *Strangers from a different shore: A history of Asian Americans.* Boston: Little, Brown.

Thornton, Russell. (1987) *American Indian holocaust and survival: A population history since 1492.* Norman, OK: University of Oklahoma Press.

United Nations. (1993). *Report on world situation 1993* (No. E93.IV.2). New York: Bureau of Social Affairs, UN Secretariat.

Weiner, M. (1997). *Japan's minorities: The illusion of homogeneity.* New York: St. Martin's Press.

Yang, Philip. (1995). *Post-1965 immigration to the United States: Structural determinants.* Wesport, CT: Praeger.

Yang, Philip. (2000). *Ethnic studies: Issues and approaches.* New York: State University of New York Press.

Yoshino, K. (1992). *Cultural nationalism in contemporary Japan.* London: Routledge.

PART III

Cultures in Conflict: Case Studies

CHAPTER 6

Cultural Continuities beneath the Conflict between Radical Islam and Pro-Western Forces: The Case of Iran

Fathali M. Moghaddam

Since the 1970s, a series of events, including the 1979 Iranian revolution and the 9/11 terrorist attacks, have highlighted conflicts between radical Islam and pro-Western forces, both inside and outside the West. These conflicts are often seen as being associated with historic changes, such as the change from a pro-Western regime to an anti-Western one in Iran in 1979, and from an anti-Western regime to a pro-Western one after the fall of the Taliban in Afghanistan in 2002. The focus on change has been particularly underlined by use of terms such as "revolution" and "regime change," and by heightened attention to what is formal, explicit, and more readily tangible. The thesis in this chapter is that the focus on change has sometimes been misguided, leading us to neglect fundamentally important cultural continuities beneath the conflict between radical Islam and pro-Western forces. Further, I argue that the importance of cultural continuities is evident in deeper explorations of revolutions and regime changes in other contexts.

In his analysis of the French revolution, Schama (1989) has identified important ways in which, at a deep level, behavior in social, political, economic, and other major domains continued in basically the same manner after the revolution. Such continuity persisted despite surface appearances of change, and despite monumental efforts on the part of various groups to smash the old regime and to put aside the old ways of doing things. Schama's (1989) analysis is in line with critical reassessments of revolutions in other societies, including Mexico (Middlebrook, 1995), Iran (Arjomand, 1988a), China (Salisbury, 1992), and Russia (Figes & Kolonitskii, 1999), where a surprising level of continuity is identified by researchers from different disciplines, starting with working assumptions that are also somewhat different. Middlebrook (1995) termed this the "paradox of revolution," as reflected in the old saying that "the more things change, the more they stay the same": the revolutionaries who take over the reigns of power often find themselves following along the same paths as the regime they replaced. A perhaps even more important, but still neglected, part of this paradox is the persistence of everyday social practices that are part of the normative system and seem particularly immune to the pressures associated with change, but which eventually have an impact on the macro political system.

In previous discussions of the paradox of revolution, I argued that part of the explanation for this well-established phenomenon is a rift between change in the formal, macro systems, such as the formal system of government and formal laws, and change in the informal, micro systems, such as the norms and rules that actually regulate everyday behavior (Moghaddam & Crystal, 1997; Moghaddam & Harré, 1996). The relationships between these two domains is dynamic, complex, and multidirectional. Changes at the formal macro level of political, economic, and legal systems does not necessarily cause changes in the micro level of informal systems. For example, formal changes in rights and duties, as reflected in "black letter law" do not necessarily cause corresponding changes in actual behavior in everyday life, and the dynamic relationship between formal and informal rights and duties has to be understood in cultural context, culture being a meaning system (Moghaddam, 2000; Moghaddam, Slocum, Finkel, More, & Harré, 2000).

Toward further exploring the paradox of revolution, I focused on the difference in the speed of change at the macro formal level and the micro informal level. As the collapse of communism in the former USSR and Eastern Europe clearly showed, formal political, economic, and legal systems can collapse almost overnight. The destruction of the Berlin Wall was visible evidence of this sudden change. On paper, at least, dozens of countries quickly went from communism to democracy, with similarly speedy changes in formal economic and legal systems. However, actual change in everyday behavior has been much slower. Even in the united Germany, where enormous resources have been used to try to bring about behavioral change, East and West are still in some fundamental ways different in informal everyday life. This rift in the speed of change led me to propose a micro/macro universal law: "the maximum speed of change at the macro level of legal, political, and economic systems is faster than the maximum speed of change at the micro level of everyday behavior" (Moghaddam, 2002, p. 33).

In attempting to understand revolutions and change, then, I have placed considerable emphasis on, first, the informal normative system regulating everyday life as opposed to the formal macro system that exists on paper and, second, on continuities in social life that transcend formal changes of political, economic, and legal systems. My objective in the present discussion is to examine important continuities that have fundamentally influenced developments in Iran, particularly in the modern era that includes the revolution of 1978–79 and the spread of Islamic fundamentalism in the Middle East and elsewhere. The reason for focusing on Iran is that "there is no other country where the ulama (religious scholars) have entered into nearly the amount of protest one finds in Iranian history" (Keddie & Cole, 1986, p. 10). The Iranian revolution and the establishment of the Islamic Republic of Iran have served directly and indirectly to inspire, encourage, and nourish Islamic fundamentalist movements worldwide. My thesis is that an analysis of these events that focuses on the macro formal system leads to an incomplete and at times misleading picture, and that greater attention should be given to the informal micro normative system.

Toward this goal, I shall rely in particular on two concepts that enable finer and more critical cultural analysis: *carriers*, the means by which styles of thinking and doing are sustained from generation to generation, and *cultural surplus*, that part of a meaning system that is additional to (i.e., above and beyond) what is needed for mere survival in a given context (Moghaddam, in press). Illustrative examples will demonstrate that the concepts of carriers and cultural surplus are particularly useful in better understanding intergroup conflict, such as those involved in revolutions and the clashes between Islamic fundamentalists and Western and pro-Western forces.

THEORETICAL FRAMEWORK

I begin by briefly outlining the theoretical framework for this analysis (a more extensive account is available in Moghaddam, 2002). Although this framework is cultural and evolutionary, the theoretical focus is on explaining stability rather than change per se. This is an important if subtle shift, because to explain why things change is not necessarily the same as explaining why things do not change. For example, to explain why a revolution brings about certain types of political change, such as change in a formal system from one party to multiparty, is not necessarily to explain why certain other types of change do not come about, such as the evolution of everyday social relations supportive of, and in harmony with, multiparty political systems. The main theoretical focus has so far remained on explaining why change has taken place, rather than on why it has not, and these questions do not always point to the same issues or answers.

Primitive Social Relations and Cultural Surplus

In any context, human groups require certain *primitive social relations* in order to survive; I refer to these as primitive because they are the forms of social relations most likely to evolve first within a given context. For example, in order to be able to communicate effectively with one another, verbally and/or nonverbally, group members must effectively practice turn taking. This requires each person to take turns in saying things to others and in listening to others. Turn taking arises as a primitive in the sense that it lays the foundation for more complex communications patterns. If a person refuses to let others have a turn to speak, or if a person refuses to take a turn to speak, then basic communications break down. Even leaders who run their groups with dictatorial power have to practice turn taking in some form; otherwise, they will not be able to effectively communicate their commands and gather information about how their commands have been carried out.

Turn taking represents an important continuity in behavior, linking twenty-first-century humans with their primitive ancestors. Just as we do today, our hunter-gatherer ancestors practiced turn taking in communications tens of thousands of years ago. The informal norms and rules regulating turn taking later formed the basis for formal rules governing turn taking. For example, this is illustrated by turn taking in the cross-examination of witnesses in the formal law courts, and in term limits for political positions, which results in turn taking in political power, at least in most modern democracies (Moghaddam & Lvina, 2002). It has been argued that trust, reciprocity, and leadership are also essential for human survival, and thus qualify as primitive social relations (Moghaddam, 2002).

Leadership is particularly interesting, because although certain aspects of leader-follower relations have changed and are probably new to modern democracies, in other respects leadership has remained the same throughout human history. In terms of changes, modern democracies involve elected political leaders, and universal franchise is new to our era, as is the idea of term limits applied to the highest political office. But there are also important continuities, in the sense that only a few examples exist of social groups without leaders (e.g., Middleton & Tait, 1958). Indeed, Freud argued that only groups with leaders can achieve high levels of organization and performance (see Taylor & Moghaddam, 1994, chap. 2). Some form of effective leadership seems to be universally required for the survival of human groups.

The acquisition of primitive social relations enabled certain groups to survive, and also formed the platform on which a cultural surplus eventually developed. With respect to the evolution of cultural surplus on the basis of turn taking as a primitive social relation, there have evolved countless cultural practices, from turn taking at traffic stops to turn taking in complex multiparty political debates, which are additions to the basic minimal social relation needed for mere survival. Cultural surpluses also evolved in domains that are directly linked to physical survival, such as the need to eat. Human groups must achieve certain primitive social relations in order to successfully gather food and eat in a collectivity, and this basic survival activity eventually led to successive cultural surpluses, leading in the West to haute cuisine and the complex sets of rules that come under the label of table manners. The history of food in human societies (for example, see Fernandez-Armesto, 2002) is in this sense a history of cultural surpluses in behavior related to cooking and eating.

The gains achieved through previous cultural surpluses are already present when an individual is born. The continuity of cultural surpluses is achieved through carriers, such as flags. For example, in the United States the American flag, "Old Glory," is an important carrier, sustaining what it means to be American from generation to generation. All those who want to become American, including immigrants, have to learn certain attitudes and behaviors in relation to this flag.

Continuity of Cultural Surplus: The Case of Carriers and Religion

The power of carriers is their flexibility; anything can serve as a carrier to sustain meaning systems, and if a carrier fails to serve this role effectively, it can be abandoned, and if necessary replaced. For example, during the 1960s some feminists in Western societies adopted bra burning as a carrier for a brief period, but this did not prove to be effective and was abandoned. Similarly, some African Americans adopted the Afro hairstyle as a carrier, but this, too, was abandoned. For both women and African Americans, certain leaders, such as Gloria Steinem and Martin Luther King Jr. proved to be more effective carriers. Changes in carriers become particularly evident during revolutionary times, when one group wins power from another. After a successful revolution, one of the first things changed is the national flag, often the most important carrier in a modern state.

Among the most pervasive and powerful carriers are those that sustain religions. For example, a fundamentally important carrier in Christianity is the crucifix. Looked at by a person who does not understand Christian values and history, a crucifix may be just two pieces of wood joined together in the shape of a cross. There is nothing inherently special about this object. Indeed, it may appear to be an unimportant item, with no obvious function. However, for a practicing Christian, the crucifix is one of the most important carriers helping to sustain and ensure the continuation of Christianity. Because of this carrier role, the crucifix becomes a focus for power struggles between groups. For example, at Georgetown University, a Catholic institution where I am a professor, there has been a struggle between those who support having crucifixes displayed in class-rooms and those who are opposed to this practice. Both groups obviously recognize the important carrier role of the crucifix; otherwise, they would not fight over two pieces of wood joined together in the shape of a cross. Similarly, the flag of the Old Confederacy in the Southern part of the United States is "just a piece of cloth," but African Americans have fought to have this flag set aside, because they recognize it as a carrier of values associated with slavery. Thus, of central importance is the cultural mean-ing of a carrier as subjectively understood by people, rather than any objective or strictly practical characteristics it might have.

In this discussion, I shall focus particularly on the role of two carriers central to the Islamic movement (1) leadership, and (2) the veil prescribed for use by women. Although almost all human societies have leaders, there is considerable variation in style of leadership across cultures, and my focus will be on the continuity of style of leadership in Iran. With respect to the Islamic veil, which from one perspective is just a piece of cloth, again the emphasis will be on the role of this carrier in sustaining particular aspects of a meaning system.

THE IRANIAN REVOLUTION, CARRIERS, AND CULTURAL SURPLUS

A variety of competing interpretations and ideologies are available for assessing the Iranian revolution of 1978–79 (for examples, see Algar, 1983; Arjomand, 1988a; Khomeini, 2002; Motahhari, 1986; Parsa, 1989), a survey of such interpretations and ideologies being beyond the scope of this chap-ter. My main objective is to highlight certain continuities achieved through carriers, continuities that span across pre- and postrevolution Iran and that underline fundamental ways in which life remained the same after the revolution. In this analysis, I pay close attention to informal normative systems, the way things actually get done and meaning systems as they are, rather than to formal systems, or the way things are officially sup-posed to be done. This cultural approach is in line with developments in a number of specialties, giving greater importance to social-cultural rather than formal-material aspects of life, such as the focus on social capital in political science (Putnam, 2000) and discussions of human capital in eco-nomics (Jones, 1987).

Context and Background

Modern Iran covers a territory of 628,000 square miles, an area larger than France, Italy, and Spain combined. At the time of the revolution in

1978–79, the population in Iran numbered around thirty-six million, and in 2002 it is close to seventy million. The discovery and excavation of oil in Iran in the early 1900s eventually formed the economic basis for the modern Iranian state, with the Qajar dynasty (1796–1921) being succeeded by the Pahlavi dynasty (1926–78). The revolution of 1978 toppled Moham-mad Reza Shah (1941–79), and brought into place an Islamic Republic, thus ending a supposedly unbroken line of monarchy going back 2,500 years (for a more detailed background discussion, see Mackay, 1998).

LEADERSHIP, CARRIERS, AND CULTURAL SURPLUS

Leadership is a primitive social relation that emerged early in the evo-lution of human social life. The role of leader in such early groups was probably particularly essential in organizing defense, flight from enemies, and hunting. Elementary leadership characteristics are reflected in the rank order that emerges among animals as well as humans, including children (Savin-Williams, 1979). The coming together of a group of indi-viduals for the first time typically involves an initial period of competition, after which a pecking order is established. In a cross-cultural study in-volving comparisons across European children, Japanese children, and children of Bushmen in central Kalahari, Hold (1977) identified a number of common characteristics among high-ranking and low-ranking children in all three groups. Of particular importance for our discussion are the high-ranking children, potential leaders, who were more likely to initiate activities, mediate in conflicts, protect weaker members, and act as the decision maker in the distribution of resources (e.g., candy). Interestingly, the notion of pecking order was first empirically demonstrated in a pio-neering study on rank order among chickens (for a broader discussion, see Eibl-Eibesfeldt, 1989, pp. 297–314), and a number of the elementary characteristics of leadership are found among human and nonhuman primates.

Leadership Style As Cultural Surplus

Although the primitive social relation of leadership was common to most and perhaps all surviving human groups, particular forms of lead-ership style evolved and were sustained by carriers as part of a cultural surplus in each group. Such leadership style can only be understood by considering the relationship between leaders and followers, rather than by focusing on leaders in isolation. More specifically, attention must be given to the details of everyday social practices among followers in their relationships with the leader. These everyday practices are informal and can continue across generations, able to survive attempts to change the official system of governance and formal relationship between leaders and followers. For example, the informal system of creating obligations in others, especially leaders, is practiced in a number of societies, particularly Eastern ones. Yang (1994) has studied this practice in China, where it is termed *Guanxixue,* and specifically involves "the exchange of gifts, favors, and banquets; the cultivation of personal relationships and networks of mutual dependence; and the manufacturing of obligations and indebtedness" (p. 6). By going out of their way to create obligations in leaders, as when a factory worker does huge personal favors for the family of the factory manager, followers can influence leader behavior.

A second strategy for assessing leadership style is to attend to the implicit and informal system, rather than the explicit and formal system. For example, according to the formal rhetoric in China, the practice of *Guanxixue* is a relic of the past that has been stamped out, or at least is almost ended. But a detailed look at everyday social practices as they actually are suggests this practice to be continuing, despite serious efforts to end it by the communist regime. Thus, attention to leader-follower relationships and to everyday social practices as they actually exist leads to the identification of a surprising level of continuity.

In the context of Iran, also, by paying close attention to leader-follower relationships, as well as to everyday social practices, we identify a surprisingly high level of continuity across pre- and postrevolution eras. The 1978–79 revolution formally changed the political system of Iran from monarchy to Islamic Republic. The Safavid rulers (1501–1722) made Shiism the state religion of Iran, Shia being the minority religion in the world context, comprising about 15 percent of all Muslims, with most of the rest being Sunni Muslims. On the surface, the 1978–79 revolution fundamentally changed the political landscape in Iran, because it set aside the monarchy and established religious authority as the absolute power. However, in terms of deeper leader-follower relations, the situation in Iran is characterized by continuity rather than change. To recognize the nature of this process, it is necessary to consider some details of the practice of Shiism in Iran.

A fundamentally important feature of Shiism as traditionally practiced in Iran is that it comprises an informal normative system, rather than a formally organized system (this is for the most part still true of post-1978 Iran). For example, there is no formal Shii church, with an identifiable organizational chart and formal hierarchy as in the case of the Christian church. Similarly, the system of training for *talabeh,* "theology students," in the *madrasa,* "Islamic schools," tends still to be informal and unstructured compared with the Christian educational system. Similarly, the process through which Islamic mullas come to acquire titles such as Hujjat al-Islam or Ayatollah or Grand Ayatollah is, again, informal and unstructured compared with the Christian system, with its explicit and well-known bureaucracies for appointing bishops, the pope, and so on. The informality of Shiism in Iran, as compared with the formal and explicit system of the secular government in Iran with the monarch at its head, has meant that leadership has been analyzed in connection with the secular rather than the religious system. A major point I want to illustrate and highlight is that leadership in Iran must be considered in the context of religion, and not just the monarchy and the formal secular state. It is through attention to leader-follower relations in Shiism as practiced in Iran that we can best explain continuity in leadership style in Iran.

The key to leader-follower relations in Islam, as practiced by Sunni and Shia alike, is found in Verse 4:59 in the Quran, the Muslim holy book, which commands believers to obey God, to obey the Messenger, and to obey "those in authority among you" (see Arjomand, 1988c, p. 1). Muslim ulama (religious scholars) have debated the exact interpretation of "those in authority among you." A tension has existed historically, between the authority of religion and temporal authority, in Western terms, the church versus the state. Whereas in the United States and most other Western democracies, as well as some non-Western ones, church and state are explicitly separated, at least on paper, in Iran, the relationship between religion and temporal authority has been much more intimate and interwoven. Those who interpret this relationship to have been competitive must acknowledge that religious authority has become dominant and monopolistic in postrevolution Iran.

The authority of religion, and the influence of religious leaders, has been considerably strengthened in Iran through the particular characteristics of Shia practice. Each practicing Shia Muslim is obligated to select a *marja-i-taqlid,* "a source of imitation." This *marja-i-taqlid* is selected from among the ulama and is used as a reference point, a guidepost, on each and every single issue and decision. Each practicing Shia Muslim is obligated to pay Islamic taxes (these are additional to, and separate from, government taxes) directly to the clergy, and typically such taxes are paid to the person selected as one's *marja-i-taqlid.* Thus, the authority of Islamic authorities in Shia Iran has been based on a strong and independent or freestanding foundation. On the one hand, the laymen are obligated to adopt a *marja-i-taqlid* as a source of imitation; integral to this relationship is a legal and moral obligation for the follower to obey the leader. On the other hand, the follower is obligated to pay taxes directly to the leadership, thus helping to maintain the ulama financially independent from the secular powers.

A third key feature of the leader-follower relationship in Shia Islam as practiced in Iran can best be understood through the concept of *ijtihad,* involving the interpretation of legal norms through jurisprudence and more generally the interpretation of holy scripture. The Quran is still read in classical Arabic, a language only a small minority understand in Iran, which is predominantly Persian speaking (no doubt this reminds Christians of the pre-Reformation era, when the Bible was still not translated from Latin into local languages, and those clergy who were educated were among the very small minority who could read and understand the Bible in Latin). Through many years of study and devotion, religious scholars may reach a stage when they join the *mujtahidin*, those who have the authority to interpret holy scripture. Thus, the Shia masses have a particularly dependent relationship with the *mujtahidin*, because the ordinary Shia believer is unable to read and understand the holy book of Islam in Arabic, and even if some believers could read the Arabic text they would still have to rely on the *mujtahidin* to interpret the text for them and to resolve contemporary issues through the application of such interpretations.

These broad and central characteristics of Shia Islam as practiced in Iran support a certain style of leader-follower relationship, and this style is further strengthened by more fine-grained, detailed features of everyday social practices. An example is the practice of daily prayers, every Muslim being obligated to say prayers five times each day, at specified times: when the sky is filled with light but before actual sunrise, immediately after midday, sometime between three and five o'clock in the afternoon, after sunset but before darkness, and any hour of darkness. The daily prayer in Islam is a highly structured, repetitive, collective activity. It is collective first in the sense that all Muslims follow the same procedures for ritually cleaning themselves before each prayer, all face in the direction of Mecca, and all recite the same prayers in Arabic. Thus, each individual goes through the same prayer rituals at the same time as all other Muslims, and this shared activity underlines the collective rather than individualistic nature of the experience. A second way in which the daily prayer is collective is that Muslims are encouraged to say their prayers in the company of other Muslims, and the attendance of community prayer is an obligation for the noon prayer on Fridays. This coming together is an opportunity for the community, and particularly the Imam leading the prayer, to exert influence on individuals and to strengthen conformity and obedience. A third way in which the daily prayer is collective is that five times a day the muezzin call the faithful to prayer, traditionally by calling out from the high minarets of mosques, and in recent years by calling through loudspeaker systems. In this way, everyone present in the Islamic world experiences the call to prayer five times every day and is reminded of the overarching power and reach of the mosque, even if they themselves do not attend prayers.

Integration and Interim Conclusion

Leadership is conceptualized as a primitive social relation, a behavioral characteristic essential for effective functioning and survival for human groups, particularly in ecological conditions that require more complex organization. On the basis of this primitive social relation of leadership, there evolves a cultural surplus that varies in fundamental ways across cultures. To understand the nature of this cultural surplus in Iran, I examined follower-leader relations, rather than leadership in isolation, and highlighted aspects of the informal rather than the formal system, giving particular importance to everyday practices in Shia Islam as practiced in Iran. An extensive array of carriers serves to sustain the follower-leader relationship characteristic of Shiism in Iran. These carriers vary with respect to their pull, load, and flexibility. A number of carriers, such as the daily Islamic prayer, are low on flexibility, in the sense that their form and meaning is fairly well established and unbending, but very high on pull and load, meaning that they are highly effective in sustaining continuity and meaning across generations. The daily prayer involves rituals that have to be performed five times a day, with specific meanings to each part of each ritual, and this repetitive social practice serves to sustain continuity, particularly upholding the collective, community-based nature of social life.

Other carriers, such as the *marja-i-taqlid*, are more flexible. Over the last several hundred years, the scope of authority of the *mujtahid* has varied, becoming broader at times but narrower at other times. Through the influence of Ayatollah Ruhallah Khomeini and others, a very broad interpretation of the powers of the *mujtahid* has been dominant since the 1978 revolution, so broad that *the marja-i-taqlid* is now placed above all other secular and religious powers. This principle of leadership by a *mujtahid* recognized as the supreme *marja-i-taqlid* is referred to as *vilayat al-faqih*, authority of the jurist, and is at the heart of the Constitution of the Islamic Republic of Iran. In the Preamble to the Constitution, it is stated:

In keeping with the principles of governance and the perpetual necessity of leadership, the Constitution provides for the establishment of leadership by a faqih possessing the necessary qualifications and recognized as leader by the people. . . . Such leadership will prevent any deviation by the various organs of the State from their essential Islamic duties. (Arjomand, 1988b, pp. 373–374)

Thus, the supreme leader of the Islamic Republic is the leading *marja-i-taqlid*, or a council of *mujtahid* if one outstanding leader is not recognized above all others. Because all laws and regulations must be based on Islamic criteria (Article 4), the *marja-i-taqlid*, supported by a Guardian Council and other faithful Muslims, acts as the final judge as to which laws, regulations, decisions, and so on, will receive final approval and go into effect. This "judgment from above" trumps the popular vote, because although the president of the Republic, the representatives of the national consultative assembly, and other representatives are voted on by the people, they have to be approved by religious authorities, the most important being the supreme *marja-i-taqlid*. There have been many examples of the popular vote being overturned by the religious leadership.

It is timely at this juncture to look across from religious to secular leadership in Iran and identify a fundamental similarity and continuity:

The similarity of the leadership role attained by Khomeini and by the shah is remarkable. . . . the opinion they expressed on any subject (and they expressed opinions on just about every aspect of life) was treated as the final authoritative word, not to be questioned under any circumstances. It was as if these leaders had risen above the level of mere mortals. To criticize them was not just wrong; it was to commit sacrilege. This infallibility was in both of their cases associated with lifelong supreme power. (Moghaddam, 2002, p. 25)

In conclusion, then, despite the vehement opposition of Ayatollah Khomeini and the shah to one another, their leadership style and relationship with followers was based on the same cultural surplus. The everyday social practices that upheld the one also upheld the other.

THE ISLAMIC VEIL: CARRIER AND CULTURAL SURPLUS

Any serious attempt to understand the Islamic fundamentalism movement in Iran and the current conflicts involving Islamic fundamentalists in the Middle East and elsewhere must take into consideration the situation and treatment of women. The modern Western attitude toward gender roles, and the spread of these attitudes to Islamic societies, is viewed by Islamic fundamentalists as a direct threat, and one that must from their viewpoint be thwarted effectively. In this section of the discussion, I begin by elaborating on minimal social relations in the domain of gender roles, and then I discuss the role of the Islamic veil as a carrier used to sustain a particular cultural surplus in Iran and other parts of the world.

Gender Roles, Minimal Social Relations, and Cultural Surplus

The survival of any human group depends on successful procreation and nurturance of the young. Each generation must achieve a certain minimal set of behaviors that enable males and females to have offspring, and to socialize the next generation toward having and supporting offspring. Such minimal social relations must provide for the safety and nourishment needs of pregnant mothers and the young. Any situation in which this is not achieved threatens the survival of the group. These shared requirements create certain universals in gender relations. For example, even in societies in which women are kept in near slavery conditions, they are valued for their role in procreation and are provided certain safeguards as mothers.

Beyond this minimal level of behavior required for survival, there are enormous cross-cultural variations in the way gender roles and gender relations are organized. Such variations are part of the cultural surplus in any society, and the nature of cultural surpluses differs across cultures. For example, there are numerous ways in which male dominance is maintained in different societies, including the deprivation of property and voting rights, as was the case in most Western societies until early in the twentieth century, and more direct physical interventions such as female circumcision as still practiced in some Islamic societies (see Moghaddam, 1998, chap. 12). Practices such as foot binding and female circumcision have both practical and symbolic importance in intergroup relations: they serve to impose a severe physical limitation on females in conformity with norms established by males, and so have a direct practical impact; but they also serve as a symbolic reminder of male superiority and male-female differences according to the dominant male ideology.

The Islamic veil functions as a fundamentally important carrier in Iran and many other countries. Most important, the veil sustains values and perpetuates central traditions, particularly those related to gender roles and the limited role of women in the public sphere. Second, the normative use of the veil is a visible and public expression of the dominance of Islamic ideology in a society. Third, the veil serves as a clear visible line between the in-group (Islamic societies) and out-groups (non-Islamic societies). In order to clarify the carrier role of the veil, in the next section I briefly review the fight over the veil in recent Iranian history.

The Veil in Iran

Competing groups have interpreted the veil differently in Iran, but explicitly or implicitly, all view it as a carrier of Islamic values. Islamic traditionalists and fundamentalists have argued that the veil protects women and allows them to escape being treated as sexual objects. From this perspective, the veil also prevents men from being distracted and getting into trouble, it being their nature to be sexually attracted to women. As one mulla put it, a woman should cover herself "because a fight might start if a beautiful woman is seen: the eyes that see her will cause the heart to want her" (Loeffler, 1988, p. 20). Women rather than men wear the veil because men are more easily distracted by the opposite sex than are women, but men should also dress modestly. Those who oppose the veil, most of whom argue for a separation of church and state, view the veil as a means by which the second-class status of women is maintained and the activities of women in the public sphere are severely limited.

Both the pro-Islamic and pro-modernist forces are headed by elite groups of men, and the tug-of-war over the veil has for the most part involved elite men making decisions for women. The first serious efforts to change the gender role of women were made by Reza Shah (ruled 1926–41), who attempted to forcibly make women *behejab*, "without the veil," as part of his modernization program. The veil was torn away from the heads of any women who dared to appear *bahejab*, "with veil," in public. At the same time, pressure was placed on men to change from traditional to modern Western clothes. In making these changes, Reza Shah was moving against traditional Islamic forces, including of course the leading Ayatollahs of the day, but he was also moving against the wishes of many traditionalist fathers, husbands, brothers, sons, and other male family members, who did not want the women in their families to become *behejab* and active in the public sphere.

When Reza Shah was forced to abdicate in 1941, his son became Shah but at the time lacked the power to continue the modernization program begun by his father. The policy of forced unveiling of women in public was abandoned, and traditionalists gained ground once more. A small group of women, mostly from the upper classes and living in urban centers, continued to appear in public without the veil, but the majority of women went back to the veil, under varying degrees of direct and indirect social pressure. After the pro-democracy movement led by Mossadeq failed in 1951, and another uprising was thwarted in 1963, Mohammed Reza Shah (ruled 1941–79) used Iran's increasing oil revenues to bolster his support and dominate power at the national level. During the 1960s and early 1970s, increasing urbanization and Westernization was associated with the greater activities of women in the public sphere, mostly without the veil. By the early 1970s, middle- and upper-class women, as well as many working class women, appeared in public without the veil, particularly in the larger urban centers. Indeed, women who wanted to participate in the profitable new modern economy had little choice but to appear in public without the veil.

But this government pressure on women to appear in public without the veil continued side by side with a pressure in the opposite direction from Islamic traditionalists and fundamentalists, who often ruled the private sphere of the home and the family. Thus, during this period in Iran, some women would remove the veil in some public contexts because of the need to conform to government-supported norms in the public sphere, but put the veil back on at other times because of the necessity to conform to traditional norms imposed by their own family members.

From around 1977, people in Iran began to participate in large demonstrations against the Shah. These demonstrations included many different groups with various ideologies, from left to right on the political spectrum. However, it was Ayatollah Khomeini and the Islamic clerics who stole the thunder from the other groups and took over the leadership of the revolution against the Shah. In order to participate in demonstrations, many women who had previously abandoned the veil now again put on the veil, because the norm for the large demonstrations was now that women should wear the veil. A month after the Shah's downfall, Ayatollah Khomeini called for women to be *bahejab*, with veil, again. Despite some opposition, within a year women in Iran found themselves forced by law to be veiled when appearing in public (see Moghissi, 1995).

Integration and Interim Conclusion

Certain minimal social relations must be achieved in gender relations in order for a human group to survive; but beyond this minimum, variations abound in cultural surpluses in the domain of gender relations. In this discussion, I focused on a very important carrier, the veil, that sustains and perpetuates the cultural surplus pertaining to gender relations in Iran and elsewhere. In some respects, the veil served in the Iranian revolution of 1978–79 the kind of function that the red flag served in the Russian revolution of 1917. Most important, the veil served to unify all of the different Islamic factions, from the so-called Islamic Marxists of the left to the ultraconservative Islamic groups of the right. All the multitudes of Islamic groups could identify with the veil and see it as a symbol of "their" revolution, just as many groups could project their revolutionary ideals onto the red flag during the Russian revolution (Figes & Kolonitskii, 1999).

The veil has also achieved extremely high carrier load and carrier pull. On the one hand, the meaning load of the veil has been tremendously high. In a sense, the veil has come to stand in for the revolution. The veil has a highly visible meaning load in two senses. First, the veil is highly visible, literally speaking. Second, the impact of the veil in changing gender relations and limiting the activities of females in the public sphere has also been highly visible. The carrier pull of the veil is evident in its anchoring power; gender roles are tied down by the veil. Women are not able to operate as equal competitors with men in the public domain, but are forced to stand back and play a complementary public role. Thus, the veil anchors males and females in Iran (and elsewhere) to traditional gender roles.

GENERAL CONCLUSION

The tragedy of 9/11 has led to a great deal of interest in conflict between radical Islam and pro-Western forces, particularly as influenced by the countries of the Near East and Middle East. However, there is a danger that this conflict will remain an enigma, because of a lack of sufficient attention to continuity rather than to change, and to the informal and implicit normative system rather than to the formal and explicit.

In this discussion, I have explored follower-leader relations and the Islamic veil as important aspects of the cultural surplus in Iran. In fundamental ways, my discussion of both follower-leader relations and the Islamic veil highlights continuity rather than change, pointing out the way that things do not, rather than do, change. This focus on stability is a key to understanding relations between macro- and micro-level processes, particularly in the Islamic societies. A recent United Nations report written by a group of distinguished Arab intellectuals states, "The wave of democracy that transformed governance in most of Latin America and East Asia in the 1980s, and Eastern Europe and much of Central Asia in the 1980s and early 1990s, has barely reached the Arab States" (United Nations Development Program, 2002). In order to understand these continuities, it is necessary to focus on factors associated with stability, and not just factors associated with change.

REFERENCES

Algar, H. (1983). *The roots of the Islamic revolution*. Markham, Canada: The Open Press.

Arjomand, A. A. (1988a). *The turban for the crown*. New York: Oxford University Press.

Arjomand, A. A. (Ed.). (1988b). *Authority and political culture in Shi'ism*. Albany, NY: SUNY Press.

Arjomand, A. A. (1988c). Introduction: Shi'ism, authority, and political culture. In A. A. Arjomand (Ed.), *Authority and political culture in Shi'ism* (pp. 1–22). Albany, NY: SUNY Press.

Eibl-Eibesfeldt, I. (1989). *Human ethology*. New York: Aldine de Gruyter.

Fernandez-Armesto, F. (2002). *Near a thousand tables: A history of food*. London: Free Press.

Figes, O., & Kolonitskii, B. (1999). *Interpreting the Russian revolution: The language and symbols of 1917*. New Haven, CT: Yale University Press.

Hold, B. (1977). Rank and behavior: An ethological study of pre-school children. *Homo, 28*, 158–188.

Jones, E. L. (1987). *The European miracle: Environments, economies, and geopolitics in the history of Europe and Asia* (2nd ed,). Cambridge: Cambridge University Press.

Keddie, N. R., & Cole, J. R. I. (1986). Introduction. In J. R. I. Cole & N. R. Keddie (Eds.), *Shi'ism and social protest* (pp. 1–29). New Haven, CT: Yale University Press.

Khomeini, R. (2002). *Islam and revolution*. Translated by A. Algar. London: Kegan Paul.

Loeffler, R. (1988). *Islam in practice: Religious beliefs in a Persian village.* Albany, NY: SUNY Press.

Mackay, S. (1998). *The Iranians: Persia, Islam, and the soul of the nation.* New York: Plenum.

Middlebrook, K. J. (1995). *The paradox of revolution: Labor, state, and authoritarianism in Mexico.* Baltimore: Johns Hopkins University Press.

Middleton, J., & Tait, D. (1958). *Tribes without rulers: Studies in African segmentary systems.* London: Routledge & Kegan Paul.

Moghaddam, F. M. (1998). *Social psychology: Exploring universals across cultures.* New York: Freeman.

Moghaddam, F. M. (2000). Toward a cultural theory of human rights. *Theory & Psychology, 10,* 291–312.

Moghaddam, F. M. (2002). *The individual and society: A cultural integration.* New York: Worth.

Moghaddam, F. M. (in press). Cultural surplus, social mobility, and minorities. *Culture & Psychology.*

Moghaddam, F. M., & Crystal, D. (1997). Revolutions, Samurai, and reductons: Change and continuity in Iran and Japan. *Journal of Political Psychology, 18,* 355–384.

Moghaddam, F. M., & Harré, R. (1996). Psychological limits to political revolution: An application of social reducton theory. In E. Hasselberg, L. Martienssen, & F. Radtke (Eds.), *The concept of dialogue at the end of the 20th century* (pp. 230–240). Berlin: Hegel Institute.

Moghaddam, F. M., & Lvina, E. (2002). Toward a psychology of societal change and stability: The case of human rights and duties. *International Journal of Group Tensions, 31,* 31–51.

Moghaddam, F. M., Slocum, N. R., Finkel, N., More, T., & Harré, R. (2000). Toward a cultural theory of human duties. *Culture & Psychology, 6,* 275–302.

Moghissi, H. (1995). Public life and women's resistance. In S. Rahnema & S. Behdad (Eds.), *Iran after the revolution: Crisis of an Islamic state* (pp. 251–267). London: I.B. Tauris.

Motahhari, M. (1986). *Social and historical change: An Islamic perspective.* Berkeley, CA: Mizan Press.

Parsa, M. (1989). *Social origin of the Iranian Revolution.* New York: Rutgers University Press.

Putnam, R. D. (2000). *Bowling alone: The collapse and revival of American community.* New York: Simon & Schuster.

Salisbury, H. E. (1992). *The new emperors: China in the era of Mao and Deng.* New York: Avon.

Savin-Williams, R. C. (1979). Dominance hierarchies in groups of early adolescents. *Child Development, 50,* 923–935.

Schama, S. (1989). *Citizens: A chronicle of the French Revolution.* New York: Vintage.

Taylor, D. M., & Moghaddam, F. M. (1994). *Theories of intergroup relations: International social psychological perspectives* (2nd ed.). Westport, CT: Praeger.

United Nations Development Program. (2002). *Arab Human Development Report*. New York: Author.

Yang, M. M. (1994). *Gifts, favors, and banquets: The art of social relationships in China*. Ithaca, NY: Cornell University Press.

CHAPTER 7

Conflict, Identity, and Ethos: The Israeli-Palestinian Case

Neta Oren, Daniel Bar-Tal, and Ohad David

This chapter focuses on the relationship between identity and conflicts, which we believe is mutual and complex. On the one hand, elements related to identity can collide and cause eruption and evolvement of a conflict, but on the other hand, protracted and intense conflict that lasts many decades has a profound effect on identity. In fact, these relations can be seen over time as circular because elements of identity may cause conflict, and then, as the intensive conflict continues through the years, it has great influence on the shaped identity, which in turn has an effect on the conflict's continuation.

With regard to the effect of identity on the evolvement of intensive conflicts, it is well noted that in most cases, contradictions in identity elements played a crucial role in the eruption of conflicts (see Agnew, 1989; Ross, 1998). However, we will primarily focus on the latter part of the equation. We claim that, through the course of an intensive conflict, each of the rival parties evolves an ethos of conflict which supplies content to the meaning of the group's social identity, and serves as the epistemic basis for the conflict. Moreover, the societal beliefs of the two ethoses are in opposition and provide contradictory views to group members, and these views fuel the continuation of the conflict. In this chapter, we first describe the nature of social identity and its relations to ethos. Then we describe opposing societal beliefs in the ethoses as held by rival groups. Next, we illustrate the present conception by describing the contradictory parts in the ethos of conflict held by the Israeli Jews and the Palestinians. Finally, we conclude by pointing out the necessary steps to be taken when groups in intensive conflict begin the long process of reconciliation.

IDENTITY AND ETHOS IN INTRACTABLE CONFLICTS

Conflicts are part of every intergroup relationship and therefore many of them erupt continuously in this world. But especially troubling are enduring and intensive conflicts (intractable conflicts)[1] over contradictory goals and interests that are considered essential for group survival (Azar, 1990; Bar-Tal, 1998a; Goertz & Diehl, 1993; Kriesberg, 1998). In many of these conflicts, the existential contradictory goals concern issues related to *identity*. A determinative element in the "being" of any group or society,[2] including a nation, is its *social identity*, defined psychologically as "that part of an individual's self-concept which derives from his knowledge of his membership of a social group (or groups) together with the value and emotional significance attached to that membership" (Tajfel, 1978, p. 63). Only when a collective of individuals share the idea that they are members of society and that the society is a reality for them does a society exist. Of special importance in this context is their perception that there are similar individuals, who share the same notion of being members of society, whereas other individuals are different and therefore belong to other groups.

The perception of similarity is based, among other elements, on shared beliefs (Bar-Tal, 1990, 1998a; Giddens, 1984; Griswold, 1994; Hoebel, 1960). Of interest for this paper are shared societal beliefs[3] that provide a dominant orientation to the society and contribute the epistemic basis of the social identity of its members. The totality of these beliefs constitutes ethos, defined as "the configuration of central societal beliefs that provide particular orientation to a society" (Bar-Tal, 2000a). The particular contents of societal beliefs of the ethos evolve under the influence of the particular conditions in which the society lives and the particular collective experiences that shape the society. Ethos, then, combines dominant societal beliefs in a particular structure, and gives meaning to the societal life of a particular society. It constitutes an important basis of content for social identity (see, e.g., McClosky & Zaller, 1984, who analyze the beliefs about democracy and capitalism in the American ethos). We focus on a particular ethos—the ethos of conflict—as the fundamental part of social identity that gives meaning to the conditions of intractable conflict in which the group lives. This ethos evolves because an intractable conflict lasts at least a period of a generation and many of them last many decades and even centuries. Bar-Tal (1998a) identified eight themes of societal beliefs as constituting the ethos of conflict: Societal beliefs about the just nature of one's own goals, about the negative image of the opponent, victimization, positive collective-image, security, patriotism, unity, and peace. Of these themes, this paper addresses only the first three, which are central in the Israeli and the Palestinian ethos, and play a crucial role in the maintenance of intractable conflict.

We propose that these societal beliefs of ethos of conflict, which evolve in societies involved in intractable conflict, have double implications: on the one hand, the societal beliefs are functional in allowing the groups involved to adapt to the lasting stressful and demanding conditions of intractable conflict, but on the other hand, they cause continuation of the conflict. The evolved societal beliefs are in many respects mirror images of both societies involved in intractable conflict. Both societies evolve societal beliefs in justness of the conflict, delegitimization, and victimization. The societal beliefs of one group are in direct conflict with those of the other group. The societal beliefs in the justness of the goals refers to the upholding of a group's own goals and the negation of the rival's goals. Societal beliefs in delegitimization and victimhood serve as mirror images in their content. Often the groups use even the same labels for delegitimization, but always view themselves as victims. We will demonstrate these contradictions in the case of the Palestinian-Israeli conflict. But first we will describe the conflict.

For more than 80 years, Palestinian nationalism and Zionism, the Jewish national movement, have clashed recurrently over the right for self-determination, statehood, and territory. This is a case in which elements of national identity provided the foundations for the eruption of conflict (Kelman, 1999). For a long time, the conflict seemed irreconcilable and total. The dispute concerned elementary issues, involving basic existential needs of each side, and it was impossible to find an agreeable solution for both parties. Thus, it is not surprising that the sides involved perceived the conflict as being of zero sum nature and they mobilized all possible resources in order to win. But the coming of President Anwar Sadat of Egypt to Jerusalem in November 1977 signaled the possibility of resolving this conflict peacefully and began to change its intractable character. The next breakthrough took place in 1993 when Israel and the Palestinian Liberation Organization signed an agreement of mutual recognition, known as the Oslo Accord. This was followed by a peace treaty with Jordan and the establishment of the Palestinian authority in the West Bank and Gaza Strip. But in 2000, following the failure of the negotiation between the Palestinians and Israelis in Camp David and the eruption of violence in September, the Palestinian-Israeli peace process collapsed and both sides returned to violent confrontation. During the decades of the intractable conflict, the Jewish and the Palestinian societies in the Middle East developed ethos of conflict (see Rouhana & Bar-Tal, 1998a). The Jewish Israeli ethos of conflict was described in detail previously (Bar-Tal, 2000a; Bar-Tal & Oren, 2000). We will focus now on three opposing societal beliefs of the ethos of conflict and analyze the nature of their contradiction.

THE CONTRADICTORY SOCIETAL BELIEFS OF ETHOS OF CONFLICT AS HELD BY THE ISRAELI JEWS AND THE PALESTINIANS

In this section we will discuss the contradictory contents of the three themes of societal beliefs described earlier. We will base our analysis on two sources. One source is Palestinian and Israeli school textbooks, as they provide an excellent illustration of institutionalized societal beliefs (Apple & Christian-Smith, 1991; Bourdieu, 1973; Luke, 1988). The other source is the national public polls carried out among the Palestinians and the Israeli Jews that shed light on the societal beliefs held by society members. Of special significance is the public opinion surveys that were performed jointly from December 1997 to December 2001 by the Palestinian and Is-raeli research institutes, using an identical questionnaire developed by the Jerusalem Media and Communication Center (JMCC) and the Tami Stein-metz Center for Peace Research at Tel Aviv University (see Tables 7.1–7.5).

SOCIETAL BELIEFS ABOUT THE JUSTNESS OF ONE'S OWN GOALS

Societal beliefs about the just nature of one's own goals explain and justify the goals that are challenged by the opponent in the conflict. These beliefs outline the reasons for the supreme and existential importance of the goals, stressing that failure to achieve them may threaten the existence of the group. In addition, the societal beliefs disregard the goals of the other side, describing them as unjustified and unreasonable.

Israeli Societal Beliefs

In the case of Jews, their return to territory known over the last centuries as Palestine, to establish their own state after 2,000 years of exile, was inspired by the nationalist ideology of Zionism. This ideology provided Jews with the goals and their justifications (Avineri, 1981; Vital, 1982). The goals referred first of all to the rights of establishing a Jewish state in the old homeland of Israel, and historical, theological, national, existential, political, societal, and cultural arguments were used to justify them. Within the theme of justness of Jewish Israeli goals, special efforts were made through the years to refute the Palestinian claims.

This goal continues to be a central theme in Israeli culture (Galnoor, 1982; Liebman & Don-Yehiya, 1983), but the territorial dimension of the Jewish state became a central controversy since its outset. The alternatives were more Jewish sovereignty in less territory, or more territory at the cost of sovereignty (Horowitz & Lissak, 1978). The conquest of Sinai, the Gaza Strip, the West Bank, and the Golan Heights in the 1967 war brought the territorial aspect of the Israeli goals into focus, as Israeli Jews confronted the dilemma of choosing between keeping the conquered territories and losing the Jewish majority and democratic nature of the state, or relinquishing the territories that allowed them to keep the democratic and Jewish nature of the state.

The beliefs about justness in one's own goals have been found in Israeli textbooks, which justified the Jewish people's claim to the land and at the same time discredited any parallel Arab claims. Firer (1985), analyzing history school textbooks used between 1900 and 1984, found that a number of justifications were used. The basic justification referred to the historical origin of the Jews in Israel (Eretz Israel, i.e., "the land of Israel"), where their nation originated and they lived for many centuries until they were forcibly exiled. In this line, their return to Eretz Israel was presented as the rightful regaining of their homeland. In addition, Firer found other, complementary justifications: the rights of the Jewish people to lead a normal life in a country of their own, which was denied to the Diaspora Jews; the continuous spiritual contact with Eretz Israel that the Jews kept throughout their exile; and the continued Jewish presence in Eretz Israel throughout history. The same schoolbooks denied Arab rights to the land of Israel. This was done, according to Firer (1985), through the delegitimization of Arabs, the denial of a national Palestinian movement, and in general the refusal to recognize a Palestinian entity (see also the study by Podeh, 2002). Bezalel (1989), analyzing Hebrew readers from the late 1950s until the 1980s, found in her study a similar approach. Another study of geography textbooks between 1882 and 1989 done by Bar-Gal (1993a) indicates that they were also dominated by justification of the return of the Jews to their homeland, implying that they cared about the country and successfully turned the swamps and the desert into blossoming land. On the other hand, the books delegitimized Arabs' claims to the same land. The implied message was that the Arabs neglected the country, did not cultivate the land, and were characterized by primitivism and backwardness. Only after the 1970s did some books begin to acknowledge the Palestinian claim but considered the Jewish rights to be more just. Podeh (2002), who continued the analysis of the history textbooks into the late 1990s, found that the last generation of books was considerably different than those used through many decades. These books present a more balanced picture of the conflict and describe the rise of Palestinian nationalism; a few even consider the desirability of establishing a Palestinian state.

Of special interest is the question of the boundaries of Israel as they appear in the geography school textbooks, because, as we pointed out earlier, the territorial aspect of the Israeli goals has become a central controversy in the Israeli-Palestinian conflict. Bar-Gal (1993b) found that the Israeli geography textbooks distinguish between three kinds of borders:

historical, natural, and political. Until the 1960s, these books saw the land of Israel extending along *both* banks of the Jordan River as one geographical unit with natural borders. The authors of these books explained the gap between the historical, political, and natural borders as temporary, one that Zionist activity will eventually close. After the 1960s, however, the Israeli geography textbooks present an unclear map of the borders, and there is a subtle avoidance of any discussion of this question.

Findings of public polls of the Jewish population in Israel indicate that societal beliefs about the Israeli goal of having a Jewish state is held by almost all of the Jewish individuals in the society. In a 1988 survey, 97 percent of the responders said that it was important or very important to them that the Jewish character of the state be preserved (Shamir & Shamir, 2000). As for the territorial aspect, when the Israeli Jews were asked in June 1967—several days after the 1967 war ended—whether Israel should keep or return the West Bank that was captured from Jordan, 86 percent responded that Israel should keep it. Nevertheless, in subsequent years, there has been a gradual trend toward greater willingness to return the West Bank as part of peace agreement; by 1994, for example, only 35 percent of the responders wanted to keep it (Arian, 1995). Moreover, when asked to indicate a preference for either the goal of having Israel with a Jewish majority or the goal of having Greater Israel, since 1988 most Israeli Jews assign a higher value to the Jewish majority state than to a Greater Israel (Shamir & Shamir, 2000). In this line, according to polls conducted by the Tami Steinmetz Center for Peace Research in 1999, most of the Israeli Jews (72 percent) opposed Israel's withdrawal *from all* of the territory in the West Bank. Israeli Jews differentiate among different captured territories: for example, fewer Israeli Jews are ready to withdraw from the parts of the West Bank that are settled by Jews, especially those close to the 1967 borders, and a great majority of the public is less willing to make concessions with regard to Jerusalem. There is a consensus that Jerusalem should remain united under Israeli control; according to polls conducted by the Tami Steinmetz Center, as late as 1999, 72.5 percent of the Israeli Jews wanted Jerusalem to be the unified capital of the Jewish state (see Table 7.1).

The polls also indicate that the majority of the Israelis are opposed to one of the major goals of the Palestinians: to fulfill the right of the refugees' return to the State of Israel (see Zakay, Klar, & Sharvit, 2002). Only 8 percent of Israeli Jews in 1999 agreed to the Palestinian goal of letting the Palestinian refugees settle in the State of Israel. The poll indicated that 52.6 percent of the Israelis wanted refugees to be settled in the place of their present residence, and 31 percent wanted them to be settled within the Palestinian state (see Table 7.2).

Table 7.1
The Best and Final Solution to the Jerusalem Problem

	Israeli Jews n = 502	Palestinians n = 1199
Unified Jerusalem (East and West) as capital of Israel.	81.0	0.8
West Jerusalem is the capital of Israel. The Old City is under a joint sovereignty, and East Jerusalem is under Palestinian sovereignty.	6.7	4.4
East Jerusalem as the capital of the Palestinian state and West Jerusalem as the capital of the State of Israel.	4.0	18.6
Jerusalem as an open city and capital of the two states.	3.0	7.6
International Jerusalem.	4.2	9.1
Unified Jerusalem (East and West) as the capital of Palestine.	1.1	32.9
Capital of Muslims	--	25.0
Other		0.3
Don't know		1.3

Source: Israeli-Palestinian People to People Peace Index, carried out by The Tami Steinmetz Center for Peace Research at Tel-Aviv University, and Jerusalem Media and Communication Center in 1999. The data appeared in The Tami Steinmetz Center's web site at www.tau.ac.il/peace/Peace_Index/IPPPPI

Palestinian Societal Beliefs

In contrast, the Palestinian ethos presents the Palestinians as the true native inhabitants of the same territory claimed by the Israeli Jews. The Palestinian goal, as opposed to the Israeli goal, is to establish a Palestinian state in this territory. Another goal declared by the Palestinians is the right of the Palestinian refugees to return to their land, a goal that contradicts the Israelis' aspirations to have a Jewish state with a Jewish majority. The Palestinians use their own historical, legal, demographical, societal, and cultural arguments to justify these goals. From the historical point of view,

Table 7.2
Where Should the Palestinian Refugee Be Permanently Settled?

	Israeli Jews $n = 502$	Palestinians $n = 1199$
Mainly in their original homes inside 1948 Palestine (Israel).	7.8	71.3
Mainly in places within the Palestinians state.	31.1	21.1
Mainly in their present place of residence in the Middle East or elsewhere.	52.6	5.3
Don't know	8.5	2.3

they claim that they lived in this territory for a long time and have endured repeated foreign occupations, the latest one being the Zionist occupation and the resulting expulsion of refugees. From a social and cultural point of view, during those years a Palestinian identity was created, a nation with its own language (Palestinian dialect of Arabic) and folklore, with villages and cities, intellectual and professional classes, and a highly developed national consciousness. Demographically, until the establishment of Israel in 1948, there was an Arab majority in Palestine (Said, 1979). Politically, the Palestinians claim to have the right to self-determination and legally, this right and the right of Palestinian refugees to return to their land are embedded in international legal covenants (e.g., article 13 of the Universal Declaration of Human Rights from 1948, and the International Covenant on Civil and Political Rights from 1966) and numerous United Nations resolutions (e.g., the UN General Assembly resolution number 194, affirming the right of the Palestinians to return to their homes, from 1948; Khalidi, 1997; Said, 1979). Special efforts are made to counter the Israeli claims, ranging from presenting the Israelis as foreign invaders to Palestine, like the Crusaders, or the western colonists to disregard and even deny the Holocaust (Nordbruch, 2002).

As is the case for Israeli textbooks, these beliefs and justifications are found in Palestinian textbooks. The textbooks present the Palestinian uniqueness, which, according to the Palestinian Curriculum Development Center, "derives from the Palestinian history and struggle to maintain cultural and religious rights" (Nordbruch, 2002). The idea of the uniqueness of the Palestinians can be found, for example, in sixth-grade textbooks, such as in the following paragraph:

The Palestinian society is distinct, through its history 1. Agriculturally: 70% of Palestinian society owns farmland and rely on it for their daily livelihood. 2. Nationally: all of its history is one of battle and heroism in the struggle against British rule and Israeli occupation. The Palestinian society carried out several rebellions and sacrificed thousands of martyrs and wounded. 3. [The Palestinian society is] educated: The Palestinian people throughout their long history focused on learning and knowledge as a weapon to counter challenges of poverty, expulsion and dispersion. 4. Pan-Arab Nationalism (Qawmi): The flag of the Palestinian national movement is the Arab flag, its hymn is the Arab hymn, and Arab unity is the wish of the Palestinian people. 5. Tolerance: Brotherly love and tolerance between Muslims and Christians prevails in the Palestinian society. 6. Proud in its heritage: The national dress and traditional songs, which have been preserved by the people, are proof of their pride in the heritage. 7. Overtaken by Expulsion and Dispersion: The Palestinian people were expelled from their land by the Israeli occupation of Palestine, were exposed to massacres, and [were] forced to leave to the surrounding countries.[4]

Contrary to Israeli claims, the textbooks present Palestine as part of the Arab world since biblical times. The Arab nation appears as a timeless entity, and this timeless element is ethnic and territorial; the sixth-grade unit on "the Arabs before Islam" presents a map of the Arab world that includes the current borders of Syria, Iraq, and mandatory Palestine, and the lesson speaks of Nabatean and other ancient pre-Islamic civilizations, and those civilizations are treated as Arabs (Brown, in press).

Like the Israeli textbooks, the Palestinian textbooks present an unclear map of the borders of Palestine. They include many maps of mandatory Palestine that are historical or topographical in order to avoid drawing political boundaries. Even maps of a later period do not indicate the existence of the state of Israel. Some maps mark the West Bank and Gaza Strip with different colors but do not explain what they signify. According to Brown (in press), because there is a lack of any legitimate borders, the books dodge the issue. Nordbruch (2002) interprets it differently: "The absence of Israel in graphics or illustrations suggests a Palestinian entity that comprises all the territories of the British Mandate" (p. 10; i.e., all of current Israel and not just the West Bank and Gaza). Both authors agree, however, that, as for Jerusalem, the Palestinian textbooks make it clear that Jerusalem has been an Arab city since ancient times. A unit on Jerusalem describes it as an Arab city since its founding by the "Arab Canaanites" and claim that Ibrahim [Abraham] paid a tax that was paid by non-Muslims under Muslim rule to the local king (Brown, in press). Also, in various illustrations appears the slogan "Jerusalem is Ours" (Nordbruch, 2002).

Findings of public polls among the Palestinians indicate that these societal beliefs about the Palestinian goals are held by most of the Palestinian society members. According to polls conducted by JMCC in 1999, 78.3 percent of the Palestinians wanted either a Palestinian or an Islamic state in the entire territory west of the Jordan River (see Table 7.3). Also, 32.9

Table 7.3
The Preferred Solution to the Israeli-Palestinian Conflict

	Israeli Jews *n* = 502	Palestinians *n* = 1199
A confederation between Israel and the Palestinian state	7.8	3.6
A Jewish state in the entire territory west of the Jordan River	63.2	1.2
A Palestinian state in the entire territory west of the Jordan River	1.5	35.5
An Islamic state in the entire territory, west of the Jordan River	1.0	42.8
An independent Palestinian state with entire sovereignty		6.6
A confederation with Jordan		1.2
The Jews leave Palestine		1.2
Other	10.9	1.8
There is no solution to the conflict	5.0	4.8
Don't know	10.6	1.3

percent of the respondents wanted a unified Jerusalem (East and West) as the capital of Palestine, and another 25 percent prefer the solution of Jerusalem as the capital of Muslims (see Table 7.1). Finally, 71.3 percent of the Palestinians prefer that Palestinian refugees return to their place of origin in Israel as a solution to the refugee problem (see Table 7.2).

In sum, we find that the societal beliefs about the justness in having the whole country as a national homeland are central in the Jewish and Palestinian ethos and give meaning to their respective national identities. However, over the years there has developed a tendency to compromise on those goals. For example, there has been a gradual shift in the direction of acceptance of the idea of a Palestinian state in the West Bank and Gaza Strip only, which is a compromise between the Palestinian goal of a Palestinian state in the entire territory west of the Jordan River, and the Israeli goal of an Israeli state in the same area. Among the Israelis, support for this idea increased from 20 percent in 1987 to 44 percent in 1998 (Arian, 1999). According to polls conducted by JMCC and the Tami Steinmetz

Center, in 1999, 58 percent of the Israelis and 46 percent of the Palestinians supported the two-state solution (see Table 7.4). Another compromise solution, which is less acceptable, is a binational state in which the Palestinians and the Israelis will have equal representation in the various institutions of government. In 1999, 15 percent of the Israelis and 20 percent of the Palestinians supported this idea (see Table 7.4).

SOCIETAL BELIEFS ABOUT DELEGITIMIZATION OF THE OPPONENT

Societal beliefs about the negative image of the opponent portray the opponent in a negative view, often in delegitimizing terms by denying humanity from the adversary (Bar-Tal, 1990; Stagner, 1967; White, 1970). In fact, these beliefs are part of the negative psychological intergroup repertoire that groups in intractable conflict have about each other. This repertoire not only includes beliefs (i.e., stereotypes), but also negative attitudes, affect, and emotions.

Israeli Societal Beliefs

In the Israeli case, Arabs in general have been labeled as being primitive, dirty, stupid, easily agitated, and violent. Over time, as the conflict deepened and became violent, Arabs were perceived as killers, a bloodthirsty mob, rioters, treacherous, untrustworthy, cowards, cruel, and wicked. In addition, Arabs were blamed for the continuation of the conflict and for the eruption of all of the wars and military acts, and were presented as intransigent and refusing a peaceful resolution of the conflict They were also portrayed as striving to annihilate the state of Israel, and to drive the Jewish population into the sea (see Bar-Tal & Teichman, in press).

Table 7.4
The Support for Compromises in the Israeli-Palestinian Conflict

	Israeli Jews n = 502	Palestinians n = 1199
Prefer the two-state solution	57.9	46.2
Prefer the binational solution	15.3	20.6
Prefer another solution	11.1	13.8
There is no solution to the conflict	7.5	14.0
Don't know	8.3	5.4

Those beliefs about Arabs were transmitted through institutionalized channels, like the school textbook. Firer (1985) found that from 1930, as the violent conflict escalated, history school textbooks referred to the Arabs as "robbers, vandals, primitives and easily agitated" (Firer, 1985, p. 128). Also, the books portrayed Arabs as being ungrateful to the Jews who had come to contribute to the development of the country, whereas the Arab leaders were thought to incite the Arab people against the Jewish settlement. With regard to the Arab population, the books focused on fellahin (Arab peasants), who were generally presented as primitive and backward (see also Podeh, 2002). After the establishment of the State of Israel until the early 1970s, the school textbooks continued to present Arabs negatively. Bar-Gal's analysis of geography school textbooks published in Palestine (1993a, 1994) showed similar findings. He summarized his analysis of Arab representation in geography books by pointing out that throughout many decades, Arabs have been represented in terms of the following characteristics: "unenlightened, inferior, fatalistic, unproductive, apathetic, with the need of a strong paternalism ... They are divided, tribal, exotic, people of the backward East, poor, sick, dirty, noisy, colored. Arabs are not progressive; they multiply fast, ungrateful, not part of us, non-Jews. They commit arson and murder, they destroy, are easily inflamed, and vengeful" (Bar-Gal, 1993a, p. 189).

Delegitimization of Arabs was also common in Hebrew readers. Zohar (1972), analyzing widely used school readers published in the 1950s and 1960s, found that Arab society was represented as primitive, backward, and passive. The most frequent representation of Arabs was as the enemy, but their national aspirations and the context of the conflict between the two national movements were never mentioned. The books used the label "enemy" in a depersonalized and undifferentiated way, which implied threat: "the enemy wanted" or "the enemy thought." In general, the textbooks tended to describe the acts of Arabs as hostile, deviant, cruel, immoral, and unfair, with the intention to hurt Jews and to annihilate the State of Israel. Within this frame of reference, Arabs were delegitimized by the use of such labels as "robbers," "wicked ones," "bloodthirsty mob," "killers," "gangs," or "rioters."

In the 1970s, the delegitimizing descriptions, noted earlier, had almost disappeared from the textbooks, but the negative stereotyping remained (e.g., Bar-Tal & Zoltack, 1989; Firer, 1985). Podeh (2002) noted that from the late 1970s, the history textbooks began to acknowledge the existence of Palestinian nationalism, used less pejorative terminology in their description of the Arabs' violent resistance to Jewish immigration and settlement, and began to present the origin of the Palestinian refugee problems in a more balanced way. Recently, Bar-Tal (1998b) analyzed the content of all school textbooks used in all school grades (1 to 12) in history, geography, civic studies, and Hebrew (readers), approved by the Ministry of Education for use in schools in 1994–95 and which referred to Arabs, or to the Arab-Jewish conflict. In general, the analysis shows that there is sporadic delegitimization of Arabs, negative stereotyping is prevalent, and positive stereotypes are rare.

Although no survey study investigated the perception of the Palestinians by the Israeli Jews until the late 1990s, there are a number of studies showing that the Palestinians were stereotyped negatively (see Bar-Tal & Teichman, in press). When a public poll was done during the peace process in 1997 and 1999, the results showed that most of the respondents did not hold negative views of the Palestinians, but at the end of 2000, with the eruption of violence between the two sides, the situation was changing toward a more negative image of the opponent. In 1997, only 39 percent of the Israeli Jewish respondents described the Palestinians as violent, 42 percent regarded Palestinians as dishonest, and 37 percent regarded them as unintelligent. Nevertheless, by the end of 2000, 68 percent of the Israeli Jewish respondents perceived the Palestinians as violent, and 51 percent perceived them as dishonest (see Table 7.5).

Palestinian Societal Beliefs

In many aspects, the Palestinian delegitimization of Jews is a mirror image in its content to the Israeli delegitimization of the Arabs (see Bar-Tal, 1988); Jews were given labels such as deceitful, treacherous, thief, and disloyal. They were seen as aggressors and robbers, and as an enemy whose aim is to annihilate the Palestinians. In addition, they were perceived as racist, fascist, and colonialist, and were even compared with the Nazis.

Many of these beliefs appeared in Jordanian and Egyptian textbooks

Table 7.5
Images of the Palestinians and Israelis

The images of the Palestinian in Israeli eyes			
	1997	1999	2000
Violent	39	37	68
Dishonest	42	35	51
Unintelligent	37	30	*
Weak	*	*	35
The images of the Israelis in Palestinian eyes			
Violent	77	75	94
Dishonest	62	67	81
Unintelligent	12	15	*
Weak	*	*	23

Note: *The question wasn't asked.

that were used by Palestinian schools in the West Bank and Gaza Strip through the decades since 1948, including the period of Israeli occupation since 1967, and were also distributed by the Palestinian National Authority. The books included statements that describe the Jews as disloyal and treacherous, as in the following: "Treachery and disloyalty are character traits of the Jews and therefore one should beware of them" (*Islamic Education* for Ninth Grade, p. 87, quoted in the Center for Monitoring the Impact of Peace [CMIP], 2001), or "In many cases these Jews acted according to their known cunning and deceit, and they incited wars [between Arab tribes]" (*Islamic Education* for Ninth Grade, p. 78, quoted in CMIP, 2001). This ninth-grade book also contained the following statement: "One must beware of the Jews, for they are treacherous and disloyal" (*Islamic Education* for Ninth Grade, p. 79, quoted in CMIP, 2001).

The Jews in these books were described as an enemy and aggressor, whose aim is to destroy and conquer Palestine. For example, a history book for tenth grade describes Zionism as "a political, aggressive and colonialist movement, which calls for the Judaisation of Palestine by the expulsion of its Arab inhabitants" (*Modern Arab History and Contemporary Problems*, Part Two, for Tenth Grade, p. 49, quoted in CMIP, 2001).

As can be seen from the last citation, the Zionists were characterized as colonialists and even worse than the Western imperialists. The tenth-grade history book mentioned earlier claimed: "The colonial powers regarded the Zionist Movement as the means for the attainment of their greedy colonial aspirations and saw Palestine as the base for the setting up of a Jewish state, thus tearing the Arab Homeland asunder and imposing their rule on it in order to **exploit** its natural resources. The European colonial powers spread the idea of Zionism among the Jews" (*Modern Arab History and Contemporary Problems*, Part II, for Tenth Grade, p. 48, quoted in CMIP, 2001). Later in the book, a table is presented that compares Zionism with imperialism. The table indicates that Zionism differs from imperialism because the former "believes in the elimination of the original inhabitants," whereas the latter "has not gone as far as the elimination of original inhabitants." Also, Zionism is "based on the foundation of false religious and historical rights," whereas imperialism is "based on foundations of economic interests" (*Modern Arab History* for Twelfth Grade, Part I, p. 123, quoted in CMIP, 2001). Zionism was also compared with the Nazi movement; a twelfth-grade history book, for example, declares: "The clearest examples of racist belief and racial discrimination in the world are Nazism and Zionism" (*Modern Arab History* for Twelfth Grade, Part I, p. 123, quoted in CMIP, 2001).

However, from 1994, the newly created Palestinian Ministry of Education began to introduce a new curriculum. In 1994, it composed a set of textbooks for the first six grades as a supplement for the Jordanian and Egyptian books. In 2000, new textbooks for the elementary schools were written by the Palestinian Ministry of Education. As Brown (in press) and Nordbruch (2002) point out, although these books discuss current problems of the Palestinians and talk about occupation and colonialism, they ignore the existence of Israel.

Findings of public polls among Palestinians indicate that most of the Palestinians hold a negative image of the Israelis. In 1997, according to polls conducted by JMCC, almost all Palestinians (89 percent) believed that the government of Israel does not truly want peace (whereas half of the Israelis, as described earlier, thought that the Palestinian Authority truly wants peace). But when it comes to the intentions of the Israeli people, 51 percent of Palestinians believed that the Israelis truly desire peace. As for negative stereotypes, the findings indicate that a large majority of Palestinians in 1997 perceived Israelis as violent (77 percent) and unfair (62 percent) but intelligent (71 percent). At the end of 2000, 94 percent of the Palestinians perceived the Israelis as violent and 81 percent perceived them as dishonest (see Table 7.5).

SOCIETAL BELIEFS ABOUT VICTIMIZATION

Societal beliefs about victimization are formed over a long period of violence as a result of society's sufferings and losses. The formation of these beliefs is based on beliefs about the justness of the society's own goals and about positive self-image, while emphasizing the wickedness of the opponent's goals and delegitimizing the opponent's characteristics (Frank, 1967).

Israeli Societal Beliefs

The Israeli ethos presents the Israelis as victims of unjust deeds and atrocities perpetrated by the Arabs. From the early encounter with Arabs, Israeli Jews perceived the attempts to harm Jews physically, to stop their immigration, or to prevent their settling as evidence of their victimization. These beliefs were greatly reinforced following the establishment of the state of Israel, when the Palestinians and the Arab states tried to annihilate the new state and continued to express their wish with active attempts during the first decades of its existence. The wars fought, the Arab embargo on the Israeli trade, and the terrorist attacks on the Israeli and non-Israeli Jews—all confirmed to the Israeli Jews their victimhood. These beliefs were reinforced by the Jewish tradition to view Jews as victims of the hostile world (Bar-Tal & Antebi, 1992; Liebman, 1978). This perception has been based on constant and continuous persecutions, libels, special taxation, restriction, forced conversions, expulsions, and pogroms that Jews experienced throughout their history, with the climax of a systematic genocide (Holocaust) that took place in the twentieth century.

The beliefs of victimization were conveyed to Israeli children through school textbooks. According to Firer (1985), history textbooks used in 1948–67 presented a picture of the Jewish people as victims of anti-Semitism. Jewish history was presented as an unbroken sequence of pogroms, special taxation, libel, and forced conversion, with the Holocaust forming the climax. While writing on the Arab-Israeli wars, Israelis were presented as the weak side that reacted to the violence of many stronger enemies. The War of Independence was presented as a struggle between the few and the many that began with attacks by Arabs gangs and was followed by the invasion of seven Arab states. Similarly, the other wars were described as acts of Arab mal-intention and aggression. The books spoke about Arabs' anti-Semitism and hatred of Jews as the motivating forces in the violence they initiated.

Bar-Tal (1998b), who analyzed the contents of all school textbooks used in 1994–95, found that victimization of the Jews was a leading theme in the readers and history books. Those books present the continuity of this phenomenon throughout Jewish history, some going as far back as ancient Egypt. The victimization of the Jews is also presented in the context of the Israeli-Arab conflict. It is always the Arabs who initiate violence against Jews, who are then forced to defend themselves.

Although there is no data about Jews' self-perception as a victim, there are findings that clearly indicate that they feel a potential victim by attributing mal-intentions to Arabs. Between 1986 and 2002, at least 50 percent of the Jews in Israel, and often over 60 percent and 70 percent, believed that the real objective of the Arab people is at least to destroy the state of Israel, and more than half of them believed that, in addition, Arabs also strive to annihilate the great majority of the Jewish population in Israel (see also Arian, 1995).

Palestinian Societal Beliefs

The Palestinian ethos, in contrast, presents the Palestinians as the victims of the Israeli-Palestinian conflict, especially in the 1948 and 1967 wars, when, according to this ethos, a significant portion of the Palestinian population was terrorized by the Israeli military forces into leaving their homes. Contrary to the Israeli ethos, the Arabs present their involvement in the Israeli-Arab wars as a reaction to Israeli aggression. For example, they claim that what Israelis call the Arab states invasion in 1948 was actually a defensive attempt to hold onto the areas allotted by the Partition Plan to the Palestinian state. Historically, the Palestinians see themselves as victims of repeated foreign invasions, specifically Western colonialism, of which Zionism is a prime example.

Some of the preceding views are found in the Palestinian textbooks. These books describe common experiences of sorrow as the major theme in the life of the Palestinian nation. The books refer to such experiences as the British occupation and the British Mandate, along with the Zionist settlement policies before and after the establishment of Israel. Students are instructed to mention incidents of violence that "our people" have been exposed to from enemies, and students are then asked how the enemies and occupiers have dealt with the inhabitants of occupied countries. First-grade children are exposed to harsh images from the Palestinian tragedy as a nation under occupation who lives in refugee camps; in a short story, a mother in a camp loses all hope when the rain comes through her roof. She expresses the thought that it would have been better to die than to have come to the camp. Sixth-grade books include a unit covering life in Israeli prisons. Another is devoted to an author describing his flight from Jaffa in 1948: he boards a boat with his Palestinian history books, only to see them tossed into the sea (all examples are from Brown, in press). No polls by the Palestinians were found about self-perception as a victim.

CONCLUSION

The presented analysis suggests that parties in intractable conflict, as Palestinians and Israeli Jews are, hold an ethos of conflict, which is one of the major foundations for its continuation. Moreover, three themes of the ethos are in direct contradiction between the two groups. Societal beliefs in the justness of one's own goals provide the epistemic rationale for the outbreak of the conflict and later continue to maintain it. The societal beliefs about the opponent's delegitimization and one's own victimhood evolve during the conflict and later serve as an inseparable part of the psychological intergroup repertoire that underlies the conflict. The contents of these two themes are a mirror image, as both sides often use the same labels and justifications.

We can easily infer that as long as the parties continue to hold these societal beliefs, peaceful resolution is an impossible mission. A peaceful resolution and the follow-up process of reconciliation require at least a modification of these three societal beliefs. Of special importance is changing the beliefs about the goals of societal conflict, because they stand as the clearest obstacle to any compromises that are a necessary condition for a peaceful resolution of the conflict (Bar-Tal, Kruglanski, & Klar, 1989). The compromises require that new goals be formulated—goals that will be accepted by the other party. The offered compromises have to be seen as minimal required conditions by the other party for the peaceful settlement of the conflict. In addition, parties in conflict have to form a new goal of having peaceful relations. This is another necessary condition for the parties' movement towards peace.

These changes have to be accompanied by a major modification of the perception of the rival. The peace process requires a cessation of delegitimization and even negative stereotyping, and instead a formation of legitimization and personalization of the opponent. Legitimization allows one to view the opponent as belonging to the category of acceptable groups with whom maintaining peaceful relations is desired. Personalization enables one to see members of the rival group as humane individuals, who have legitimate needs and goals. The new beliefs should also contain a balanced stereotype consisting of positive and negative characteristics and a differentiating perception of the group that acknowledges its heterogeneous composition. These new perceptions are necessary for the evolvement of trust, sensitivity to the rival's needs, and respect, which are required for negotiation and eventually for reconciliation. In addition, parties in conflict have to realize that both societies were victims of the conflict, as both suffered heavy losses and destruction.

The described required changes for the peace process indicate that the ethos of conflict has to change and instead a new ethos has to emerge—the ethos of peace. This is not a simple process, as during their long period of violent confrontations, the parties in conflict evolved and institutionalized an ethos of conflict, which penetrated to the societal fabric and was maintained by society's institutions and channels of communication (Bar-Tal, 2000b). Moreover, this ethos expressed the social identity of the society in conflict. It provided the explanation of the past and direction for future actions. Its change is also a change in the meanings of identity—a process that not only takes a long time, but also meets with resistance from various groups within the society, which may resort to violence.

The collapse of the Israeli-Palestinian peace process testifies to the difficulty of evolving an ethos of peace. Years of indoctrination leave their mark, and any cue that reminds the societies about their past conflict easily arouses the opposing societal beliefs that fuel the conflict. Fear, hatred, and mistrust easily reappear, while trust and sensitivity to the other's needs and personalization are built over a long period of time and need the supporting context of intergroup relations. The ethos of conflict, supported by different groups in a society, is alive and alternative societal beliefs penetrate very slowly into the societal fabric to give new meaning to identity.

Still, the success of different societies, which had been engulfed by intractable conflict (see South African or Northern Irish cases) but made the needed changes to embark on the road to peaceful resolution of their conflict, is evidence that these changes are possible. The required changes include cessation of violence, dedicated leadership to peace, ongoing meetings between representatives of the two societies, consistent gestures and acts showing peaceful intentions, persistent support of peace by various organizations, joint projects that solidify the peace, and institution-alized changes that continuously form a climate of peace.

NOTES

1. On the extreme end of the tractability-intractability dimension, in-tractable conflicts are formally defined as being total, violent, of zero sum nature, and perceived as irreconcilable; as lasting at least a generation; as involving all society members; and as requiring great investments (Bar-Tal, 1998a; Kriesberg, 1998).

2. The term "society," which denotes a large, stable social system with boundaries that differentiate it from other societies, will be used through-out this paper. Societies consist of collectives that have a clear sense of social identity and that evolve tradition, culture, collective memory, belief systems, social structures, and institutions (Giddens, 1984; Griswold, 1994).

3. Societal beliefs are defined as cognitions, shared by society members, on issues that are of special concern for the particular society (Bar-Tal, 2000a). These beliefs are formed on the basis of collective experience, serve to make sense of as well as to create a shared reality, and contribute to the sense of uniqueness of the society members. Societal beliefs are organized in themes and include such elements as goals, values, collective memory, collective image, and so on.

4. *National Education*, Textbook for the Sixth Grade, 2000–2001, p. 13 (as cited in Nordbruch, 2002).

REFERENCES

Agnew, J. (1989). Beyond reason: Spatial and temporal sources of ethnic conflicts. In L. Kriesberg, T. Northrup, & S. J. Thorsan (Eds.), *Intrac-table conflicts and their transformation* (pp. 41–52). Syracuse, NY: Syracuse University Press.

Apple, M., & Christian-Smith, L. K. (Eds.). (1991). *The politics of the textbook.* New York: Routledge.

Arian, A. (1995). *Security threatened: Surveying Israeli opinion on peace and war.* Cambridge, UK: Cambridge University Press.

Arian, A. (1999). *Security threatened.* Tel-Aviv, Israel: Papirus. (In Hebrew)

Avineri, S. (1981). *The making of modern Zionism: The intellectual origins of the Jewish State.* London: Weidenfeld and Nicolson.

Azar, E. E. (1990). *The management of protracted social conflict.* Hampshire, UK: Dartmouth Publishing.

Bar-Gal, Y. (1993a). *Homeland and geography in a hundred years of Zionist education.* Tel Aviv, Israel: Am Oved. (In Hebrew)

Bar-Gal, Y. (1993b). Boundaries as a topic in geographic education. *Political Geography, 12,* 421–435.

Bar-Gal, Y. (1994). The image of the "Palestinian" in geography textbooks in Israel. *Journal of Geography, 93,* 224–232.

Bar-Tal, D. (1988). Delegitimizing relations between Israeli Jews and Palestinians: A social psychological analysis. In J. Hofman (Ed.), *Arab-Jewish relations in Israel: A quest in human understanding* (pp. 217–248). Bristol, IN: Wyndham Hall Press.

Bar-Tal, D. (1990). Causes and consequences of delegitimization: Models of conflict and ethnocentrism. *Journal of Social Issues, 46*(1), 65–81.

Bar-Tal, D. (1998a). Societal beliefs in times of intractable conflict: The Israeli case. *International Journal of Conflict Management, 9,* 22–50.

Bar-Tal, D. (1998b). The rocky road toward peace: Societal beliefs functional to intractable conflict in Israeli school textbooks. *Journal of Peace Research, 35,* 723–742.

Bar-Tal, D. (2000a). *Shared beliefs in a society: Social psychological analysis.* Thousands Oaks, CA: Sage.

Bar-Tal, D. (2000b). From intractable conflict through conflict resolution to reconciliation: Psychological analysis. *Political Psychology, 21,* 351–365.

Bar-Tal, D., & Antebi, D. (1992). Siege mentality in Israel. *International Journal of Intercultural Relations, 16,* 251–275.

Bar-Tal, D., Kruglanski, A. W., & Klar, Y. (1989). Conflict termination: An epistemological analysis of international cases. *Political Psychology, 10,* 233–255.

Bar-Tal, D., & Oren, N. (2000). *Ethos as an expression of identity: Its changes in transition from conflict to peace in the Israeli case* (Discussion paper No. 83). Jerusalem: The Leonard Davis Institute for International Relations: The Hebrew University of Jerusalem.

Bar-Tal, D., & Teichman, Y. (in press). *Stereotypes and prejudice in conflict: The case of the perceptions of Arabs in the Israeli society.* Cambridge, UK: Cambridge University Press.

Bar-Tal, D., & Zoltak, S. (1989). Images of an Arab and Jewish-Arab relations in school readers. *Megamot, 32,* 301–317. (In Hebrew)

Bezalel, Y. (1989). *Changes in Zionist values as reflected in elementary school literature and language readers from the late fifties to the mid eighties.* Master's thesis, Ben Gurion University of the Negev, Beer Sheva, Israel.

Bourdieu, P. (1973). Cultural reproduction and social reproduction. In R. Brown (Ed.), *Knowledge, education and cultural change* (pp. 71–112). London: Tavistock.

Brown, N. (in press). *Politics under the Palestinian National Authority: Resuming Arab Palestine.* Berkeley, CA: Berkley University Press.

Center for Monitoring the Impact of Peace. (2001). *Palestinian Authority school books.* New York: Author. (also on-line at www.edume.org)

Firer, R. (1985). *The Agents of Zionist Education.* Tel Aviv, Israel: Sifriyat Poalim. (In Hebrew)

Frank, J. D. (1967). *Sanity and survival: Psychological aspects of war and peace.* New York: Vintage.

Galnoor, I. (1982). *Steering the polity: Communication and politics in Israel.* Beverly Hills, CA: Sage.

Giddens, A. (1984). *The constitution of society.* Cambridge: Polity.

Goertz, G., & Diehl, P. F. (1993). Enduring rivalries: Theoretical constructs and empirical patterns. *International Studies Quarterly, 37,* 147–171.

Griswold, W. (1994). *Cultures and societies in a changing world.* Thousand Oaks, CA: Pine Forge Press.

Hoebel, E. A. (1960). The nature of culture. In H. L. Shapiro (Ed.), *Man, culture, and society* (pp. 168–181). New York: Oxford University Press.

Horowitz, D., & Lissak, M. (1978). *Origins of the Israeli polity.* Chicago: University of Chicago Press.

Kelman, H. C. (1999). The interdependence of Israeli and Palestinian identities: The role of the other in existential conflicts. *Journal of Social Issues, 55*(3), 581–600.

Khalidi, R. (1997). *Palestinian identity: The construction of modern national consciousness.* New York: Columbia University Press.

Kriesberg, L. (1998). Intractable conflicts. In E. Weiner (Ed.), *The handbook of interethnic coexistence* (pp. 332–342). New York: Continuum.

Liebman, C. (1978). Myth, tradition and values in Israeli society. *Midstream, 24,* 44–53.

Liebman, C. S., & Don-Yehiya, E. (1983). *Civil religion in Israel: Traditional Judaism and political culture in the Jewish state.* Berkeley, CA: University of California Press.

Luke, A. (1988). *Literacy, textbooks, and ideology.* London: Falmer.

McClosky, H., & Zaller, J. (1984). *The American ethos: Public attitudes toward capitalism and democracy.* Cambridge, MA: Harvard University Press.

Nordbruch, G. (2002). *Narrating Palestinian nationalism—A study of the new Palestinian textbooks.* Washington, DC: The Middle East Media Research Institute (MEMRI).

Podeh, E. (2002). *The Arab-Israeli conflict in Israeli history textbooks, 1948–2000.* Westport, CT: Bergin & Garvey.

Ross, M. H. (1998). The cultural dynamics of ethnic conflict. In D. Jacquin, A. Oros, & M. Verweij (Eds.), *Culture in world politics* (pp. 156–186). Houndmills, UK: Macmillan.

Rouhana, N., & Bar-Tal, D. (1998). Psychological dynamics of intractable conflicts: The Israeli-Palestinian case. *American Psychologist, 53,* 761–770.

Said, E. (1979). *The question of Palestine.* New York: Vintage Books.

Shamir, J., & Shamir, M. (2000). *The anatomy of public opinion.* Ann Arbor, MI: University of Michigan Press.

Stagner, R. (1967). *Psychological aspects of international conflict.* Belmont, CA: Brooks/Cole.

Tajfel, H. (1978). Social categorization, social identity and social comparison. In H. Tajfel (Ed.), *Differentiation between social groups* (pp. 61–76). London: Academic Press.

Vital, D. (1982). *Zionism: The formative years.* Oxford: Clarendon Press.

White, R. K. (1970). *Nobody wanted war: Misperception in Vietnam and other wars.* Garden City, NY: Doubleday.

Zakay, D., Klar, Y., & Sharvit, K. (2002). Jewish Israelis on the "right of return." *Palestine-Israel Journal, 9,* 58–66.

Zohar, N. (1972). *An image of the Arab in readers.* Unpublished master's thesis, Hebrew University, Jerusalem. (In Hebrew)

CHAPTER 8

The Cultural Bases of Ethnocentrism: Comparing White Afrikaners and European New Zealanders

John Duckitt

Social scientists have neglected the study of the cultural bases of ethnocentrism, prejudice, and group conflict. One possible reason for this may be the intellectual dominance of relativist thinking on culture, at least in Western democratic societies. From a relativist perspective, it would be unjustifiable to classify cultures or societies along value-laded dimensions such as ethnocentrism or prejudice. For this reason, perhaps, the study of the causes of prejudice and ethnocentrism has tended to focus on less problematic questions.

One such question has been that of individual differences in prejudice: why do certain individuals seem more disposed than others to be generally prejudiced and ethnocentric? The neglected question of culture is analogous to this question, except that here the unit of analysis is not the individual, but the social or cultural group. What characteristics of social and cultural groups might make them disposed to be generally more or less hostile and rejecting to out-groups, minorities, and deviants, and more prone to conflict with out-groups?

Social scientists have so rarely posed this question that few studies offer evidence directly bearing on it. One study that did was conducted by Bond (1988), who investigated cultural values across 22 countries. His findings showed that societal and cultural groups did differ in ethnocentrism, and these differences were related to their basic values and attitudes. Two distinct cultural value dimensions emerged in the research, with ethnocentric values and attitudes strongly defining one of these two dimensions. This dimension was named "social integration" at one pole, where it was characterized by tolerance for others loading together with openness to change. The opposing pole was termed "cultural inward-ness," and characterized by a sense of superiority over others loading together with traditionalism and authoritarianism. Thus, it was the more authoritarian and traditionalist cultures and societies that seemed to be less tolerant of deviance and more rejecting of out-groups.

It is interesting that this finding directly parallels findings obtained in research on individual differences and prejudice. Here, research on the authoritarian "personality" (Adorno, Frenkel-Brunswick, Levinson, & Sanford, 1950; Altemeyer, 1996) had already shown that individuals hold-ing authoritarian social attitudes were also disposed to be generally more prejudiced and ethnocentric. Bond's findings suggest that when such au-thoritarian attitudes and values come to be widely held and normative in a society, they will form a distinctive cultural pattern that may make the society generally more ethnocentric and prejudiced.

This chapter will suggest that there may be two such distinct social or cultural patterns that make societies generally ethnocentric and preju-diced, with each characterized by particular values, social or ideological attitudes, and worldviews that are widely held and normative in those societies. These two cultural patterns are extrapolated from research that has shown that two kinds of ideological beliefs predispose individuals to be generally ethnocentric and prejudiced, and that these two kinds of ideological beliefs seem to be causally associated with particular social worldviews, personality dispositions, and socialization experiences. Evi-dence will then be reviewed suggesting that societies in which these ideo-logical beliefs and their associated worldviews, personality dispositions, and socialization patterns have become widespread and normative will also be characterized by greater ethnocentrism and prejudice. And finally, one highly ethnocentric society, White Afrikaners in South Africa, will be empirically compared with a relatively tolerant and nonethnocentric cul-ture, European or Pakeha New Zealanders, to show that they do indeed differ as predicted on the theoretical constructs of ideological attitude, worldview, personality, and socialization, and that these differences do seem to account for their differences in ethnocentrism.

IDEOLOGICAL BELIEFS AND ETHNOCENTRISM IN INDIVIDUALS

A great deal of research has shown that two distinct kinds of social or ideological attitudes held by individuals, authoritarian and social domi-nance attitudes, are powerfully associated with prejudice and ethnocen-trism. The study of authoritarian attitudes began with the classic investigation of anti-Semitism by Adorno et al. (1950). They found that anti-Semitism tended to be just one component of a broader syndrome of social attitudes involving generalized prejudice against out-groups and minorities, ethnocentric in-group glorification, politico-economic conservatism, and a set of social or ideological attitudes they described as implicitly pro-fascist and antidemocratic. They developed their F ("fascist") scale to measure these implicitly pro-fascist and antidemocratic attitudes. They also suggested that an "authoritarian personality" must underlie and give coherence to this covariation of social and intergroup attitudes. However, they never measured this authoritarian personality dimension directly and simply assumed that their F scale would be measuring it indirectly.

Although the F scale was initially widely used, it was later largely abandoned because of important psychometric weaknesses and because it included too many empirically divergent facets to be adequately unidimensional (Altemeyer, 1996). Today, is has been replaced by Altemeyer's (1996) Right Wing Authoritarianism (RWA) scale, which encompassed only three central facets of authoritarian attitudes: conventionalism, authoritarian submission, and authoritarian aggression. Research by Altemeyer (1996, 1998) and others (see Stone, Lederer, & Christie, 1993) has shown that the RWA scale is unidimensional and reliable, and it powerfully predicts generalized prejudice and ethnocentrism.

During the 1990s, Sidanius and Pratto proposed a second social attitude construct, Social Dominance Orientation (SDO), measured by their SDO scale, which was also powerfully associated with prejudice and ethnocentrism (Pratto, Sidanius, Stallworth, & Malle, 1994; Sidanius & Pratto, 1999). They described SDO as a "general attitudinal orientation toward intergroup relations, reflecting whether one generally prefers such relations to be equal, versus hierarchical" (Pratto et al., p. 742). Research has indicated that the SDO and RWA scales are either not correlated or only weakly correlated, suggesting that they measure two quite different social attitude dimensions. They therefore predict prejudice independently of each other (Altemeyer, 1998; McFarland, 1998; Pratto et al.).

Because Adorno et al. (1950) had originally thought that their F scale reflected an underlying authoritarian personality dimension, the RWA scale, and occasionally even the SDO scale, has sometimes been loosely referred to as measuring personality dimensions (cf. Altemeyer, 1998). However, commentators have frequently pointed out that the items of the RWA scale, and its predecessor, the F scale, do not pertain to personality traits and behavior at all, but are statements of social attitude and belief of a broadly ideological nature (cf. Stone et al., 1993, p. 232). This is clear from RWA items such as "What our country really needs is a strong, determined leader who will crush evil, and take us back to the true path" and "Everyone should have their own lifestyle, religious beliefs, and sexual preferences, even if it makes them different from everyone else" (Altemeyer, 1996). Similarly, the items of the SDO scale, such as "We should strive to make incomes as equal as possible" and "Inferior groups should stay in their place" (Pratto et al., 1994), are also clearly statements of social attitude and belief.

If SDO and RWA are ideological belief or social attitude dimensions and not personality trait dimensions, then similar dimensions to SDO and RWA should have emerged in the research literature investigating sociopolitical attitudes. A recent review of this literature did indeed show that investigations of the structure of sociopolitical attitudes have typically revealed two roughly orthogonal dimensions, with one corresponding closely to RWA, and the other to SDO (Duckitt, 2001, see Table 3). The RWA-like dimension has been labeled social conservatism or traditionalism at one pole versus openness, autonomy, liberalism, or personal freedom at the other pole. The SDO-like dimension has been labeled economic conservatism, power, belief in hierarchy, or inequality at its one pole versus egalitarianism, humanitarianism, social welfare, or social concern at its other pole. Empirical studies have confirmed the association. Thus, measures of socially conservative sociopolitical attitudes have correlated powerfully with the RWA scale and scaled with it as a single general factor or dimension. For example, Saucier (2000) in a large-scale study of sociopolitical attitudes obtained a correlation of .77 between the RWA scale and a well-established attitudinal measure of social conservatism.

IDEOLOGICAL SOCIAL ATTITUDES AND CULTURAL VALUE DIMENSIONS

In the past two decades, cross-cultural investigations of cultural values have produced remarkably convergent findings showing that essentially similar basic value dimensions differentiate cultures and societies as entities, and individuals within societies (Fiske, Kitayama, Markus, & Nisbett, 1998). The two most central cultural value dimensions that have emerged directly parallel the two social attitude dimensions of RWA and SDO.

The most methodologically sophisticated investigation has been that by Schwartz (1996), whose data from 54 countries and 44,000 participants indicated a circular ordering of value types around two basic dimensions: conservation (conformity, security, tradition) versus openness (hedonism, self-direction, autonomy), and self-enhancement (achievement, power) versus self-transcendence (universalism, benevolence). These two pivotal dimensions were found to describe both individual differences within cultures or societies, and country differences—though the actual structuring of value types was simpler at the societal or country level (with 7 value types for societies as opposed to 10 for individuals) and some of the labels used at individual and societal levels differed. The correspondence between these two cultural value dimensions and the two social attitude dimensions of RWA and SDO has been empirically confirmed by Altemeyer's (1998) finding of highly significant correlations between Schwartz's individual difference value types and RWA and SDO. The conservation value types (traditionalism, conformity) correlated positively and the openness values (hedonism, self-direction) correlated negatively with RWA, but were uncorrelated with SDO. Power values correlated positively and universalism values negatively with SDO, whereas neither correlated with RWA.

Similar dimensions have emerged from other investigations of cultural values. For example, the two most important dimensions from Hofstede's (1980) earlier investigation using only country-level data were individualism-collectivism (corresponding to Schwartz's conservation versus openness, or RWA) and power distance (corresponding to Schwartz's hierarchy versus egalitarianism, or SDO).

These findings suggest that individual differences and differences between societies and cultures can be described and measured on essentially similar value/attitude dimensions. They also indicate that the two social attitude or ideological dimensions measured by RWA and SDO, which have been shown to be pivotal in predicting prejudice and ethnocentrism, correspond very closely to basic cultural value dimensions that appear to have validity across cultures. This suggests that societies in which either authoritarian attitudes and conservative (collectivist) values or social dominance beliefs and power (high power distance) values are dominant and normative may also be disposed to ethnocentrism, prejudice, and group conflict. Evidence supporting this will be reviewed later in this chapter. First, however, a broader conceptual framework will be described that suggests that authoritarian and social dominance attitudes express motivational goals that have become highly salient for individuals or groups, and that these motivational goals have been made salient by certain socialization experiences, personality dispositions, and social worldview beliefs.

A MOTIVATIONAL BASIS FOR SOCIOCULTURAL ATTITUDES AND ETHNOCENTRISM

Psychological anthropologists, notably D'Andrade (1992) and Strauss (1992), have proposed that strongly held social values and attitudes express motivational goals that are highly salient for individuals or groups. They argue that these motivational goals will be salient because cultural socialization will have resulted in individuals or groups acquiring particular social schemas, or shared ways of perceiving reality. It is these shared perceptions of reality, or social worldviews (Ross, 1993), that then activate and make salient particular motivational goals.

This conceptual framework can be readily applied to the two ideological social attitude dimensions of RWA and SDO and their associated cultural values of collectivist-traditionalism and hierarchy-power, respectively. Thus, these two sociocultural attitude and value patterns can be seen as expressions of motivational goals that are made salient for individuals or societies by particular sociocultural worldviews, which in turn result from cultural socialization creating particular dispositional tendencies in people to interpret the social world in characteristic ways. These two patterns are summarized in Table 8.1 and each is described in more detail following.

Authoritarian-Conservative Attitudes and "Threat-Cohesion" Cultures

In the case of the authoritarian-conservative dimension, high RWA would express the motivational goal of social cohesion (to provide social security, stability, and control) made salient by the social worldview of the world as a dangerous and threatening place. Low RWA would express the opposing motivational goal of personal freedom and individual autonomy, made salient by a view of the social world as safe, secure, and stable. The predisposing personality disposition seems likely to be that of social conformity versus autonomy. Being higher in dispositional social conformity would create a greater readiness to perceive threats to the existing conventional social order and so to see the social world as dan-

Table 8.1
Two Sets of Psychological Dimensions Underlying Prejudice and Ethnocentrism, with Causality from Left to Right

Socialization	Personality	Worldview	Motivational goal	Ideological beliefs
Strict, punitive	Conforming	Threatening/ dangerous	Social cohesion	Authoritarian/ conservative
versus	versus	versus	versus	versus
Tolerant, indulgent	Autonomous	Safe/secure	Personal freedom	Openness
Unaffectionate	Tough-minded	Competitive-jungle	Superiority /dominance	Social dominance
versus	versus	versus	versus	versus
Affectionate	Tender-minded	Cooperative-harmony	Altruistic concern	Egalitarianism-humanitarianism

gerous and threatening. High social conformity should also have a direct impact on authoritarian attitudes by itself creating personal needs for security, order, stability, and control that would also make the motivational goal of social cohesion highly salient for the individual. Numerous studies have supported the core propositions here. First, findings indicate that social threat and a view of the world as dangerous and threatening is strongly associated with authoritarian-conservative social attitudes (e.g., Altemeyer, 1996; Doty, Peterson, & Winter, 1991; Sales, 1973). Second, evidence also indicates an association between authoritarianism and a need for social cohesion (Duckitt, 1992).

What kind of cultural socialization would produce socially conforming personalities? Adorno et al. (1950) linked strict, punitive parental socialization to the formation of authoritarian social attitudes. Others have also reported evidence supporting this (Milburn, Conrad, Sala, & Carberry, 1995). Cross-cultural evidence has shown that this seems to hold at the cultural or group level as well (e.g., Thomas, 1987). A major cross-cultural investigation by Ross (1993) found that preindustrial societies that were ethnocentric and conflict prone tended to be characterized by two distinct dimensions of childhood socialization. One socialization dimension was characterized by punitive, strict versus permissive, indulgent socialization, which fits with the kind of socialization Adorno et al. (1950) suggested would underlie authoritarianism.

The overall causal sequence characterizing these "threat-cohesion" societies or cultures can be summarized as follows. These societies will encourage strict, punitive socialization that tends to produce persons higher on social conformity. Such personalities will tend to be more sensitive to threats to conventional society and therefore be more likely to see the social world as dangerous and threatening. Socially conforming personality dispositions and viewing the social world as dangerous and threatening will make salient the motivational goal of social cohesion (and through it social security, stability, order, and control) that then becomes expressed in collectivist cultural values and conservative-authoritarian ideological attitudes. Such individuals and societies will therefore tend to be characterized by more ethnocentric and prejudiced attitudes.

Social Dominance Attitudes and "Competitive-Dominance" Cultures

In the case of the second ideological social attitude dimension, high SDO would express the motivational goals of power and dominance over others, whereas low SDO would express the opposing motivational goal of altruistic and egalitarian social concern for others. What kinds of worldviews would make these motivational goals important for individuals or groups? A strong relationship has been shown between the SDO scale and measures that express a view of the social world as a competitive jungle characterized by a ruthlessly amoral Darwinian struggle for resources and power (e.g., "It's a dog-eat-dog world where you have to be ruthless at times") such as Altemeyer's (1998) Personal Power, Meanness and Dominance scale and his Exploitive Manipulative Amoral Dishonesty scale, which contain items drawn largely from the older Machiavellianism scale. Sidanius, Pratto, and Bobo (1994) also found that items expressing a ruthlessly competitive view of the world ("Winning is more important than how the game is played") scaled together with more typical SDO scale items expressing a belief in social inequality.

SDO has also been empirically linked with the personality dimension of tough versus tender-mindedness, characterized by traits of being hard, tough, ruthless, and unfeeling to others, as opposed to compassionate, generous, caring, and altruistic (McFarland, 1998; Pratto et al., 1994; Sidanius & Pratto, 1999). This suggests that tough-minded personalities would tend to adopt a view of the world as a ruthlessly competitive jungle in which the strong win and the weak lose, which would tend to activate the motivational goals of power, dominance, and superiority over others expressed in high SDO. Tender-minded personalities, on the other hand, would tend to adopt the directly opposing view of the social world as a place of cooperative and altruistic harmony in which people care for, help, and share with each other. This would make salient the motivational goal of altruistic social concern, which would be expressed in low SDO. The second cultural socialization dimension that characterized cultures high on ethnocentrism and conflict that was identified in Ross's (1993) cross-cultural research described earlier was that of unaffectionate as opposed to affectionate child-rearing practices, and it seems likely that unaffectionate child-rearing practices would produce tough-minded as opposed to tender-minded personalities.

A second causal sequence linking cultural socialization to the ideological attitudes and social values acquired by individuals is therefore suggested here. In "competitive-dominance" cultures or societies, unaffectionate childhood socialization practices will be favored and produce personalities higher on tough-mindedness. Such persons will be more disposed to see the social world as a competitive jungle. This worldview will then make salient the motivational goals of seeking power and dominance over others that find expression in social values and attitudes expressing beliefs in inequality and social dominance. These ideological attitudes in individuals will incline them to adopt ethnocentric and prejudiced attitudes. Societies or cultures in which these ideological attitudes are widely shared and have become the dominant ideologies will therefore be particularly prone to more ethnocentric and prejudiced attitudes to outgroups and minorities and to a greater tendency to stigmatize and reject deviants.

RESEARCH ON WORLDVIEW, IDEOLOGICAL ATTITUDES, AND ETHNOCENTRISM IN INDIVIDUALS

The hypothesized causal framework summarized in Table 8.1 has been tested in research on individuals. First, three studies showed that the personality dimensions of social conformity and tough-mindedness could be reliably measured and related as expected to ideological attitudes (Duckitt, 2001, Study 1). Both personality constructs were measured by asking participants to rate how "characteristic or uncharacteristic" personality trait terms were "of their personality and behavior." For social conformity, examples were "obedient," "respectful," "unpredictable," and "rebellious," and for tough-mindedness, examples were "ruthless," "brutal," "soft-hearted," and "sympathetic." The Social Conformity Scale was strongly correlated with RWA but not with SDO, whereas the Tough-mindedness Scale was correlated with SDO but not with RWA.

Second, four studies using structural equation modeling with latent variables produced results that were consistent with the causal relationships proposed between the two socialization, two personality, two worldview, and two ideological attitude dimensions with each other and with intergroup attitudes for large samples in New Zealand, South Africa, and the United States (Duckitt, 2001; Duckitt, Wagner, du Plessis, & Birum, 2002). These findings suggested that there did indeed appear to be two causal pathways to the holding of ethnocentric and prejudiced attitudes. One pathway was characterized by strict and punitive childhood socialization seemingly producing more socially conforming personality dispositions, a tendency to believe that the social world was a dangerous and threatening place, and authoritarian and conservative social attitudes. The second pathway was characterized by unaffectionate childhood socialization seemingly producing more tough-minded personality dispositions, leading to the adoption of a view of the social world as a ruthlessly competitive jungle, and to ideological beliefs in social dominance and inequality.

Third, experimental evidence suggests that when social environments change drastically and seemingly irrevocably, sudden and dramatic changes in social worldviews may occur that would produce equally dramatic changes in ideological beliefs. Altemeyer (1996), for example, found that when students were given scenarios in which a future Canadian society had experienced a long decline and was in economic and political crisis with massively escalating crime, unemployment, and terrorism, their RWA scores increased dramatically. More recently, Duckitt and Fisher (in press) replicated this by showing that similar threatening future scenarios for New Zealand also increased RWA, and that the effect on RWA was entirely mediated through an increased view of the world as dangerous and threatening. These findings have a direct historical parallel with the catastrophic political and economic situation triggered by the Great Depression in 1930s Germany that catapulted the Nazis from political obscurity to state power in only a few years and culminated in world war and the holocaust against the Jews.

RESEARCH ON ETHNOCENTRIC CULTURES AND SOCIETIES

It is well established that processes operative at the individual or interpersonal level may not also operate at the group level. However, there is evidence indicating that cultures and societies that are high on the social worldview and ideological attitude dimensions of threat-cohesion or competitive-dominance do indeed seem to be more prone to ethnocentrism, prejudice, and conflict proneness. For example, the following four studies have demonstrated how societies characterized by threat-cohesion or competitive-dominance or both tend to be higher in ethnocentrism and conflict proneness:

- Bond's (1988) investigation of cultural values across 22 countries, which has already been noted, showed that cultures that were more authoritarian and traditionalist, and therefore higher in threat-cohesion, were also less tolerant of deviance and more rejecting of out-groups.

- Bonta (1997) studied completely peaceful societies in which aggression, intergroup hostility, and conflict were almost totally absent. He found that the most salient characteristic of these societies was a powerful normative emphasis on cooperation, with any kind of competitiveness being completely eschewed. Thus, these societies seemed to be exceptionally low on competitive-dominance.

- Ross's (1993) research, which has also been noted, showed that in preindustrial societies, punitive, strict socialization, which should be associated with threat-cohesion, and unaffectionate socialization, which should be associated with competitive-dominance, were both independently predictive of the degree to which these societies were conflict prone and ethnocentric.

- Meloen (2000) compared 63 countries and found that the higher they were on Hofstede's two cultural value dimensions of collectivism (i.e., threat-cohesion) and power distance (i.e., competitive-dominance), the more they were characterized by undemocratic practices and the more likely they were to have been involved in military conflict.

Competitive-Dominance Cultures and Ethnocentrism

Ethnographic studies have provided more in-depth descriptions of societies, cultures, or subcultures characterized by competitive-dominance or threat-cohesion. For example, the violence and ethnocentrism of competitive-dominance cultures have been documented in the American South (Nisbett & Cohen, 1996), in Fascist movements (Billig, 1978), in the post-Vietnam paramilitary subcultures of America (Gibson, 1994), and in violent underclass and gang subcultures (Toch, 1992). These subcultures are typically characterized by a view of the social world as a competitive jungle in which power, toughness, machismo, defense of one's honor, and dominance become important values and goals. These seem to be central features of cultures of honor and warrior cultures.

McNeil (1961, as cited in Van der Dennen, 1987), describing his experiences in living with a group of 70 aggressive and antisocial boys, noted how at first contact they immediately began a pattern of militant interpersonal and intergroup probing to establish an aggressive pecking order of dominance and submission. Toch (1992) and others (Staub, 1996) have also described such cultures of power, toughness, and machismo, in which defense of one's honor and the establishment of dominance becomes a central value. In such cultures, the social world seems to be sharply divided into those who are strong and superior and those who are derogated as weak, inferior, and unworthy.

Historically, very high levels of anti-Black prejudice and higher levels of prejudice to other out-groups such as Jews and immigrants have characterized the American South. In their book *Culture of Honor: The Psychology of Violence in the South,* Nisbett and Cohen (1996) have shown how the culture of the South is characterized by an overriding importance to men of strength, power, and toughness, and being ready in any situation to respond to any challenge to one's honor in order to maintain respect from others. They argue that this culture emerged from an economy of cattle herding and relative lawlessness. In this competitive-jungle situation, self-preservation and the preservation of ones' property required strength, toughness, and a readiness to retaliate violently if challenged. Nisbett and Cohen (1996) have argued that this culture accounts for the higher levels of certain kinds of violence in the South. Clearly, it could also account for the higher levels of ethnocentrism and prejudice characterizing the South.

Threat-Cohesion Cultures and Ethnocentrism: White Afrikaners and New Zealanders

Threat-cohesion cultures seem quite different from competitive-dominance cultures. Altemeyer (1996), for example, has noted how authoritarian belief systems are characterized by fundamentalist religiosity, moral self-righteousness, and a pervasive intolerance of nonconformity and deviance. These were prominent features of the White Afrikaner culture that gave rise to apartheid in South Africa.

MacCrone (1937) has described how this culture was originally forged in the South African frontier situation. Once the Dutch colonists had spread from the original settlement at the Cape to the interior, the frontier situation and an enduring conflict with the more numerous indigenous African peoples and the British colonial power developed. The essential characteristics of the frontier situation were isolation, danger, war, and extreme insecurity. This created a society characterized by a sense of omnipresent threat and vulnerability with an intense emphasis on group cohesion, conservatism, conformity, and a pervasive ethnocentrism. In threat-cohesion cultures such as this, the all-important social distinction therefore seems to be between "us" who are decent, normal, and good, and "them" who are threatening, bad, deviant, disruptive, and immoral.

The characterization of White Afrikaner ethnocentrism as a product of a threat-cohesion culture suggests several hypotheses that might indicate whether the constructs of social worldview and ideological attitudes can be used to describe and explain social group as well as individual differences. Previous research has shown that White Afrikaners tend to be particularly high on authoritarianism, ethnocentrism, and anti-Black prejudice (cf. review in Duckitt, 1992, chap. 9). European/Pakeha New Zealanders, on the other hand, tend to be generally low in prejudice, and New Zealand is a reasonably tolerant, multicultural society in which intergroup relations, though strained at times, are not seriously antagonistic.

White Afrikaners should therefore be significantly more ethnocentric than European New Zealanders. However, if White Afrikaners' ethnocentrism is an expression of a threat-cohesion culture, then they should be markedly higher than New Zealanders on authoritarianism and dangerous world beliefs, but not necessarily higher on social dominance and a competitive-jungle worldview. Similarly, White Afrikaners should be higher on the personality dimension of social conformity and on strict, punitive socialization than European-Pakeha New Zealanders, but not necessarily higher on tough-mindedness or on unaffectionate socialization. Moreover, if Afrikaners' heightened ethnocentrism is the expression of a threat-cohesion culture, then controlling for authoritarianism and dangerous world beliefs should eliminate the difference between the two groups in ethnocentrism, whereas controlling social dominance and a competitive-jungle worldview should not.

In order to test these hypotheses, data were reanalyzed from two earlier studies that had each independently tested the framework in Table 8.1 for individuals (see Duckitt, 2001; Duckitt et al., 2002). These two studies, one of White Afrikaners in South Africa and the other of European New Zealanders, used equivalent samples of undergraduate psychology students and the same measures of socialization, personality, social worldviews, and ideological attitudes, and were both conducted in 1999. These data were reanalyzed to directly compare the two samples. This would indicate if White Afrikaner South Africans were indeed higher than European New Zealanders on the socialization, personality, worldview, and ideological attitudes dimensions characteristic of a threat-cohesion culture, and if these differences would account for the White Afrikaners' higher levels of ethnocentrism and prejudice than the European New Zealanders, as the framework outlined in Table 8.1 would predict.

The 236 European-Pakeha New Zealand students were from the University of Auckland, and the 227 White Afrikaner undergraduate students from the University of Pretoria. Auckland is the largest city in New Zealand and Pretoria the capital city of South Africa. The measures, which are described more fully elsewhere (Duckitt, 2001; Duckitt et al., 2002), and an illustrative item from each were as follows:

1. Strict socialization was measured using three items (e.g., "I was strictly disciplined while I was growing up").

2. Unaffectionate socialization was measured using five items (e.g., "I grew up in caring and loving environment").

3. Social Conformity was measured by ratings on 14 trait items (e.g., "obedient," "nonconforming").

4. Tough-mindedness was measured by ratings on 16 trait items (e.g., "hardhearted," "kind").

5. Belief in a Dangerous World was measured by nine items, with most taken from Altemeyer's Beliefs in a Dangerous World scale (e.g., "Any day now chaos and anarchy could erupt around us. All the signs are pointing to it").

6. Belief in a Competitive-Jungle World was measured by 12 items, with most selected or adapted from Altemeyer's (1998) PP-MAD or E-MAD scales (e.g., "Winning is not the first thing, it's the only thing").

7. RWA was measured by eight items from Altemeyer's scale (e.g., "What our country really needs is a strong determined leader who will crush evil and take us back to our true path").

8. SDO was measured by 10 items from Pratto et al.'s (1994) scale (e.g., "Inferior groups should stay in their place").

9. Ethnocentrism. The questionnaires for both samples included pro-in-group (pro-Afrikaner and pro-Pakeha) and anti-out-group attitudes. Unfortunately, the pro-in-group measures in the two studies had different items, and the out-groups were necessarily different as well. Thus, in South Africa, out-group attitudes were measured to two Black groups, Africans and Indians (items shown in Duckitt et al., 2002), whereas in New Zealand, they were measured to the three main ethnic minorities, that is, Maori, Asians, and Polynesians (items shown in Duckitt, 2001). This meant it was not possible to compare the two samples on exactly the same measure of ethnocentrism. However, the response scales to the items of the pro-in-group and anti-out-group attitude measures were the same in both studies (nine point scales from +4 to –4). This meant that summing pro-in-group and anti-out-group attitudes (with in-group and out-group attitudes equally weighted) and dividing by the total number of items would give a very crude common index (on a scale of +4 to –4) of the

degree to which White Afrikaners and European New Zealanders were endorsing ethnocentric (pro-in-group and anti-out-group) sentiments in general.

Table 8.2 shows the means for the two groups on this index of ethnocentrism and their means for the two ideological attitude, two social worldview, two personality, and two socialization scales. To facilitate interpretation, we divided the means for all of the measures by the number

Table 8.2
Ethnocentrism, Social Worldview, Ideological Attitudes, Personality, and Socialization Item Response Scale Mean Scores for White Afrikaners (n = 224–227) and European/Pakeha New Zealanders (n = 231–236)

Measures	White Afrikaners		NZ Europeans			
	Mean	SD	Mean	SD	$\underline{F}$	$\underline{D}$
Ethnocentrism index	1.91	1.69	.03	1.66	143.10	.98
Ideological attitudes						
RWA	1.68	1.20	-1.21	1.23	650.84	1.53
SDO	-.82	1.45	-1.18	1.14	9.12	.28
Social worldviews						
Dangerous World	1.56	1.43	-.16	1.24	189.23	1.08
Competitive World	-2.15	1.05	-1.51	1.14	38.91	-.56
Personality						
Social Conformity	.19	.98	-.20	1.14	15.30	.36
Tough-mindedness	-2.84	1.50	-2.53	.97	6.80	-.24
Socialization						
Strict	.41	1.85	-.62	1.84	36.73	.54
Unaffectionate	-2.75	1.30	-2.38	1.60	7.46	-.25

Notes: All effects are significant at $p < .01$. The item means range from +4 (highest) through 0 (scale midpoint) to -4 (lowest).

of items in the measure so that all of the means shown are on the same standard response scale of $+4$ to -4. Because the samples were large, small differences would be statistically significant; therefore, Cohen's (1988) d was computed to give an index of effect size, with d values of .20, .50, and .80 usually viewed as denoting weak, moderate, and strong effects, respectively.

Table 8.2 shows that Afrikaners' mean score on the ethnocentrism index was very much higher than that for European New Zealanders, with Cohen's d indicating a very powerful effect. Despite the crudeness of the ethnocentrism index, the absolute values of the means for the two groups also seemed to provide clear support for its validity, because the mean for Afrikaners was over a standard deviation above the index's midpoint, suggesting a highly ethnocentric sample, whereas the New Zealanders' mean was almost exactly at the midpoint, suggesting a sample that was not particularly ethnocentric.

As predicted from the characterization of Afrikaners as a threat-cohesion culture, Afrikaners were also much higher on Dangerous World beliefs and RWA, with both effects very powerful. In contrast, Afrikaners were moderately *lower* on the Competitive-Jungle Worldview scale. Although Afrikaners were significantly higher on SDO, the effect was slight (Cohen's d indicating a weak effect), and when RWA was statistically controlled using analysis of covariance, the mean SDO scores for Afrikaners (adjusted $M = -1.47$) was significantly lower than that for the New Zealand Europeans (adjusted $M = -1.18$; $F = 29.7$, $p < .0001$). In contrast, controlling SDO left the difference between the two groups in RWA unchanged.

It was predicted that the heightened ethnocentrism of threat-cohesion cultures would be entirely accounted for by these cultures being higher on RWA and Dangerous World beliefs. Thus, controlling for Dangerous World beliefs and RWA should entirely eliminate the difference between Afrikaners and New Zealanders in ethnocentrism. This was confirmed by an analysis of covariance showing that when RWA and Dangerous World beliefs were controlled, the ethnocentrism means for the two groups were similar and the difference statistically nonsignificant (Afrikaner adjusted $M = 1.04$, New Zealand European adjusted $M = .93$; $F = .36$, $p = .55$).

Finally, as expected for a threat-cohesion culture, Afrikaners were significantly higher that New Zealanders on the personality trait scale of Social Conformity and on the Strict Socialization scale. In contrast, Afrikaners were not higher and indeed were significantly lower than New Zealanders on the Tough-mindedness scale and on the Unaffectionate Socialization scale.

These findings therefore support the view that Afrikaner ethnocentrism seems to be specifically threat-cohesion driven, and therefore characterized by authoritarian attitudes, a view of the world as dangerous and threatening, higher levels of social conformity, and strict parental social-ization. Afrikaners were either no higher, or lower, than New Zealanders on social dominance attitudes, a view of the world as a competitive jungle, tough-mindedness, or unaffectionate socialization. Indeed, with differences in ideological attitudes and social worldview statistically controlled, Afrikaners tended to be no higher in ethnocentrism than European New Zealanders.

CONCLUSIONS

Overall, the theoretical framework described in this chapter, although originally proposed to explain individual differences in people's propensity to adopt and hold prejudiced and ethnocentric attitudes, also seems to have promise for explaining how social groups such as societies and cultures may be more or less prone to prejudice and ethnocentrism. Specifically, the framework suggests that there are two sociocultural patterns that tend to be associated with ethnocentrism in social groups.

First, threat-cohesion societies will tend to be characterized by a widespread acceptance of a view of the social world as a threatening and dangerous place (as opposed to a safe and secure place) with the dominant ideological beliefs being authoritarian-conservative (as opposed to liberalism and personal autonomy). These societies value group cohesion, stability, order, and control. The cultural pattern favors strict childhood socialization and sees the ideal personality as one characterized by social conformity. The heightened ethnocentrism and prejudice in these societies seems likely to be directed against those internal deviants or out-groups who seem to threaten cohesion, security, order, and stability. This suggests it will be those who are culturally or socially different, deviant, or socially disruptive and threatening who are more likely to be stigmatized or the targets of prejudice in these societies. In Western Europe, for example, which is more collectivist than the United States, the most socially problematic prejudice tends to be that directed toward "foreigners," that is, those who are culturally and ethnically different (Pettigrew, 1998).

Second, competitive-dominance societies are characterized by the widespread acceptance of a view of the social world as a competitive jungle, where the strong and able win and the weak and less able lose. The dominant ideology expresses belief in inequality and hierarchy, where the more able are deservingly dominant and the less able are subordinate. These societies value power, success, strength, and dominance. The cultural pattern favors relatively unaffectionate rather than affectionate childhood socialization and sees the ideal personality as tough, hard, and ruthless rather than as gentle, soft-hearted, and compassionate. These high power cultures seem likely to be most prejudiced against disadvantaged or socially subordinate out-groups and minorities, who would be seen as weak, incompetent, and inferior. In North America, for example, which is characterized by greater social inequality and competitiveness than that in Western Europe, the most problematic social prejudice seems to be selectively directed against African Americans who constitute the most disadvantaged and socially subordinate ethnic group in American society.

Finally, it should be noted that such group level effects should be sharper for smaller, more homogeneous social groups than for large complex societies. Nevertheless, the research by Hofstede (1980) and Schwartz (1996) has shown systematic patterns of value differentiation even at the country level, and Meloen (2001) has also shown that these patterns were systematically associated with country differences in ethnocentrism. However, the interpretation of findings from such large, heterogeneous groups should always be subject to the caveat that they would inevitably be reflecting very broad, overall effects that could be substantially moderated by subgroup differentiation.

REFERENCES

Adorno, T., Frenkel-Brunswick, E., Levinson, D., & Sanford, N. (1950). *The authoritarian personality.* New York: Harper.

Altemeyer, B. (1996). *The authoritarian specter.* Cambridge, MA: Harvard University Press.

Altemeyer, B. (1998). *The other "authoritarian personality."* In M. P. Zanna (Ed.), *Advances in Experimental Social Psychology* (Vol. 30, pp. 47–92). San Diego, CA: Academic Press.

Billig, M. (1978). *Fascists: A social psychological view of the National Front.* London: Academic.

Bond, M. (1988). Finding universal dimensions of individual variation in multi-cultural studies of values: The Rokeach and Chinese value surveys. *Journal of Personality and Social Psychology, 55,* 1009–1015.

Bonta, B. (1997). Cooperation and competition in peaceful societies. *Psychological Bulletin, 121,* 299–320.

Cohen, J. (1988). Statistical power analysis for the behavioral sciences (2nd ed.). Hillsdale, NJ: Erlbaum.

D'Andrade, R. (1992). Schemas and motivation. In R. D'Andrade & C. Strauss (Eds.), *Human motives and cultural models* (pp. 23–44). Cambridge, UK: Cambridge University Press.

Doty, R., Peterson, B., & Winter, D. (1991). Threat and authoritarianism in the United States, 1978–1987. *Journal of Personality and Social Psychology, 61,* 629–640.

Duckitt, J. (1992). *The social psychology of prejudice.* New York: Praeger.

Duckitt, J. (2001). A dual process cognitive-motivational theory of ideology and prejudice. In M. Zanna (Ed.), *Advances in experimental social psychology* (Vol. 33, pp. 41–113). San Diego, CA: Academic Press.

Duckitt, J., & Fisher, K. (in press). The impact of social threat on worldview and ideological attitudes. *Political Psychology.*

Duckitt, J., Wagner, C., du Plessis, I., & Birum, I. (2002). The psychological bases of ideology and prejudice: Testing a dual process model. *Journal of Personality and Social Psychology, 83,* 75–93.

Fiske, A., Kitayama, S., Markus, H., & Nisbett, R. (1998). The cultural matrix of social psychology. In D. Gilbert, S. Fiske, & G. Lindzey (Eds.), *The handbook of social psychology,* (4th ed., Vol. 2, pp. 915–981). New York: McGraw-Hill.

Gibson, J. (1994). *Warrior dreams: Paramilitary culture in post-Vietnam.* New York: Hill and Wang.

Hofstede, G. (1980). *Culture's consequences.* Beverly Hills, CA: Sage.

MacCrone, I. (1937). *Race attitudes in South Africa.* London: Oxford University Press.

McFarland, S. (1998). *Toward a typology of prejudiced persons.* Paper presented at the annual meeting of the International Society of Political Psychology, Montreal, Canada.

Meloen, J. (2000). The political culture of state authoritarianism. In S. Renshon & J. Duckitt (Eds.), *Political psychology: Cultural and crosscultural foundations* (pp. 108–127). New York: New York University Press.

Milburn, M., Conrad, S., Sala, F., & Carberry, S. (1995). Childhood punishment, denial, and political attitudes. *Political Psychology, 16,* 447–478.

Nisbett, R., & Cohen, D. (1996). Culture of honor: The psychology of violence in the South. Boulder, CO: Westview.

Pettigrew, T. (1998). Intergroup contact theory. *Annual Review of Psychology, 49,* 65–85.

Pratto, F., Sidanius, J., Stallworth, L., & Malle, B. (1994). Social dominance orientation: A personality variable predicting social and political attitudes. *Journal of Personality and Social Psychology, 67,* 741–763.

Ross, M. (1993). *The culture of conflict.* New Haven, CT: Yale University Press.

Sales, S. (1973). Threat as a factor in authoritarianism. *Journal of Personality and Social Psychology, 28,* 44–57.

Saucier, G. (2000). Isms and the structure of social attitudes. *Journal of Personality and Social Psychology, 78,* 366–385.

Schwartz, S. (1996). Value priorities and behavior: Applying a theory of integrated value systems. In C. Seligman, J. Olson, & M. Zanna (Eds.), *The psychology of values: The Ontario symposium.* (Vol. 8, pp. 1–24). Hillsdale, NJ: Erlbaum.

Sidanius, J., & Pratto, F. (1999). *Social dominance: An intergroup theory of social hierarchy and oppression.* Cambridge, UK: Cambridge University Press.

Sidanius, J., Pratto, F., & Bobo, L. (1994). Social dominance orientation and the political psychology of gender: A case of invariance? *Journal of Personality and Social Psychology, 67,* 998–1011.

Staub, E. (1996). Cultural-societal roots of violence. *American Psychologist, 51,* 117–132.

Stone, W., Lederer, G., & Christie, R. (1993). The status of authoritarianism. In W. Stone, G. Lederer, & R. Christie (Eds.), *Strength and weakness: The authoritarian personality today.* (pp. 229–245). New York: Springer.

Strauss, C. (1992). Models and motives. In R. D'Andrade & C. Strauss (Eds.), *Human motives and cultural models* (pp. 1–20). Cambridge, UK: Cambridge University Press.

Toch, H. (1992). *Violent men.* Washington, DC: American Psychological Association.

Thomas, D. (1987). Authoritarianism and child-rearing practices. *Australian Psychologist, 22,* 197–201.

Van der Dennen, J. (1987). Ethnocentrism and ingroup-outgroup differentiation. In V. Reynolds, V. Falger, & I. Vine (Eds.), *The sociobiology of ethnocentrism.* London: Croom Helm.

CHAPTER 9

Interethnic Relations in the Baltic States: Between Confrontation and Integration

Juris G. Draguns

INTRODUCTION

In 1991, the three Baltic countries, Estonia, Latvia, and Lithuania, regained their independence, after being occupied by and annexed to the Soviet Union for half a century. One of the most painful legacies of Soviet rule was a major demographic shift in the ethnic composition of the population in Estonia and Latvia and, to a lesser extent, in Lithuania. In 1940, ethnic Latvians constituted 77 percent and ethnic Estonians 88 percent of the inhabitants of their respective countries. By 1991, the corresponding figures had shrunk to 52 and 61 percent, respectively. Over the same period, the percentage of ethnic Russians had increased from 14 to 34 in Latvia and from 8 to 30 in Estonia (Kirch & Kirch, 1992; Mežs, 1992; Taagepera, 1993; Woods, 1998), mostly through migration from Russia and the other republics of the Soviet Union. Local population was substantially depleted through arrests and deportations to Siberia and Kazakhstan, and in some cases migrants were literally assigned housing in the homes of the deportees. After the Soviet Union collapsed, this situation appeared to be tailor-made for a violent confrontation. However, during the ensuing 12 years, no bloodshed has occurred. Even an outspoken critic of the Baltic governments' ethnic policies has conceded that "absence of interethnic violence and bloodshed is our incontestable achievement, to the credit of all inhabitants of Latvia" (Tsilevich, 1998, p. 53).[1]

Against this background, Clemens (2001) has recently wondered how and why Baltic states have managed to avoid such calamities as ethnic cleansing, social unrest, and armed conflict. Yet, there have been few attempts (e.g., Haas, 1996) to account for this paradoxical phenomenon. In this chapter, a few further steps will be taken toward an admittedly post hoc explanation of the peaceful transition in the Baltic region. To this end, historical information will be briefly provided, and a look will be taken at the accumulated findings, by psychologists and other social scientists, supplemented by the author's observations during his 10 visits to the Baltics between 1991 and 2002. Promising programs toward the resolution of the ethnic impasse will also be described.

HISTORICAL INFORMATION

After several centuries of foreign domination, the three Baltic countries emerged as free democratic states at the end of World War I and became full-fledged members of the world community of nations. In recognition of the multiethnic character of their population, all three states enacted rather liberal legislation guaranteeing cultural and educational rights to the linguistic and ethnic minorities within their borders. It would be an exaggeration to say that friction was entirely eliminated or that complete harmony ensued. However, several observers (e.g., Feigmane, 2000; von Rauch, 1974) concur that the cultural and educational provisions were exemplary for their time; they contributed greatly to nipping ethnic animosity in the bud. The situation changed abruptly during the Second World War as the three states were occupied and annexed by the Soviet Union, which was replaced as occupier by Nazi Germany; both imposed unimaginable suffering upon large segments of the population. The Holocaust of the Jewish population under the Nazis was preceded and followed by mass persecution of political and class enemies, real and imagined, by the Soviet regime. Soviets targeted persons of all nationalities. Thus, Russian intelligentsia in the Baltic States was decimated (Lieven, 1994). The demographic effect was especially devastating upon ethnic Estonians, Latvians, and Lithuanians; among the deported, arrested, and executed were disproportionate numbers of talented, enterprising, and productive individuals. Baltic nationalities came close to becoming minorities in their own lands. Their languages were relegated to a subsidiary position; official and/or important business was increasingly conducted in Russian, and learning it started virtually in kindergarten. The prospect for long-term survival of distinctive Estonian, Latvian, and Lithuanian cultures looked bleak. Yet, somehow the Baltic nations "managed, despite all odds, to regenerate themselves into self-reliant, buoyant, and consolidated entities whose identity has become so solidly indestructible that nothing short of a truly genocidal exercise could undermine it" (Shtromas, 1986, p. 208). As the Soviet regime was liberalized, fear of persecution vanished, national self-expression blossomed, and political demands came to be openly expressed.

RETURN TO INDEPENDENCE: THE PAINFUL
PROCESS OF SEPARATING FROM A SUPERPOWER

By the late 1980s, the Baltic region was in turmoil. What could only be whispered a few years ago was now shouted from the rooftops. In the spring of 1991, led by Lithuania, the freely elected parliaments of the three republics declared their annexation to the Soviet Union null and void and reasserted national independence. Hundreds of thousands of people streamed into streets and squares in order to voice their demands insistently, yet peacefully. A total of 700,000 persons gathered in Riga, Latvia, roughly one-fourth of the population of the republic (Levits, 1991). In Vilnius, Lithuania, a standoff of hundreds of thousands of unarmed civilians against the Soviet military ended in bloodshed; 15 persons were killed and many more injured by soldiers (Lieven, 1994). In more scattered violence in Riga, seven people were shot dead by Soviet special police, including two ethnically Russian police lieutenants who had rallied to the Latvian side (Dreifelds, 1992; Lieven, 1994). Barricades were constructed in the three capitals. Manned by unarmed volunteers, they were intended to serve as impediments to the movement of tanks and troops to government and public buildings. Concurrently, Soviet authorities tried to mobilize ethnic Russians in defense of the Soviet regime. These efforts at producing ethnic polarization turned out to be counterproductive. Protest strikes were called in all three countries. Yet, only a small fraction of ethnic Russian workers responded (Gerner & Hedlund, 1993; Lieven, 1994; Taagepera, 1993). In Vilnius, no more than 10,000 people turned up at a counterdemonstration in support of Soviet power. In fact, repression kindled a wave of solidarity that swept across all social barriers, including ethnicity. It has been estimated that 15 percent of the people guarding the barricades were Russian in ethnicity, and the percentage of ethnically Russian supporters of and active participants in the struggle for independence kept rising during the three years of transition. Kionka (1990, as cited in Gerner & Hedlund, 1993) concluded that "Moscow has grossly overestimated its basis of support among Estonia's non-indigenous peoples" (p. 29).

In the spring of 1991, voters in the Baltic states were asked to declare themselves for or against independence. Exceeding the most sanguine expectations of the pro-independence forces, 90 percent of voters in Lithuania, 78 percent in Estonia, and 74 percent in Latvia endorsed independence (Taagepera, 1993). In all three referendums, the percentages of "yes" votes surpassed those of indigenous nationality. Thus, as many as 30–50 percent of ethnic Russian voters opted for separation from the Soviet Union (Lieven, 1994; Savoskul, 2001). In Daugavpils, Latvia's second-largest city, where in 1991, 14 percent of the population was Latvian and 58 percent Russian, 51 percent of the voters chose independence (Mežs, 1992).

INTERETHNIC RELATIONS AFTER INDEPENDENCE: CONFLICT AVERTED, BUT RESOLUTION NOT YET ACHIEVED

From Euphoria to Reality: Complications and Disappointments

The collapse of the Soviet hard-liners' coup in August 1991 removed the remaining obstacles to the restoration of Baltic independence. Thus, sooner than they had dared to hope, the Baltic peoples' cherished dreams came true. Russian-speaking minorities in their midst were, however, faced with a host of complexities and ambiguities. For hard-core supporters of the Soviet regime, the reawakening was rude and traumatic. Many more people thought they had moved to an outlying part of their own country; suddenly they found themselves in a foreign land with a political system and language of its own (Chinn & Kaiser, 1996). Russophone residents now faced issues such as whether they should leave or stay and to what extent, if any, they should accommodate to their new language, cultural, and political situation. More subtly, questions of personal and ethnic identity were likely to arise: Who am I now that the Soviet Union is no more? Where do I belong? How do I define myself ethnically and civically? What about me has remained unchanged, and what, if anything, has disappeared? Bergquist and Weiss (1994) had the opportunity to conduct systematic open-ended interviews with both Russians and Estonians shortly after Estonia regained independence. They noted a gamut of reactions from confusion, almost to the point of disorientation, to hints of exhilaration.

Before independence, many Russian speakers, especially those sympathetic to the Baltic cause, expected easy and swift access to citizenship. They were encouraged in this hope by pronouncements of some of the Baltic pro-independence leaders. Known sometimes as the zero option, this procedure was enacted into law only in Lithuania, where the influx of settlers from Russia and other parts of the Soviet Union was modest. As a result of this legislation, by 1994, 95 percent of the post-1945 migrants were granted Lithuanian citizenship (Chinn & Kaiser, 1996). Thus, a major frustration was removed, but other tensions were not eliminated. Surprisingly, recent survey data even attest to a higher level of dissatisfaction and a greater sense of insecurity among Russians in Lithuania than in Estonia, perhaps because the Russian-speaking community in Lithuania is smaller (Savoskul, 2001).

Why has Lithuania's example not been emulated in Latvia and Estonia? For one, the sheer size of the task as well as its complexity would be daunting. The two nations faced the challenge of absorbing several hundred thousand migrants and their descendants. Even those politicians who had espoused the zero option began to backtrack; others quit politics in disgust over what they felt was the breach of implied promise of easy and quick naturalization (Kostoe, 1995). Initial citizenship legislation in both Latvia and Estonia was limited to restoring the status quo; citizens in 1940 and their descendants were reaffirmed in their rights and obligations. It is important to emphasize that this provision extended to persons of all ethnicities; it is not true that Russians were barred from citizenship on the basis of ethnicity. Only the citizenship as of 1940 mattered and Russians' percentage among citizens and voters after 1991 was somewhat higher than before 1940 (Savoskul, 2001).

As for opening the door to new citizens, laws were hesitantly and grudgingly enacted. Their initial provisions were highly restrictive in terms of years of residence and annual quotas for the number of persons to be naturalized. Language proficiency examinations were also instituted. Some say that the tests were too difficult, especially for the elderly and persons of limited education. As a result, many prospective candidates felt discouraged and gave up trying. The implicit message they perceived was that they were not welcome in the community of citizens. Only a trickle of people applied, not even filling the small annual windows. More recently, naturalization procedures have been streamlined and liberalized in both Estonia and Latvia. By now, the number of naturalized citizens is steadily increasing. However, for the foreseeable future, the majority of Soviet-era migrants and many of their descendants will remain permanent residents, more as a matter of choice than because of any difficulties in scaling the naturalization hurdle. Moreover, Estonia—but not Latvia—has enacted legislation that allows noncitizens to vote in local elections, though not to run for office.

Other grievances continue to fester. In Latvia especially, the Russophone community is troubled by uncertainties regarding public schooling in Russian. Current legislation stipulates a transition from Russian to Latvian as the principal medium of instruction in high schools for Russian students, with eventually only Russian language, literature, history, and culture to be taught in Russian. These provisions are widely endorsed by the Latvian population, but are resented by most ethnic Russians, including teachers and students, as coercive and pedagogically ineffective. At the same time, Russian language instruction in grade schools continues, the Russophone Baltic Russian Institute offers accredited university-level programs in most major cities of the Baltic states, and an excellent Russian professional theater in Riga is thriving, with government support.

Language laws, which in both countries restrict the use of Russian in business records, correspondence, street signs, product labels, posters, and other public uses have also generated resentment. Some of the more extreme provisions have been revoked or mitigated, with forceful encouragement by advisors and observers from the Council of Europe. Again, attitudes toward these modifications diverge across ethnic lines; whereas many Russians applaud them, the bulk of Estonian and Latvian public opinion resents them as extraneous interference.

In the field of employment, the collapse of the Soviet-era defense-related and heavy industry enterprises has disproportionately affected Russian workers brought in from the interior of the Soviet Union (Savoskul, 2001). However, Lithuanian, Latvian, and Estonian employees have also been displaced in large numbers. Ethnic discrimination in hiring practices is often alleged, but no wholesale dismissals on ethnic grounds have occurred. In a survey, one-half of the Russian respondents raised fairness issues at their places of employment, compared with one-third of their Latvian counterparts (Savoskul, 2001). State employees and others whose jobs involve contact with the public are required to pass a language proficiency examination in Latvian or Estonian. In both countries, however, the grace period for complying with this requirement was repeatedly extended. At the same time, Russian ownership of small, medium, and large businesses is widespread, and some observers say that business is dominated by Russians. The prevailing, and possibly stereotypic, view is that ethnic Russians tend to focus their career aspirations upon the private sector as opposed to public employment.

BALTIC NATIONALS' PERSPECTIVE: TRAUMATIC PAST, AMBIGUOUS PRESENT, UNCERTAIN FUTURE

In August 1991, after independence was secured, there was little rejoicing in the Baltics. The three nations had survived, but the burden of 50 years of war and external rule weighed heavily upon them. It is difficult to overestimate the amount and intensity of suffering the Baltic peoples had endured. A Russian ethnographer who had studied and done research in Latvia described the consequences of Soviet rule as follows: "The barbaric utilization of Latvia's natural resources, the irresponsible actions of the all-union economic ministries that have stimulated large scale migrations, cutting people off from their ecological niches and pushing them into alien socio-cultural environments, the absence of any real possibilities to influence decisions, and a national policy of unification which has resulted in Latvians finding themselves on the verge of becoming a national minority" (Ustinova, 1992, p. 107).

Deportations, arrests, and executions of the Stalin era affected directly or indirectly virtually every family in the three republics. After Stalin's death in 1953, mass persecution ceased, but more insidious stresses continued. Glorification and promotion of everything Russian was pursued, concomitant with denigration of achievements of the Baltic peoples, especially during their brief period of independence. On the practical level, newcomers from the interior of the USSR were given preference in housing, a scarce commodity in the Soviet system. In the seven largest cities of the republic including the capital, ethnic Latvians became a minority (Mežs, 1992). In the Estonian city of Narva, the percentage of Estonian nationals shrank to less than 10 percent (Taagepera, 1993). Under these circumstances, resentment, threat orientation, and insecurity were commonly experienced. Sometimes, these sentiments were displaced onto Russian-speaking residents, including both beneficiaries and victims of the Soviet regime. In any case, this frame of mind goes a long way to explain why quick and painless integration of the Russian-speaking minorities failed to take place.

INTERETHNIC COMPARISONS IN THE BALTICS: SOME DIFFERENCES, MUCH OVERLAP

Under the Soviets, ethno-cultural comparison was not encouraged. Instead, the official rhetoric proclaimed that all the problems of a multiethnic society had been solved, and any remaining ethnic differences were trivial. During the 1990s, however, a body of findings has come into being. Without pretense at a comprehensive review, a few illustrative studies are summarized as follows.

An early study by Hansen and Štšipletsova (1994) explored Estonian high school students' stereotypes of Russians. Although global evaluations were negative, specific attributions were mixed. Russians were rated as good-natured, warm, hospitable, and talented, yet lazy, disorganized, and uncultured. These characterizations are paralleled by the general observations by Haas (1996), who noted that "Estonians are inclined to see Russians as more friendly, outgoing, funloving, spontaneous, and spiritual than themselves [and] Russians tend to acknowledge that Estonians are diligent, responsible, efficient, and orderly" (p. 53). More recently, Valk (2001) amplified these impressions. On the basis of both verbal ratings and preferred residential distance, Russian stereotypes by Estonian adolescents were found to be negative, yet Russians were also rated as helpful, sympathetic, friendly, and cheerful. In fact, their scores on these traits were higher than those of the other five nationalities compared, including Estonians. Negative evaluations were focused upon the historical and political impact of Russia (and the Soviet Union) on Estonia, and especially so by those Estonians who strongly identify with their nation.

In a large-scale study at the University of Latvia by Dimdins (1998), Russian respondents showed higher ethnic identification and evaluated Latvians more stereotypically, as compared with the evaluation of Russians by their Latvian counterparts. In value ratings, however, both groups tended to be similar, a finding corroborated in another part of Latvia by different measures (Ruža, 2001). Dimdins concluded that even in the absence of value differences, group consciousness tends to exaggerate differences between "us and "them" and promote polarization, and that it is slow to change. From a different perspective, Volkan and Harris (1993) discovered another obstacle to constructive intergroup communication while conducting experiential interethnic discussion groups: projective identification, which involves the attribution of the objects of an in-group's insecurity to behaviors and intentions of the out-group and creates the illusion of "understanding" and "knowing" the out-group's members. Discussions promoted by Volkan and Harris were instrumental not only in identifying this mechanism, but also in helping overcome it.

In a comparison of Latvian and Russian adolescents in high schools in Riga, Robinson and Breslav (1996) hypothesized that relative deprivation of Russian students subsequent to the shift in power from the USSR to independent Latvia would negatively affect their self-concept. However, results demonstrated the robustness of self-evaluation and its imperviousness to both political shifts and the shrinkage of material resources, which both ethnic groups experienced in the early postindependence years. Aasland (2002) utilized extensive survey data in order to ascertain whether mostly Russophone noncitizens in Estonia and Latvia experienced greater social exclusion from the labor market, civic participation, and political life. Compared with citizens, such a discrepancy was found in Estonia but not in Latvia. According to Aasland, even this finding is not necessarily traceable to state policies, which are not more restrictive in Estonia than in Latvia, but may reflect economic changes, such as the decline in the volume of trade with Russia, which may have disproportionately affected noncitizens. Moreover, Aasland concluded, low educational level is a more important determinant of social exclusion than citizenship.

In a recent survey of Latvian university students (Vaivars, 2000), more Russian respondents voiced readiness to engage in close relations, from personal friendships to marriage, with Latvians than did their Latvian counterparts with Russians. Overshadowing this difference, 70 to 90 percent of the total sample expressed motivation to expand their relationships across ethnic lines. Social contact with the other group and living close to them, for example in student dormitories, emerged as the best predictor of such intentions. Younger and well-educated people appear to be inclined to reach out across the ethnic divide in all three of the Baltic states. Moreover, general observations (e.g., Gordon, 1984; Kostoe, 1995), self-reports (e.g., Lieven, 1994), and research data (Realo & Allik, 1999) converge in suggesting a considerable degree of acculturation to the "indigenous" Baltic values and attitudes within the Russian-speaking segment of the population. Thus, Realo and Allik (1999) found ethnic Russians in the Estonian city of Narva to be less collectivistic than respondents in Moscow. The alternative interpretation proposed by the investigators was that individualism may promote migration.

Another source of relevant data can be found in opinion polls on a host of topics. Polling has been a well developed and methodologically sophisticated enterprise in the Baltic region for close to two decades, antedating independence. Differences between titular national groups and Russian minority often emerge, in conjunction with considerable overlap. Not unexpectedly, at the dawn of independence, Russian and Estonian respondents differed both in their judgments concerning recent historical events and in their outlook for the future (Kirch & Kirch, 1992). Moreover, considerable divergence in the evaluation of Soviet rule continues. Many Baltic Russians, especially the migrants among them, refer to the sovietization of the Baltic countries as "liberation" (Karklins, 1986); they bristle when the local population calls it "occupation." Perhaps on no other day is this division as marked as it is on May 9, celebrated in the Soviet era as the Victory Day in World War II. To large segments of the Russian population, it commemorates glory, heroism, and sacrifice in defeating Nazi invaders; to many Estonians, Latvians, and Lithuanians, it marks the reimposition of alien rule and evokes the suffering of the ensuing 45 years.

Shortly after independence, Russian respondents voiced more pessimistic expectations about the future and harbored more positive images of the past than did their Latvian counterparts (Kirby, 1995). Estonians placed a higher value upon freedom and a lower value upon equality in comparison with Russians. Baltic nationals in all three countries endorse the prospect of NATO membership in greater numbers than do members of the Russian minority. Somewhat paradoxically, the picture is reversed in relation to the desire for joining the European Union (Norgaard et al., 1999), perhaps because of Russian hopes of European support for their educational and cultural aspirations.

More recently, however, a divergence of ethnic attitudes on this issue has occurred. Upon a thorough analysis of the results of the referendums on joining the European Union (EU), Mežs (2003) concluded that in all of the three Baltic countries the overwhelming majority of voters of titular nationality endorsed EU membership. Conversely, the majority of ethnically Russian electorate voted against entry into the European Union. A similar trend toward ethnic polarization was observed in the 2002 parliamentary elections in Latvia (Rozenvalds, 2002), with Latvian and Russian voters opting for different parties with a minimal overlap. There is no evidence as yet that this split has spilled over into other areas of life, such as cultural, social, and economic.

The attitudes and opinions just described are illustrative; limited by time, place, and sampling; and subject to shifts and fluctuations with changes in context and circumstances. However, it is the author's impression that the edge of ethnic confrontation is gradually being blunted.

Traumatic events of the Soviet era are less painfully recalled by younger people, and fears of Russian aggression are receding. The increase of ethnic Latvians from 52 to 58 percent and of Estonians from 61 to 66 percent in their respective countries by 2000 has contributed to reducing concerns about Baltic peoples' physical and cultural survival. In two of seven of Latvia's major cities, there is once again an ethnically Latvian majority, although the percentage of Latvians in the capital, Riga, barely exceeds 40 percent. The frequent complaint that Russians refuse to learn Estonian/Latvian/Lithuanian is losing some of its validity. In Latvia, the proportion of self-declared Russian speakers of Latvian has doubled in the last 10 years from 26 to 53 percent. As a consequence, the country is becoming bilingual, with 79 percent of the population claiming proficiency in Latvian and 81 percent in Russian (Mežs, 2002). Still, many Latvians are worried about their language's future as a medium of communication in all spheres of life, including schools and government (Mežs, 2002).

Moreover, attitudes are often subtle, differentiated, and complex. As reported by Tsilevitch (1998), a Danish opinion poll in Latvia has identified a sizable segment of ethnic Latvians who profess no anti-Russian prejudice in personal dealings, even including marriage, yet insist on special political rights and safeguards for the Latvian population. Conversely, in the same survey, a subgroup of Latvians advocated political equality regardless of ethnicity, yet indicated a preference for association and relationships within their own Latvian milieu.

In a survey of 1,000 persons in Daugavpils, a city with a highly heterogeneous population, (Peipina, 2001), 72 percent of Latvians and an identical percentage of Russians characterized ethnic relations as good and existing problems as solvable. Between 1993 and 1997, these figures rose from 59 percent for Russians and 61 percent for Latvians. Yet, only 20 percent of Latvians and 8 percent of Russians pronounced themselves entirely satisfied with the current interethnic situation. Russians' complaints were focused upon the division of the population into citizens and noncitizens, whereas Latvians decried the slow pace of integrating Russians into Latvian society and the absence of adequate safeguards for the status of Latvian as an official language.

Facilitating Constructive Ethnic Interaction: Promising Programs and Initiatives

Psychologists and other social scientists have not limited themselves to observing and describing the interethnic scene in the Baltic region. Several innovative programs have been developed in order to transcend confrontation and to promote constructive interaction, in keeping with Amir's (1969) contact hypothesis.

Prominent among these efforts is Vamik Volkan's extension of his ethno-

political discussion groups to the Baltics. Volkan, a psychoanalyst by training, integrated his psychodynamic orientation with the objectives and
experiences of unofficial diplomacy in order to bring together members
of antagonistic ethnic groups for face-to-face discussions. Once free flow
of communication is established, attempts are made to find common
ground, to develop empathy for the feelings of the persons across the
ethnic barrier, to promote mutual understanding, and to facilitate reconciliation (Volkan, 1999). Facilitators refrain from taking sides, but promote
the search for solutions and structure the discussion. They serve as cata-
lysts for the group process, which remains open-ended and is not predetermined by explicit goals nor constrained by a tight agenda. The
complexity and uniqueness of Volkan's projects is such that it defies the
imposition of formal research designs. Extensive qualitative information
is available on the process and outcome of these interventions. In the Baltic
area, these programs were first implemented in Lithuania (Volkan & Harris, 1992) and Latvia (Volkan & Harris, 1993) on a time-limited basis for
the purpose of mitigating ethnic friction in the aftermath of the Soviet
Union's disintegration. In Estonia, ethno-political discussions were inau-
gurated in three ethnically mixed locations, characterized by the potential
for conflict between Estonian and Russian residents and a paucity of opportunities for constructive dialogue. These communities also faced stag-
gering social and economic problems, and no apparent solution was in
sight. At all three sites, attitudes of the participants toward members of
the other ethnic group have undergone a transformation and major practical improvements were achieved through joint interethnic efforts. The
results of these experiences have reverberated through the communities
and may facilitate further improvement in the interethnic climate.

Volkan's objectives are compatible with those of the Multinational Culture Center (MCC) in Daugavpils, designed to promote the tenets of multiculturalism and to facilitate exchange of information and increased
contact among that Latvian city's six major ethnic groups. In the conception of its founder, Priedītis (2001), MCC aspires to help move Latvian
society from its current state of "grudging toleration" (p. 39)[2] to one of
genuine tolerance.

Not far from Daugavpils, the town of Kraslava is the site of the unique
multiethnic Rainbow School, which aims to equip its graduates with a
thorough grounding in Latvian language and culture, in combination with
intensive study of their respective national heritage and language. The
product of this educational experience is envisaged as a multicultural individual who combines thorough cultural and language competence in
Latvian and internalization of shared Latvian values with knowledge of
and respect for the language and heritage of his or her own ethnic group.
Furthermore, such a person is expected to have international language
skills, to be both socially sensitive and interpersonally effective, and to

foster the actualization of his or her culturally integrated self (Fleišmans, 1994). Makarevich (2001) found that the experience at Rainbow School has shifted students' personal constructs toward affiliation and away from aggression in comparison with students of a standard high school.

Analyzing ethnic tolerance as a phenomenon and concept, studying it empirically, and promoting it through action research are the declared objectives of an interdisciplinary group of investigators at Daugavpils Pedagogical University (Makarevich, 2001). Sebre (2000) found a significant positive correlation among Latvian participants between the experience of political persecution by the Soviets and ethnic pride, and emotional, physical, and sexual abuse emerged as significant, though indirect, antecedents of ethnic intolerance, mediated by dissociation, hostility, and resentment. Although their antecedents were different, a low significant correlation also linked ethnic pride and ethnic intolerance.

WHY HAS VIOLENT CONFRONTATION BEEN AVOIDED?

The beginnings of Baltic national reassertion go back to the late 1980s. Since then, there have been plenty of opportunities for ethnic polarization with resulting violence and bloodshed. Why have these eruptions failed to occur in the Baltic region, even though some well informed and perceptive observers envisaged such a possibility (e.g., Lieven, 1994)?

First, there is neither the opportunity nor the temptation to seek an absolute resolution of the ethnic dilemma through the use of force. The population of the Baltic states is highly urbanized, and guerrilla warfare is unthinkable. Tensions have never reached a fever pitch, and various grievances and frustrations are invariably held in check by the specter of bloodshed, which is dreaded by all segments of the Baltic population. This attitude goes beyond the recognition of the futility of violence. There is a widespread if intuitive awareness that the fragile recovery of the Baltic nations would be imperiled and their very survival would be put at risk. At different degrees of explicitness, many people realize that violence produces unintended consequences, but brings no solution to accumulated problems. No amount of coercion can compel hundreds of thousands of migrants to leave nor can the status quo before the collapse of the Soviet Union be reimposed. Baltic independence movements opted for a nonviolent strategy, and even radicals on both sides stepped away from the brink at several crucial points during the preindependence struggle and thereafter. In Haas's (1996) view, the willingness of Estonian authorities to be flexible and to consider the feelings of Russian-speaking residents has been an important factor in reducing tensions. There may be variations among the three states; however, the awareness that it is dangerous to push an issue to its extreme is widespread in all segments of the Baltic population and power structure.

Second, residential proximity of the local nations and Russians may have also contributed to de-escalating tensions at crucial moments. Housing of Russians and local nationals is not consistently separated, although rows of shoddily constructed apartment houses on the outskirts of Riga and Tallinn have a predominantly Russian occupancy. Nonetheless, ethnic mixture in housing is characteristic. Proximity breeds contact and contact acts as an antidote against hostile confrontation, especially if it occurs on an egalitarian basis and in a variety of contexts (Amir, 1969). These conditions prevent a rigid division into in-groups and out-groups and act as a brake against dehumanizing or demonizing members of the other ethnicity.

Third, as already pointed out, stereotypes of the other ethnic group in the Baltics are neither monolithic nor uniformly negative. In reference to Estonia, Haas (1996) stated that "individual Russians are accepted as close colleagues, good neighbors, or attractive dating partners even by Estonians who resent their presence as colonizers" (p. 53). Moreover, Russians settled in the three republics over a period of several centuries, in a variety of capacities, and for a host of reasons, and negative attitudes toward some Russians resist blanket generalization. Participants in demonstrations in the preindependence years remember ethnic Russians marching and standing with them, a fact curiously glossed over by Baltic radical nationalists and Soviet apologists alike. And even the deportees who returned after decades in the Siberian Arctic report compassion by some ordinary Russian (and Siberian native) people (e.g., Taagepera, 1993; Volkan & Harris, 1993). Thus, personal interactions between Balts and Russians proceed more smoothly than the strained relationship on the group level would suggest. During my 10 visits to Riga, I have never observed an altercation on an ethnic basis, and the level of civility and helpfulness in social interaction both within and across ethnic groups tends to be high. There are, however, credible reports of some local Russians tongue lashing and even threatening the returning overseas Latvians for their "refusal" to use Russian, a language which most of them have never learned.

Fourth, regardless of ethnicity, the inhabitants of the Baltic region are locked into economic interdependence. Mass departure by Russians would have catastrophic consequences for the Baltic economies. Equally unrealistic are the appeals of some disgruntled Russian spokespersons for the boycott of Latvian businesses because of their alleged refusal to respond to requests for service in Russian. In the market economy, both consumers and producers seek the best deal available, and the language used in the transaction is a minor consideration. Economic consideration may have helped slow down repatriation of Russians to a trickle, and political upheavals and economic uncertainties in Russia are perceived by potential repatriates as major obstacles to their return (Savoskul, 2001). By analogy with the classical experiment by Sherif and Sherif (1966), both the majority and the minority find themselves in a common predicament, grappling with a difficult economic situation in a complex and ambiguous sociopolitical context. A lot of issues must be faced, negotiated, and accommodated on a day-to-day basis. In the process, confrontation, competition, and antagonism do not disappear, but they may be subordinated to the pursuit of vital supra-ordinate goals. Pressing practical problems, such as the revitalization of the economy, the protection of the environment, and various municipal issues are tasks around which all ethnic groups may coalesce (Draguns, 1996).

BETWEEN FEAR AND HOPE: TOWARD INTEGRATION?

The prospect that Estonians and Latvians dread is being submerged by their more numerous and powerful neighbors and eventually losing not only their national sovereignty, but also their distinctive languages and cultures. Insecurities of Russian residents in all three Baltic countries also focus on language and identity loss, but are coupled with fears of social and economic marginalization. So far, the experience of the postindependence period has served to reduce, but not to eliminate, these concerns. Deeply embedded in the consciousness of many individuals is the conception of the ethnic conflict as a zero-sum game. As the status of the other group's language is strengthened and secured, the position of one's own group is expected to suffer. The alternative to this view, more often implied than directly expressed, is to provide safeguards and to work simultaneously for the attainment of both groups' legitimate and realistic objectives. This is more easily said than done, but it is possible to envisage promoting the goal of a national state with one official language, yet multiple opportunities for all residents to cultivate their heritage and use their own languages in many spheres of life. In fact, on the declarative level, this is the policy of all three states.

To sum up, during the difficult transition from subjugation to independence, the people of the Baltic states have managed to avoid overt and prolonged ethnic strife. The time, however, has been too short to produce a stable and equitable solution to the problems faced by the principal ethnic components of the population of the Baltic region. On the psychological level, subtle problems persist, and the sense of ethnic identity of the majority and minority groups is easily threatened. The paradox of the Baltic situation is that most of the people have found their own way of interacting with members of the other ethnic group without much anxiety or hostility, whereas, on the sociopolitical level, insecurities and resentments persist. A differentiated and complex perception of individuals, self-control in action and verbal expression, modulation of intensity of interethnic contacts, and the realization of the dangers of ethnic conflict have all contributed to preventing disruption so far. A continuing need remains for building bridges across the ethnic divide, in the form of opportunities for emotionally safe and spontaneous social interaction. In such an atmosphere, looking at a situation from the other group's point of view, and eventually feeling empathy with its members, may be an ambitious but realizable objective. In the process, controversy, conflict, and divergence of goals and interests will inevitably come to the fore; they must be faced, tolerated, and yet not be allowed to escalate in an uncontrolled manner. Rather, grievances should ideally be nipped in the bud, or, more realistically, recognized and addressed at an early stage. The eventual aim is a gradual change of fundamental attitudes toward self and others as well as the burning issues of the day, including the sociopolitical situation in one's country of birth or residence. Baltic nationals and the Russians in their midst have no alternative to coexistence. They face a long and tortuous road together "until the Russians in the Baltic learn to live without an empire and the Balts learn to live with the Russians" (Lieven, 1994, p. 384).

NOTES

1. Translated from Russian by the author.

2. Author's translation from Latvian of *netoleranta iecietiba*, literally "intolerant toleration."

REFERENCES

Aasland, A. (2002). Citizenship status and social exclusion in Estonia and Latvia. *Journal of Baltic Studies, 33*, 57–77.

Amir, Y. (1969). Contact hypothesis in ethnic relations. *Psychological Bulletin, 71*, 319–343.

Bergquist, W., & Weiss, B. (1994). *Freedom! Narratives of change in Hungary and Estonia.* San Francisco: Jossey-Bass.

Chinn, J., & Kaiser, R. (1996). *Russians as the new minority. Ethnicity and nationalism in the Soviet successor states.* Boulder, CO: Westview Press.

Clemens, W. C., Jr. (2001). *The Baltic transformed: Complexity theory and European security.* Lanham, UK: Rowman & Littlefield.

Dimdins, G. (1998). A study of ethnic identification and in-group bias, and importance of values among Latvian and Russian students living in Latvia. Master's thesis, Stockholm University, Sweden.

Draguns, J. G. (1996). Solving the problems within a multicultural society. What can cross-cultural psychology contribute? In A. Prieditis (Ed.), *Multiculturalism in Latvia* (pp. 83–96). Daugavpils, Latvia: AKA.

Dreifelds, J. (1992). Latvia: Chronicle of an independence movement. In M. Rezun (Ed.), *Nationalism and the breakup of an empire. Russia and its periphery* (pp. 43–56). Westport, CT: Praeger.

Feigmane, T. (2000). *Russkiye v dovoyennoy Latvii na puti k integratsiii* [Russians in prewar Latvia on the road to integration]. Riga, Latvia: Baltic Russian Institute.

Fleišmans, A. (1994). O kontseptsii obrozovaniya v nashem litsei [About the educational conception in our high school]. *Kultūra un Vārds, 1*(2), 2.

Gerner, K., & Hedlund, S. (1993). *The Baltic States and the end of the Soviet empire.* London: Routledge.

Gordon, F. (1984). "Rossijane" un "latvijci" [Russian and Latvian nationals]. *Latvija šodien, 12,* 9–10.

Haas, A. (1996). Non-violence in ethnic relations in Estonia. *Journal of Baltic Studies, 27,* 47–67.

Hansen, H., & Štšipletsova, T. (1994). O natsional'nikh stereotipakh [About national stereotypes]. *Kultūra un Vārds, 1*(1) 3, 13.

Karklins, R. (1986). *Ethnic relations in the USSR. The perspective from below.* Boston: Allen & Unwin.

Kirby, D. (1995). *The Baltic world 1772–1993. Europe's northern periphery in an age of change.* London: Longman.

Kirch, A., & Kirch, M. (1992). National minorities in Estonia. In K. Rupesinghe, P. King, & O. Vorkunova (Eds.), *Ethnicity and conflict in a post-Communist world. The Soviet Union, Eastern Europe, and China* (pp. 89–106). New York: St. Martin's Press.

Kostoe, P. (1995). *Russians in the former Soviet republics.* Bloomington, IN: Indiana University Press.

Levits, E. (1991). Lettland unter der Sowjetherrschaft und auf dem Wege zur Unabhangigkeit (Latvia under the Soviet rule and on the road toward independence), In B. Meissner (Ed.), *Die Baltischen Nationnen: Estland, Lettland, Litauen* (Second Edition), (pp. 139–222). Cologne, Germany: Markus Verlag.

Lieven, A. (1994). *The Baltic Revolution: Estonia, Latvia, Lithuania and the path to independence,* (2nd ed.). New Haven, CT: Yale University Press.

Makarevich, V. (2001). Tolerance as a psychological problem. In V. Makarevičs (Ed.), *Tolerance un citas psiholoģiskas un pedagoģiskas problēmas* (pp. 29–38). Daugavpils, Latvia: Saule.

Mežs, I. (1992). *Latvieši Latvijā: Etnodemogrāfisks apskats* [Latvians in Latvia: An ethnodemographic survey]. Kalamazoo, MI: Latvian Studies Center.

Mežs, I. (2002, June 12). Latviešu valoda krustceļos [Latvian language at the crossroads] *Diena,* p. 14.

Mežs, I. (2003, September 26). Etniskie balsojumi par ES (Ethnic voting on the EU). *Diena*, p. 2.

Norgaard, O., Johannsen, L., Skak, M., & Sorensen, R. H. (1999). *The Baltic States after independence* (2nd ed.). Cheltenham, UK: Edward Elgar.

Peipina, O. (2001). Nacionālas identifikācijas un sociālas atsvešinātības problēmas sociālo pārmaiņu apstākļos [Problems of national identification and social alienation under conditions of social change]. In V. Makarevičs (Ed.), *Tolerance un citas psiholoģiskas un pedagoģiskas problēmas* (pp. 43–49). Daugavpils, Latvia: Saule.

Priedītis, A. (2001). Netoleranta iecietība [Intolerant toleration]. In V. Makarevičs (Ed.), *Tolerance un citas psiholoģiskas un pedagoģiskas problēmas* (pp. 39–42). Daugavpils, Latvia: Saule.

Realo, A., & Allik, J. (1999). A cross-cultural study of collectivism: A comparison of American, Estonian, and Russian students. *Journal of Social Psychology, 39*, 133–142.

Robinson, W. P., & Breslav, G. (1996). Academic achievement and self-concept of Latvian adolescents in a changed social context. *European Journal of Psychology in Education, 11*, 399–410.

Rozenvalds, J. (2002, November 15). Interview (in Russian). *Chas*, p. 5.

Ruža, A. (2001). Value orientations in the tolerant relations. In V. Makarevičs (Ed.), *Tolerance un citas psiholoģiskas un pedagoģiskas problēmas* (pp. 29–38). Daugavpils, Latvia: Saule.

Savoskul, S. S. (2001). *Russkiye novogo zarubezh'ia: Vybor sud'by* [Russians of the new abroad: Choice of destiny]. Moscow: Nauka.

Sebre, S. (2000). Dissociation, hostility, resentment and intolerance in relation to familial and political abuse. *Journal of Baltic Psychology, 1*, 27–45.

Sherif, M., & Sherif, C. (1966). *In common predicament: Social psychology of intergroup conflict and cooperation*. Boston: Houghton Mifflin.

Shtromas, A. (1986). The Baltic States. In R. Conquest (Ed.), *The last empire. Nationality and the Soviet future* (pp. 183–217). Stanford, CA: Hoover Institution Press.

Taagepera, R. (1993). *Estonia: Return to independence*. Boulder, CO: Westview Press.

Tsilevich, B. L. (1998). *Al'ternativa* [The alternative]. Riga, Latvia: Insight.

Ustinova, M. (1992). Causes of inter-ethnic conflict in Latvia. In K. Rupesinghe, P. King, & O. Vorkunova (Eds.), *Ethnicity and conflict in a post-Communist world. The Soviet Union, Eastern Europe, and China* (pp. 106–112). New York: St. Martin's Press.

Vaivars, J. (2000). Different nationalities' integration of first year university students. Paper presented at Fourth International Baltic Psychology Conference, Riga, Latvia.

Valk, A. (2001). *Two facets of ethnic identity: Pride and differentiation*. Tartu, Estonia: Tartu University Press.

Volkan, V. (1999). The Tree Model: A comprehensive psychopolitical approach to unofficial diplomacy and the reduction of ethnic tension. *Mind and Human Interaction, 10,* 142–210.

Volkan, V., & Harris, M. (1992). Negotiating a peaceful separation: A psychopolitical analysis of current relationships between Russia and the Baltic States. *Mind and Human Interaction,* 4(1), 20–39.

Volkan, V., & Harris, M. (1993). Vaccinating the political process: A second psychopolitical analysis of relationship between Russia and the Baltic States. *Mind and Human Interaction,* 4(4), 169–190.

von Rauch, G. (1974). *The Baltic States: The years of independence. 1917–1940.* Berkeley, CA: University of California Press.

Woods, S. A. (1998). Ethnicity and nationalism in contemporary Estonia. In C. Williams & T. D. Sfikas (Eds.), *Ethnicity and nationalism in Russia, the CIS and the Baltic States* (pp. 265–286). Aldershot, UK: Ashgate.

CHAPTER 10

The Ethnic and Cultural Process of Zhongguo (China) As a Central Kingdom

Naran Bilik, Yueh-Ting Lee, Kan Shi, and Hanh Huy Phan

Much cross-cultural research has suggested that nationality is different from, but related to, ethnicity (Hsu, 1981a; Lee, 2002b; Lee, McCauley, & Draguns, 1999; Lee, Moghaddam, McCauley & Worchel, this volume). It is uncommon for a nation to have only one ethnic group today. Typically, countries (or nation-states) have multiple ethnic and cultural groups, and different ethnic groups exist in different nations and countries. For example, the Han Chinese and Jews live in most of the world whereas in China and in Israel, there are ethnic groups other than the Han Chinese and Jews. In this chapter, we will focus on the historical process, psychological categorization, and complexity of different ethnicities (*minzu*) within China.

PART 1: A NEW LOOK AT MULTI-ETHNIC GROUPS IN CHINA TODAY

Known as the Central Kingdom for thousands of years, China (also known as Zongguo) has a long history and a rich culture. Today, China has 56 *minzu* (which used to be translated as "nationalities")[1]: 55 officially recognized national minorities plus the Han Chinese as a majority group. The Han and those 55 minority groups are called *Zhong Hua Minzu*, which is a name for a big Chinese family. The population distribution of all Chinese ethnic groups is as follows (Census Office in the State Department in China, 2002)[2]:

01 Han   (1,137,386,112)

02 Mongol   (5,813,947)

03 Hui   (9,816,805)

04 Tibetan   (5,416,021)

05 Uygur   (8,399,393)

06 Miao or Hmong   (8,940,116)

07 Yi   (7,762,272)

08 Zhuang   (16,178,811)

09 Buyei   (2,971,460)

10 Korean   (1,923,842)

11 Manchu   (10,682,262)

12 Dong   (2,960,293)

13 Yao   (2,637,421)

14 Bai   (1,858,063)

15 Tujia   (8,028,133)

16 Hani   (1,439,673)

17 Kazak   (1,250,458)

18 Dai   (1,158,989)

19 Li   (1,247,814)

20 Lisu   (634,912)

21 Wa   (396,610)

22 She   (709,592)

23 Gaoshan   (4,461 within mainland China/inland)

24 Lahu   (453,705)

25 Shui   (406,902)

26 Dongxiang   (513,805)

27 Naxi   (308,839)

28 Jingpo   (132,143)

29 Kirgiz   (160,823)

30 Tu   (241,198)

31 Daur   (132,394)

32 Mulao   (207,352)

33 Qiang   (306,072)

34 Blang	(91,882)
35 Salar	(104,503)
36 Maonan	(107,166)
37 Gelao	(579,357)
38 Xibe	(188,824)
39 Achang	(33,936)
40 Pumi	(33,600)
41 Tajik	(41,028)
42 Nu	(28,759)
43 Uzbek	(12,370)
44 Russ	(15,609)
45 Eweki	(30,505)
46 Deang	(17,935)
47 Baonan	(16,505)
48 Yugur	(13,719)
49 Jing	(22,517)
50 Tatar	(4,890)
51 Derong	(7,426)
52 Oroqen	(8,196)
53 Hezhe	(4,640)
54 Monba	(8,923)
55 Lhoba	(2,965)
56 Jino	(20,899)

These 56 formal *minzu* groups are identified and recognized as official groups today. The largest administrative ethnic minorities in China are the Zhuang in Guangxi Province (in southern China), the Manchu (in northeast China), the Hui and the Mongols (in northern China), Yi (in southwest China), the Miao (also known as the Hmong outside China, who are in southwest China), the Tibetans (west of China), and the Uygur (in Xinjiang, northwest China).

However, two issues must be clarified here. First, it is unknown how many ethnic groups constituted China before 1949, when the Communist Party took power. Second, today in Taiwan, which is considered part of

China, there are two major categories of ethnic groups: mountain people (e.g., Atayal, Seedeq, Saisiyat, Bunnun, Tsou, Kanakanabu, Rukai, Paiwan, Puyama, Ami, and Yami) and people from the plains in central Taiwan or near the Sun-Moon Lake (e.g., Kavalan, Pazeh, and Sao; Gong Ben & Wei, 2001).

Ethnicity in China has undergone complex changes. For more than 5,000 years, there have been three dilemmas or conflicts in the Central Kingdom (zongguo; see Xia, 1985; Yuan, 1988). The first conflict was between the major ethnic groups (i.e., mainly the people of Huaxia who later developed into the Han people, the Mongols, and the Manchus, both of whom once ruled the whole of China) and those non-Han groups beyond the pale of direct influences from the center. The second conflict involved the earthbound north and the seaward south. The third conflict involved China as an Eastern country and major Western powers (e.g., Britain, Russia, United States, Spain, Italy, Germany, Belgian, and Netherlands).

Ethnicity in China has been created as a result of multiple interactions within time and space, something that stands between "physics-biology" and "linguistics-psychology," and between body and soul. Related to categorization (or recategorization), ethnicity is considered "Thirdness," which is an ongoing nonstatic process. In line with Charles Peirce, ethnic Thirdness can be understood as follows: "The first is agent, the second patient, the third is the action by which the former influences the latter" (see Hoopes, 1991, pp. 186–202). The meaning of ethnicity in China resides in the marginal fuzzy areas where history, power, and culture interact. In China, ethnicity makes sense only when one (agent) contacts another (patient) through interpretation (action). Consistent with the thirdness perspective, social identification and categorization address ethnic group membership as well as cognitive and evaluative awareness of both one's group categories and identity, as proposed by Tajfel (1981). Chinese ethnic group development will be discussed later in terms of Peirce's Thirdness and Tajfel's social identity or categorization.

PART 2: ANCIENT ETHNIC RELATIONS BETWEEN THE CENTRAL KINGDOM AND PERIPHERAL GROUPS

The Central Kingdom's Ethnocentralism and In-Group–Out-Group Boundaries

According to *Shanhaijing,* or *Records of Ancient Mountains, Seas and Oceans* (Shang Hai Jing, c. 2200 B.C./1925; Xu, 1991), the ancient Central Kingdom (China) was surrounded by the Great Wilderness (*dahuang*), where half-man and half-animal barbarians lived. The people of the ethnic groups from the center of civilization confronted the barbaric people from the peripheral region. This symbolized the lingering division between normal or civilized in-group members and abnormal or uncivilized out-group members. Although Westerners misunderstood it as ethnocentrism or cultural intolerance toward the outsiders in China (e.g., Dikötter, 1992, p. 6), the book demonstrated diverse totems, lifestyles, and identities of ethnic groups outside the Central Kingdom over 4,000 years ago (Chinese Shanghaijing Scholarly Society, 1986; Xu, 1991). *Shanhaijing* recorded ethnographic diversity and various lifestyles of different tribes around the world. Diverse cultural examples include the description of a tribe of one-eyed people (*Yimuguo*), as well as a country of three-headed barbarians (*Sanshouguo*).

The Central Kingdom comprised the *"da hanzu zhuyi"* (i.e., "Hano-centralism") when the Han Chinese were in power. Ethnicity and culture were stereotypically exchangeable and interrelated (see Lee, Moghaddam, McCauley & Worchel, this volume). In ancient China, it was said that if he is not of our race or ethnicity, he is sure to have a different mind. In other words, people in different racial or ethnic groups have different behavior, cognition, and cultural beliefs and values. The central or most important culture was based on the Han's culture and values along the Yellow River as a center. Other peoples in the four directions (i.e., outside the Central Kingdom) were portrayed or stereotyped differently. Although biologically or genetically they are more similar to, than different from, each other (Cavalli-Sforza, Menozzi, & Piazza , 1994), people in the east of Han or China were stereotyped as Dong Yi, including today's Koreans (see http://ist-socrates.berkeley.edu/~korea/history.html; http://ist-socrates.berkeley.edu/~korea/Nat'nalist_Chronology.html; Sima, 100 B.C./1994); people in the south were stereotyped as Nan Man; people in the west were described as Xi Rong; and people in the north were described as Bei Di.[3] These peripheral groups were often negatively stereotyped as out-group members by those in the Central Kingdom (e.g., the Han Chinese), but both the peripheral and central ethnic groups have today shared much in common as a result of the mutual influence of thousands of years of war, trade, and migration (Lee, 2002b; Yuan, 1988), despite the apparent linguistic and cultural differences.

Socialization, acculturation and ethnic recategorization made ethnic mobility relatively easy in ancient China. As Confucius put it, "human nature is pretty similar, but cultures or customs make a difference among humans" (B. J. Yang, 1965). In other words, "People are similar by nature, but through habituation become quite different from each other" (see http://www.human.toyogakuen-u.ac.jp/~acmuller/contao/analects.htm). People outside the Central Kingdom could become Han Chinese after they learned and followed "Chinese ways." Han Chinese people could become outside barbarians if they lost their Chinese ways.

However, the Han Chinese way was not always accepted by those peripheral people because of different "human desires to be right" (Lee,
2002a, 2002b; Lee, Takako, Ottati, & Yan, this volume). Therefore, the Chinese history has been a history of ethnic conflict between those in the
Central Kingdom and those outside of it for more than 5,500 years (see
Xia, 1985; Yuan, 1988). First, for example, as per legend, there was a war
between three big ethnic groups (Emperors Yan, Huang, and Chi You)
around 6,000 years ago. Emperor Huang (also known as the Yellow Emperor) defeated the ethnic groups of Yan and Chi You, whose offspring
escaped either to the north or northeast, or to the south and southwest
(such as the Lee, Yue or Vietnamese, Hmong, Laotians; see Hsu, 1981b;
Wang 2000a, 2000b; D. Y. Wang & Song, 1998; Yuan, 1988). Although the
continent in China was united, often ethnic wars and natural disasters
(especially floods) made the offspring who migrated challenge the Central
Kingdom.

Second, the cases of Korea and Vietnam are examples of the conflict
between the Central Kingdom and its peripheral ethnic or cultural groups.
In various dynasties, different Chinese emperors in the Central Kingdom
attempted to conquer Vietnam and Korea (including both South and
North Korea) so as to enlarge the Central Kingdom. In the Korean bio-
graphical chapter 55, volume 115, of the *Grand Historical Record* by Sima
Qian (100 b.c./1994), Korea was perceived as a part of the Central Kingdom (2,200 years ago). It was called the State of Yen. The ruler of the Yen
State was designated by the emperor in the Qin and Han dynasties. Sima
Qian (100 b.c./1994) also wrote about Vietnam (Nan Yue, see vols. 113
and 116), which was perceived as a part of the Central Kingdom. The
Central Chinese Kingdom repeatedly invaded peripheral ethnic groups
(see http://ist-socrates.berkeley.edu/~korea/history.html for Korean history, and see http://www.bvom.com/resource/vn_history.asp?pContent
= Ancient_Time for Vietnamese history). When conquered or defeated,
the peripheral rulers in Korea or Vietnam became part of the Central Kingdom and were expected to pay annual tributes to the Central Kingdom.
When the Central Kingdom was weak politically or militarily, those peripheral ethnic groups often refused to pay any tributes to the Central
Kingdom and attempted to become independent. For instance, although
the Central Kingdom had much impact on peripheral Vietnamese politics,
law, education, literature, and language (http://www.1upinfo.com/coun
try-guide-study/Vietnam/vietnam13.html), the Vietnamese people as a
marginalized ethnic group sometimes refused or at other times selectively
accepted, and often modified, aspects of the Han Chinese culture, stead-
fastly maintaining a uniquely Vietnamese sense of identity and culture.
Many other peripheral ethnic groups also maintained their own identity
and cultures. People in the Central Kingdom tended to perceive themselves as superior to the peripheral groups.[4]

Third, inspection of China's history points to the confrontations between the Center and the northern peripherals, largely divided by the Great Wall. According to Arthur Waldron (1990), the widely embraced images and discourses of the Great Wall of China are the creation of a mythological history. A closer examination revealed that the Great Wall of China represents multiple efforts at wall building with variations in time and space and vicissitudes in dynastic policies toward those northern steppe groups. This history also highlights the trails of dual interactions between the Center and the northern margin, and between the Central Kingdom and other ethnic groups outside of it, such as wars between the nomadic Hun (Xiongnu or Hsiung-nu) and the sedentary Qin and Han from the second century B.C. to the second century A.D. The Great Wall, however, does not have symbolic meaning for multiple succeeding dynasties. The Mongols, who penetrated the Great Wall, might not have thought seriously about the Wall's significance.

Fourth, the Turkic empire emerged from the steppe in the sixth and seventh centuries (Yu, 1999). The Turkic people have contributed to the Sui and Tang dynasties with their political, military, cultural, and even genetic elements, giving the Central Kingdom a tremendous vitality of culture and prosperity of social life. In the Tang dynasty (about A.D. 700), the troops from the Central Kingdom were ordered and sent to fight against peripheral Turkic ethnic groups. After being defeated and driven out of Northwest Xinjiang, most of the Turks escaped west and went to the Mediterranean and Black Seas, staying in what is now Turkey. Some of the Turks stayed in central Asia (Yu, 1999). They escaped partially because of the conflict between the Central Kingdom and the peripheral Turks, who are also ancestors of the Uygurs, Khazaks, and many other northwestern groups today.

Fifth, the Central Kingdom has never comprised only the Han ethnic Chinese group. Different ethnic groups sometimes replaced each other as rulers. In the twelfth and thirteenth centuries, the Mongols in the north conquered China plus much of Europe. The Mongols changed their status as the marginal ethnic group to the Central Kingdom. After being driven out of the hinterland, the Mongols continued to challenge the Ming dynasty, who overthrew them (about A.D. 1400). People in the Ming dynasty (who were the Han Chinese) were in the Central Kingdom until they were finally conquered by the semi-nomadic Manchurians, a northeastern people who in 1644 overthrew the Ming and established the Qing in the Central Kingdom lasting for around 250 years.

Finally, outsiders in the west and southwest also defied the Central Kingdom. For example, the name K'unlun, now universally accepted as referring to the mountain system overlooking the southern edge of the Taklamakan desert from the massive heights of Tibet, was originally not a geographical name, but a tribal name associated with the edge of the

Ordos region of Inner Mongolia (Lattimore, 1951, p. 163). During the process of nation building in modern China, the *r-ma* people became Qiang, and Qiang as an ethnic name "traveled" far into the west together with the national border (M. Wang, 1999).

The differentiation between zhongguo in-group and out-group members was vague ethnically and culturally. The Han and non-Han ethnicity evolved as a flexible process. Those in the Central Kingdom tended to be ethnocentric when in power. The Han Chinese had never been in the Central Kingdom constantly; ethnic groups in and outside the Central Kingdom were changeable and moved around through contact (e.g., war or fighting).

PART 3: MODERN ETHNIC RECATEGORIZATION
AND CHANGE IN CHINA

The Crisis of the Central Kingdom and Western Challenge:
The Notion of Nation-State

It was not until the Western notion of nation-state was introduced that the boundary of the Central Kingdom was seen as clear rather than vague. Before that, the importance of the Central Kingdom (zhongguo) seems to be emphasized more than the boundaries of the Kingdom.

Since the Opium Wars in the first half of the eighteenth century, the Central Kingdom was continually exposed to unequal treaties, internal concessions, extraterritoriality, indemnity, and foreign control over the maritime customs. At the same time, however, the Central Kingdom was also exposed to foreign ideas, especially the most important conception of the nation-state. Darwinism became popular among the academic circle, who advocated for racial survival and improvement. When in power, the Han Chinese were prejudiced against Manchurians, Mongols, and other northern people. Sun Yat-sen, a Cantonese (a Yue or Nan Man) who spent many years in America and Japan, started a revolution under the slogan of "driving out the Manchurians, and restoring the Central Kingdom" (Lee, 2002a). He fought for a modern China or Central Kingdom as a nation-state. From this time on, in a dramatic turn, rice-growing southerners took away central power from grain-consuming northerners. Seaward people have won an upper hand over the earthbound people.

However, the northern nomads were unfamiliar to seaward people. It took a while before Sun Yat-sen changed his slogan to "co-existence of five peoples" (*wuzu gonghe*) after he overthrew the Manchu rulers (Lee, 2002a). Here the old puzzle of "where China ends" still existed. Dr. Sun, though recognizing the existence of the four peoples of Manchurian, Mongol, Muslim, and Tibetan origin, said, "Although there are a little over ten million non-Han in China, including Mongols, Manchus, Tibetans, and

Tatars, their number is small compared with the purely Han population. . . . China is one nationality" (Dreyer, 1976, p. 16). Facing Western invasion of the Central Kingdom, Sun Yat-sen changed his focus to the Western powers away from the ethnic groups within and outside the Central Kingdom in the East. Seaward people, led by Sun Yat-sen and others, have restored China to its Han-centered position, replacing the Manchurians who came from the North like the Mongols. Dr. Sun's notion of "race" or "nation" has undergone tremendous changes at different stages of the Chinese Revolution. His successor, Chiang Kia-shek, followed this policy by claiming that all inhabitants of China had a common ancestry (Chiang Kai-shek, 1947, pp. 12–13), which is consistent with other recent research (Lee, 2002a) that demonstrated that there was more in-group homogeneity (i.e., similarities) than heterogeneity (or differences) among them.

Marxism, the "Four Commons," and Communist Impact on Chinese Ethnicity

The loss of Jiang Kai-Shek in 1949 marked the beginning of the Chinese Communist Party, which took power over China as the Central Kingdom. Marxism, Maoism, and other communist ideologies are the foundations by which the government deals with different ethnic relations in China. Combining historical materialism with dialectical materialism, the core of Marxism had so deeply influenced China for half a century that there was no place for nationalism. Marx used the term "nation" interchangeably with "society," "state," and "ruling class" (Dreyer, 1976, p. 44). Ethno-nationalistic elements such as language and culture are secondary to international class interest and proletarian consciousness. Economic progress may eventually eliminate ethno-national boundaries. Nationalism changes nature depending on the stage of society. Nationalism is progressive for feudal society; nationalism is reactionary for bourgeois-capitalist society.

National consciousness, according to Marx, is a manifestation of the bourgeois state of society (Dreyer, 1976, p. 43). It is the Soviet leaders, however, who dealt head-on with ethnic-nationalistic problems. Following Karl Marx, Stalin formalized the "four commons" as a definition of nation:

A nation is a historically evolved, stable community of language, territory, economic life, and psychological make-up manifested in a community of culture. (Stalin, 1942, p. 12)

Stalin's four commons has one very important condition. All of the four should come together to define a nation: "It is sufficient for a single one of the characteristics to be absent and the nation ceases to be nation"

(Stalin, 1942, p. 12). By the time the Chinese Communist Party embraced Marxism, there had been a major transition from cultural centrism to social Darwinism. Marxist materialism, however, added a vital turn to the exclusive racial discourse: an inclusive nation-state is more important for political and economic progress.

The Chinese Communist Party based its own theories and practice on the Stalinist four commons in dealing with ethnic problems, but not without major modifications. After the communist takeover in 1949, under the influence of the Soviet nationality theories, the Chinese people launched a Nationality/Ethnicity Identification Program in their own way, as can be seen following.

Nationality/Ethnicity Identification Program

Why was it important to establish the Nationality/Ethnicity Identification Program in China? On the one hand, it was due to the influence of the Soviet Union (e.g., Stalin's four commons). On the other hand, no one knew exactly how many ethnic or cultural groups the People's Republic of China had in 1949 when the Chinese Communist Party took power. There were over 400 different ethnic groups that registered for a Beijing conference in the early 1950s (Q. Yang, 1998, p. 185), which was considered a big headache, or confusion, in the eyes of the Chinese government. For example, many big tribal groups and family clans who spoke different dialects claimed themselves to be ethnic minorities. It was very difficult to select representatives from ethnic groups if there were no officially recognized or identified ethnic groups. The government could not promote equality policies or provide privileges for all ethnic groups if there were hundreds of different ethnic groups.

Thus in 1953, the Chinese government invited thousands of professors and scientists in the social sciences (e.g., anthropologists, ethnologists, archaeologists, historians, linguists, psychologists, sociologists), students, cadres, and Communist Party members to participate in this program. The Chinese government sent them out to investigate national minorities. Ethnic groups were identified based on the similarities of their language, history, ancestry, physical appearance, geography, economics, cultural customs, values, beliefs, lifestyle, psychological behavior, personality, and ethnic relations. An important aspect was that those investigators conducted fieldwork, consulting with all of the different ethnic groups. The input or preference of each ethnic group played a very important role in the decision about what they were called ethnically. If there was an agreement between native self-naming and fieldwork results (or scientific standards), the identification of an ethnic group was completed. By 1979, a total of 55 national minorities had been identified as beneficiaries of preferential policies (Q. Yang, 1998, p. 186).

Ethnicity (or Nationality) Policies in China

Chinese ethnic policies were influenced by Marxism, Leninism, and Maoism for half a century, but they were quite different from the policies in the United States and in the previous Soviet Union. Before and after the Cultural Revolution, many positive policies and measures came into force: each minority group that lives in a small community was represented at the People's Congress of that locality; presses and universities for publications and ethnic language education were established. In May 1951, the central government ordered local residents to remove "all signs, place names, tablet inscriptions, and billboards that carry derogatory terms or show discrimination against minority nationalities" (Ma, 1989, p. 22).

Moreover, according to the Regional National Autonomous Law of China, which was passed by the Twentieth Conference of the Standing Committee of the Ninth National People's Congress on February 28, 2001, nationality or ethnicity policies are summarized as follows:

1. Equality and Harmony. The rights for all ethnic groups in China must be respected and protected on an equal basis. The government should promote and strengthen harmony and peace between all ethnic groups.

2. Self-Governance and Self-Autonomy. Regional self-governments are established in areas where minority nationalities (or ethnicities) live in their communities. These governments, apart from exercising the functions and powers of normal state bureaucracies, also exercise the functions and powers of autonomous self-government within the limits prescribed by the Constitution and state laws.

3. Training and Promoting Minority Leaders. It is crucially important to select and train those excellent minority people as leaders. These excellent leaders function as bridges between the minority and majority groups.

4. Freedom of Languages. Languages are part of the identity of ethnic groups. The Chinese government allows and encourages the minority groups to use and develop their own languages.

5. Respect Cultural Practices. Each minority group has its own customs or style in marriage, reproduction, funerals, food, festivals, housing, dress, holidays, taboos, and other habits. All these cultural practices must be respected.

6. Religious Beliefs. Minority groups have their own religious beliefs. These beliefs are expected not to interfere with other beliefs or society. They have religious freedom, but religions cannot be used to deceive or exploit other people.

7. Help in Their Economic and Educational Development. The government should help ethnic minority groups in their economic and educational success. This includes financial support for those minority groups.

8. Ethnic Conflict Resolution. It is imperative to gain support from a majority of people in an ethnic minority group and to isolate the very few who cause disharmony as trouble-makers or separatists.

However, a cautionary note should be made. Although these policies sound reasonable and humanitarian, the way that they are implemented may be sometimes problematic and controversial (as can be seen following). Thus, ethnic issues in China still face a lot of challenges, which will be addressed in the following section.

PART 4: CONCEPTUAL, PRACTICAL, AND THEORETICAL APPROACHES TO CHINESE ETHNICITY

Conceptual Discussion of Nationality, Ethnicity, and *Minzu*

The minority *minzu* in China should be included in a unified Chinese nation-state. China has 55 minority nationalities or ethnicities (*Zhonghua Minzu you wushiwuge shaoshuminzu*). The Chinese Communist Party granted those minority *minzu* equal status *minzu* to the Han, giving precedence to the principle of unity and equality. However, the concept of *Minzu* was historically complicated.

At an earlier stage, between the 1950s and early 1980s, a modified Soviet model, which ranked minorities hierarchically from *natsia* to *norodnost'* to tribe, was adopted in China's nationality identification project that laid emphasis on equality rather than hierarchy, granting all groups, including the majority Han, the status of *minzu*. The Soviet government, even under Stalin's rule, has given some large minority groups the status of *natsia* (nation) within the centralized federation system (USSR). Earlier on, the Communist Party of China did think of adopting the Soviet model and letting some large minority groups enjoy the status of a republic armed with the right of secession. Later, however, it gave up such thinking because of the historical and situational differences between Russia and China. The equal minority status of *minzu* at that time was an important component of the United Front in fighting against the Japanese invaders and the Kuomingtang. Additionally, in the late 1940s, both in Xinjiang and Inner Mongolia, the Uygurs and Mongolians formed their own independent governments, which were supported by the Third International headed by the Soviet Union, or by the Japanese, or on their own. All of these self-governing bodies finally joined in New China. At a later stage, with economic reform (in the 1980s), China opened up to the West and put a priority on economic development. A market economy would challenge the preferential treatment of minorities. The translation problem of *minzu* into "nationality" did not seriously arise until then.

About 10 years ago, the Foreign Ministry of China issued a document requiring the replacement of the term "nationality," the traditional standard English translation of the Chinese word *minzu*, with the term "ethnic group." The ministry argued that the term "nationality" also refers to citizenship and causes confusion. There were over 400 groups that claimed to be ethnic minority groups when the Identification Projected started, although only 55 of them were recognized and given preferential treatment, including allowance for childbirth and social promotion.

Since the mid-1990s, in many English versions of official documents, the fashionable term "ethnic group" has replaced the original English term "nationality" for *Minzu*. This is not a simple linguistic practice. Encountering the eight-power alliances in the Opium War of the 1800s, China came upon the notion of "nation-state." When interacting with the Soviets during a large part of the twentieth century, China made Marxism-Leninism its basis in theory and practice for ethnic issues. At the turn of the century, when China faced the West again, China looked at her own confusing nationalistic image in this particular mirror for the first time in many years. Struggling for a negotiated meaning of *minzu* in a rapidly changing world, China had to go over the implications of all of the classifications of ethnic groups for both conception and practice.

The translation of the Chinese term *Minzu* as a political-social practice has a history of over one hundred years. It is a history of confrontations, conflicts, compromises, and competition between China and the West. The term *Minzu* in its extant meaning did not come into Chinese discourse until late nineteenth century (Han & Li, 1985, p. 4). From the start, there had been tension or confusion between the signifier and the signified, between notion and reality, and between word and thing. During the 1960s, several scholarly discussions took place to locate the term *Minzu* and its translation in foreign languages (Han & Li, 1985, p. 3). Professor Lin Yue-hwa suggested that *Minzu* should be used for different references that point to communities at different social stages in a Western language (Lin, 1963). Whether *Minzu* should be translated to "nationality," "ethnic group," or simply *"minzu,"* is still controversial in China.[5] Minority universities, such as the Central University of (for) Nationalities in Beijing, still use the term "nationality" as the equivalent to *Minzu*. Academic debates are still ongoing.

Ethnic Challenges within the Central Kingdom Today

The ending of the cold war has finally recast ideological boundaries into state/cultural boundaries. The collapse of the Soviet block might have much to do with ethnic conflicts. Similarly, some separatists in Xinjiang (northwest of China) near Russia are trying by all means, including the setting off of bombs, to press for an independent Eastern Turkistan, "convincing Beijing that its fears regarding Uygur separatism and the increasing influence from the newly independent Turkic states on its borders were well-founded" (Gladney, 1994, p. 183), as part of pan-Turkism (Yu, 1999). The Chinese government has recently officially recognized the dangerous presence of terrorists in Xinjiang. Some scholars seem to partially argue that the market economy is one of fair play into which all should enter with equal opportunities (Li et al., 1992). Minority nationals, according to the mainstream ideology, here are expected to give up their privileges and learn from the Han for their vision, intelligence, industriousness, and especially their language (Bilik, 1992).

As an ethnic identity, language is a concern. On October 31, 2000, the Standing Committee of the Ninth National People's Congress passed a law on the legal status of Chinese as the only language for nationwide use in China. This law has also reconfirmed the legal status of the largest of the minority languages as general media within autonomous regions and administrative units. Most local officials in minority regions would choose to ignore minority languages and opt to strengthen Chinese education. For example, in Xinjiang, many Han educators, including some Uygur officials and educators, believe that Chinese should replace Uygur in university teaching.

Coinciding with the construction and excavation of new and old Han cultural symbols, the Mongols, the Uygurs, the Yis, the Naxis, and many other minorities groups are building and reviving their own languages and cultural symbols. The Genghis Khan Mausoleum has been refurbished; many new mosques have appeared; and a Yi scholar has declared that the Chinese civilization originated from the Yi ten-month calendar and its associated Yi culture (Liu, 1985). The Naxi have been rebuilding their Dongba culture,[6] and the Miao (or Hmong) have been practicing worship for their claimed ancestor Chi You, a defeated arch enemy to the Yellow King of the Han according to legend.

Terrorist attacks have taken place in Xinjiang and ethnic violence has happened in Tibet. For example, the ethnic situation in Xinjiang seems to be very salient. The Afghan conflict also has very strong implications for the political life of Xin Jiang. In the 1980s, Afghan militia drove out the Russian invaders and saved their motherland from becoming a colony of Russia. Majority Muslims regarded the victory of Afghanistan against the former Soviet Union superpower as the victory of Islam against the enemies of Islam. Muslims in China, especially in Xinjiang, regard the history of Afghan fighting with respect and admiration. These sentiments, combined with the ever-increasing migration of the Chinese community into Xinjiang and the failure of government agents to solve ethnic conflicts properly, make the ethnic issues in Xinjiang more complicated and troublesome.

In a generally stable situation, these events cause headaches for the central and local governments and relevant Han communities alike. The Central Kingdom (Zhong Guo) faces a lot of ethnic challenges before a peaceful and harmonious relationship can occur.

Theoretical Perspective 1: Ethnicity in China and Thirdness

The idea of Thirdness[7] is a contribution by Charles Pierce to the symbolic study of human society. It is more often referred to as "interpretant." Peirce holds a ternary view of a sign, which surpasses the difficulty of the Saussurian dualistic approach to language[8] in explaining ethnographic data. Foucault's notions of "discursive practice" and "power" (Dreyfus and Rabinow, 1983), Bourdieu's notions of "praxis" and "habitus" (1977, 1990), and Maturana and Varela's theory of "structural coupling"[9] all agree with the idea of Thirdness—a process that mediates between the signifier and the signified to create plausible meaning. This is the power of negotiation. Ethnicity in China, past and present, is better understood with the help of the idea of Thirdness.

Ethnicity is created along the Great Wall, a symbolic Thirdness, where nomads negotiate with peasants, where the culture of land confronts the culture of water, and from where the boundaries of a New China as an emerging modern nation-state extend to hundreds of miles beyond. Chinggis Khan and Nurhachi, the founding fathers of the Mongols and the Manchurians, both came from the Margin, and were connected to the steppe people and the Chinese sphere of civilization. They were middlemen of Thirdness and knew their opportunities well.

The physical confrontations with the eight-power alliances have changed the discourse of ethnicity in China forever. Since then, new ideas, new objects, and new images have swarmed in to adapt to and change Chinese reality, turning the Chinese discourse of ethnicity from dialogue to polyphonic discussion and disputes. People created what they lacked. Each major confrontation would bring about some core concepts, creating new landscapes. The meaning of ethnicity in China is developing and changing, the direction and degree of which depends on the ongoing, continuous interaction between the history of structural coupling (historical Thirdness) on one hand, and structural negotiations between more than two systems (discursive Thirdness) on the other hand. It is interactive and open, but remotely, sometimes closely, bounded by social memories, cultural traditions, the configuration of power relations, and the manifestation of biological needs. Although ethnicity as "technology of classification" and as one way of identifying "we-group," "you-group," and "they-group" will remain and reinvent itself, whether ethnic groups can coexist peacefully depends on their skill of negotiation and tolerance toward differences.

In summary, Chinese ethnicity is related to the evolutionary processes and complexity of the Han and non-Han groups. But ethnicity is a changing and flexible process as a result of conflict between the Central Kingdom and its marginal peoples, and between Eastern China and Western powers.

Theoretical Perspective 2: Social Identity and Recategorization

Social identity theory was originally proposed by Tajfel and Turner (Tajfel, 1981; Tajfel & Turner, 1986), but was also developed by other social psychologists (e.g., Abrams & Hogg, 1990; Brewer, 2001; Brown, 2000; Capozza & Brown, 2000; Lee, 1993; Lee & Ottati, 1995; Worchel, chap. 15 this volume). This theory holds that (ethnic) group members attempt to see their group differentiated from other groups and are motivated to preserve and achieve positive group distinctiveness, which in turns serves to protect or enhance a positive social identity for group members (Tajfel, 1981). People's individual knowledge or self-concept (that he or she belongs to certain social categories) is derived from awareness of the membership in a social group or groups and from recognition of the values and emotional significance of that membership. Group membership influences personal perception and behavior, and social interaction and group comparison also affects identity and membership.

Consistent with social identity theory by Tajfel and Turner (1986), recent studies by Samuel Gaetner, John Dividio, and their colleagues showed that categorization and recategorization enhance intergroup cooperation and reduce bias (e.g., Anastasio, Bachman, Gaertner, & Dovidio, 1997; Dovidio, Gaetner, Validzic, & Matoka, et al., 1997; Gaertner et al., 2000; Gaertner, Mann, Murrell, & Dovidio, 2001; Seta, Seta, & Culver, 2000). For example, in the experiment by Gaertner et al. (2001), recategorization treatments induced members of two three-person groups to conceive of memberships either as one six-person group or as six separate individuals. Their findings revealed that the one-group and separate-individuals conditions, as compared with the control condition (i.e., the aggregate compared with a control condition designed to maintain initial group boundaries), reduced intergroup bias. Furthermore, these recategorized conditions reduced bias in different ways. The one-group representation reduced bias primarily by increasing the attractiveness of former outgroup members, whereas the separate-individuals representation primarily decreased the attractiveness of former in-group members.

Social identity theory and the recategorization model account for at least three cases related to Chinese ethnic processes, complexity, and development. First, Confucian cultural values facilitate Chinese ethnic identity formation and recategorization. As Confucius put it, "People are similar by nature, but through habituation become quite different from each other" (see http://www.human.toyogakuen-u.ac.jp/~acmuller/contao/analects.htm). Those people outside the Central Kingdom could become the Han Chinese after they learned and followed Chinese ways. The Han Chinese would become outside barbarians if they lost their Chinese ways. This is just an example of recategorization and identity formation.

Second, Sun Yat-sen perceived the Manchu ethnic group and the Manchu government as his enemies before 1911. When he succeeded in overthrowing the Manchu government (i.e., the Qing dynasty), he recategorized or redefined all different ethnic groups in China as in-group members when Western powers invaded China. Facing Western invasion of the Central Kingdom, Sun Yat-sen changed his focus to the Western powers from the ethnic groups within and outside the Central Kingdom in the East (Lee, 2002a). Sun Yat-sen's notion of race or nation has undergone tremendous changes at different stages of his life.

Third, regarding the Chinese Nationality/Ethnicity Identification Program, over 400 ethnic groups in the 1950s were recategorized into 56 ethnic groups (the Han Chinese as the majority and 55 Chinese minorities). In a way, the program is consistent with social identity development and enhances intergroup cooperation and reduces intergroup bias. According to Turner (1984), five distinctive features of group behavior include: (1) perceived similarities between members; (2) mutual attraction and esteem (cohesiveness); (3) cooperation and altruism; (4) shared uniformities in attitudes and behavior (collective or unified actions and beliefs, conformity to group norms, etc.); and (5) emotional contagion and empathy (p. 528). The categorization and recategorization process (e.g., Chinese Nationality/Ethnicity Identification Program) directly enhances perceived similarities and harmony between group members as a function of shared self-stereotyping and membership.

PART 5: CONCLUSION[10]

When people from various ethnic and cultural groups are in contact, auto-stereotypes (i.e., self-perception) and hetero-stereotypes (i.e., perception of others or out-group members) occur automatically (Kluckhohn & Murray, 1965; Lee, 2001; Lee & Ottati, 1993; Lee et al., 1999; Lee, Jussim, & McCauley, 1995; Ottati & Lee, 1995). This is because people are different in many ways for different purposes (Ichheiser, 1949, 1972; F. L. K. Hsu, 1981a; Lee, 1996; Mead, 1953; Zhang et al., 1999). Ethnic identity or group personality (including national characteristics and stereotypes) may be developed based on those actual or perceived differences, for example, social differentiation, social comparison, and social categorization and recategorization. Further, the formation or development of ethnicity or ethnic identity/stereotypes is perhaps an ongoing process (similar to Thirdness, as discussed earlier). Ethnic identity in the Central Kingdom (or zhongguo) is no exception.

Because the Central Kingdom was repeatedly defeated during the Opium Wars (1840s), China started to embrace in conception and practice the nation-state ideology. Sun Yat-sen and the Communists redefined or recategorized the Central Kingdom and its ethnic configuration in their own ways. New versions of taxonomy of ethnicities or *Minzu*, which came out as a result of a market economy, modernization, and cultural interaction, are posing challenges to ethnic and cultural identity within the Central Kingdom (zhongguo).

Rooted in the Thirdness theory and social recategorization model, the concept of ethnicity (or ethnic identity), or zhongguo culture, is a changing process (i.e., Thirdness) in China. To understand it, we must first understand Chinese history, behavior, beliefs, and politics. This very process of change and flexibility shows that there is no ethnic group free from the influence of other ethnic groups. Ethnographically, the concept of zhongguo Ren (i.e., Chinese), which includes the Han, the Mongols, the Manchurians, the Zhuang, the Hmong, the Tibetan, the Uygur, and many others, was a symbolic and evolutionary process of almost all ethnic groups in China (Lee, 2002a).

This process has been the case for thousands of years. Specifically, China's history has been a process of conflict, negotiation, change, invention, imagination, group identification, comparison, social categorization, and recategorization. Although such a process is increasingly open and accessible to the world, it is far from being easily and clearly comprehensible. The boundaries of the Central Kingdom (or zhongguo) are changeable. In addition to the Han, other ethnic groups, including the Mongols and the Manchurians, have established their central reign in the Central Kingdom, becoming rulers of China and all of the ethnic groups within its boundaries. The center and the peripheral were relative and mutual, depending on how they are perceived and how they are categorized and recategorized with regard to their ethnic identity or membership.

ACKNOWLEDGMENTS

Thanks are extended to Ms. Fan Hongxia who helped in the project and Stephen Worchel, Clark McCauley, Fathali Moghaddam, Fredrick Slocum, and Kimberly O'Farrell who offered us many insightful comments on previous versions of this chapter.

NOTES

1. The translation itself is a "translingual practice" (Liu, 1995), closely linked to the history, power, and culture of China. Although China used to distinguish peoples in the world by the yardstick of "civilizations," this was replaced with the Western conception of sovereignty in modern history. For more discussion on *Minzu*, please refer to part 4 of this chapter.

2. Census Office in the State Department in China and Bureau of Chinese Population Statistics (2002). The order of the ethnic groups in the following list are based on the original Chinese.

3. Although these names may contain a negative meaning for some marginal groups, the original names might be related to the characteristics of each group. For example, people in the West or East were associated with the usage of their weapons (Hsu, 1981b; Sima, 100 B.C./1994). More information can be found in Hsu's book (1981b).

4. After being dominated by the Central Kingdom for a long time, the ethnic Vietnamese group gained political (and tributary) independence from the Central Kingdom. Vietnam's long-standing association with China provides a testimony to the fierce sense of separate identity and culture the Vietnamese have always felt, a trait that would evolve into a strong sense of nationalism that would, after traumatic interventions by the French and Americans, result in the unified nation of Vietnam.

5. Actually, the ambiguity of *Minzu* is a positive cure for either Hano-centralism or discrimination based on sociocultural development, which might hurt the feelings of the minority *Minzu*. Between the 1960s and 1990s, the official English translation of *Minzu* has always been "nationality" for both Han and minorities. When the last nationality, Jinuo, was officially recognized, "55" seemed to be fixed with political input and preferential treatment as the quantity of national minorities in China. This administrative version of 55 nationalities is now in conflict with the number of claims for ethnic identities from the locals. In Taiwan, the local government recognized over 10 ethnic groups, and on the mainland, groups belong to the single category of Gaoshan; in Hong Kong and China's coastal regions, people use *zuqun* (ethnic group) to refer the local subgroups of Hans, such as the Hakka.

6. Dongba, once used by ancestors of the Naxi, a southwestern minority group in China, is a pictographic writing that dates back to antique times.

7. "Thirdness" is more often referred to as "interpretant" by Peirce. Interpretant is an abstract conception that denotes the open process of interpretation.

8. Saussure (1916/1959) regards a sign as a twofold entity of signifier and signified, or form and meaning.

9. "We speak of structural coupling whenever there is a history of recurrent interactions leading to the structural congruence between two (or more) systems" (Maturana and Varela, 1998, p. 75). One of several illustrations of their view is of the protozoan-engulfing amoeba: the presence of the protozoan generates a concentration of substances in the environment. These substances are capable of interacting with the amoeba membrane, triggering changes in the consistency of the protoplasm, which results in the formation of a pseudo pod.

10. This chapter presents brief statistics only. The detailed results, including specific tests for group differences, are available upon request. To

save space, they are not presented here. Also, references to the Koreans here primarily means South Koreans.

REFERENCES

Abrams, D., & Hogg, M. A. (1990). *Social identity theory: Constructive and critical advances*. New York: Springer-Verlag.

Anastasio, P., Bachman, B., Gaetner, S., & Dovidio, J. (1997). Categorization, recategorization and common in-group identity. In R. Spears, P. Oakes, N. Ellemers, and S. A. Haslam. (Eds.), *The social psychology of stereotyping and group life* (pp. 236–256). Malden, MA: Blackwell.

Bilik, N. (1992). Language education, intellectuals and symbolic representation: Being an Urban Mongolian in a new configuration of social evolution. In W. Safran (Ed.), *Nationalism and ethnoregional identities in China* (pp. 47–67). London: Frank Cass.

Bourdieu, P. (1977). *Outline of a theory of practice*. Cambridge, UK: Cambridge University Press.

Bourdieu, P. (1990). *The logic of practice*. Stanford, CA: Stanford University Press.

Brewer, M. B. (2001). The many faces of social identity: Implications for political psychology. *Political Psychology, 22*, 115–125.

Brown, R. (2000). Social identity theory: Past achievements, current problems and future challenges. *European Journal of Social Psychology, 30*(6), 745–778.

Capozza, D., & Brown, R. (2000). *Social identity processes: Trends in theory and research*. London, UK: Sage.

Cavalli-Sforza, L. L, Menozzi, P., & Piazza, A. (1994). *History and geography of human genes*. Princeton, NJ: Princeton University Press.

Census Office in the State Department in China and Bureau of Chinese Population Statistics. (2002). *Census Statistics Chinese 2000 Population*. Beijing, China: Chinese Statistical Publishing House.

Chiang, Kai-shek. (1947). *China's destiny* (Wang Chung-hui, Trans.). New York: Macmillan.

Chinese Shanhaijing Scholarly Society. (1986). *New findings of Shanhaijing*. Chengdu, China: Sichuan Social Sciences Publishing House. (In Chinese)

Dikötter, F. (1992). *The discourse of race in modern China*. Stanford, CA: Stanford University Press.

Dovidio, J. F., Gaertner, S., Validzic, A., Matoka, K. et al., (1997). Extending the benefits of recategorization: Evaluations, self-disclosure, and helping. *Journal of Experimental Social Psychology, 33*(4), 401–420.

Dreyer, J. (1976). *China's forty million*. Cambridge, MA and London: Harvard University Press.

Dreyfus, H., & Rabinow, P. (1983). *Michel Foucault: Beyond structuralism and hermeneutics* (2nd ed.). Chicago: The University of Chicago Press.

Gaertner, S., Mann, J., Murrell, A., & Dovidio, J. F. (2001). Reducing intergroup bias: The benefits of recategorization. In M. Hogg & D. Abrams (Eds.), *Intergroup Relations* (pp. 356–369). Philadelphia: Psychology Press.

Gaetner, S., Dovidio, J. F., Banker, B., Houlette, M., Johnson, K., & McGlynn, E. (2000). Reducing intergroup conflict: From superordinate goals to decategorization, recategorization, and mutual differentiation. [Special issue: One hundred years of group research]. *Group Dynamics, 4*(1), 98–114.

Gladney, D. (1994). Ethnicity in China: The new politics of difference. In W. Joseph (Ed.), *China briefing* (pp. 171–192). Boulder, CO: Westview Press.

Gong Ben, Y. R., & Wei, G. B. (2001). Native ethnic groups in Taiwan. Taiwan: Cheng Xin.

Han, J., & Li, Y. (1985). *Textual materials for the origin of the Chinese term Minzu* [*Hanwen Minzu yi ci kao yuan ziliao*]. Beijing, China: Department of Nationality Theories, Institute of Nationality Studies, Chinese Academy of Social Sciences.

Hoopes, J. (Ed.). (1991). *Peirce on signs*. Chapel Hill, NC, and London: The University of North Carolina Press.

Hsu, F. L. K. (1981a). *Americans and Chinese: Passage to differences*. Honolulu, HI: University Press of Hawaii.

Hsu, P. S. S. (1981b). *Chinese discovery of America*. Hong Kong: Southeast Asian Research Institute.

Ichheiser, G. (1949). Sociopsychological and cultural factors in race relations. *American Journal of Sociology, 54*, 395–401.

Ichheiser, G. (1972). *Appearances and realities: Misunderstanding in human relations*. San Francisco: Jossey-Bass.

Kluckhohn, C., & Murray, H. (1965). *Personality in nature, society and culture* (3rd ed.). New York: Knopf.

Lattimore, O. (1951). *Inner Asian frontiers of China* (2nd ed.). New York: Captol Publishing Co., Inc. Irvington-on-Hudson, and American Geographical Society.

Lee, Y.-T. (1993). In-group preference and homogeneity among African American and Chinese American students. *The Journal of Social Psychology, 133*(2), 225–235.

Lee, Y.-T. (1996). It is difference, not prejudice, that engenders intergroup tension: Revisiting Ichheiserian research. *American Psychologist 51*(3), 267–268.

Lee, Y.-T. (2001). *"Unique" similarities between Ancient Chinese and Native American cultures: Paleo-psychological beliefs and cultural meanings beyond time and space*. Paper presented at the Annual Conference of

Association of Chinese Social Scientists (in USA) at the University of Bridgeport, October 26–27, Bridgeport, CT.

Lee, Y.-T. (2002a). *Dr. Sun Yat-sen's ethnic desire to be right and strengthening Zhongguo Minzu spiritual beliefs system.* Paper presented at the conference of the China Reunification Alliance in July in Taipei, Taiwan, China.

Lee, Y.-T. (2002b). *Psychological analyses of ethnicities and beliefs: Sino-American cultural comparison.* Unpublished book manuscript (in Chinese). Mankato, Minnesota State University.

Lee, Y.-T., Jussim, L., & McCauley, C. (1995). *Stereotype accuracy: Toward appreciating group differences.* Washington, DC: American Psychological Association.

Lee, Y.-T., McCauley, C. R., & Draguns, J. (Eds.). (1999). *Personality and person perception across cultures.* Mahwah, NJ: Lawrence Erlbaum Associates.

Lee, Y.-T., & Ottati, V., (1993). Determinants of in-group and out-group perception of heterogeneity: An investigation of Chinese-American stereotypes. *Journal of Cross-Cultural Psychology, 24,* 298–318.

Lee, Y.-T., & Ottati, V. (1995). Perceived group homogeneity as a function of group membership salience and stereotype threats. *Personality and Social Psychology Bulletin 21*(6), 612–621.

Li, R. et al. (1992). *Shaoshuminzu hanyu jiaoxue yanjiu* [A study of Chinese teaching for minorities]. Urumqi, China: Xinjiang Education Publishing House.

Lin, Y. (1963). *Guanyu "Minzu" yici de shiyong he yiming de wenti* [About the problems of the synonyms and the use of the term *Minzu*]. *MinzuLishi Yanjiu, 2,* 171–190.

Liu, Lydia H. (1995). *Translingual practice.* Stanford, CA: Stanford University Press.

Ma, Y. (Ed.). (1989). *China's minority nationalities.* Beijing, China: Foreign Languages Press.

Maturana, H., & Varela, F. (1998). *The tree of knowledge* (Rev. ed.). Boston & London: Shambhala.

Mead, M. (1953). National character. In A. L. Kroeber (Ed.), *Anthropology today* (pp. 642–667). Chicago, IL: University of Chicago Press.

Ottati, V., & Lee, Y.-T. (1995). Accuracy: A neglected component of stereotype research. In Y.-T. Lee, L. Jussim, & C. McCauley (Eds.), *Stereotype accuracy: Toward appreciating group differences* . Washington, DC: The American Psychological Association.

Saussure, F. (1916/1959). *Course in general linguistics.* New York: McGraw-Hill.

Seta, C. E., Seta, J. J., & Culver, J. (2000). Recategorization as a method for promoting intergroup cooperation: Group status matters. *Social Cognition, 18*(4), 354–376.

Shan Hai Jing [Record of mountains and seas/oceans]. (c. 2200 B.C./1925). Shanghai: Jing Zhang Press. (In Chinese)

Sima, Q. (100 B.C./1994). *Shi Ji* [*The Grand Historical Record*]. Yin Chuan, China: Nin Xia People's Publishers. (In Chinese)

Stalin, J. (1942). *Marxism and the national question: Selected writings and speeches.* New York: International Publishers.

Tajfel, H. (1981). *Human groups and social categories.* Cambridge, UK: Cambridge University Press.

Tajfel, H., & Turner, J. C. (1986). The social identity theory of intergroup behavior. In S. Worchel & W. G. Austin (Eds.), *Psychology of intergroup relations* (pp. 7–24). Chicago, IL: Nelson-Hall.

Turner, J. C. (1984). Social identification and psychological group formation. In H. Tajfel (Ed.), *Social dimension* (Vol. 2, pp. 518–538). London: Cambridge University Press.

Waldron, A. (1990). *The Great Wall of China.* Cambridge, UK: Cambridge University Press.

Wang, D. Y. (2000a). *Chinese dragon culture.* Beijing, China: Chinese Society's Press. (In Chinese)

Wang, D. Y. (2000b). *The Times of Shan Huang Wu Di.* Beijing, China: Chinese Society's Press.

Wang, D. Y., & Song, B. Z. (1998). *Illustrations of American totems.* Beijing, China: People's Art Publishers. (In Chinese).

Wang, M. (1999). Genji Gushi: Qiangzu de Dixiong Gushi [A history of root: The sibling story of the Qiang]. In Yinggui Huang (Ed.), *Shijiang, Lishi yü Jiyi [Time, history and memory]*), (pp. 283–341). Taipei: Institute of Ethnology, Academia Sinica.

Xia, N. (1985). *Origins of Chinese civilization.* Beijing: Chinese Archaeological Publishing House. (In Chinese)

Xu, X. Z. (1991). *The origin of the book Shan Hai Jing.* Wuhan, China: Wuhan Publishing House. (In Chinese)

Yang, B. J. (1965). *Lunyu (Confucian aphorism) and its interpretation.* Beijing: Chinese Book Publishing Bureau.

Yang, Q. (1998). *Min Zu Xue Gai Lun* [Introduction to ethnology]. Shanghai, China: Shanghai Social Science Publishing House. (In Chinese)

Yu, J.-H. (1999). *Min Zu Zhu Yi* [Nationalism]. Shanghai, China: Xuelin Publishing House. (In Chinese)

Yuan, K. (1988). *Chinese history of mythology.* Shanghai, China: Shanghai Literature. (In Chinese)

Zhang, K., Lee, Y.-T., Liu, F., & McCauley, C. (1999). Chinese-American differences: A Chinese view. In Y.-T. Lee, C. McCauley, & J. Dragnus (Eds.), *Personality and person perceptions across cultures* (pp. 127–138). Mahwah, NJ: Lawrence Erlbaum Associates.

CHAPTER 11

Perception and Interpretation of Terrorism, Justice, and Conflict: Three Cultures and Two Sides of One Coin

Yueh-Ting Lee, Seiji Takaku, Victor Ottati, and Gonggu Yan

How do people see and interpret violence or conflict when it occurs? Why does it occur again and again? Although these are fundamental questions about human nature, psychologists and other social scientists cannot afford to avoid these tough and painful issues. We may not be able to build a perfect utopia, but it is imperative that we seek to increase understanding of human conflict and develop strategies to reduce it. In this chapter, we will focus on how people of different cultures see and interpret the events surrounding September 11, 2001 (for more detail, see Barringer, 2001). For example, how do people perceive Americans bombing in Afghanistan? Is the September 11 attack perceived as a heroic or a terrorist behavior? Is the American military response to this event a terrorist act or a necessary and justified reaction? Who should be responsible for the conflict or violence that has occurred?

Simply speaking, we attempt to address three general questions in the current chapter. First, we briefly report the results of an exploratory survey regarding perceptions and interpretations of the 9–11 event, as well as perceptions of what constitutes "terrorism" and "justice" in three different cultures (i.e., Christian, Chinese, and Islamic).[1] The results of this exploratory analysis lead directly to our second concern, namely, why do these three cultures perceive and interpret the 9–11 event, terrorism, conflict, and violence differently? In this second section, we consider the universal nature of the human need for justice as well as cultural differences that might account for intercultural differences in the way that terrorism, justice, and conflict are perceived. Finally, we conclude by highlighting some important lessons to be gleaned from this research.

PART 1: EXPLORATORY SURVEY RESULTS
REGARDING PERCEPTIONS OF TERRORISM,
JUSTICE, AND CONFLICT IN THREE CULTURES

Approximately two months after the 9–11 event in 2001, participants were recruited from three different cultures (N = 79 self-identified Christian Americans; N = 54 Islamic subjects from Pakistan, Egypt, and Bangladesh; and N = 93 Chinese students primarily from China). All of these participants were college students whose age ranged from 18 to 26 years.[2] The American sample was recruited from a midwestern university, and the Islamic sample was obtained from a midwestern university's foreign student office. The Chinese sample was recruited primarily from a university in Mainland China. The Christian American sample was recruited from an introductory psychology class. The Chinese students were recruited from a psychology class and also from students in the libraries. The Islamic students were recruited by an Islamic graduate assistant who approached them in the dorms, the university library, or the cafeteria. There were no significant differences among the three samples with regard to age, gender, or education. Thus, this sampling strategy enabled us to compare the three cultures while controlling for these factors.

1. How Was the Survey Administered?

A "Terrorism, Justice and Peace" questionnaire was administered to the three samples. The response scales of the questionnaire items ranged from 1 (strongly disagree) to 5 (strongly agree). The survey contained three basic sections, with numerous filler items inserted throughout to hide the purpose of the study. In Section 1, the items included "The USA may be also responsible for what happened on September 11," "I think that the attackers on September 11 should be condemned," "The USA's bombing of Afghanistan and other countries should be condemned," "I think it was a heroic act that the American air-fighters and soldiers dropped bombs on other countries (e.g., in Afghanistan, Iraq, or Yugoslavia)," "I think it was a heroic act that non-American attackers (probably Muslims) used Boeing airplanes to attack the World Trade Center and Pentagon," "I think it was a terrorist behavior that non-American attackers (probably Muslims) used Boeing airplanes to attack the World Trade Center and Pentagon," and "I think it was a terrorist behavior when the American air-fighters and soldiers dropped bombs onto other countries (e.g., Afghanistan, Iraq, or Yugoslavia)." Section 2 of the survey included nine items that are described in detail in Table 11.1.

Section 3 of the survey actually contained a pre-postexperimental design that enabled us to examine how attitudes toward the 9–11 event and related issues might be impacted by exposure to an ancient metaphor or

Table 11.1
Mean Tri-cultural Perception of War/Violence, Peace, and Justice

Item No.	Eastern (e.g., Chinese) (N = 92)	Judeo-Christian (e.g., White Americans) (N = 79)	Islamic (e.g. Pakistan Egypt) (N = 54)	F-values (df = 2, 222)	p <
1.	2.41a	2.91b	1.94c	11.49	.000
2.	1.46 a	2.06 b	1.50 a	7.81	.001
3.	1.96 a	3.29 b	2.02 a	33.22	.000
4.	3.04 a	3.53 b	3.04 a	3.30	.04
5.	2.74 a	3.80 b	3.20 a	14.80	.000
6.	1.63 a	2.43 b	1.78 a	13.51	.000
7.	3.45 a	2.18 b	3.50 a	34.06	.000
8.	2.48 a	3.44 b	2.59 a	14.85	.000
9.	3.43 a	2.71 b	3.89 a	28.00	.000

Notes:

Measure of the Perception of War/Violence, Peace, and Justice:

By Tukey HSD test, mean numbers with different subscripts mean they differ at least at the alpha level of .05. Higher numbers mean more agreement.

1. If justice is done, America has to wage a world war against Osama bin Laden and Taliban or other Islamic people in the Middle East.

2. It does not matter how many civilians in Afghanistan will be killed as long as America can get rid of those attackers involving the 9–11 event.

3. I think violence (or war in Afghanistan) is justifiable, though violence may produce more violence.

4. It is just to punish or kill those who were directly or indirectly related to the 9–11 event.

5. It is important for America to fight back at all cost against those attackers involving the 9–11 event.

6. The best way for America to deal with terrorism is to act just as tough (including using mass destruction weapons—e.g., nuclear or biological weapons in return) as they do.

7. It is the American government's fault that the 9–11 event occurred.

8. It is imperative to fight against those who attacked USA, no matter how long this war lasts.

9. The USA's bombing on Afghanistan and other countries should be condemned.

analogy. In this section, participants responded to the following three items: (1) "The USA may be also responsible for what happened on September 11"; (2) "I think that the attackers on September 11 should be 100% (or fully) condemned"; and (3) "I think it is unwise for the USA to station American troops for their own interest in the Middle East (e.g., in Saudi Arabia) and elsewhere." Again, these questions were embedded within a section containing multiple filler items. We then asked our participants to read and consider the following analogy that was derived from an ancient writing and to answer the questions that follow:[3]

A problem, no matter what kind, is a manifest effect produced by the combination of an inherent and external cause. Here is a glass of water. *Let's suppose that there is some sediment at the bottom. If you stir the contents, the water will become dirty. In this case, the sediment is the inherent cause and the act of stirring is the external cause.* Suppose we have a husband (or Group X) and wife (or Group Y) who lead a cat-and-dog existence. Each insists the other is to blame. That's like saying, "because you stirred the water, it became dirty!" *But, no matter how hard you stir, if there is no sediment the water will remain clear. People often fail to notice the sediment in their own lives and simply accuse others of stirring up the water. In other words, they are not aware that the cause of their unhappiness lies within themselves and that they are merely experiencing the effect of that cause after it has been activated by someone else.* (Emphasis added.)(Causton, 1995, p. 170)

After reading this analogy, participants responded to each of the following five questions on a scale ranging from 1 (strongly disagree) to 5 (strongly agree).

a. Based on the above ancient analogy, I think the USA may be also responsible for what happened on September 11 (i.e., US responsibility).

b. Based on the above ancient analogy, I think that the attackers on September 11 should be 100% (or fully) condemned (i.e., condemning 9–11 attack).

c. Based on the above ancient analogy, I think it unwise for the USA to station American troops for their own interest in the Middle East (e.g., in Saudi Arabia) and elsewhere (i.e., US unwise stationing).

2. What Results Were Obtained from the Survey?

Effect of Culture on Perceptions of Violence and Responsibility

The results of this cross-cultural survey demonstrated that participants from different cultures perceived and interpreted the 9–11 event and other violence in different ways. For example, when participants were presented with "I think it was a terrorist behavior when the American air-fighters and soldiers dropped bombs onto other countries (e.g., Afghanistan, Iraq, or Yugoslavia)," Islamic ($M = 3.68$) and Chinese ($M = 3.88$) participants were more likely to agree than Christian Americans [$M = 2.84$, F (2, 220) $= 14.36$, $p < .001$]. The post-hoc Tukey HSD (Honestly Significant Difference) test did not show any significant difference between Islamic and Chinese respondents ($p > .05$), who differed from the Christian Americans ($ps < .05$).

Intercultural differences also emerged in response to the statement "I think it was a terrorist behavior that non-American attackers (probably Muslims) used Boeing airplanes to attack the World Trade Center and Pentagon." In this case, Christian Americans agreed significantly more ($M = 4.35$) than did the Chinese ($M = 4.03$), and the Chinese, in turn, agreed significantly more than did the Islamic respondents [$M = 3.69$, F (2, 220) $= 5.02$, $p < .01$]. The post-hoc Tukey HSD revealed that all of these means differed, $ps < .05$.

Should the USA also be held responsible for what happened on September 11? Although Christian Americans were not likely to endorse this item ($M = 2.80$), Chinese ($M = 3.99$) and Islamic ($M = 3.80$) participants were more likely to believe that the United States should bear some of the responsibility for what happened on 9–11 [F (2, 220) $= 29.07$, $p < .001$]. The post-hoc Tukey HSD test did not show any significant difference between Islamic and Chinese respondents ($p > .05$), who differed from Christian Americans ($ps < .05$).

Effect of Culture on Perceptions of War, Peace, and Justice

The data in Table 11.1 reveal significant intercultural differences with regard to perceptions of justice and war and how these relate to the 9–11 attack. The average response to these items suggests that Christian Americans ($M = 3.19$) were more likely to favor fighting back for "justice" and punishing the terrorists than were the Chinese ($M = 2.28$) or Islamic ($M = 2.29$) participants [F (2, 221) $= 41.51$, $p < .0001$]. The post-hoc Tukey HSD test did not show any significant difference between Islamic and Chinese respondents ($p > .05$), who differed from Christian Americans ($ps < .05$). Specific results can be examined in Table 11.1.

The results in Table 11.1 also demonstrate that both Islamic and Chinese participants strongly opposed American bombing and killing in Afghanistan, whereas Christian Americans tended to be more accepting of such acts.

Effects of Culture and Exposure to an Ancient Analogy

We performed a 3 (cultures) × 2 (before and after reading the ancient analogy) multivariate analysis of variance (MANOVA) on the three dependent measures assessed before and after participants read the ancient analogy. Using the Wilks' Lambda test (Λ), there was no significant interaction between culture and pre- and post-reading [F (2, 218) $= 1.51$,

$p = .18$, ns]. This means that the ancient analogy impacted the three cultures similarly. However, there was a significant main effect or difference between pre-reading and post-reading [$F(2, 218) = 12.24, p = .0001$]. The results in Table 11.2 show that (1) participants across all three cultures were more likely to agree that Americans should also be held responsible for the 9–11 events after reading the ancient analogy than before reading it, (2) participants were less likely to fully condemn the 9–11 attackers after reading the analogy than before reading it, and (3) participants were less likely to endorse Americans stationing their troops in the Middle East after reading than before reading the ancient analogy. Thus, the analogy appears to have increased the likelihood that participants would agree the conflict was caused by both parties (i.e., "it takes two to tango" in the Western sense, or "one palm cannot clap" in an Eastern sense).

PART 2: WHY WERE TERRORISM, JUSTICE, AND CONFLICT SEEN DIFFERENTLY?

1. The Human Need for Justice

Before we discuss why participants from three cultures saw and interpreted terrorism, justice, and violence differently, we would like to use the example of how people judge President George W. Bush. Is Mr. George W. Bush a good leader? The answer to this question will vary tremendously among people within and across cultures. Within the USA, liberal democrats will tend to evaluate Bush's leadership performance negatively,

Table 11.2
Conflict Is Caused by Two Parties: It Takes Two to Tango

| | Reading the Ancient Analogy | | | | |
| | Before | After | Λ-value | F-value | p < |
	Mean (SD)	Mean (SD)		(df =1, 218)	
US Responsibility	3.53 (1.18)	3.90 (1.25)	.952	11.08	.000
Condemning 9-11 attack	3.86(1.14)	3.49 (1.36)	.937	14.76	.000
US unwise stationing	3.40 (1.20)	3.66 (1.30)	.975	5.64	.01

Note: Higher scores mean more agreement.

whereas conservative Republicans will tend to evaluate his performance quite positively. In the eyes of some people residing in Muslim culture, George W. Bush is seen as a devil. One person's meat is another person's poison.

Although human perceptions vary across individuals and cultures, people from all cultures share a desire to be "right" (DBR) in terms of behavior and judgment. Of course, a Christian is apt to believe that the Christian belief system is superior to other religious belief systems. It is "right" to practice Christianity. Likewise, a devout Muslim tends to see the Muslim faith as superior to other spiritual belief systems. It is "right" to follow Islamic religion. The same can be said of Hindus, Buddhists, Daoists (or Taoists), Confucianists, or any other spiritual group. However, all of these spiritual groups share a DBR, both spiritually and psychologically. That is, all of these groups share a concern with believing in what is right and acting in a fair and righteous manner (Lee, Albright, & Malloy, 2001; Lee, Kleinbach, Hu, Peng, & Chen, 1996). In some instances, this concern motivates aggressive or violent behavior (Geen, 1998).

Can we set universally acceptable criteria for what is right, just, good, or evil for all human behavior and judgment? Perhaps we cannot do so. Different cultures have different criteria or standards (e.g., norms, values, and belief systems) for what is right or wrong. What is right or acceptable in one culture may not necessarily be right or acceptable in another culture. The Holy Bible may be the right book for Christians to follow, whereas the Qur'an may be the right book for Muslims to follow. For traditional Chinese, books such as the *Analects of Confucius* or the *Dao De Jing* may contain the right answer to many life questions. Likewise, for Buddhists, reading the *Lotus Sutra* may provide the right answer in their struggle for enlightenment. These holy books provide their followers with knowledge, beliefs, and a value system that affects their behavior and judgment.

The DBR can be seen as a need for fairness or justice. Thus, a related question involves whether we can provide universally acceptable standards for justice for all people around the world. Unfortunately, this is not likely to be easily accomplished. Although all human beings share a general desire for justice, specific standards of justice are subjective. That is, "justice standards are a socially created reality" (Tyler & Smith, 1998, p. 595), which is culturally specific (Lee et al., 1996; Lee, Pepitone, & Albright, 1997). Of course, a tendency to justify in-group favoritism might elicit divergent perceptions of an event even when comparing the perceptions of different groups that share a common standard of justice. In the case of 9–11, however, we speculate that intercultural differences in the interpretation of this event are rooted (at least partly) in cultural differences regarding specific standards of justice.

2. Not Necessarily Prejudice but Perceived Differences May Lead to Human Conflict

What occurred on September 11, 2001, was seen as a terrorist act by some participants but was also seen as a heroic act by other participants. Why is one person's meat another person's poison? Different people have different tastes and perceptions. Human beings are extremely diverse and cultures can differ from each other in fundamental ways. Conflicts may not always originate from blind prejudice (i.e., negative attitudes toward members of certain groups; see Lee, Jussim, & McCauley, 1995). To the contrary, actual or perceived group differences (Ichheiser, 1948, 1970; Lee, 1996; Lee et al., 1995; Lee, McCauley, & Draguns, 1999), or a lack of tolerance for these differences, may often constitute a more fundamental cause of conflict.[4] We are different in numerous respects and for many reasons (e.g., socioculturally, economically, spiritually, psychologically, politically, and perhaps genetically). Perhaps, as John Lennon's song "Imagine" suggests, the answer is to transcend or simply ignore these differences. The lyrics suggest that the transcendence of perceived or actual differences among different groups (or categories), can lead to a reduction of conflict and a life of peace.

John Lennon imagined a world that transcends categorization and differentiation. Unfortunately, it may be impossible for people to completely transcend, suppress, or ignore real category differences (e.g., ethnicity, race, religion, class, nationality). Furthermore, even if one controls for differences in culture, race, ethnicity, nationality, class, and religion, there are thousands of other differences that differentiate groups of people (e.g., gender, language, age, height, weight, personality type, motivation for power, birthday, birthplace, political attitudes). Even within an all White, European, Christian, and middle-class culture, differences between various subgroups are apt to engender conflict. This is especially true when people fail to understand or appreciate their differences. As Ichheiser (1948) articulated long ago:

This, to my mind, should be the basis of an intelligent intercultural and interracial education. For denying differences which are actually there means making propaganda for misunderstanding each other. And the inevitable result of this is, in collective terms, an increase of intergroup tension—for the concealed and denied differences remain, and are more disturbing than if they were openly admitted. And in individual terms, the result is neurosis which develops if we conceal, or deny, what we really are. (p. 451)

All this suggests that group differences are inevitable, and that understanding and appreciating these differences may be the key to human harmony and peace.

3. Meaning and the Interpretation of Behavior: The Cultural Stereotype Accuracy-Meaning Model (CSAM)

Because social groups possess real differences, perceptions or stereotypes of social groups can vary in terms of their degree of accuracy (see Lee & Duenas, 1995; Ottati & Lee, 1995; Ryan & Bogart, 2001). The ability to gauge stereotype accuracy, however, is by no means a simple problem. For one thing, group characteristics can change across time and circumstance (see Baron, 1995; McArthur & Baron, 1983; Peterson, 1999). For example, the stereotype of the Chinese as superstitious may have been accurate in the 1930s, but is probably no longer accurate today (Lee, 1995; Lee & Ottati, 1995, 2002). A second concern involves the distinction between simply perceiving a behavior and interpreting a behavior. According to Lee and Duenas's (1995) "cultural stereotype accuracy-meaning" model (CSAM), two groups can perceive a behavior in an accurate or convergent manner, but nevertheless interpret the behavior differently (see also Kenny's 1994 weighted average model). For example, in the eyes of urban Americans, rural Chinese who only bathe once a month in the winter are dirty. In the eyes of the rural Chinese, however, urban Americans who bathe every day possess a virtual obsession with cleanliness. These types of divergent perceptions undoubtedly arise because these two groups possess distinct standards of comparison (see Ashmore & Longo, 1995; Biernat, 1995 for a discussion of how shifting standards impact stereotypic beliefs). That is, although the two groups may perceive the behavior identically in absolute terms, they may interpret it differently in relative terms because of their use of different standards of comparison.

The essence of understanding stereotype accuracy may lie in clarifying the distinction between low-level perception and the more abstract *meanings* or *interpretations* that people from different cultures attach to their perceptions (see Lee, 1993; Ottati & Lee, 1995). If members from two different cultural groups are unable to achieve a certain degree of mutual understanding, it is likely that stereotypic beliefs about the out-group will be more negative than those of the in-group. A variety of motivational models of prejudice predict this pattern of in-group favoritism and out-group derogation, and such a pattern is consistent with the assumption that intergroup perceptions possess a component of bias or distortion. However, stereotypic beliefs can also possess an accuracy component even when these motivational processes are at work. A good example of this tendency was demonstrated long ago by E. M. Bruner (1956). In an anthropological investigation, Bruner (1956) examined stereotypic perceptions between Hidatsa Indians and local ranchers of European extraction (i.e., the Yankees) in the Dakotas. According to Campbell (1967), the moral requirement of immediate sharing was fully imperative for the Hidatsa Indians, as was the imperative of thrift and providence among the Yankees. Both groups accurately perceived these cultural differences, but used different labels to interpret them. That is, the Hidatsa Indians regarded their own behavior as generous and unselfish while regarding the Yankees as stingy and selfish. On the other hand, the Yankees considered their own behavior as thrifty and provident while considering the Hidatsa Indians as profligate and improvident. These labels, though indicative of ingroup favoritism, are also consistent with the CSAM theory (Lee & Duenas, 1995). That is, the two groups both perceived their behavior in an accurate and convergent manner, but nevertheless interpreted this behavior differently. An analogous tendency might underlie intercultural differences in the interpretation of events surrounding 9–11. Namely, even if two cultures agree about the objective nature of the 9–11 attack (e.g., the number of civilian casualties), they may disagree when making attributions of causality and responsibility or when forming interpretations of the 9–11 event.

4. The Definition of "Terrorism" Is Subjective and Based on Interest, Power, and Specific Time and Context

Consistent with the CSAM model, the concept of "terrorism" is subjectively defined and open to interpretation. People from one culture may label a certain behavior as "terrorism," whereas those from another culture might label the same behavior as "heroism." This does not prevent government bodies, however, from trying to provide an official or objective definition of terrorism. The U.S. Department of Defense, for example, defines terrorism as "the unlawful use of or threat of use of force or violence against individuals or property, to governments or societies, often to achieve political, religious, or ideological objectives" (U.S. Department of Defense, 1990). Based on U.S. government documents, Henderson (2001) defines terrorism as "premeditated, politically motivated violence perpetrated against noncombatant targets by sub national groups or clandestine agents, usually intended to influence an audience, and the term 'international terrorism' means terrorism involving citizens or the territory of more than one country" (Henderson, p. 4).

Many variations in the use of the label "terrorism" are neglected by the official definitions provided earlier (see Hoffman, 1998, 2001). One involves historical changes in the way terrorism has been assumed to relate to social power. The word "terrorism" was introduced in 1795, and was used to denote acts of intimidation against civilians by their government (i.e., top-down, see Akhtar, 2001, p. 350). That is, terrorism referred to powerful group members oppressing less powerful group members. Today the meaning of terrorism has changed considerably. That is, terrorism typically involves a less powerful group performing violent acts toward a more powerful group (i.e., bottom-up). Examples include the Oklahoma bombing by Timothy McVeigh, the Palestinian bombing of buses to kill Israelis (Juergensmeyer, 2000), and the 9–11 attack.

Of course, the label "terrorist" is invariably applied to an individual or a group by others and is rarely a self-assigned designation. Moreover, use of the term "terrorism" is related to specific interests (Akhtar, 2001, p. 351). The same individual might be declared a terrorist by the group targeted by an assault and a hero by those whose interests are represented by that individual's actions. For example, a Christian extremist who bombs an abortion clinic might perceive himself as a "soldier for Christ" rather than seeing himself as a terrorist. When an Arab student blew up himself and many other Israelis on a bus (August 21, 1995), it was viewed as a terrorist act by most Israelis and Americans (see Juergensmeyer, 2000, pp. 71–72), but was seen as an *istishhadi* ("self-chosen martyrdom" in Arabic) by a number of Palestinians.

The use of the label "terrorism" also varies as a function of time and historical context. Yesterday's terrorism might well be tomorrow's heroism. Nelson Mandela, who organized violence against the White government in South Africa in the 1960s, was put into jail. He is now a prominent hero in South Africa. Yasser Arafat, the leader of the Palestine Liberation Organization—regarded by many as a terrorist organization, later became a Nobel laureate for world peace.

Almost all religious groups have used violence to achieve their goals. Examples include the Christian Militia, Christian antiabortion activists, Zion extremists (i.e., radical Jews who killed others betraying Zion), extremists of Sikhism or Muslim (see Cromer, 2001; Juergensmeyer, 2000), and members of a Hindu-Buddhist group who placed nerve gas in a Tokyo subway. Thus, although different civilizations (e.g., Christian, Islamic, and Confucian) often converge in their endorsement of peace and harmony (Vieceli, 2001), different cultures or civilizations also tend to clash (Huntington, 1996).

The September 11 attack on the United States represents a prime example of cultural clash. This attack has been viewed as terrorism within the United States, Europe, and elsewhere. However, Muslims (e.g., Pakistan students in our survey) appear to view this attack as an act of heroism. A given behavior can elicit divergent attributions and interpretations that are virtually opposite in meaning. The "terrorist" interpretation suggests that the September 11 attack was unjustified and immoral, whereas the "heroism" interpretation suggests that this act was justified and morally defensible. Divergence of interpretation is also apparent when considering the U.S. response to the September 11 attack. Throughout the United States, Europe, and elsewhere, the U.S. bombing of Afghanistan has been viewed as a justified act of retribution and a heroic means of preventing future terrorism.

There is indeed something about the concept of "terrorism" that virtually guarantees this form of oppositional interpretation. For, if there is no social group that views a terrorist act as justified, the act probably fails to meet the criteria of a bona fide terrorist act. If there exists no social group that believes a given killing is justified, the killing is simply labeled "murder," not "terrorism." In this sense, it is virtually guaranteed that terrorism and heroism serve as two sides of one interpretational coin.

5. Eastern and Western View of Conflict: Perceptions of Causality

Differences in the way Americans, Chinese, and Pakistani participants interpreted the 9–11 event may be rooted in alternative conceptualizations of causality (Weiner, 1995). Patterns of causal attribution can vary tremendously from culture to culture (Nisbett, Peng, Choi, & Norenzayan, 2001; Takaku, Weiner, & Ohbuchi, 2001). According to recent studies by Richard Nisbett and his colleagues, the East Asian view of causality is *holistic*, marked by a tendency to attend to the entire field when making causal attributions. This way of viewing causality has been labeled *dialectical reasoning* (or Yin-Yang thinking as per Lee, 2000). It includes the principles of change, contradiction, and interrelation. A violent situation can change into a peaceful one (i.e., change); a terrorist act can be viewed as an act of heroism (i.e., contradiction); and the 9–11 event involves two parties ("it takes two to tango"—i.e., interrelation).

The origin of this type of reasoning can be traced to many ancient philosophies in the East. These include Confucianism, Daoism, and Buddhism. On the other hand, the Western view of causality is *analytic*, attending to specific objects in question, and attempting to understand them by using various laws of *formal logic* (i.e., the laws of identity, noncontradiction, and the excluded middle). Western formal logic is rooted in the philosophy of Aristotle. The main differences between these two forms of philosophical approaches and how they can produce different ways of conceptualizing a conflict situation can be made apparent in the following examples.

Example 1. Because *the law of identity* assumes that "A must be A regardless of the context," a wrongdoer must be a wrongdoer regardless of the context. However, because *the principle of change* assumes that life is a constant passing from one stage of being to another (so that to be is not to be, and not to be is to be), to be a wrongdoer is not to be a wrongdoer, and not to be a wrongdoer is to be a wrongdoer depending on the context.

Example 2. Because *the law of noncontradiction* assumes that "A cannot equal not-A," a wrongdoer cannot become a not-wrongdoer (i.e., a victim). However, because *the principle of contradiction* assumes that "A can equal not-A depending on the context," a wrongdoer can become a not-wrongdoer (i.e., a victim) depending on the context.

Example 3. Because *the law of the excluded middle* assumes that "A is either B or not-B," a person is either right or not right, or a wrongdoer or not a wrongdoer (i.e., a victim). However, *the principle of interrelation* assumes that "nothing is isolated and independent, but everything is connected. If we want to know something fully, we must know all of its relations—how it affects or is affected by everything" (Peng & Nisbett, 1999, p. 743). Therefore, A can be both B and not-B, or a person can be both right and not right, or a wrongdoer and not a wrongdoer (i.e., a victim).

Following these examples, it is safe to assume that some conflict situations become very difficult to resolve because of a strong tendency held by both parties involved in a conflict to perceive a victim and a wrongdoer as separate entities such that if one is a wrongdoer, then she or he cannot be anything other than a wrongdoer, and vice versa for a victim. However, if both parties involved in a conflict were to follow the principles of the Eastern dialectical reasoning, these difficult conflict situations might be resolved more easily (Takaku, 2001; Takaku et al., 2001). In fact, one of the best conflict resolution strategies used in Japanese society is to follow an old saying that goes, "In a quarrel both parties must be blamed."

Two cautionary notes are in order here. First, although Easterners tend to think in a holistic and dynamic fashion, this does not mean Westerners are unable to think in this way. For example, Americans or Europeans often say, "It takes two to tango" (Lee, 2000, p. 1066). Second, though the way people react to conflict is influenced by a culturally determined view of causality (Nisbett et al., 2001; Peng & Nisbett, 1999; Takaku et al., 2001; see also Lee & Seligman, 1997), there is probably also a universal component to such reactions that generalizes across cultures (Child, 1968; Lee, 2000; Pepitone & Triandis, 1987). In this regard, it is important to note that all three cultures (China, USA, and Pakistan) were influenced in a similar manner by the temporary situational activation of a dialectical style of reasoning. That is, all three cultures were influenced similarly by the ancient Buddhist analogy that conveyed a dialectical view of causality.

PART 3: CONCLUSIONS AND LESSONS LEARNED FROM THIS RESEARCH

The CSAM model posits that members of two cultures can observe a social behavior in a convergent and accurate manner (e.g., "Fred slapped Raymond on the back"), but may nevertheless interpret this behavior in a divergent fashion (e.g., "hostile provocation" versus "act of friendship"). These differences in interpretation or attribution result from cultural differences in value orientation, social standards, norms, or modal personality. All of these cultural differences may play a role in helping to explain why Christian Americans, Chinese, and Muslims saw and interpreted the events surrounding the September 11 attack in a divergent manner.

What lessons can be learned from these findings? First, it is clear that the concept of "terrorism" functions as an interpretation that can vary across context, interest, and culture. One group's "terrorism" is another group's "heroism." Although all cultures share a DBR, and although all cultures seek justice, perceptions of justice are a culturally and subjectively created reality. The data revealed that the September 11, 2001, attack was perceived as terrorism by Christian Americans. However, people from Islamic cultures tended to perceive it as heroism and freedom fighting, at least in a way different from Christian perception. Second, real or perceived differences in cultural perspective create these divergent interpretations as well as the intergroup conflict they engender. To deny the reality of these cultural differences, to fail to understand and appreciate these cultural differences, is to operate within an impoverished informational environment. Successful negotiation between opposing cultural groups requires that both parties strive to recognize and appreciate the other's perspective.

Finally, the aforementioned cultural differences notwithstanding, there also exists some degree of universality in human behavior. For example, our results demonstrate that Christian American, Chinese, and Muslim participants were all affected similarly by exposure to an analogy derived from an ancient Buddhist scripture that emphasizes the *shared* responsibility of two parties in conflict. In all of these groups, the ancient scripture elicited a view of the September 11 attack that emphasized the shared responsibility of all parties involved. Such findings raise the possibility that cultures in conflict can, at least temporarily, abandon their self-serving perspectives and understand each other from a more detached perspective.

ACKNOWLEDGMENTS

Part of the results in the chapter were presented at the Annual Conference of American Psychological Association, Chicago, on August 22–25, 2002. Thanks are extended to Jacqueline M. Vieceli, Fathali Moghaddam, Clark McCauley, Stephen Worchel, and other reviewers who offered us insightful comments on previous versions of this manuscript and to Ahmad Sufyan, Jovan Hernandez, and Kristin Sandberg who helped us with data collection and entry. This project was partially supported by the 2001–2002 Research Grant (to the first author) at the College of Social and Behavioral Science at Minnesota State University, Mankato.

NOTES

1. Because of the nature and limited space of this chapter, we will only report selected portions of these results. A detailed analysis of the current study is available upon request from the first author.

2. It is true that samples differed in size. But, with regard to age, gender, and education, there were no significant differences among the three samples. Thus, although the three samples are not necessarily representative of the three cultures, they permit a comparison of the three cultures that controls for these potential confounds.

3. The effect of demand characteristics is unlikely to occur for two reasons. First, our pre-reading measures were mixed with other fillers in Sections 1 and 2, which reduced the likelihood that the demand characteristics were salient (Ghiselli, Campbell, & Zedeck, 1981). Second, post hoc interviews with a subset of the participants revealed that they were not aware that we were comparing the pre- and post-responses to these particular items.

4. As a psychological process, tolerance is based on reality. That is, tolerance is assumed to be a response to the perception of actual or real group differences.

REFERENCES

Akhtar, S. (2001). The psychodynamic dimension of terrorism. *Psychiatric Annals, 29*(6), 350–356.

Ashmore, R. D., & Longo, L. C. (1995). Accuracy of stereotypes: What research on physical attractiveness can teach us. In Y.-T. Lee, L. Jussim, & C. R. McCauley (Eds.), *Stereotype accuracy: Toward appreciating group differences* (pp. 63–86). Washington, DC: American Psychological Association.

Baron, R. (1995). An ecological view of stereotype accuracy. In Y.-T. Lee, L. Jussim, & C. R. McCauley (Eds.), *Stereotype accuracy: Toward appreciating group differences* (pp. 115–140). Washington, DC: American Psychological Association.

Barringer, F. F. G. (2001, September 12). As an attack unfolds, a struggle to provide vivid images to homes. *New York Times*, p. A25.

Biernat, M. (1995). The shifting standards model: Implications of stereotype accuracy for social judgment. In Y.-T. Lee, L. Jussim, & C. R. McCauley (Eds.), *Stereotype accuracy: Toward appreciating group differences* (pp. 87–114). Washington, DC: American Psychological Association.

Bruner, E. M. (1956). Primary group experience and the process of acculturation. *American Anthropologist, 58,* 605–623.

Campbell, D. T. (1967). Stereotypes and the perception of group differences. *American Psychologist, 22,* 817–829.

Causton, R. (1995). *The Buddha in daily life: An introduction to the Buddhism of Nichiren Daishonin* (p. 170). London: Ryder.

Child, I. (1968). Personality in cultures. In E. F. Borgatta & W. W. Lambert

(Eds.), *Handbook of personality theory and research* (pp. 82–145). Chicago: Rand McNally.

Cromer, G. (2001). *Narrative of violence*. Aldershot, UK: Dartmouth.

Geen, R. G. (1998). Aggression and antisocial behavior. In D. T. Gilbert, S. T. Fiske, & G. Lindzey (Eds.), *The handbook of social psychology* (Vol. 2, pp. 317–356). New York: McGraw-Hill.

Ghiselli, E. E., Campbell, J. P., & Zedeck, S. (1981). *Measurement theory for the behavioral sciences*. San Francisco: W. H. Freeman.

Henderson, H. (2001). *Terrorism*. New York: Facts on File.

Hoffman, B. (1998). *Inside terrorism*. New York: Columbia University Press.

Hoffman, B. (2001). The mind of the terrorist: Perspectives from social psychology. *Psychiatric Annals, 29*(6), 337–342.

Huntington, S. (1996). *Clash civilizations remaking world order*. New York: Simon & Schuster.

Ichheiser, G. (1948). Are our silent presuppositions about prejudices correct? *American Psychologist, 3*(10), 451.

Ichheiser, G. (1970). *Appearance and reality*. San Francisco: Jossey-Boass.

Juergensmeyer, M. (2000). *Terror in the mind of God: The global rise of religious violence*. Berkeley, CA: University of California.

Kenny, D. (1994). *Interpersonal perception: A social relations analysis*. New York: Guilford.

Lee, Y.-T. (1993). Reaction of American minority and non-minority students to the Persian Gulf war. *The Journal of Social Psychology, 133*(5), 707–713.

Lee, Y.-T. (1995). A comparison of politics and personality in China and in the U.S.: Testing a "kernel of truth" hypothesis. *The Journal of Contemporary China, 9*, 56–68.

Lee, Y.-T. (1996). It is difference, not prejudice, that engenders intergroup tension: Revisiting Ichheiserian research. *American Psychologist 51*(3), 267–268.

Lee, Y.-T. (2000). What is missing in Chinese-Western dialectical reasoning. *American Psychologist, 55*(9), 1065–1067.

Lee, Y.-T. (2003). Daoistic humanism in ancient China: Broadening personality and counseling theories in the 21st century. *Journal of Humanistic Psychology, 43*(1), 64–85.

Lee, Y.-T., Albright, L., & Malloy, T. (2001). Social perception and stereotyping: An interpersonal and intercultural approach. *International Journal of Group Tension, 30*(2), 183–209.

Lee, Y.-T., & Duenas, G. (1995). Stereotype accuracy in multicultural business. In Y. T. Lee, L. Jussim, & C. McCauley (Eds.), *Stereotype accuracy: Toward appreciating group differences*. Washington, DC: The American Psychological Association.

Lee, Y.- T., Jussim, L., & McCauley, C. (Eds.). (1995). *Stereotype accuracy: Toward appreciating group differences.* Washington, DC: The American Psychological Association.

Lee, Y.-T., Kleinbach, R., Hu, P., Peng, Z. Z., & Chen, X. Y. (1996). Cross-cultural research on euthanasia and abortion. *The Journal of Social Issues, 52*(2), 131–148.

Lee, Y.-T., McCauley, C. R., & Draguns, J. (Eds.). (1999). *Personality and personality perception across cultures.* Mahwah, NJ: Lawrence Erlbaum Associates.

Lee, Y.-T., & Ottati, V. (1995). Perceived group homogeneity as a function of group membership salience and stereotype threats. *Personality and Social Psychology Bulletin 21*(6), 612–621.

Lee, Y.-T., & Ottati, V. (2002). Attitudes toward American immigration policy: The role of ingroup-outgroup bias, economic concern, and obedience to law. *Journal of Social Psychology, 142*(5), 617–634.

Lee, Y.-T., Pepitone, A., & Albright, L. (1997). Descriptive and prescriptive beliefs about justice: A Sino-U.S. comparison. *Cross-Cultural Research, 31*(2), 101–120.

Lee, Y.-T., & Seligman, M. E. P. (1997). Are Americans more optimistic than the Chinese? *Personality and Social Psychology Bulletin, 23*(1), 32–40.

McArthur, L. Z., & Baron, R. M. (1983). Toward an ecological theory of social perception. *Psychological Review, 90,* 215–238.

Nietzsche, F. (1966). *Beyond good and evil* (W. Kaufmann, Trans.). New York: Basic Books.

Nisbett, R., Peng, K, Choi, I., & Norenzayan, A. (2001). Culture and systems of thought: Holistic versus analytic cognition. *Psychological Review: 108*(2), 291–310.

Ottati, V., & Lee, Y.-T. (1995). Accuracy: A neglected component of stereotype research. In Y.-T. Lee, L. Jussim, & C. McCauley (Eds.), *Stereotype accuracy: Toward appreciating group differences* (pp. 29–59). Washington, DC: The American Psychological Association.

Peng, K., & Nisbett, R. (1999). Culture, dialectics, and reasoning about contradiction. *American Psychologist, 54*(9), 741–754.

Pepitone, A., & Triandis, H. (1987). On the universality of social psychological theories. *Journal of Cross-Cultural Psychology, 18*(4), 471–498.

Peterson, J. (1999). *Maps of meaning: The architecture of beliefs.* New York: Routledge.

Ryan, C. S., & Bogart, L. M. (2001). Longitudinal changes in the accuracy of new group members' in-group and out-group stereotypes. *Journal of Experimental Social Psychology, 33,* 118–133.

Takaku, S. (2001). The effects of apology and perspective taking on interpersonal forgiveness: A dissonance-attribution model of interpersonal forgiveness. *Journal of Social Psychology, 141,* 494–508.

Takaku, S., Weiner, B., & Ohbuchi, K. (2001). A cross-cultural examination of the effects of apology and perspective taking on forgiveness. *Journal of Language and Social Psychology, 20,* 144–166.

Tyler, R. T., & Smith, H. (1998). Social justice and social movement. In D. T. Gilbert, S. T. Fiske, & G. Lindzey (Eds.), *The handbook of social psychology* (Vol. 2, pp. 595–629). New York: McGraw-Hill.

U.S. Department of Defense. (1990). *Military operation in low intensity conflict* (FM 100–20 or USAFP 3–20). Washington, DC: Author.

Vieceli, J. (2001). *Challenging the "clash of civilizations": Convergence points of Christian, Islamic and Confucian teachings on war and peace.* Paper presented at the Annual Meeting of Mid-West Political Science Association, April 19–22, Palmer House, Chicago.

Weiner, B. (1995). *Judgment of responsibility: A foundation for a theory of social conduct.* New York: Guilford Press.

PART IV

Prevention and Management of Cultural Conflict and Ethnic Violence

CHAPTER 12

Intercultural Communication, Contact, and International Business Assignments

Richard W. Brislin and Joyce F. Liu

THE BUSINESS CASE FOR DIVERSITY

In the increasingly globalized and multicultural business environment of the United States, companies that cannot recognize and harness the benefits of diversity face the potential of losing their competitive edge or, more likely, fall below the status quo. In its fullest definition, diversity comprises a spectrum of differences, including physical characteristics, such as disabilities and gender; social category memberships, such as race, ethnicity, religion, or sexual orientation; and talents and perspectives, such as those gained through job experiences and training. Weighing the tangible short-term costs against their long-term benefits represents a dilemma for pursing diversity as a business strategy in a stock market environment in which success is measured on a daily basis. Such short-term costs can manifest as the diversion of resources away from operations and toward diversity management training, the creation of new diversity retention programs, and changes to policy and corporate culture.

Perhaps the first issue to consider is not the long-term benefits of diversity, but rather the costs of failing to manage it. According to the American Management Association, a conservative estimate of the cost to replace an employee is 30 percent of her annual salary, with the cost rising to as much as 150 percent of the annual salary of highly skilled employees who are in demand (Business Women's Network, 2002). With four million Americans changing jobs each month (Business Women's Network, 2002), employers are also challenged with recruiting and retaining a talented workforce. The Hudson Report forecasts that 85 percent of entrants to the workforce in 2005 will be women, minorities, and immigrants (Business Women's Network, 2002).

Job seekers also expect and desire diversity within the workplace. A New York Times Job Market survey found that, of the job seekers in New York, 94 percent would rather work in a diverse workplace, whereas only 6 percent would not (Ebenkamp, 2002). Of their respondents, 77 percent are looking for a diverse workplace in their next job, 76 percent report that diversity improves the work environment, and 55 percent consider diversity in the workplace as extremely or very important to them in the job search (Ebenkamp, 2002). Talented applicants then self-select themselves away from organizations without a record of diversity in favor of those that have that record. The human resources cost to an organization is measured by the continually shrinking pool of talent available to them.

The changing composition of the U.S. populace, along with increased reliance on international ties, further challenges the business community to respond proactively. The U.S. Census Bureau (2000b) estimates that the combined African American, Asian American, Latino/Hispanic, and Native American populations will comprise almost 33 percent of the U.S. population by 2010. Moreover, the eras since the 1970s have seen the composition of foreign-born residents in the United States move dramatically away from residents originating from Europe and toward Latin America and Asia (U.S. Census Bureau, 2000a). Such changes in the demographic topography of the United States represent the emerging markets of the twenty-first century. An organization's failure to reflect the diversity of perspectives, experiences, and intimate knowledge about those markets translates into an inability to cater to them. Moreover, the globalization of businesses is forcing organizations to merge different ethno-cultural and corporate cultures while striving to meet the needs of their changing customer base. Labor and market trends, and the need to maximize on scarce resources, are forcing organizations to become increasingly dependent on cross-functional, interdepartmental, and interorganizational alliances (Jackson, May, & Whitney, 1995), thus translating into greater diversity within working groups.

The business case for diversity is further strengthened when examining the benefits of effectively managing diversity. Following the announcement of awards for exemplary affirmative action programs, Wright, Ferris, Hiller, and Kroll (1995) found that the recipients saw significant and positive excess returns in their stock price. Conversely, companies found liable in discrimination lawsuits saw a sharp drop in their stock price following the damage award announcements (Wright et al., 1995). Organizations that have successfully managed diversity have also demonstrated a competitive edge (Colvin, 1999; Cox, 1994), and those with a strong history of diversity management have outperformed the Standard and Poor's 500 stock market average by 2.4 percent, whereas companies with poor diversity management track records underperform the average by 8 percent (Carfang, 1993).

The competitive advantage for successfully managing diversity has been attributed to lower costs due to decreased absenteeism, turnover, and job dissatisfaction, and a greater ability to respond to the diverse customer base with more creative solutions and the ability to adapt to the external environment (Wright, Pringle, & Kroll, 1994). In order for organizations to compete as producers of desirable goods and services, as well as remain employers of choice, they must be proactive in recognizing, incorporating, and supporting such diversity in business practices and the workplace.

Although the definition of diversity is broader than simply differences in race, ethnicity, or culture, the following chapter focuses specifically on ethno-cultural diversity as a starting point for a discussion about increasing positive group relations in the business setting. We emphasize diversity because of differences in culture and ethnicity, with the belief that points made here are applicable to discussions about other forms of diversity. Moreover, diversity refers to the ethno-cultural differences residing within all individuals, and not just in reference to those of the ethnic minority (Ibrahim, 1996). Ethnicity and culture include such features as shared worldviews, shared values and cognitive maps that guide behaviors, and often shared languages or dialects that allow efficient communication among individuals who claim the same ethnic or cultural background (Triandis, 1995). With certainty, such changes in the population and business landscapes will result in more interactions among people from very different ethno-cultural backgrounds (Landis & Bhagat, 1996).

There are two quite different categories of people's reactions to this increased intercultural contact (Brislin, 2000). One is negative, and it includes prejudicial attitudes, facile and harmful stereotypes, and discrimination (Allport, 1954; Brewer & Brown, 1998). The other is positive, and it includes the development of more tolerant attitudes, the pursuit of more intercultural interactions, and the generalization of positive attitudes across various cultural groups (Pettigrew, 1998). Rather than view diversity as a handicap and problem to be minimized, understanding the positive contributions of diversity can lead to its use as a source of creativity, innovation, and growth.

COGNITIVE AND SOCIAL BENEFITS OF DIVERSITY

Diversity in the workplace has been met with fears about reduced productivity, impaired performance, and hostility between colleagues (Hollister, Day, & Jesaitis, 1993). Yet empirical studies have demonstrated that diverse working groups can be as effective as ethno-culturally homogenous groups and in some cases demonstrate a clear advantage.

Given appropriate feedback and extensive opportunities to interact and modify group processes, the performance of diverse groups do not differ from homogeneous groups. Watson, Kumar, & Michaelsen (1993) compared the performance of ethno-culturally homogeneous and heterogeneous student groups on problem-solving tasks across a 15-week undergraduate course in international business. Although students in homogeneous working groups initially outperformed their culturally heterogeneous counterparts on solving international business scenarios, heterogeneous groups eventually matched the performance of the homogeneous groups on subsequent problem-solving tasks when given opportunities to discuss their performance and identify methods of improving group productivity (Watson et al., 1993). Although both homogeneous and heterogeneous groups received similar instructions to develop strategies for increasing group success, the heterogeneous groups demonstrated greater gains across working sessions. Pelled, Eisenhardt, and Xin (1999) also found that the longevity of an ethno-culturally diverse group among corporate employees—the length of time a group was retained and had collaborated on projects—moderated the amount of conflict reported by group members. The longer that group members worked together, the less conflicts they reported. Although at the outset homogenous groups demonstrated an advantage over heterogeneous groups in group productivity and success, the advantage diminished over time as the latter group became more practiced in their intragroup relations.

Diversity may also offer another distinct functional advantage over homogeneity. Individuals in heterogeneous groups originate from different backgrounds; therefore they can bring to the task different sets of experiences and cognitive styles that extend beyond those that can be offered by homogenous groups. Heterogeneous groups excel over homogenous groups at problems that are ill defined and novel, thereby maximizing on the diversity of perspectives and opinions (Filley, Hourse, & Kerr, 1976; Hambrick & Brandon, 1988; Hambrick, Davison, Snell, & Snow, 1998). The heterogeneous student working groups from Watson et al. (1993) not only matched the overall performance of their homogenous counterparts, but they also offered higher-quality solutions, a greater range of perspectives, and more alternative solutions. Task conflict—the disagreement about task issues such as goals, key decisions, procedures, and choice of action—has also been associated with increased group performance and decreased instances of groupthink (Pelled et al., 1999). The cognitive diversity within a group serves as an asset for solving novel problems that do not have a predetermined protocol or correct answer and that require extensive consideration of alternatives.

Enthusiasm for diversity, however, must also be tempered with the awareness that the context of the situation ultimately dictates the appropriate composition of the work group. For example, when the situation calls for a traditional solution to a known problem to be developed within a short period of time, a homogeneous group may be superior to a heterogeneous one. On the other hand, when the situation is novel or the problem calls for creative solutions, the heterogeneous group may be superior. Moreover, diversity must be appropriately managed. Simply bringing different people together is insufficient to facilitate progress and may even result in increased hostility and setbacks. Without diversity management initiatives, employees may come to perceive discrimination in the workplace, which has been associated with low organizational commitment and job satisfaction, and increased work tension (Sanchez & Brock, 1996). To harness diversity for its benefits, groups should be formed according to the members' functional diversity, which are differences in values, skills, abilities, and knowledge that are directly relevant to organizational performance, and given essential supervision and training on ways to best utilize those differences (Schneider & Northcraft, 1999). By thinking of diversity as a tool or an asset, it can be used at the right times, in the right ways, for the appropriate reasons.

Nonetheless, negotiating a cultural landscape differing from one's own can result in beneficial outcomes that are indicative of personal development and growth. As a result of the cultural brokering and negotiation, exposure to differing perspectives, and incorporation of appropriate feedback and conditions for cooperation, group members learn to be flexible in their communication behaviors as well as cognitions. Successful groups require members to engage in diversity management skills, including the ability to understand how one's own behavior affects others, postponing the assignment of causes to behaviors until more information is gathered, and demonstrating a willingness to communicate when disagreements between perspectives arise (Shaw & Barrett-Power, 1998). Such skills are assets that have been identified in positive interpersonal relations, similar to the skills associated with emotional intelligence such as delay of gratification and appropriate expression of affect (Goleman, 1998).

WHAT CHANGES AS A RESULT OF INTERCULTURAL INTERACTIONS?

Individuals to target as promising candidates for the diverse workplace are those who have a history of actively seeking experiences that involve extensive intercultural contact and demonstrate a desire and motivation to incorporate such contacts in their repertoire of experiences. Such individuals include international students, individuals with prior experiences as foreign exchange students, businesspeople who view overseas assignments as an important component of career development, and students who apply to graduate programs in cross-cultural counseling and clinical psychology. Researchers have been prompted to ask the question, "What changes occur as a results of these experiences?" (Cushner, 1989; Gmelch, 1997; Kagitçibasi, 1978). In comparing individuals with and without an intercultural experience, members of the former group appear to reap several benefits from exposure to a culture different from their own.

Kagitçibasi (1978) assessed the changes that occurred among Turkish adolescents who spent a year in the United States as part of a foreign exchange program. Assessment of the adolescents was conducted immediately after the one-year intercultural experience and again at one and two years after their return to Turkey. Compared with matched controls of adolescents who remained in Turkey, program participants became more world-minded, more interested in international issues, and more tolerant of views other than their own. They also became less authoritarian in their outlook, a finding that was attributed to the need to develop openness and flexibility when adjusting to other cultures (Deshpande & Viswesvaran, 1992). The program participants also increased their belief that their behaviors were internally rather than externally controlled, a change also documented by Gmelch (1997) in an analysis of the journals and travel logs of Americans studying in Austria. All of these changes were maintained two years after the program participants returned to Turkey.

The benefits of the intercultural experience arise from the need to develop interpersonal and coping skills in order to successfully establish interpersonal relationships and negotiate around an unfamiliar cultural milieu. To develop positive interpersonal relations with individuals from other cultures, people must be open to differing attitudes and personalities and must be flexible in their behaviors. If the Turkish adolescents had authoritarian outlooks, they would be challenged by the demands for openness and flexibility. When people have intercultural interactions, they inevitably encounter some difficulties and misunderstandings. But because they do not have the daily support of family members and long-time friends, they must solve their problems on their own (Cushner, 1989). As they deal effectively with difficulties, they increase their sense of internal control and efficacy. The unfamiliar culture requires individuals to challenge their existing beliefs and foster within themselves abilities and skills that can be beneficial to their future well-being.

THE CASE FOR PRESERVING ETHNO-CULTURAL IDENTITIES

An additional outcome of increased intercultural interactions is the examination of one's own identity in juxtaposition to the surrounding ethno-cultural persons and environment. Both ethnic minorities and White

Americans are in a position of comparing and contrasting their own worldviews, behaviors, and self-concepts relative to those held by persons from ethno-cultural backgrounds different from their own. According to Social Identity Theory (Tajfel, 1978), individuals seek positive self-concepts through affiliation with groups that have high status, and as a result, have emotional value attached to membership in particular groups. Social Identity Theory also attempts to predict an individual's motivation for changing or maintaining behaviors based on those group memberships (Gudykunst & Bond, 1997).

Ethnic identity is the one such form of social identity, in which one's self-concept arises from membership in an ethno-cultural or racial group (Phinney, 1990, 1993) and carries a significance and emotional value for the membership (Rotheram & Phinney, 1987). Related to the development of ethnic identity is the maintenance of a sense of pride, security, and niche in the world (Phelps et al., 1998). Individuals with higher, or more advanced stages of ethnic identity development, are characterized by an internalization of a positive evaluation of their own ethnic group, a sense of commitment and belonging to their group, and interest and involvement in activities of the group (Phinney, Cantu, & Kurtz, 1997). Ethnic identity can be an especially salient and important domain for members of ethno-cultural minority groups (Phinney et al., 1997). The conferred sense of belonging to a larger social group provides a reference by which to understand one's worldview when it is distinctly different from the dominant or majority group worldview.

An important development in the study of ethnic identity is its relationship to global self-esteem and psychological well-being. Global self-esteem enhances psychological well-being by protecting and enhancing feelings of self-worth, and engaging coping mechanisms in the event of threats to one's sense of self-worth (Rosenberg, Schooler, Schoenbach, & Rosenberg, 1995). Whereas negative attitudes about one's group may reduce self-esteem, a positive view of one's membership in an ethno-cultural group has been posited to do the opposite by enhancing self-esteem (Crocker, Luhtanen, Blaine, & Broadnaz, 1994; Martinez & Dukes, 1997; Phinney, 1993; Phinney & Chavira, 1992; Phinney et al., 1997).

The discussion of ethnic identity is not restricted to ethno-cultural minorities, as non-Hispanic, White Americans can benefit from exploration into their own identity as majority group members and Americans. Phinney et al. (1997) found that White Americans who reported a greater sense of membership to the category "American" also demonstrated higher global self-esteem. Helms (1990) also proposed that White Americans are in a position to evaluate their racial identity and social power relative to ethno-cultural minorities. By realizing and accepting the realities of the racial hierarchy within the sociopolitical and historical context and one's membership in a privileged group, White Americans are able to empathize and accept the experiences of ethnically, racially, and culturally different persons (Helms, 1990). Similar to ethno-cultural minorities, White Americans can enjoy the benefits of group affiliation as it serves to bolster aspects of psychological well-being.

The question is, How do we preserve the benefits of social identity for the individual while maximizing the cohesiveness and productivity of the corporate work group? Strong social identities that are shared between individuals may emphasize perceived differences between social groups (Messick & Mackie, 1989), thereby leading them to assume that there are incompatible and unchangeable differences, which may not actually exist (Northcraft, Polzer, Neale, & Kramer, 1995). Individuals may also be more prone to mentor and to promote others who share a similar social identity, thereby leading to homogenization within the organization (Schneider & Northcraft, 1999). In order to utilize social identities to the benefit of the organization, it is crucial that the assumptions, values, needs, and perspectives of different social groups are reinforced as being potentially similar or complementary rather than as irreconcilably discordant (Northcraft et al., 1995).

THE CONDITIONS NECESSARY FOR POSITIVE INTERCULTURAL CONTACT

Although it is easier for managers to change the demographics of the group rather than manipulate the behavioral interactions within it, such minimalistic interventions are inadequate for those seeking positive outcomes (Yu, 2002). Researchers (Allport, 1954; Amir, 1969; Pettigrew, 1998) have recommended that people move beyond the commonsense notion that bringing people from different cultures together will have positive effects. Often, contact alone can have negative impacts such as the reinforcement of stereotypes and the maintenance of power differences, especially because different ethno-cultural backgrounds come with different behavioral, attitudinal, and affective responses. Researchers have identified the necessary conditions under which contact can bring positive intercultural interactions. Although extensive lists of up to 15 conditions exist, Pettigrew (1998, p. 80) has attempted to identify the essential and necessary components for positive intercultural interactions.

Pettigrew identifies five key components, of which four were originally proposed in Allport's (1954) classic book on prejudice. First, contact should be marked by *equal status,* such that people in the contact situation are treated equally and have equal access to rewards. Some examples of rewards include promotions and training opportunities in the workplace and housing opportunities in desirable neighborhoods. Even if there are clear status differences in the larger society, administrators can often work toward equal status in a specific contact setting.

Second, people from different ethno-cultural backgrounds should work toward *common goals*. Such goals are desired by all involved parties and demand the efforts of all for their attainment. Goals can include improving products or services from an organization that results in pay increases for all workers or creating youth exchange programs that results in positive experiences for both international students and their host families (Cushner, 1989). Moreover, the employees themselves shoulder the short-term costs of introducing diversity initiatives to an organization, whereas the potential benefits generally occur at the level of the organization and are not directly received by the employee (Schneider & Northcraft, 1999). Shared goals mitigate against loss of morale from individuals involved in the intercultural exchanges by establishing immediate and tangible benefits for their participation, such as bonuses and accolades earned for group success. Shared goals, such as a shared mission statement, are ideally constructed from the equal contribution of all involved parties, thereby also highlighting the third condition: *cooperative effort.*

Efforts to attain these common goals should involve cooperative effort with minimization of competition between individuals in the contact situation. Examples are athletic teams whose members must play in a cooperative manner and must not emphasize only their own performance statistics to win, and cooperative learning groups in the classroom in which individual students receive grades based on the performance of their group members (Aronson & Patnoe, 1997).

Fourth, there should be *support from authority figures.* If teachers introduce cooperative learning, for instance, they must have the endorsement of school administrators. The administrators must convey a sense that they support positive intercultural relations and that they will back up teachers if difficulties arise, such as complaints from parents familiar with only traditional teaching styles. If business executives communicate that there is a zero-tolerance policy regarding workplace discrimination, they must follow through and demonstrate their commitment in their decisions about salary increases, promotions, and advanced training opportunities. Inadequate or lip service commitment to diversity by authority figures would only undermine efforts to increase positive intergroup relations.

Although these four basic conditions for positive intercultural contact appear simple, successful implementation of those conditions can be undermined by the failure to recognize the role of social power in organizations. Ely and Thomas (2001) illustrated the importance of recognizing these hidden issues with their case study of three organizations. "Separate but equal" departments in one organization that were divided by Black-White race boundaries were associated with low morale, poor communication, inability to openly discuss conflict issues, and resentment among employees. Additionally, one organization that justified diversity as a moral imperative produced employees who felt unvalued and undermined. Ironically, the unspoken message to the ethnic minority staff was that to be successful in the organization, they had to assimilate to White corporate culture. On the other hand, when an organization marketed diversity as a source for mutual learning and a resource for transforming work processes, employees felt valued and respected for their contributions and competence. Although conflicts continued to result from cultural differences, the sense of equal social power within the organization facilitated open discussions and conflict resolution. The first step to minimizing the destructive effects of social power on an organization is to increase awareness of the ways that it is institutionalized in its organizational chart, operations, and policy. At the interpersonal level, this sense of empowerment and respect among involved parties can be fostered by the fifth condition for positive intercultural contact: *friendship*.

Pettigrew argued that the fifth condition for the contact situation is the opportunity for individuals to form close friendships with at least one other person (Pettigrew, 1997). Friendships break down barriers between "us" and "them." Once people engage in the self-disclosure, shared activities, and affective bonds necessary for friendship, it becomes more difficult to hold prejudiced views about the out-group of which the friend is a member. At times, people who develop friendships change their categories so that the original "us" and "them" change to a more generalized "people (like myself and my friend) who engage in successful intercultural contact." They develop what is called a "third culture," one based on the shared experiences and interests in seeking intercultural contact. People who are especially interested in intercultural contact develop interpersonal relationships based on this shared interest, and actively seek out more such contact (Brislin & Yoshida, 1994; Useem & Useem, 1967).

AFTER SUCCESSFUL CONTACT: MAINTAINING INTERCULTURAL RELATIONS

The helpful insights gained from study of the contact hypothesis and from the analysis of culture-contact benefits can encourage people to form friendships and close working relationships with people from cultures other than their own. But then another challenge begins: maintaining the newly developed interpersonal relationships. One reason for why difficulties occur over time is that people do not understand the various cultural differences that can have an impact on interpersonal relationships. One field of study that can assist in the maintenance of intercultural relationships is cross-cultural training.

Cross-cultural training, also called intercultural communication training and a variant of diversity training (Brislin & Yoshida, 1994; Cushner, 1989), deals with formal efforts to encourage learning about one's own and other cultures. Such programs are planned, budgeted, staffed, and take place according to schedule, and use specially prepared educational materials. One of the most effective types of materials consists of critical incidents and explanations of them, with the explanations drawing from well-designed research on cultural differences. Critical incidents are short stories that deal with people experiencing cultural misunderstandings or challenges. They have characters, a setting, a plot line, and end with a misunderstanding or difficulty. Then, concepts are introduced that help explain the incident. One goal is to introduce the concepts so that people can use them in interpreting different potential cultural misunderstandings. Critical incidents are especially valuable because they are very similar to the way people actually talk about their intercultural experiences. People don't talk about "the necessity of support from authority figures." They do, however, tell stories about why a certain specific change in their organization did or did not occur given the presence or absence of support from authorities.

The following two critical incidents and explanations are drawn from materials we have prepared for businesspeople on overseas assignments. One key element is that there should be concepts in the critical incidents that are of interest to virtually all users. For example, users may not have had work experience in Japan, but they have surely been in work situations for which they felt unprepared. Another key element is that the explanatory concepts should be seen as helpful in understanding people's day-to-day interactions in other cultures. The following two incidents deal with an issue that all businesspeople will face: how to disagree and to argue one's point vigorously without threatening positive interpersonal relationships.

Incident One: Japanese Work Groups

"I thought I was prepared for working in Japanese groups, but I was surprised by the level of vigorous discussion." Mike Cavanagh was sharing his observations in an e-mail message to hometown friends in Anacortes, Washington. Mike had been offered a six-month consultancy by Aoyama Music in Nagoya, Japan. Aoyama had a very good reputation for making harps and executives wanted to expand its product line with other acoustic instruments. Mike had a good reputation as a maker of various stringed instruments such as guitars, ukuleles, and mandolins.

Mike learned that he would be working with a group of managers who had been at Aoyama for over 10 years and who knew each other well. Mike knew that Japan was a collectivist culture in which people achieve much of their identity through group membership. He knew that in collectivist cultures people value politeness, cooperation, and a harmonious interaction style. At meetings of the Aoyama work group, however, Mike found that team members argued vigorously, disagreed with each other, and were very forceful in putting their ideas forward.

Common to first-time experiences with intercultural interactions, Mike had discovered that his basic knowledge about cultural theories required supplementation with hands-on experience in order to fully understand the intricacies of culture. From his observations, he may have posited that any one individual in a collective culture can have interactions with people at three different levels of intimacy. If the individual does not know other people, relations can be quite formal and "standoffish." People may have little to do with each other and can be rather abrupt and pushy if they come into contact in public places such as subway trains during rush hour. If the individual knows others but does not yet have collective ties with them, interactions can be very polite and guided by a complex system of etiquette. These people might be part of a collective in later years, and politeness is expected.

For long-term members of a collective, as in this example with Aoyama, people set norms to achieve various goals. If they have known each other for many years, collective membership has been established and they don't need to always show carefully planned politeness. Instead, members may have set the norm that they need to argue vigorously about new products that will meet the demands of a fast-moving marketplace. They may not be a collective tomorrow if they don't formulate new ideas today!

This incident and analysis was developed from conversations with Garr Reynolds, a marketing manager with prior experience at a leading electronics corporation in Osaka, Japan. In addition to understanding types of relations among people, individual differences must be taken into account. Some Japanese individuals are more assertive and outspoken than others, and they may be among the first to voice public disagreements.

This incident explained some basic points about individualism and collectivism (Triandis, 1995), but also cautioned that various social contexts must be understood, and that there is always the possibility of individual differences. We also referred to individual differences in this second example that has the United States as the "receiving country," where the intercultural interactions take place. The following incident underscores the importance of examining the influence of one's own culture upon an intercultural interaction.

Incident Two: When Disagreements Threaten Self-Worth

"People have been working on marketing plans for about three months, but we'd like to hear your fresh perspectives." Dan Kagawa, born and raised in Hilo, had recently welcomed Krishna Joshi to the marketing division of a digital technology company in Honolulu. Dan knew only a few facts about Krishna's background. He was from New Delhi, India, and was from a prominent and well-respected family. He had attended the prestigious Allahabad University and wanted to develop his entrepreneurial skills by working for a small promising company in the United States.

Dan had asked Krishna to participate in a staff meeting at which the marketing of cellular phones was to be discussed. Krishna shared his view that 30-second spots on television would be most effective. Kathleen Jacobs disagreed in a direct but pleasant tone of voice. "There are real limitations to a marketing campaign based on television. Cost-effectiveness can be a big problem. I feel that we should develop radio spots and place them on stations that will attract drive-time commuters." Other ideas were shared and the meeting was adjourned without a consensus concerning a marketing strategy.

About two days later, Krishna came to Dan's office with a set of complaints. "I can't sleep. I can't eat. I can't face my coworkers in the morning. My entire sense of myself has been attacked." Dan could not understand why Krishna felt the way he did. Dan reviewed what he knew about Krishna's work and interactions with others, but could not identify a reason for his complaints.

There are several possibilities for Krishna's reactions. In India, he may not have learned to separate disagreements on issues from personal feelings about the disagreements. In many parts of the world, there is a great deal of overlap between "my opinions" and "my feelings about my self-worth." Forthright disagreements, then, can be interpreted as personal attacks. Another possibility was that Krishna is not accustomed to vigorous discussions with women. He may have known women in high school and college, but he may have rarely observed discussions in which women argued forcefully about their positions on various issues. A third possibility is that Krishna was more thin-skinned than other professionals from India. If this were the case, then he would have few opportunities to develop a thick skin, given his socialization into a prominent Indian family.

The skill of keeping disagreements separate from personal feelings is not easy to develop anywhere in the world. In some cultures, however, people become exposed to this skill as part of school activities such as debate clubs and teachers' assignments to bring in alternative viewpoints for discussions of various social issues.

In addition to dealing with cultural differences surrounding disagreements, another goal of this incident was to introduce aspects of *one's own culture* that can cause interpersonal difficulties (Triandis & Suh, 2002). If people can examine their own behavior in their own culture and can point to potential difficulties that people from other cultures might face, they may be able to prevent misunderstandings.

Critical incidents can be useful for training in the business setting, but intercultural education should not be limited to the confines of adult learning.

THE TRAINING GROUNDS FOR THE FUTURE FOR MULTICULTURALISM

Primary and secondary education settings can serve as training grounds for developing the interculturally competent workforce of the future. Education visionaries would see the trends of growing diversity across the nation and prepare students in both primary and secondary educational levels to interact in intercultural situations with their peers. Although social and economic systems are progressing toward greater global connectedness—connectedness that is being fueled by global commerce, technology, and mass media—U.S. educational institutions have been somewhat slow in recognizing the importance of preparing their students to become leaders in an increasingly multicultural and global business environment (Keohane, 1999). We propose that the internationalization of education, in other words, changing curricula, degrees, and student bodies of educational institutions to reflect the growing global connectedness (see Keohane, 1999), be incorporated in both the secondary and primary educational setting. By developing knowledge and skills to maneuver within a diverse and multicultural setting at an earlier age, students are prepared to think more critically about the complexities of diversity by the time they reach secondary and postsecondary education.

In the primary school setting, cooperative learning methods are an example of successful integration of lessons on diversity management with regular curricula. In cooperative learning methods, students of different ethnicities, sexes, and levels of achievement are organized into heterogeneous groups. Students then receive rewards and recognition based on the degree to which they can increase the academic performance of their group members. Past research has found that the cooperative learning methods that met the five necessary conditions for positive intercultural contact (see earlier; Pettigrew, 1998) resulted in changes among the group members, including increased emphasis on group goals and cooperation, increased individual accountability, gains in academic achievement for African American and Hispanic students, and the development of close, cross-ethnic friendships (see Slavin, 1995 for a review). Both ethnic minority and White American students also developed more positive racial and ethnic attitudes following participation in cooperative learning groups. The effectiveness of the cooperative learning methods demonstrate the ability to implement policies and programs that maximize on diversity and create an environment from which all ethnic groups can benefit.

The challenge to educators is to prepare students to think about problems, not only with a critical eye, but also with a cultural eye, and to develop self-awareness and maturity in the ways that they think about their own culture and the culture of those around them. Ultimately, the lessons learned in school translate into skills and savvy in the work setting.

CONCLUSIONS AND RECOMMENDATIONS

Ethno-cultural diversity serves as a vital resource for the well-being of both ethnic minorities and majority alike. In order to maximize on the benefits of multiculturalism and diversity, we recommend the following.

View Ethno-Cultural Diversity as an Asset Rather Than a Handicap

The diversity of experiences and cognitive styles that individuals bring with them can be utilized for the benefit of both the individuals themselves and the parties that recognize and foster its appropriate application. As individuals become exposed to different perspectives, their own cognitive styles become more flexible while providing significant contributions to the effectiveness of the group. Diversity can be utilized as a resource if recognized and fostered appropriately.

Make the Commitment to Diversity More Than Just Lip Service

In order for diversity to become an asset to an organization, it must be made a priority that is advanced by corporate leaders and embedded into organizational culture. Diverse working groups have demonstrated the ability to operate effectively in both the educational and occupational settings. However, the ability to become effective requires extensive opportunities for feedback, a conscious striving toward the goal of improved group functioning, and most important, time for the intercultural skills to be learned, practiced, and incorporated into group relations. The degree of commitment that an organization has to diversity must extend beyond changing hiring practices to include retention activities, such as the active use of diversity management skills and fostering of instrumental support among all staff, especially managers. Such a commitment can be demonstrated by recognizing the challenges to intercultural interactions and structuring contact situations to facilitate positive outcomes. As evidenced by work in the educational and occupational settings, meeting the five essential conditions for positive intercultural contact can result in benefits to academic, interpersonal, and productivity domains for all parties in contact. It is likely that individuals involved in such positive experiences will choose to engage in future intercultural interactions as well as to develop skills that increase their value to an organization entering the era of globalization. In light of the changing demography of the United States and the increasing likelihood for intercultural interactions, cooperation among ethno-culturally diverse individuals is favored over divisiveness.

Incorporate Complexity in Thinking about Culture

One of the challenges to successfully incorporating diversity into the workplace is the erroneous assumption that a person exactly reflects the prototypical or stereotypical representation of his or her ethnic group. The ethno-cultural identities within individuals are modified by their personal experiences, and they retain multiple social identities beyond those of their ethnic identity. Thinking complexly about culture translates into understanding a person as a unique combination of identities, experiences, and idiosyncrasies. Moreover, behaviors are often driven by the context in which they occur; therefore, failing to account for such contextual factors threatens the validity of any interpretation of a social interaction. The misuse of cultural knowledge would be in predicting a person's behaviors based on a stereotype. The proper use of cultural knowledge would be to inform and expand one's own understanding of a person's behaviors.

Support the Internationalization of Education

A challenge for employers and organizations is finding the job candidate that possesses the skills and experiences with intercultural interactions without investing in extensive training. Such candidates would likely be the graduates of programs that have responded to the call for internationalization of education. The business community can facilitate the internationalization of education by demanding changes to programs and curricula to address multiculturalism and include diversity management skills training, by recruiting from those institutions, and by mentoring promising candidates.

These recommendations and conclusions speak to one overarching theme: Progress cannot be made without a real commitment to incorporating diversity into business practices and the business landscape.

REFERENCES

Allport, G. (1954). *The nature of prejudice*. Reading, MA: Addison-Wesley.
Amir, Y. (1969). Contact hypothesis in ethnic relations. *Psychological Bulletin, 71*, 319–343.

Aronson, E., & Patnoe, S. (1997). *The jigsaw classroom* (2nd ed.). New York: Longman.

Brewer, M., & Brown, R. (1998). Intergroup relations. In D. Gilbert, S. Fiske, & G. Lindzey (Eds.), *The handbook of social psychology* (4th ed., Vol. 2, pp. 554–594). New York: McGraw-Hill.

Brislin, R. (2000). *Understanding culture's influence on behavior* (2nd ed.). Fort Worth, TX: Harcourt.

Brislin, R., & Yoshida, T. (1994). *Intercultural communication training: An introduction*. Thousand Oaks, CA: Sage.

Business Women's Network (2002). Wow Facts [HTML document]. URL: http://www.ewowfacts.com

Carfang, A. J. (1993). *Equal opportunity stock performances linked* [press release]. Chicago: Covenant Investment Management.

Colvin, G. (1999). The 50 best companies for Asians, Blacks, and Hispanics. *Fortune, July 19*, 53–57.

Cox, T. (1994). *Cultural diversity in organizations*. San Francisco: Berrett-Koehler Publishers.

Crocker, J., Luhtanen, R., Blaine, B., & Broadnaz, S. (1994). Collective self-esteem and psychological well-being among White, Black, and Asian college students. *Personality and Social Psychology Bulletin, 20*, 503–513.

Cushner, K. (1989). Assessing the impact of a culture-general assimilator. *International Journal of Intercultural Relations, 13*, 125–146.

Deshpande, S., & Viswesvaran, C. (1992). Is cross-cultural training of expatriate managers effective? A meta-analysis. *International Journal of Intercultural Relations, 16*, 295–310.

Ebenkamp, B. (2002). And you thought your job was tough. *Brandweek, 43*(11), 15.

Ely, R. J., & Thomas, D. A. (2001). Cultural diversity at work: The effects of diversity perspectives on work group processes and outcomes. *Administrative Science Quarterly, 46*, 229–273.

Filley, A., House, R., & Kerr, S. (1976). *Managerial process and organizational behavior*. Glenview, IL: Scott Foresman.

Gmelch, G. (1997). Crossing cultures: Student travel and personal development. *International Journal of Intercultural Relations, 21*, 475–490.

Goleman, D. (1998). *Working with emotional intelligence*. New York: Bantam Books.

Gudykunst, W. B., & Bond, M. H. (1997). Intergroup relations across cultures. In J. W. Berry, M. H. Segall, & C. Kagitçibasi (Eds.), *Handbook of cross-cultural psychology: Vol. 3. Social behavior and applications* (pp. 119–161). Boston: Allyn and Bacon.

Hambrick, D. C., & Brandon, G. (1988). Executive values. In D. C. Hambrick (Ed.), *The executive effect: Concepts and methods for studying top managers* (pp. 3–34). Greenwich, CT: JAI Press.

Hambrick, D. C., Davison, S. C., Snell, S. A., & Snow, C. C. (1998). When groups consist of multiple nationalities: Towards a new understanding of the implications. *Organization Studies, 19*(2), 181–205.

Helms, J. E. (1990). *Black and White racial identity: Theory, research, and practice.* New York: Greenwood Press.

Hollister, L. A., Day, N. E., & Jesaitis, P. T. (1993). Diversity programs: Key to competitiveness or just another fad? *Organization Development Journal, 11*(1), 49–59.

Ibrahim, F. A. (1996). A multicultural perspective on principle and virtue ethics. *The Counseling Psychologist, 24*(1), 78–85.

Jackson, S. E., May, K. E., & Whitney, K. (1995). Understanding the dynamics of diversity in decision-making teams. In R., Guzzo, E. Salas et al. (Eds.), *Team effectiveness and decision making in organizations* (pp. 204–261). San Francisco: Jossey-Bass.

Kagitçibasi, C. (1978). Cross-national encounters: Turkish students in the United States. *International Journal of Intercultural Relations, 2,* 141–160.

Keohane, N. O. (1999). Majoring in diversity. *Business Mexico, 8/9,* 30–31.

Landis, D., & Bhagat, R. (Eds.). (1996). *Handbook of intercultural training* (2nd ed.). Thousand Oaks, CA: Sage.

Martinez, R. O., & Dukes, R. L. (1997). The effects of ethnic identity, ethnicity, and gender on adolescent well-being. *Journal of Youth and Adolescence, 26*(5), 503–517.

Messick, D. M., & Mackie, D. M. (1989). Intergroup relations. *Annual Review of Psychology, 40,* 45–81.

Northcraft, G., Polzer, J., Neale, M., & Kramer, R. (1995). Diversity, social identity, and performance: Emergent social dynamics in cross-functional teams. In S. Jackson & M. Ruderman (Eds.), *Diversity in work groups* (pp. 69–96). Washington, DC: American Psychological Association Press.

Pelled, L. H., Eisenhardt, K. M., & Xin, K. R. (1999). Exploring the black box: An analysis of work group diversity, conflict, and performance. *Administrative Science Quarterly, 44,* 1–28.

Pettigrew, T. (1997). Generalized intergroup contact effects on prejudice. *Personality and Social Psychology Bulletin, 23,* 173–185.

Pettigrew, T. (1998). Intergroup contact theory. *Annual Review of Psychology, 49,* 65–85.

Phelps, R. E., Atschul, D. B., Wisenbaker, J. M., Day, J. F., Cooper, D., & Potter, C. G. (1998). Roommate satisfaction and ethnic identity in mixed-race and White university roommate dyads. *Journal of College Student Development, 39*(2), 194–203.

Phinney, J. (1990). Ethnic identity in adolescents and adults: A review of research. *Psychological Bulletin, 108,* 499–514.

Phinney, J. (1993). A three-stage model of ethnic identity development. In

M. B. Knight & G. Knight (Eds.), *Ethnic identity: Formation and transmission among Hispanics and other minorities.* Albany, NY: State University of New York Press.

Phinney, J. S., Cantu, C. L., & Kurtz, D. A. (1997). Ethnic and American identity as predictors of self-esteem among African American, Latino, and, White adolescents. *Journal of Youth and Adolescence, 26,* 165–185.

Phinney, J. S., & Chavira, V. (1992). Ethnic identity and self-esteem: An exploratory longitudinal study. *Journal of Adolescence, 15,* 271–281.

Rosenberg, M., Schooler, C., Schoenbach, C., & Rosenberg, F. (1995). Global self-esteem and specific self-esteem: Different concepts, different outcomes. *American Sociological Review, 60,* 141–156.

Rotheram, M., & Phinney, J. (1987). Ethnic behavior patterns as an aspect of identity. In *Children's ethnic socialization: Pluralism and development.* Newbury Park, CA: Sage.

Sanchez, J. I., & Brock, P. (1996). Outcomes of perceived discrimination among Hispanic employees: Is diversity management a luxury or necessity? *Academy of Management Journal, 39*(3), 704–719.

Schneider, S. K., & Northcraft, G. B. (1999). Three social dilemmas of workforce diversity in organizations: A social identity perspective. *Human Relations, 52*(11), 1445–1467.

Shaw, J. B., & Barrett-Power, E. (1998). The effects of diversity on small work group processes and performance. *Human Relations, 51*(10), 1307–1325.

Slavin, R. E. (1995). Cooperative learning and intergroup relations. In J. A. Banks & C. A. McGee Banks (Eds.), *Handbook of research on multicultural education* (pp. 628–634). New York: Macmillan.

Tajfel, H. (1978). Social categorization, social identity, and social comparison. In J. Turner & H. Giles (Eds.), *Intergroup behavior* (pp. 61–76). London: Academic.

Triandis, H. (1995). *Individualism and collectivism.* Boulder, CO: Westview.

Triandis, H., & Suh, E. (2002). Cultural influences on personality. *Annual Review of Psychology, 53,* 133–160.

U.S. Census Bureau (2000a). Profile of foreign-born population in the United States: 2000 [WWW document]. *Current Population Reports: Special Studies.* URL: http://www.census.gov/population/www/socdemo/foreign/ppl-145.html

U.S. Census Bureau (2000b). *Projections of the resident population by race, Hispanic origin, and nativity: Middle series, 2006–2010.* Washington, DC: Populations Projections Program, Population Division, Author.

Useem, J., & Useem, R. (1967). The interface of a binational third culture: A study of the American community in India. *Journal of Social Issues, 23*(1), 130–143.

Watson, W. E., Kumar, K., & Michaelsen, L. K. (1993). Cultural diversity's impact on interaction process and performance: Comparing homogeneous and diverse task groups. *Academy of Management Journal, 36*(3), 590–602.

Wright, P., Ferris, S. P., Hiller, J. S., & Kroll, M. (1995). Competitiveness through management of diversity: Effects on stock price valuation. *Academy of Management Journal, 38*(1), 272–287.

Wright, P., Pringle, C. D., & Kroll, M. J. (1994). *Strategic management: Text and cases.* Boston: Allyn & Bacon.

Yu, L. (2002, Winter). Does diversity drive productivity? *MIT Sloan Management Review,* 17.

CHAPTER 13

Preventing Ethnic Violence: The Role of Interdependence

Jack Levin and Gordana Rabrenovic

Warfare recently fought between ethnic groups in the Balkans, the Middle East, Asia, and other places around the world has led many observers to believe that the only resolution to ethnic conflict is a violent one. Operating under this assumption, researchers and policy makers alike have tended to focus much of their attention on the worst sorts of news about ethnic relations and to overlook positive examples.

In reality, however, at least some historical exemplars of intergroup cooperation have occurred even in circumstances not usually associated with peace and harmony. Indeed, it is possible to locate ethnic conflicts that have not escalated into full-blown violent confrontation, but have been resolved instead through a political process involving accommodation and negotiation (Gurr, 2000; Varshney, 2002).

One such example involves the central European nation of Bulgaria. Most obviously—notwithstanding its proximity to the former Yugoslavia, a potentially explosive ethnic mix, and an impoverished economy— Bulgaria represents the only country in the Balkans that has escaped serious internal conflict. Moreover, Bulgaria has a track record of ethnic tolerance that dates back at least to its Nazi alliance during World War II, when the Bulgarian people resisted Hitler's efforts to send Bulgarian Jews to death camps. Of course, Bulgaria has also had its share of ethnic conflict (e.g., with Turks and Romas), but it has also managed to resolve its hostilities in a peaceful manner.

In this chapter, we examine several cases of peaceful resolution to ethnic tensions in order to explain how and under which conditions peaceful resolution works. In addition to the Bulgarian experience during World

War II, we also examine positive examples of communal relations in contemporary India, Northern Ireland, and the United States.

A SOCIAL PSYCHOLOGICAL PERSPECTIVE

Group differences have frequently inspired ethnic violence (Lee, Jussim, & McCauley, 1995). Getting individuals to put aside their differences and work together toward the satisfaction of their common objectives has long been regarded by social psychologists as an effective strategy for inoculating a community against intergroup violence (Allport, 1954). Some of the early experiments have shown how the character of group activities can increase or decrease intergroup hostility. In a classic demonstration, Sherif and Sherif (1961) studied the development and reduction of intergroup hostility in a series of experiments that took place in an isolated summer camp for 11- and 12-year-old boys. After a period of time together, the boys were separated into two distinct groups that engaged in a tournament of zero-sum games. Intergroup hostility increased. Then, Sherif introduced the conditions for making the boys *instrumentally interdependent*. That is, they cooperated toward the satisfaction of a series of *superordinate goals*, a set of objectives greatly valued by the boys in both groups that could not be achieved without everyone working together. The results were dramatic: much of the intergroup hostility in the camp dissipated, and new friendships flourished across group lines.

Sherif's concept of superordinate goals has been applied to improve intergroup relations in ethnically diverse classrooms (Aronson & Gonzalez, 1988; Aronson & Patnoe, 1997; Brewer & Miller, 1996). In an early study, Aronson, Blaney, Sikes, Stephan, and Snapp (1974) created what they called a *jigsaw teaching technique*, whereby fifth graders participated in a small experimental classroom. Each child was sorted into a racially integrated "learning group" and was given a piece of information they had to share with their classmates in order to put the puzzle together. Not unlike Sherif's campers who worked together on shared goals, the key ingredient was that students in the learning group were forced to depend on one another in order to complete their group project and receive a grade. They were instrumentally interdependent in two ways: first, students were purposely structured around the goal of getting a good grade in the class, so that when one student gained, all of them gained. Second, their efforts were shared, so that they worked together in order to achieve their goal. They taught one another; they shared information with one another. Cooperation rather than competition was their only means for achieving a good grade in the course. After using his jigsaw method for a period of six weeks, Aronson measured any changes in the attitudes of students toward one another. As compared with children in traditional competitive classrooms, fifth graders in his jigsaw groups liked their Black and White classmates better, had more positive attitudes toward school, had better self-esteem, and performed just as well on their exams.

Interdependence also has an *affective* variant, whereby individuals from diverse backgrounds become emotionally reliant on one another. In friendship and neighborliness, individuals are mutually dependent with respect to emotional support and encouragement rather than for the satisfaction of their instrumental objectives. The interaction is informal and personalized so that it breaks through the stereotyped thinking and forms the basis for a common bond.

INTERDEPENDENCE IN BULGARIA

The Bulgarian experience during World War II provides an important illustration of the power of cooperation on intergroup relations. In 1943, the citizens of this eastern European country, an ally of the Nazis, saved the lives of almost fifty thousand Jewish citizens who awaited the trains that would have carried them to the death camp, Treblinka. King Boris III of Bulgaria had already sent 11,000 Jews from occupied territories to their death, but his Bulgarian subjects would tolerate no more.

Never seeing Jews as constituting a personal threat, average Bulgarians simply could not conceive of their Jewish friends and neighbors as evil wrongdoers and did not understand Hitler's struggle against the Jewish population of Europe. First, just like their neighbors, the Bulgarian Jews were dispersed throughout the social structure. Many had low-paying jobs and lived in poor Bulgarian neighborhoods. Unlike their counterparts in other European countries, very few Bulgarian Jews were moneylenders, bankers, or owners of large businesses. Instead, they held socioeconomic positions much like their Christian and Muslim counterparts, playing roles in a wide range of occupations including small grain merchants, retail tradesmen, maids, pushcart vendors, laborers, authors, poets, factory workers, doctors and dentists, composers, pharmacists, artists, engineers, and musicians. Second, though maintaining their religious identity, the Bulgarian Jews were structurally and culturally assimilated, having many intimate friends and acquaintances among their Christian and Muslim neighbors and looking almost exactly like other Bulgarians. Hassidic Jews did not exist; most Jews did not wear *yarmulkes* or skullcaps, eat kosher food or attend Saturday services; only Rabbis wore beards. Jews didn't live in ghettos. All of them—even those who were familiar with the Judeo-Spanish dialect of their ancestors, Ladino—spoke Bulgarian. In sum, for many Bulgarians, the Jews "were like everybody else." Thus, in terms of socioeconomic status and cultural values, Bulgarian Jews were hardly regarded as a threat to the population of Christians and Muslims (Todorov, 1999).

Still, because he joined the Nazi movement relatively early, the Bulgarian tsar's alliance with Hitler brought Nazi ideology into Bulgaria and, with it, a number of new laws in the 1930s that restricted the rights of Jewish residents. By 1943, therefore, there were no Jews in the Assembly, press corps, diplomatic corps, officers' corps, state police apparatus, teaching corps, or civil service—in places where Bulgarian Jews might have cooperated with Christians and Muslims on a formal level. But influential groups in society—the physicians and lawyers, the academics and writers, and the Church leaders—confronted the government many times in order to fight with complete commitment against anti-Jewish measures (Bar-Zohar, 1998).

Those Bulgarians who participated in public affairs but lacked decision-making powers nevertheless sought to use their influence. There were letters of protest, telephone calls, and debates in the Assembly. The Union of Lawyers referred to an article in the Bulgarian Constitution, in which all individuals were regarded as equal in law. The leadership of the Bulgarian Orthodox Church pointed to the "words of our Savior in whose eyes all are children of one heavenly Father" (Todorov, 1999, p. 55). The Bulgarian Writers' Union reminded Bulgarians of their own victimization under the Turks. Assembly members emphasized the suffering of the victims, that they were surely to be transported not to labor camps but to their certain death.

The absence of any Jewish Bulgarians in formal organizations during the critical period when their fate was being negotiated precluded the possibility of Christians and Jews cooperating in an instrumental sense. Thus, it required a grassroots community movement to convince the leadership of Bulgarian society that its Jews should not be deported. There were protests from influential leaders in the Bulgarian Orthodox Church and from the professional organizations of doctors, lawyers, and authors. A bill was introduced in Parliament by its vice president to ignore Hitler's decree. Yet the underlying impetus for tolerance originated in the minds and hearts of ordinary people. Many average Bulgarian Christians chose to wear the yellow Star of David, a symbol that was required by law of its Jewish citizens to wear in order to identify them for deportation. Many average citizens tore down Nazi flags flying from public buildings. Many risked their lives to protect Jewish Bulgarians from anti-Semitic gangs.

According to Jacky and Lisa Comforty (2001) in their documentary film entitled *The Optimists*, Bulgarian Christians, Muslims, and Jews had lived side by side for hundreds of years, prior to Nazi Germany making its influence felt across Europe. Through the centuries, religious groups in Bulgaria coexisted in relative peace, friendship, and harmony. As depicted in *The Optimists*, for example, Mordechai Arbel, one of the almost 50,000 Bulgarian Jews who escaped Hitler's final solution, articulated just how much Jews and Christians crossed ethnic lines in their friendships: "Actually, I didn't know who was Jewish and who was not Jewish because the non-Jewish friends participated actively in the Jewish holidays and we participated very very actively in the Bulgarian holidays. So we knew that in this and this house, they do it the Bulgarian way, and in this and this house they did it the Jewish way. But the company was mixed, and there were no real differences." A Jewish Bulgarian woman in the film added, "Most of my girlfriends were Bulgarian Christians and they treated me like a sister. There was no isolation from society. On the contrary, you felt embraced by society."

INSTRUMENTAL INTERDEPENDENCE AND RACE RELATIONS IN JASPER, TEXAS

Communities differ with respect to how their members respond to acts of intergroup violence. When two groups have a long-standing tradition of separation and hostility, even a single event can be seen as intolerable and deserving of retaliation by members of the victim's group. Yet serious intergroup incidents do not always escalate into violence. Under certain conditions, a tragic event may even facilitate reconciliation and cooperation between groups.

In the aftermath of the vicious 1998 murder of James Byrd in Jasper, Texas, community responses were actually quite reasonable and patient. The three white supremacists who were eventually convicted of Byrd's murder—John King, Lawrence Brewer, and Shawn Berry—beat the Black hitchhiker until he was unconscious, chained him to their pickup truck, and then dragged him down the road for more than two miles to his death. Investigators discovered a Ku Klux Klan manual among the possessions carried by one of the assailants; and the other two wore white supremacist body tattoos depicting the Confederate Knights of America. King, Brewer, and Berry were definitely ardent admirers of the Klan who used white supremacist propaganda and enjoyed being identified with white supremacy symbols of power.

Given the history of racism in the Deep South, it might seem that the brutal murder of a Black resident in a small and impoverished southern town would precipitate a melee or a riot. Yet, rather than divide the community on racial grounds, the murder of James Byrd actually served to bring the Black and White residents of Jasper together. In the aftermath of the slaying, townspeople reported going out of their way to cross racial lines in greeting residents and feeling a new street-level friendliness toward members of the other race. Even the perpetrators' family members recognized the need for civility. Following the trial and conviction of the first defendant, his father phoned the local radio station, not to hurl racial accusations, but to urge townspeople to "fill the void made by his mess with love and tolerance" (Shlachter, 1999).

Just as in many other southern communities, Blacks and Whites in Jasper had not always been sympathetic toward one another (Temple-Raston, 2002). The legacy of Jim Crow segregation continued to color the informal relations between Blacks and Whites, keeping them apart in their everyday lives. One issue that had long symbolized the community's struggle with race relations was the town's cemetery, where a fence down the middle separated Whites buried on one side from Blacks buried on the other. After Byrd's murder, however, the town came to an agreement to integrate its cemetery. Many residents of Jasper, Black and White, joined together to pull out the posts and tear down the fence (Labalme, 1999).

The political leaders in Jasper had strong credibility among both its Black and its White residents. Local government had long been racially integrated. Black residents who comprised some 45 percent of the town's population occupied the position of mayor, two of the five city council positions, and the directorship of the Deep East Texas Council of Governments. In addition, school principals and the administrator of the largest hospital were Black. Even in the almost total absence of interracial friendships, Blacks and Whites in Jasper had developed a tradition of cooperating at the formal level.

Jasper's leadership inspired new areas of reconciliation and nonviolence. The community's White sheriff went out of his way to inspire confidence among Black residents in the aftermath of Byrd's slaying. Within 24 hours, he had arrested two suspects and then immediately requested the assistance of the FBI. Moreover, Jasper's local 6,000-watt radio station kept residents informed in an evenhanded way about developments related to the murder and the trials, assuring that racially dangerous rumors and anxieties never had an opportunity to spread (Shlachter, 1999). An important point to make is that Jasper, Texas, represented a primary source of community identification for Black and White residents alike—all of them felt a common bond that transcended racial differences. Even extremists on both sides of the racial ledger were genuinely embarrassed by the cruelty and sadism of James Byrd's murder. They seemed to unite across racial lines against the very strong stigma imposed on their community by members of the outside world. Interrace unity was possible because many of the town's formal organizations had brought together representatives of both groups who were already accustomed to working together (Levin & Rabrenovic, 2001).

INSTRUMENTAL INTERDEPENDENCE AND ETHNIC CONFLICT IN NORTHERN IRELAND

In divided societies in which ethnic violence can and often does rip society apart, it is difficult to sustain friendship ties between the members of different ethnic groups. Even interethnic marriages may not survive in places with extreme hostility. In order to protect themselves from the violence, people often choose to live in segregated communities. The avoidance of the members of other groups decreases the contact between them and consequently the possibility for conflict to develop. Thus, in many places, "walls make good neighbors."

Even in the most divided societies, however, it is not always possible to avoid contact. Therefore, the members of different ethnic groups may engage in selective relationships. Consequently, even in deeply divided societies like Northern Ireland, there are examples of interpersonal contacts across religious lines. Catholics and Protestant may live in segregated neighborhoods, but they might drink in the same pubs or share the use and management of some of the same local facilities and programs (Darby, 1986). Middle-class communities seem to be more likely to have cross-ethnic or religious organizations whose activities cut across religious barriers than the communities where poor people live. In middle-class communities, residents are often actively involved in organizations such as golf and tennis clubs, business organizations, and cultural clubs that address their common social, economic, and cultural needs and concerns.

One such community in Northern Ireland is Dunville (fictional name). Although you cannot call Dunville exactly an integrated community, there is a common infrastructure that allows Catholics and Protestants to co-exist, and consequently to protect themselves from communal violence. Dunville's middle-class residents own their homes in integrated neighborhoods. Also, Catholic business families are actively involved in the commercial life of the town and are engaged in mutually beneficial relationships with Protestant businesses. It is not contact per se, but a common interest in maintaining their business success that has led Catholics and Protestants to negotiate potentially divisive issues such as the routes of political demonstrations (Darby, 1986).

The members of both religious groups in Dunville have shared local shops and offices. Both Catholics and Protestants, for the most part, have used local pubs, clubs, and recreational facilities as community amenities. Although the local newspaper supported a Protestant, unionist agenda, it did made an effort to reach a Catholic audience by reporting Gaelic football matches and was consequently read by Catholics as well. The existence of instrumental ties has led to the development of affective relationships among some of the residents who have participated, across religious lines, in each other's christenings, marriages, and wakes.

Other researchers also confirm that ethnic riots have been rare in prosperous neighborhoods of Northern Ireland (Harris, 1972; Jackson, 1971). This is attributed in part to the residents' consciousness of the potential lost to their individual property as well as to the business life of their towns. The business and professional contacts that are established in formal interaction among residents are instrumental in protecting their personal livelihood and are used to maintained ethnic peace in times of crisis.

INTERDEPENDENT CIVIC ENGAGEMENT IN CALICUT

The conflict between Hindus and Muslims in Kashmir, India, has made ethnic violence in this south Asian country highly visible to observers around the world. The Hindu-Muslim cleavage widened dramatically after the separation of Pakistan from India in 1947 and continued to grow through the 1990s. Although highly localized, the ethnic riots that have periodically broken out in Indian communities have involved great losses to both life and property. In addition, rioting has spawned a rise of nationalistic political parties that further radicalized the Hindu and Muslim local populations.

In his research in India, however, Varshney (2002) was able to identify certain Indian localities in which residents successfully resisted the push toward intergroup violence. He attributes the absence of violence between Hindus and Muslims in such communities to the existence of local associations whose members come from different ethnic or religious groups in order to pursue a variety of superordinate goals. As civic organizations, they occupy the space between the government and the private family life in promoting public activities and common interests. Although affective relationships are important for maintaining integrated communities, Varshney argues, it is formal intergroup organizations that are more effective because of their greater resilience to outside threats. These formal ties are, moreover, substantially absent from those communities in which intergroup violence has occurred on a large scale.

In Calicut, a town in the southern state of Kerala, for example, Hindu, Muslim, and Christian residents live in integrated communities that are connected by their joint participation in formal organizations such as business groups, labor unions, professional associations, and social and cultural organizations. Calicut's Muslim population represents about 37 percent of the town's population, and over the last 20 years has made steady progress in joining the town's middle class. In addition, the community also has several important Muslim political, social, and cultural institutions and organizations such as the Muslim League, the Muslim Educational Society, the Muslim Service Society, and Farook College, the first Muslim college in Kerala. Therefore, the Muslims in Calicut have a strong ethnic identity. But this identity has not led to the development of separatist political activities. On the contrary, the Muslim League is a partner in local government and is able to use its position to provide benefits for its constituency such as state pensions for Muslim clerics and contracts for Muslim businessmen. The Muslim politicians in Calicut benefit from the stability of their community and are thus less likely to use divisive nationalistic strategies and create communal animosity (Varshney, 2002).

Muslims, Hindus, and Christians in Calicut have many points of co-operation—both instrumental and affective—in both formal and informal settings. In a survey conducted by Varshney, 83 percent of respondents reported that they eat with members of other religious groups in social settings, 90 percent reported that their children play together, and 84 percent reported that they visit each other regularly (Varshney, 2002). In addition, the residents of Calicut participate across religious groups in activities of many civic organizations and associations such as trade associations, Lions and Rotary Clubs, and reading and art clubs.

Calicut's economy is based on merchandise trade, and most of the traders and workers belong to one of the many trade associations and trade unions in the community. Historically, relationships among merchants were based on trust and did not require formal contracts. The trade associations have members from all religious groups. For example, in 1995, 11 of 26 trade associations registered with the Federation of Traders' Associations had Hindu, Muslim, and Christian officeholders: "If the president of the association was from one community, the general secretary was from the other" (Varshney, 2002, p. 127). Similarly, the members of the largest trade unions come from all religious groups. They might join political organizations within their own ethnic group, but when it comes to protecting their labor rights and wages, they join the organizations that they think will represent them better.

One of the explanations for the existence of instrumental interdependence in Calicut is that the caste differences among residents were perceived as more important than their religious differences. Because it was historically organized around issues of social justice, the political life of Calicut allowed Hindus and Muslims to forge common bonds around shared social and economic interests. The Muslims were seen as another caste that was put down by Brahmins. Caste divisions thus overshadowed religious divisions.

When religious tensions in the wider society reached Calicut, the residents were able to resist taking a "divide and conquer" political and economic stance by creating city-level peace committees that focused on what was viewed as good for the community as a whole. The political leaders of both groups, Muslims and Hindus, joined these committees and helped maintain peace. Moreover, the peace committees managed ethnic tensions by becoming a source of accurate information on various rumors circulating in the town that might otherwise have threatened the peace. Such formal organizations "became a forum for everybody to speak and express their anger; they have a sense of participation to all major local actors; and they provided links all the way down to the neighborhood level" (Varshney, 2002, p. 124).

THE IMPORTANCE OF CLASS IN MANAGING ETHNIC CONFLICT

Even Indian communities that do not have the rich affective connections of the residents of Calicut have maintained ethnic peace in times of crisis. The existence of Hindu-Muslim business connections in Surat, a town in the state of Gujarat, led to the formation of joint business organizations that were instrumental in protecting the old city, where most organizational members lived, from the devastating ethnic riots of 1992–93. These riots took place in Surat shantytowns and were triggered by the destruction of the Baburi mosque in Ayodhya. One hundred ninety-seven people were killed, 175 of whom were Muslim (Varshney, 2002, p. 239).

However, there were no human losses in Surat's old city. Similarly to Calicut, the business organizations there sponsored peace committees to respond to the crisis. Some Hindu residents joined the peace committees because they felt a moral obligation to protect the life of their Muslim neighbors. Although sympathetic to Hindu nationalism, other Hindus felt that their age-old business connections were more important for their economic well-being than uncertain political benefits from the riots (Varshney, 2002). Interdependence between Hindu and Muslim businesses thus became a protective force.

On the other hand, the poor residents of Surat lived in highly ethnically segregated slums. Labor contractors, working with specific ethnic groups or through ethnic networks, recruited impoverished residents for their jobs. The result was an ethnically segmented labor market with very few contacts between workers of different ethnic backgrounds. Consequently, there were no intercommunal worker's organizations. When the riots broke, there were no peace committees to intervene, and the loss of human life and property was huge.

This example confirms a more general conclusion, namely, that the poor are more likely than their wealthier counterparts in a community to suffer the consequences of ethnic tensions. As in Northern Ireland, the middle-class residents in India were more likely to develop intercommunal formal organizations to protect their common interests. That does not mean, however, that the poor cannot develop common interests and establish interdependent relationships.

Research in the United States, for example, shows how social institutions mediate relationships among the poor people in the community. In his analysis of the work of People United for a Better Oakland (PUEBLO), an organization in Oakland, California, Delgado (1993) describes how the residents of poor neighborhoods in that city were able to establish formal alliances around their common needs.

The goal of the organization was to force local human service organizations and the city government to better respond to the needs of Oakland's diverse residents. It addressed issues in education, health care, and environmental protection. It launched campaigns, like the Campaign for Accessible Health Care, to increase the number of multilingual employees in county facilities and make free immunizations available to county residents. The organization also tapped outside resources. The combination of "formal skills training, exposure to other social movement activists, and structured internal discussions developed a leadership core in PUEBLO able to envision and develop a multiracial organization with a broad-based representation" (Delgado, 1993, p. 121). The organization also developed access to national networks, making it able to obtain results of research on health care and environmental issues and to use these results in the struggle for better services.

CONCLUSION

What are the conditions under which ethnic violence can be averted? Based on a social psychological perspective, our analysis of historical examples suggests that intergroup violence is less likely to erupt where interdependence has become institutionalized. Bulgarian Jews and Christians mingled together in both public and private life; and the interdependence that developed between them helped to prevent the emergence of strong anti-Semitism. Political conditions provided additional opportunities for action as well. The Bulgarian parliament had enough autonomy and was able to use it effectively to influence the monarch. Also, the Bulgarian Orthodox Church took an active and public stand against the deportation of Jews.

In the Bulgarian experience, it was the political influence of formal organizations—occupational associations, parliament, the church hierarchy—that played a critical role in terms of influencing King Boris to withdraw his order that sent Jews to death camps. Yet, the Bulgarian example also suggests that instrumental interdependence cannot always be depended on to inoculate a people against victimization. Bulgarian Jews were not permitted by law to cooperate with their non-Jewish counterparts in most formal organizations. Thus, affective interdependence in the form of close friendships and neighborliness at a grassroots level was absolutely essential in saving Bulgarian Jews from certain death. The influence of ordinary Bulgarian citizens on behalf of their Jewish friends and neighbors was so strong and widespread that it eventually forced Bulgarian's formal political institutions to defy Hitler's decree. In the absence of affective interdependence, it seems highly unlikely that Bulgaria's formal organizations, totally lacking in Jewish representation, would have found the collective will to take such a courageous stance against Nazism.

There are also circumstances in which affective interdependence simply does not exist. The Black and White residents of Jasper, Texas, were almost totally lacking in friendships that crossed racial lines—their social segregation a holdover from the Jim Crow era, especially prevalent in rural areas of the South, when informal contacts between Blacks and Whites were almost totally prohibited both by custom and law. In Jasper after the murder of James Byrd, cooperation that cross-cut racial lines was therefore based not on having mutually supportive informal ties, but on working together around shared objectives in local political organizations. In Jasper, it was the existence of instrumental interdependence that helped to maintain peace between Black and White residents.

Moreover, instrumental interdependence seems to have a particularly strong impact on intergroup relations in large and complex societies, where integration depends on the cooperation of individuals who perform specialized tasks. In what Durkheim (1893/1960) referred to as *an organically integrated society,* members cannot be counted on to hold common values or to be deeply involved with their community. Informal relations therefore lack the influence of their formal counterparts. This seems to have been the situation between Muslims and Hindus in certain areas of India, especially in urban areas, where cooperation in formal organizations appeared to be much more effective than informal ties in terms of limiting intergroup violence.

Socioeconomic differences may facilitate or retard opportunities for cooperation to occur between the members of different ethnic groups. In particular, class-based interests seem to protect middle-class communities from experiencing the large-scale ethnic violence occurring in many impoverished neighborhoods. Even in Northern Ireland, the economic investment of Protestant and Catholic residents in their communities through homeownership and businesses created strong incentives to work together toward preventing ethnic violence. In contrast, residents of Northern Ireland's working-class neighborhoods had a much harder time articulating their own class interests, forming intercommunal organizations, or developing affective ties. Their class interests were more easily obscured by their ethnic and religious differences.

The existence of a civic infrastructure consisting of independent political parties and civic organizations as well as the separation between government and religious organizations help to create a more democratic social context in which individuals have room for action. In India, Hindu and Muslim residents who joined many of their communities' civic organizations were able to organize against ethnic tensions and provocations and ultimately to prevent violence from occurring. In a similar way, the Bulgarian state was allied with the Nazis, but it was never occupied. As a result, democratic institutions were allowed some degree of freedom to make important decisions, even those that might have been offensive to the German government. This would not have been possible under authoritarian rule.

There is relatively little compelling evidence in the literature to indicate that individuals who interact cooperatively with some members of a group will generalize their positive attitudes to other members of that group or to the group as a whole (Aronson & Gonzalez, 1988; Aronson & Patnoe, 1997; Miller, 2002). Although interesting theoretically, however, the prevention of violent behavior between groups may not depend in the least on the members of society generalizing from intimates or associates. Friendship as a basis for assisting a vulnerable group to avert disaster may aim at protecting only those within an individual's small circle of friends and neighbors, but generate policies that affect every member of the vulnerable group. Similarly, formal interdependence may be motivated by a desire to protect successful relationships across groups; however, the political actions necessary to defend such relationships also assist those not involved in formal intergroup relations. In Bulgaria, for example, individual Christian citizens meant only to rescue their Jewish close friends, but hardly all Jews.

Interdependence appears to have a powerful impact on the quality of intergroup relations, but it also has its limitations. Because communities are limited by their local cultural, political, and economic context, ethnic peace is almost always fragile. It flourishes in societies that nurture civic culture and democratic political institutions. Indeed, in the presence of autocratic rule, strong formal and informal relationships between groups may be all but irrelevant.

Moreover, in times of economic instability, structural change, or political turmoil, the members of the majority group often react to a real or perceived threat to their position in society by turning against the members of minority groups in their midst. Operating under a zero-sum definition of the situation, members of the dominant group may try to limit the minority's civil rights and access to their country's economic resources. The inability of the formal governing structure to protect the human rights of all residents and to address growing social inequalities can become the root cause of many ethnic conflicts (Levin & McDevitt, 2002; Levin & Rabrenovic, 2001). Under such conditions, it may be impossible for residents to maintain their expressive and instrumental ties across ethnic lines. In order to maintain ethnic peace, therefore, we must also maintain opportunities for interdependence to develop among diverse members of a community.

REFERENCES

Allport, G. W. (1954). *The Nature of prejudice.* Reading, MA: Addison-Wesley.
Aronson, E., Blaney, N., Sikes, J., Stephan, C., & Snapp, M. (1974). Busing

and racial tension: The jigsaw route to learning and liking. *Psychology Today, 8,* 43–59.

Aronson, E., & Gonzalez, A. (1988). Desegregation, jigsaw, and the Mexican-American experience. In P. Katz & D. Taylor (Eds.), *Eliminating racism: Profiles in controversy.* New York: Plenum Publishing.

Aronson, E., & Patnoe, S. (1997). *The jigsaw classroom.* New York: Longman.

Bar-Zohar, M. (1998). *Beyond Hitler's grasp: The heroic rescue of Bulgaria's Jews.* Avon, MA: Adams Media.

Brewer, M. B., & Miller, N. (1996). *Intergroup relations.* Ann Arbor, MI: Brooks/Cole.

Comforty, J., & Comforty, L. (2001). *The optimists: The story of the rescue of the Bulgarian Jews from the Holocaust.* Van Nuys, CA: Comforty Media Concepts.

Darby, J. (1986). *Intimidation and the control of conflict in Northern Ireland.* Syracuse, NY: Syracuse University Press.

Delgado, G. (1993). Building multiracial alliances: The case of people united for a better Oakland. In R. Fisher & J. Kling (Eds.), *Mobilizing the community: Local politics in the era of the global city. Urban Affairs Annual Review, 41,* 103–148.

Durkheim, E. (1893, 1960). *The division of labor in society* (G. Simpson, Trans.). New York: Free Press.

Gurr, T. R. (2000, May/June). Ethnic warfare on the wane. *Foreign Affairs, 79*(3), 52–64.

Harris, E. (1972). *Prejudice and tolerance in Ulster.* Manchester, UK: Manchester University Press.

Jackson, H. (1971). *The Two Irelands: A dual study in inter-group tensions.* London: Minority Rights Group.

Labalme, J. (1999, November 17). Discussion focuses on hate crimes. *Indianapolis Star,* p. B1.

Lee, Yueh-Ting, Jussim, Lee, & McCauley, Clark. (1995). *Stereotype accuracy: Toward appreciating group differences.* Washington, DC: American Psychological Association.

Levin, J., & McDevitt, J. (2002). *Hate crimes revisited: America's war on those who are different.* Boulder, CO: Westview Press.

Levin J., & Rabrenovic, G. (2001, December). Hate crimes and ethnic conflict: An introduction. *American Behavioral Scientist, 45*(4), 574–587.

Miller, Norman. (2002, Summer). Personalization and the promise of contact theory. *Journal of Social Issues, 58*(2), 387–410.

Sherif, M., & Sherif, C. (1961). *Intergroup conflict and cooperation: The robbers cave experiment.* Norman, OK: University of Oklahoma.

Shlachter, B. (1999, February 27). Jasper breathes a sigh of relief. [Online]. *Fort Worth Star-Telegram.* www.dfw.com.

Temple-Raston, D. (2002). *A death in Texas*. New York: Henry Holt.
Todorov, T. (1999). *The fragility of goodness: Why Bulgaria's Jews survived the Holocaust*. Princeton, NJ: Princeton University Press.
Varshney, A. (2002). *Ethnic conflict and civic life: Hindus and Muslims in India*. New Haven, CT: Yale University Press.

CHAPTER 14

Why Does Violence Trump Peace Building? Negativity Bias in Intergroup Relations

Clark McCauley and Joseph G. Bock

This chapter addresses a problem often noted but seldom theorized by those working for peace and conflict resolution. After years of progress in building positive interethnic relations, the resulting goodwill can evaporate after a single incident of intergroup violence. We describe this problem in the case of an aid agency working in Ahmedabad, India (Bock, 1995), and briefly mention similar difficulties in other contexts. We hypothesize that this experience can be understood as one aspect of a very general phenomenon of "negativity bias": the human tendency to react more to negative events than to positive events. For intergroup relations, negativity bias means that building intergroup harmony is not enough; active intervention is required for defusing incitements to violence. Initiation of negative events is not usually under the control of those working for peace, but reaction to these events can be usefully prepared.

AHMEDABAD: A CASE HISTORY OF DISAPPOINTMENT

The Setting

Ahmedabad is the commercial capital of the state of Gujarat, on the northwest coast of India. The city has a population of close to 2.9 million, of which roughly 20 percent is Muslim and 70 percent is Hindu (National Institute of Urban Affairs, 1994). Other religious groups, present in small percentages, include Buddhists, Christians, Jains, Sikhs, and Zoroastrians.

Politically, the state of Gujarat has been a stronghold of the secular Congress (I) Party. But, in recent years, this party has lost its political lead to the nationalistic-Hindu Bharatiya Janata Party.

It is estimated that over 40 percent of Ahmedabad's population lives in slums. Many of the slum dwellers are migrants from rural areas suffering from food insecurity. They live in shacks as squatters.

Interethnic violence has been a persistent problem in Ahmedabad, particularly between Hindus and Muslims, a sort of micro-manifestation of the international enmity between India (which is predominantly Hindu) and Pakistan (which is predominantly Muslim). There are three main factors that contribute to interethnic conflict between Hindus and Muslims in India. First, there is the history of antagonism following Islamic proselytizing after the Muslim conquest of India in the eighth century. Some historians have alleged that this antagonism was exacerbated by a British colonial "divide-and-rule" approach. Second are psychological and ethical differences associated with two different worldviews. Although Hinduism articulates what many perceive as a polytheistic theology, Islam is vehemently monotheistic. And, finally, there are economic factors. In India, Muslims tend to have lower incomes than do Hindus (Patel, 1995, pp. 371–375).

Major riots occurred in Ahmedabad in 1969, causing nearly 660 deaths, 1,084 injuries, and the displacement of 27,750 people (Khan, 2000, p. 19). Substantial riots erupted again in November–December 1990, killing 105 people and injuring 177. After Hindu militants destroyed a mosque in the northern city of Ayodha, riots during December 1992 and January 1993 (including in two of the slums referred to following—Maahajan-no-Vando and Sankalitnagar) killed 95 people and injured 143. Most recently, in 2002, following the fatal burning of 58 Hindu train passengers returning from a pilgrimage to Ayodha, over 600 people in Ahmedabad died in interethnic bloodletting, and an estimated 50,000 Muslims fled their homes for safety ("India's Hindus and Muslims," 2002; Khan 2000, pp. 19–20; Patel, 1995, p. 375).

It is believed widely that riots in the Ahmedabad slums are cultivated deliberately by three different groups. The first are politicians who attempt to make the ruling party seem weak or incapable of governing. Second are real estate developers who use a riot to clear people off of "squatted" land. Real estate developers are able to take over and develop this land, thereby bypassing the legal protection of "squatters' rights." And third are bootleggers in this state in which liquor is illegal (in contrast to many other Indian states where liquor is legal). Rival bootleggers can attack one another through the "destruction of turf," rather like the violence exhibited in the United States by rival drug-dealing groups and other organized crime operations.

These groups are led by violence-promoting leaders who orchestrate incitement activities and promulgate venomous rhetoric to foster ethnic nationalism. Leaders tend to employ the services of operatives skilled in the art of promoting violence; these "riot engineers" often work as mercenaries who, rather than fighting wars, implement campaigns designed to foster bloodshed (Brass, 1997). As reported by Nandy: "Over the years the role of organisation and rational cost-calculations have expanded enormously. During the 1980s, . . . Bhiwandi, Delhi and Ahmedabad have seen fully planned and expertly executed pogroms [violence aimed at one religious group] run by hired psychopaths . . . who not only start and sustain mob violence but do so without necessarily believing in much of the fanaticism, stereotyping and prejudice they spread, promote or sustain" (1995, p. 59). Put another way, although they may use religious symbols and rhetoric to foment ethnic nationalism, their fidelity to the religion they are exploiting is often lacking. They may appear to be "fundamentalists," when, in fact, they lack religious conviction (see Williams, 1994, p. 796).

Although there are numerous examples of how riot engineers foment violence, some of the approaches identified in Ahmedabad include: (1) hurling rocks into a slum and then spreading rumors that they were thrown by those of a different faith; (2) propagating hate-filled rumors as to how Muslims cheered for the Pakistani cricket team after it defeated India's team; and (3) desecrating publicly a holy book, like the Koran, while creating the appearance that Hindus did it out of disrespect for Muslims. This third tactic, deploying religious symbols in the cause of violence, seems to have the greatest potency in inciting violence, particularly when conducted on religious holidays or during religious festivals.

The existence of political and economic interests that profit from ethnic riots, and the employment of riot engineers to instigate such riots, cannot alone explain the repeated and large-scale killing that takes place in these riots. The riot engineers do not, after all, conduct the riots; they instigate others to do the killing, burning, and looting. The question remains as to how this instigation is so frequently and bloodily successful.

This question must be asked particularly when rioting occurs against a background of years of organized peace building in the same slums in which the rioting occurs.

The Aid Agency

Saint Xavier's Social Service Society ("St. Xavier's") was founded in the early 1970s by a Jesuit priest, Fr. Ramiro Erviti, in response to the flooding of the Sabarmati River, which flows through Ahmedabad. From this beginning, Saint Xavier's has continued to provide relief and development assistance to the poorest people of Ahmedabad. Fr. Erviti died suddenly in 1986 and was replaced in 1987 by Fr. Cedric Prakash, who also served as Coordinator of Social Works for the Ahmedabad Diocese. St. Xavier's received financial support mainly from various Catholic nongovernmental organizations in Europe and received food aid support from Catholic Relief Services of the United States.

During the 1990s, St. Xavier's had an annual budget of roughly $100,000 to $125,000, with an additional $1 million in food commodities for institutional feeding and food-for-work projects, both in Ahmedabad and in surrounding areas. Its staff has averaged around 20 full-time people, with other health workers employed on a part-time, contractual basis. In India, this is a relatively large operation for an indigenous aid agency and the size of the operation affords St. Xavier's a role in various civic organizations, including those formed to prevent interethnic conflict.

St. Xavier's has focused the majority of its work in three large, flood-prone slums: Sankalitnagar, Mahajan-no-Vando, and Nagori Kabarasthan. The average family income in these slums is roughly $40–50 per month. Family dwellings tend to be around 10 feet by 12 feet in size and are made of discarded materials, such as cardboard and scrap metal.

Types of Programs

The assistance provided by St. Xavier's in these slums has included community health services, flood relief, education, human rights advocacy, establishment of women's committees, and programs focused on improving the environment. In addition to these traditional relief and development activities, St. Xavier's, starting in 1991, began to focus on violence prevention in order to counter ongoing ethnic tensions.

Fr. Prakash has categorized St. Xavier's violence-prevention activities as either *promotive* or *preemptive. Promotive* activities were designed to foster interethnic good will. These have included sponsoring and organizing various activities with an interfaith harmony theme, including street plays, creative competition for children (such as art and poetry contests), an annual people's festival, and other events organized by community committees designed to promote interethnic good will. St. Xavier's has also integrated interfaith harmony themes implicitly into their other more traditional relief and development programs by, for instance, linking together Hindus and Muslims in a common educational project.

Preemptive activities, on the other hand, are designed to arrest incipient violence. These activities are less devoted to promoting interethnic good will than to counteracting incitement. St. Xavier's has used four kinds of preemptive activities. First is "myth busting" when riot engineers have spread venomous, malicious rumors based on half-truths or lies. These rumors are often spread through the distribution of handbills. Community peace committees organized by St. Xavier's have intervened quickly to develop a factual account of alleged out-group violations (rock throwing, Muslims cheering for Pakistan) and then have communicated widely their findings. Second, St. Xavier's has provided safe haven to groups threatened with imminent violence. For instance, St. Xavier's secured refuge in a school building for a group of Muslims who were being attacked by a group of Hindus. Third, St. Xavier's has urged influential community leaders to intervene to deflate bigoted, hate-filled hysteria when it starts to mount. Finally, St. Xavier's has requested police intervention to head off incipient intergroup violence.

Effectiveness of Promotive and Preemptive Interventions

St. Xavier's programs have had some success in promoting interethnic good will. Evidence of this success includes: (1) the exchange of ceremonial bracelets called *rakhis* between Hindu women and Muslim men in Mahajan-no-Vando in 1993, a tradition that signifies a respectful, protective sister-brother relationship; (2) the majority Hindus helping minority Muslims to get food and water when the government has imposed a curfew in anticipation of a riot; (3) the widespread use of a harmony song promoted by St. Xavier's, both by individuals in the three slum areas and by the media;[1] and (4) people of one faith sitting protectively in the front doorway of those of a threatened faith when tension is high.

Preemptive activities have also had some success. For instance, when riot engineers spread a rumor that local Muslims were cheering for Pakistan when Pakistan's cricket team beat India's, the community peace committees were able to prevent violence by publicizing the fact that local Muslims had not, in general, been rooting for Pakistan. The committees argued effectively that the applause was simply an expression of awe at one individual's skillful play.

But there has been failure as well. For instance, in December of 1992, following the destruction of a mosque in Ayodha by Hindu militants, rioting erupted in Sankalitnagar and Mahajan-no-Vando. Staff members of St. Xavier's were driven out of the slums, despite having done substantial promotive work there. Commenting on this, the director of St. Xavier's wrote in his annual report, referring to the Sankalitnagar slum, that the incident "shook the very foundations of years of innovative and pioneering work done by the organization. . . . we were aghast as the minority community (which constituted a majority there)—hounded out the other few, who did not subscribe to their creed—and burnt most houses. We asked ourselves—'what has happened to the community organizations, which were so carefully nurtured over the years. . . .' Somewhere, something seriously had gone wrong" (Prakash, 1993).

Experience at St. Xavier's indicates the particular power of religious symbols: success in defusing conflict based on a secular symbol (national cricket team) but failure when the instigation to conflict was based on an attack on a religious symbol (Ayodha mosque). When religious symbols were manipulated by riot engineers, the staff members of St. Xavier's and the various community peace committees found themselves unable to counteract collective violence. In only one instance were they successful when a religious symbol was involved, and that was when they combined their own preemptive activities with a plea for timely intervention by the police. The incitement involved the construction of a Hindu temple near a fire brigade station, which was provocative to nearby Muslims because it was erected on public property. In this instance, the police inserted themselves physically between the violence-prone Hindus and Muslims, preventing violence.

Focusing on Violence Preemption: An Example

Experience at St. Xavier's pointed to two conclusions. First, long and intense work in promoting intergroup harmony could be undone within hours of an incitement to violence. Second, at least on some occasions, this incitement could be answered with interventions aimed at preempting violence, although incitement based on manipulation of religious symbols seemed particularly difficult to counteract effectively. The relative success of violence preemption stood out against a background of investment in harmony promotion; St. Xavier's had for many years emphasized peace-building activities with relatively little attention to violence prevention. Experience seemed to suggest that a more balanced promotive-preemptive approach might be more fruitful.

From this perspective, a pilot project was developed in Palestine/Israel in 1999 to focus on preemptive activities that would emphasize mobilizing religion and religious symbols in responding to incitement to violence. Paralleling the Oslo Accords that had established an anti-incitement committee composed of officials from the Israeli government, the Palestinian Authority, and prominent U.S. citizens,[2] the pilot project aimed at developing an unofficial version to parallel the official committee, mirroring in anti-incitement what has been done in diplomacy. Whereas in the latter case this has been called "Track II Diplomacy," the pilot project was referred to as "Track II Anti-incitement" (Bock, 2001).

The initial phase of the project was primarily to undertake action research. Eighteen students were recruited to conduct this research from Bethlehem, Hebrew, and Hebron universities. Half were Israelis; half were Palestinians. There were an equal number of Christians, Jews, and Muslims and an equal number of men and women. In addition, three religious leaders—a mufti, a rabbi, and a priest—were brought into the project to help guide the students and to provide theological depth.

The project was launched at the Tantur Ecumenical Institute that borders Bethlehem and Jerusalem, a relatively neutral setting. A series of workshops were held. Initially, students spent a considerable amount of time discussing their different perspectives and relating their experiences. Later, there was considerable discussion about preemptive approaches and the potential role of religious leaders. A recent example of a preemptive intervention was presented: A Jewish rabbi who confronted a Jewish militant group that was about to thrust the head of a pig (an animal repugnant to Muslims as well as to Jews) onto the Al-Aqsa Mosque in the Old City of Jerusalem, Sephardi Chief Rabbi Eliahu Bakshi-Doron, wrote to the Chairman of the Palestinian Authority, Yasser Arafat, condemning the plan, stating, "We were sad to hear of the criminal plot by extremists who wished to harm the faith and faithful and inflame relations between the religions. We denounce any attempt and evil thought which could put off peace and friendship." He also extended warm greetings to the Muslim faithful during their holy month of Ramadan (Atallah, 1998; Wohlgelernter & Rudge, 1997).

The rabbi's letter was publicized and served to defuse the mounting Jewish-Muslim tension. What was noteworthy about this was that a prominent religious leader had preempted violence effectively, by acting publicly and using his theological legitimacy to confront those of his same faith who were being aggressive toward another group.

As the project unfolded and research findings were presented, two conclusions presented themselves. The first was that preemption had been viewed too narrowly. The problem was more accurately understood as interethnic hostility and aggression, and the students had uncovered many different forms of it: written (in various publications); verbal (especially at places of worship); electronic (a startling amount was found on the Internet); and symbolic (such as the construction of a mosque near the Church of the Annunciation in Nazareth, which strained Muslim-Christian relations considerably). What became clear is that violence, which is physical aggression, needs to be viewed as but one aspect of the problem and that trying to arrest violence only at the last moment is too limiting. Rather, it became increasingly clear that preemption should include measures that can be taken against hostile sentiments and behaviors that occur early in the pathway to violence (Tambiah, 1986).

The second conclusion was that, for maximum effect, counteracting aggression associated with religious difference probably needs to occur intrareligiously. When Palestinian students focused on aggression by Jews, the Jewish students felt uncomfortable. They argued that it would be much more constructive to focus on aggression by those of one's own faith. This is consistent with the recommendation of the Carnegie Commission on Preventing Deadly Conflict, which argued for more substantial efforts by religious leaders in confronting their aggressive coreligionists (1997, pp. xii and 114).

The Track II Anti-Incitement Project has not been abandoned, although, at the time of this writing, implementation has broken down in the midst of the Second Intifada. The breakdown is, like the riots after the destruction of the Ayodha temple, an example of an attempt to preempt violence lost in an incitement to violence based in the manipulation of religious symbols: The Second Intifada began with Ariel Sharon's visit to the Temple Mount in Jerusalem. But the early stages of the Track II project succeeded at least in suggesting that preemption may work better if religious leaders focus on their coreligionists in standing up against aggression in all of its forms at early stages of interethnic tension. That is, preemption could perhaps be better understood as within-group intervention rather than intergroup intervention.

PREEMPTION VERSUS PROMOTION: WHY IS INCITEMENT STRONGER THAN PEACE BUILDING?

We believe that the experience of St. Xavier's is all too common. Long-term, creative, grassroots interventions to promote harmonious intergroup contact are often lost in the reaction to a single negative event, whether rumor (throwing stones, cheering the enemy) or fact (destruction of a mosque). Echoing Father Cedric Prakash, who was then director of St. Xavier's, we must ask what has gone wrong. A clue emerges from occasional successes in heading off intergroup violence: preemption of violence seems to be required no matter how successful the promotion of intergroup harmony has been. It appears that increasing positive intergroup relations is not enough to control the impact of an incitement to violence.

Here we propose that doing good is a weak antidote to hostility and violence because of negativity bias: negative events generally dominate positive events in human perception and judgment. In support of this contention, we will offer a brief overview of research in psychology that has been more extensively reviewed elsewhere (Baumeister, Bratslavsky, Finkenauer, & Vohs, 2001; Rozin & Royzman, 2001). We recognize at the outset that this evidence has come from research in individual psychology rather than from research in intergroup relations. Nevertheless, the consistency of the evidence at the individual level is sufficiently great that we are confident in projecting the same tendency to the group level.

Negative Versus Positive Events Equated for Objective Value

A particularly clear demonstration of negativity bias emerges from research showing the greater subjective intensity of negative events compared with positive events of objectively the same intensity. One example of this kind involves comparing reactions to gains and losses of the same amount of money. Gain of a thousand dollars is typically rated less good than the loss of a thousand dollars is rated bad, for instance. When the same outcome can be framed as either loss or gain (e.g., 10 percent who take a drug die, versus 90 percent who recover), the outcome framed as loss is typically seen as worse (Tversky & Kahneman, 1991).

Negative Versus Positive Events in Everyday Experience

Although the comparison of extremes is difficult, the worst negative events seem to be worse than the best positive events are good. What positive event can balance the death of a loved one? Indeed there is a special name and special concern for the impact of extreme negative events. The impact is referred to as "trauma" with the implication that the effect of the traumatizing event is indelible. The concept of trauma is invoked for horrific events of abuse or loss, especially when such events occur to children. There seems to be nothing like a parallel positive event that is so positive that its effect is indelible, or, if there are such events, they are rare enough that there is no special word to refer to their positive impact.

More Attention to Negative Emotions and Events

Negative emotions seem to be more differentiated linguistically than positive emotions. Averill (1980) undertook an exhaustive listing of emotion words in English, and found that 68 percent of the 558 words referred to negative emotional experience. Another measure of attention to negative events is the amount of time and effort spent interpreting these events. Weiner (1985) reviewed 17 studies of causal attribution and found that, whenever positive events were contrasted with negative events, the negative events elicited more attempts at explanation.

Many have noticed that television, radio, and newspapers offer a preponderance of negative events in the news. To some degree, this attention may have to do with the visual excitement of fires, floods, and accidents in comparison with the visual boredom of new buildings, happy graduates, and families reunited. But it is not clear that radio, with no visuals to offer, is any less focused on negative events than television and newspapers.

More Empathy for Suffering than for Success

Empathy, sympathy, and compassion are concepts that share the idea of an observer's negative affective reaction to the negative situation of another. Rozin and Royzman (2001) point out that one can imagine a parallel response in the positive domain: a positive affective reaction to the success or glory of another. But Royzman and Kumar (2001) review evidence indicating that negative empathic responses are more common, more differentiated, and more likely to go beyond family and friends than positive empathic responses. That is, positive empathy tends to occur only when the successful other is very close to the self, whereas negative empathy can occur when the suffering other is a stranger.

Positive Versus Negative Information in Impression Formation

Perhaps the oldest and best-known examples of negativity bias come from studies of impression formation (Asch, 1946). A common paradigm in this literature is to obtain evaluative ratings (on a good-bad scale) of individual personality traits such as warm, cold, honest, and dishonest. Then new raters are asked to imagine meeting someone who is warm but dishonest, or someone who is cold but honest; and to rate the person imagined (also on a good-bad scale). The typical result is that the evaluation of the combination is much closer to the rating of the negative trait in isolation than to the rating of the positive trait in isolation. Sometimes the rating of the combination is indistinguishable from the rating of the negative trait in isolation, and indeed occasionally the rating of the combination of a positive and negative trait is worse than the rating of the negative trait in isolation (Rokeach & Rothman, 1965)!

This literature has been reviewed a number of times over the years, and each review comes to the same conclusion: negative information about a person has much more impact on the overall impression than positive information, even when the goodness and badness of the information is rated equally when the information is rated in isolation. This phenomenon is commonly referred to as "positive-negative asymmetry" (Peeters, 1989).

Positive Versus Negative Behavior in Moral Judgment

Moral judgment may be considered a special case of impression formation, in which more is known about the person being judged than is usually known in impression formation experiments and in which the evaluation of interest is explicitly a judgment of moral worth. Moral judgment is inevitably a judgment in which both good and bad behaviors—positive and negative events—have to be integrated into an overall judgment. This conclusion follows from the fact that real people are mixtures of good and bad behaviors; we all have at least some behaviors to be ashamed of and some redeeming behaviors to set against our crimes.

Unfortunately, philosophical discourse and psychological research both suffer the defect of having focused on moral judgment of single acts or offenses, rather than on moral trajectories or character (Kupperman, 1991).

In a rare exception, Rozin and Royzman (2001) report an unpublished survey suggesting that the typical undergraduate would not forgive a convicted murderer unless the murderer subsequently saved at least 25 lives. The salience of the tragic flaw in literature (Macbeth) and in politics (President Clinton) suggests that moral judgment of character, when investigated, will show negativity bias that equals or even exceeds the negativity bias found in the more abstract literature of impression formation.

Positive Versus Negative Events in Relationships

Both positive and negative events in a relationship can affect satisfaction with and continuation of the relationship. But negative events have consistently been found to be more powerful. Research with couples, for instance, found that negative interpersonal behaviors were more powerful than positive behaviors (behaviors coded from videotapes of couples' interactions) as predictors of overall relationship quality (Gottman, 1994). In particular, Gottman found that negative reciprocity in videotaped interactions predicted marital distress two years after the videos were made, whereas reciprocity of positive affect did not reduce the likelihood of distress. In other words, returning positive for positive in taped interaction was not related to marital satisfacton, but returning negative for negative was a powerful warning sign. Gottman proposes that a relationship is unlikely to succeed unless the ratio of positive-to-negative behaviors is at least five to one.

Summing Up Negativity Bias

The evidence just reviewed gives some indication of the extent to which negative events overpower positive events in human perception, attention, and judgment. People are not averaging machines in which positive and negative information is given equal weight; instead, bad dominates good in the same way that a cockroach makes a glass of juice undrinkable. The origin of negativity bias is not clear (Baumeister et al., 2001; Rozin & Royzman, 2001), although it seems plausible that biological survival may be forwarded by greater attention to negative events.

THE IMPLICATIONS OF NEGATIVITY BIAS FOR CONFLICT RESOLUTION

The experience of St. Xavier's points to what we believe is an all-too-common pattern: years of patient work in resolving conflicts and building interethnic harmony can be swept away in hours or even minutes by the occurrence of some new incitement to hostility and violence. The incitement is usually a perception of out-group threat or violence against the in-group. Following Fr. Prakash, the question we want to ask is how a relatively large investment of resources in peace building can be undermined with such an apparently trivial investment in incitement to violence.

Of course, a history of intergroup hostility and violence is important in multiplying the impact of any incitement to violence. As Horowitz (2001) suggests, this history is what makes it easy to interpret a particular incitement as intended and representative. That is, the history makes it more difficult to see a particular incident of stone throwing or assault or rape or symbol violation as the work of a criminal few. It is the history of conflict that makes it easy to attribute the incitement to the entire out-group.

Sometimes, as in the case of the rumor of Muslims cheering for Pakistan over India in cricket, the power of the incitement can be undermined by rumor busting. Sometimes an intergroup attribution of the incitement can be blocked, if leaders of the malefactors' own group will disavow them as criminals or otherwise unrepresentative of their group. Sometimes the power of incitement can be countered by police or military power deployed to prevent violence.

But sometimes, as in the case of the destruction of the Ayodha mosque, the facts of the incitement are not easily challenged, the malefactors are not easily cut off as unrepresentative criminals, and the local police power is unwilling or unable to control initiation and escalation of intergroup violence. Both the successes and the failures, we argue, reveal the nature of the problem for peace building: peace building usually means encouraging positive intergroup events, but only active inhibition of verbal and physical aggression can succeed against incitements to violence.

We propose that the psychology of this imbalance is the psychology of negativity bias. When it comes to evaluating combinations of positive and negative events, negative events dominate the overall impression. It is true that the research cited for negativity bias is almost always to do with evaluating individuals rather than groups. Only the research on evaluating marital relationships gets explicitly beyond the individual level of analysis. As described earlier, this research finds negativity bias so strong that one investigator suggests that a successful relationship requires a ratio of positive to negative that is at least five to one. We expect a similar or even stronger imbalance when future research examines negativity bias in judgments of ethnic out-groups.

Thus, we believe that negativity bias is an important part of the explanation of the relative weakness of peace building and the relative power of incitements to violence. Once recognized, this problem leads to explicit investment of resources in preventing or countering the negative intergroup events that incite violence. Preparations for rumor busting, mobilizing moral authority against violence, encouraging individual rather than group attributions for wrongdoing, and even building relationships with police—require resources and attention to the extent that intergroup relations are dominated by negative events.

CONCLUSION

It would be an overgeneralization to conclude that peace building interventions in ethnic conflict should be abandoned. Clearly, intergroup dialogue and cooperative activities to build harmony are useful and have their place (Maoz, 2000). Yet our analysis suggests that the effectiveness of promotive activities hinges on whether they are linked to preemptive interventions that are designed to arrest aggression and prevent violence at an early stage. If preemptive activities are undertaken only in the immediate threat of violence, then preemption, too, is likely to be of limited effectiveness. Rather, the focus should be on counteracting interethnic aggression even when it is only modestly exhibited in words or pictures. Even symbolic aggression lays a foundation of threat that can be exploited by riot engineers who are skillful in manipulating cultural and religious symbols.

In the application of a preemptive strategy against violence, there seem to be three possible levels to consider (our thanks to Paul Rozin for this formulation). The first and most difficult is to prevent the kind of threat or attack that is seen as an incitement to violence. This is very difficult, because incitement is an obvious and reliable strategy for blocking peace. A minority opposed to a political solution of intergroup conflict will often try to block accord by means of some kind of violent act that incites additional hostility and violence.

The second level is to interpret a threat or attack at the individual level as the responsibility of individual perpetrators, rather than at the level of one group threatening or attacking another. When two groups suffer from a history of hostility and violence, this kind of moral reframing will also be difficult but, as noted in several of our examples, can at least sometimes be effective.

The third level requires preparation of police or military force to preempt violence. As Horowitz (2001) notes, even the most bloodthirsty rioters are usually careful to attack only where they have numerical superiority and a confidence that police will be absent or sympathetic. The last bulwark against intergroup violence is thus a confidence on both sides of a conflict that police or military will be ready to act against those who would use violence. This again is a difficult prescription, which amounts to seeking responsible government with police and judiciary that are independent of political sympathies.

Despite these difficulties, a greater focus on preempting aggression and violence may be necessary for effective peace keeping.

ACKNOWLEDGMENTS

The authors would like to acknowledge the support of their collaboration by the Solomon Asch Center for Study of Ethnopolitical Conflict.

NOTES

1. Following is a transliteration of the song from Gujarati into English: "Here is the message of communal harmony . . . Allah and Ishwar are one . . . Do not fight over a temple or mosque. . . Politicians fight for power . . . The huts of the poor are set aflame . . . The lust for power is the fuel . . . Look at what has happened to our city . . . For someone's fault someone else is punished . . . If we, the people, live in harmony . . . Nobody will dare to disunite us . . . This is the message of communal harmony."

2. The Accord read, "the Palestinian side will issue a decree prohibiting all forms of incitement to violence or terror, and establishing mechanisms for acting systematically against all expressions or threats of violence or terror. This decree will be comparable to the existing Israeli legislation which deals with the same subject. . . . A US-Palestinian-Israeli committee will meet on a regular basis to monitor cases of possible incitement to violence or terror and to make recommendations and reports on how to prevent such incitement. The Israeli, Palestinian and US sides will each appoint a media specialist, a law enforcement representative, an educational specialist and a current or former elected official to the committee" (Interim Agreement, September 28, 1995, provided by Ralph Amelan of the U.S. Embassy in Tel Aviv, Oct. 15, 1999).

It should be noted that the effectiveness of this committee was compromised significantly by the perception among Palestinians that its work would inevitably amount to a one-sided accusatory exercise, with criticism generally being made toward them. According to Ben Ziff, formerly of the U.S. Consulate in Jerusalem, and Julie Conners of the U.S. Embassy / Tel Aviv, anti-incitement is becoming a focus of the U.S. diplomatic corps, especially in reference to parts of Africa and the Balkans. Interestingly, the U.S. military is now focusing some of its training on anti-incitement (Ben Ziff and Julie Conners, personal communication, 1999–2000, Jerusalem).

REFERENCES

Asch, S. (1946). Forming impressions of personality. *Journal of Abnormal and Social Psychology, 41,* 258–290.

Atallah, N. (1998, January 2). Muslim leaders shaken by Al-Aqsa pig plot. *Jerusalem Times,* p. 1.

Averill, J. R. (1980). On the paucity of positive emotions. In K. Blankstein, P. Pliner, & J. Polivy (Eds.), *Advances in the study of communication and affect.* (Vol. 6, p. 745). New York: Plenum.

Baumeister, R. F., Bratslavsky, E., Finkenauer, C., & Vohs, K. D. (2001). Bad is stronger than good. *Review of General Psychology, 5*(4), 323–370.

Bock, J. G. (1995). *Local capacities for peace project, case study #1.* [On-line]. Available: http://www.cdainc.com/pubs/case1.htm

Bock, J. G. (2001). Track II anti-incitement. *New Routes: A Journal of Peace Research and Action, 6*(1), 28–34. (Published by the Life & Peace Institute, Uppsala, Sweden).

Brass, Paul R. (1997). *Theft of an idol: Text and context in the representation of collective violence.* Princeton, NJ: Princeton University Press.

Carnegie Commission on Preventing Deadly Conflict. (1997). *Preventing deadly conflict: Final report.* Washington, DC: Carnegie Corporation of New York.

Gottman, J. (1994). *Why marriages succeed or fail.* New York: Simon and Shuster.

Horowitz, D. L. (2001). *The deadly ethnic riot.* Berkeley, CA: University of California Press.

India's Hindus and Muslims: After the slaughter, what hope? (2002, March 9). *The Economist,* pp. 45–46.

Khan, Sophia. (2000). *Changing social dynamics: A case study of social relationships among different communities of Ahmedabad.* New Delhi: Oxfam India Trust.

Kupperman, J. J. (1991). *Character.* New York: Oxford University Press.

Maoz, I. (2000). An experiment in peace: Reconciliation-aimed workshops of Jewish-Israeli and Palestinian youth. *Journal of Peace Research, 37*(6), 721–736.

Nandy, A. (1995). An anti-secularist manifesto. *Indian International Centre Quarterly, 22*(1), 35–64.

National Institute of Urban Affairs. (1994). Urban environmental maps for Bombay, Delhi, Ahmedabad, Vadodara. New Delhi, India: National Institute of Urban Affairs.

Patel, P. J. (1995). Inter-ethnic riots in contemporary India: Towards a sociological explanation. In U. Baxi & B. Parekh (Eds.), *Crisis and change in contemporary India* (pp. 370–399). New Delhi, India: Sage.

Peeters, G. (1989). Evaluative inference in social cognition: The role of direct versus indirect evaluation and positive-negative asymmetry. *European Journal of Social Psychology, 21,* 131–146.

Prakash, C. (1993). *Annual report.* Ahmedabad, India: St. Xavier's Social Services Society.

Rokeach, M., & Rothman, G. (1965). The principle of belief congruence and the congruity principle as models of cognitive interaction. *Psychological Review, 72,* 128–142.

Royzman, E., & Kumar, R. (2001). On the relative preponderance of empathetic sorrow and its relation to commonsense morality. *New Ideas in Psychology, 19*(2), 131–144.

Rozin, P., & Royzman, E. B. (2001). Negativity bias, negativity dominance and contagion. *Personality and Social Psychology Review*, 5(4), 296–320.

Tambiah, S. J. (1986). *Sri Lanka: Ethnic fratricide and the dismantling of democracy*. Chicago: University of Chicago Press.

Tversky, A., & Kahneman, D. (1991). Loss aversion in riskless choice: A reference-dependent model. *The Quarterly Journal of Economics, 106*, 1039–1061.

Weiner, B. (1985). "Spontaneous" causal thinking. *Psychological Bulletin, 97*, 74–84.

Williams, R. H. (1994). Movement dynamics and social change: Transforming fundamentalist ideology and organizations. In M. E. Marty & R. S. Abbleby (Eds.), *Accounting for fundamentalisms: The dynamic character of movements*. Chicago: University of Chicago Press.

Wohlgelernter, E., & Rudge, D. (1997, December 29). Chief rabbi condemns pig plot in letter to Arafat. *Jerusalem Post*.

CHAPTER 15

Some Unique Characteristics of Ethnic Conflict and Their Implications for Managing the Conflict

Stephen Worchel

I recently observed a group of children playing a game called Rip van Winkle in a park. The rules of the game required one participant to pretend that he or she had fallen asleep and awoken 50 years later. The young Rip would then tell the others how they and their neighborhood had changed during that period. I thought about that game several times over the next few weeks, wondering how my own world had changed over the last 50 years. After determining that I had not aged at all, I decided that the world of today had changed in nearly every aspect compared with that in the early 1950s. Methods of communication, modes of travel, the treatment of illness, and even the geographical maps of countries have undergone dramatic transformation. The slumbering Rip van Winkle would face a whole new vocabulary that included PCs, DVDs, e-mails, AIDS, and IRAs. He would run into young aliens with purple hair, earrings in their navel (or other unmentionable body parts), and tattoos creeping down their backs.

But Rip could take comfort that one aspect of the world had not changed. People in various parts of the world are still excluding or killing others because of their ethnicity. Indeed, Arab and Jew, Serb and Croat, and Greek and Turk are keeping the flame of ethnic hatred burning. The Kurds still search for a homeland. Incidents of racial violence can still be found in the United States. Ethnic and tribal warfare grip central Africa and deadly disputes paint the horizons in South Asia. Indigenous peoples in North America, New Zealand, and Australia, who once quietly accepted their place at the bottom of the social barrel, have awoken to claim land and rights that were taken from them.

PERSPECTIVES ON INTERGROUP CONFLICT: CONTRIBUTIONS FROM THE LABORATORY

The resiliency of the hatred between groups has perplexed social psychologists for decades. In the late 1950s, Muzafer Sherif and his colleagues assembled a group of "normal, well-adjusted boys of the same age, educational level, from similar sociocultural backgrounds and with no unusual features in their personal backgrounds" (Sherif, Harvey, White, Hood, & Sherif, 1961). The boys were bussed from Oklahoma City to a camp in rural Oklahoma, where they were divided into two groups. Each group was given its own bunk and distinctive clothing. The two groups then engaged in a series of encounters that brought them into direct competition with each other. As the competition escalated, so, too, did the hostility between the groups.

The Sherif camp studies laid the foundation for Realistic Conflict Theory (RCT) of intergroup relations. RCT argued that actual or perceived competition between groups leads to intergroup hostility and is the basis for prejudice (Brewer & Campbell, 1976; Horwitz & Rabbie, 1982; Kinder & Sears, 1981; Taylor & Moriarty, 1987). Competition fuels the perception that the out-group is a threat to the in-group (Bobo, 1988, 1999; Branscombe, Ellemers, Spears, & Doosje, 1999) and leads to the dehumanization (Bandura, 1999) and demonizing (Bar-Tal, 1990; White, 1984) of the out-group.

However, an interesting observation by Sherif et al. (1961) offered an additional insight into the world of intergroup conflict. They reported that soon after the two groups of campers were formed, and *before the competition began,* disparaging comments flew between the two groups. This observation suggests that group formation, not competition, may be the necessary ingredient for intergroup hostility and violence. This is the position of Social Identity Theory (SIT; Billig & Tajfel, 1973; Tajfel, 1970; Tajfel & Turner, 1979, 1986). In the tradition of psychology, SIT explains group and intergroup behavior by focusing on the psychology of the individual. According to the theory, one's self-identity is composed of two parts. The *personal identity* includes those characteristics such as physical dimensions and personality traits that are unique to the individual. The other side of the identity coin is the *social identity* that includes the social groups and categories to which one belongs. Other investigators (Brewer & Gardner, 1996; Luthanen & Crocker, 1992; Worchel & Coutant, 2001; Worchel, Iuzzini, Coutant, & Ivaldi, 2000) expanded the concept of social identity to include such aspects as the role and status one has within the in-groups. According to SIT, most individuals are motivated to hold a positive self-image. This leads them to join high-status groups and, once a member of a group, they seek to advantage that group relative to out-groups. Herein are the keys to the castle of intergroup hostility. In attempting to advantage their own group, individuals will disparage, depreciate, and delegitimize (Bar-Tal, 2000) the out-groups and give greater resources to the in-group than to the out-groups (Tajfel, 1970). This shabby treatment of the out-groups and the preference to the in-group is theoretically designed to enhance the individual's social identity.

Still concerned with identifying the basic seeds of intergroup hostility, Tajfel (1970) not only trained the scientific lens on the individual rather than on the group, but he also distilled the concept of group from a physical entity composed of people acting and interacting to people in the *minimal group*. The minimal group was a conceptual group or the cognitive image of the individuals that formed a category. The intriguing feature of much of the research on SIT was the demonstration that individuals could come to favor their own group and discriminate against other groups even when there was no interaction or acquaintance with members of either group.

Related to SIT was *social categorization theory* (Hogg, 2001; Turner, 1985) that concerned itself with how individuals became part of some groups/categories rather than others. However, rather than examine the interaction and negotiation processes that individuals undertake with groups to gain acceptance (Moreland & Levine, 1982; Worchel, Coutant-Sassic, & Grossman, 1992), social categorization theory focused on how individuals "think" their way into categories. Investigators (Abrams & Hogg, 1999; Turner, Hogg, Oakes, Reicher, & Wetherell, 1987) explicated the process by which individuals slice and dice the world into cognitive categories and locate themselves within some of the categories.

Social identity theory has spawned exciting and prolific research programs concerned with the relationship between groups and the individual's role in this relationship (Capozza & Brown, 2000; Worchel, Morales, Paez, & Deschamps, 1998). Research expanded beyond the minimal group and examined the relationship between existing groups. The theory is largely responsible for identifying the importance of identity as a basic ingredient in the relation between groups. Although SIT championed the role of individual identity, other investigators (Worchel, 1998; Worchel & Coutant, 2001; Worchel et al., 2000) suggested that the desire of groups to achieve a positive identity of their own also helped chart the course of intergroup relations. SIT and social categorization theory also emphasized the principle that individuals (and groups) respond to the world as they perceive/interpret it rather than to how it exists in dispassionate physical reality. In other words, cognition and mental activity are as important as actual events, conditions, and entities.

MOVING ON: THE SPECIAL SITUATION OF ETHNIC CONFLICT

As stimulating as the work on SIT and social categorization has been, one gets the feeling that it is incomplete. The appetite is whetted but the hunger is not satisfied. One critical issue that is not addressed by the approaches is how (when and why) individual cognition results in col-lective action (Worchel, in press). Intergroup violence involves united ac-tion of many people acting in unison against a target (out-group). The examination of individual cognitive processes does not give sufficient in-sight into how collectives form and act. The issue of collective action is a crucial one (Durkheim, 1898; Le Bon, 1895/1977; Moscovici, 1986; Reicher, 2001; Tarde, 1892). Worchel (in press) argued that an understanding of the processes involved in group formation and collective behavior requires an examination of both motivation and cognition at individual and group levels. Identifying the minimal conditions under which an individual may dislike or even aggress against members of an out-group does not paint a complete picture of intergroup conflict, especially conflict between eth-nic groups.

Conflict between ethnic groups tends to have unique characteristics that sets it apart for other types of intergroup conflict. First, it is frequently protracted, often occurring over generations. The "hot" spots of today's ethnic violence such as the Middle East, the Balkans, India/Pakistan, Iraq, Cyprus, and Central Africa have been bathed in blood for decades and sometimes generations. The violence ebbs and flows, but rarely is it set-tled. In fact, it is a challenge to identify any ethnic conflict of the past that one could view as being forever finished. Second, ethnic conflict is often violent in nature. Death and destruction are not limited to armies or com-batants, but generally consume innocent bystanders including women and children (Worchel, 1999). Indeed, the aim of the violence is not limited to conquering the other group, but is often designed to eliminate the group. Such is the nature of the aim that a unique term has been coined to describe it: genocide (Staub, 1989).

I (Worchel, 1999) attempted to explain the level of violence by referring to the unique nature of ethnic groups. I suggested that ethnic groups have characteristics that are not common to any other human group or category. My basic argument was that ethnicity is forever. Individuals are born into an ethnic category, and they can never change this distinction. They can-not be expelled from their ethnic group nor can they decline membership in this group. Once born a Kurd, always a Kurd. The salience and meaning (see chap. 1) of the ethnic identity may change, but not the basic ethnic distinction. Even enduring classifications such as religion or nationality can change by individual choice or outside force. Because of this fact, ethnic identity becomes the bedrock for one's social identity.

The immutable nature of ethnic identity gives a very distinct and dis-tressing characteristic to ethnic conflict. Large-scale confrontations such as war typically involve groups carved out on three dimensions: nation-ality, religion, and ethnicity. The prize in wars between nations is often measured in territorial gains, and with these gains come the people who inhabit that territory. National citizenship is a condition that can be changed with the stroke of a pen and the issuance of a passport. Hence, the inhabitants of a conquered land may be transformed into citizens of conquering nation. For example, former German citizens became Polish citizens as a result of redistributing land after World War II. In fact, a nation may grow in stature and strength by adding to its landmass and population. In the case of religious wars, the ultimate prize is the mind rather than the body. The strength of a religion, and possibly its "correctness," is often measured by the number of individuals who have adopted the specific religion. Therefore, one of the valued outcomes of a holy war is the number of infidels who can be converted to the victor's religion. Human history is filled with examples, often involving extreme cruelty, of the conquered being "encouraged" to adopt a new religion. (This view does not ignore the fact that religious wars are often accompanied by the slaughter of many nonbelievers.)

But, consider the situation of ethnic war. Here, no conversion is possible, regardless of the desires and willingness of the parties. The ethnic Jew cannot decide to become an ethnic Arab. The Hawaiian cannot be forced to become an ethnic Russian, no matter the means of persuasion applied. How, then, does a group win an ethnic war? The ultimate answer is to completely eliminate the opposing ethnic group, to commit genocide. A middle ground for achieving victory in an ethnic war is to pollute and dilute the ethnic pool of the vanquished. Hence, ethnic wars are often marked not only with high loss of life of the combatants, but also with the seemingly wanton killing of noncombatant women and children (Banton, 1997; Worchel, 1999). Further, comparisons of these wars also show an unusually high incidence of rape in ethnic wars; rape can be viewed as a symbolic and actual pollution of the ethnic line. The permanence of ethnic identification may help explain the reasons that these conflicts are so often violent and so difficult to resolve.

Although this discussion gives some insight into the nature of ethnic violence, several more basic questions must be asked. What constitutes ethnicity, and how does its meaning encompass the anthropological characteristics of land, language, leadership, and lifestyle? Why is ethnic conflict so common? Are there unusual or special conditions that must be examined to understand the causes of ethnic violence? The chapter now turns to these questions.

CHARACTERISTICS OF ETHNIC CONFLICT: CASTS IN STONE

Social Identity

According to SIT, the seeds of intergroup conflict are sown as soon as distinct groups are formed, either physically or cognitively. Several factors influence the erection of walls between groups or categories. For example, my colleagues and I (Worchel, 2001; Worchel & Coutant, 2001; Worchel et al., 2000) found that threats either to the individual or to the individual's group initiate the social categorization process and the formation of distinct categories. A terrorist attack on Jews in Israel leads Jews around the world to more strongly recognize their Jewish identity. The terrorist attack on the World Trade Center on 9/11 led Americans to engage in patriotic behaviors such as displaying flags. President Bush used this process to gain support for an invasion of Afghanistan and the suspension of individual rights within the United States. Several investigators have demonstrated a general link between threats to one's country and a rise in patriotism (Andrews, 1997; Kashti, 1997; Worchel & Coutant, 1997). Likewise, threats to an individual's identity can excite identification with a group and depreciation of the out-group. Brewer (1991), for example, suggested that personal failure can lead to greater identification with the ingroup.

Although social identity and social categorization processes lead to discrimination between groups formed on almost any basis, I (Worchel, 1999) have argued that these processes are especially likely to occur in the case of ethnic groups. The basis for this suggestion is that ethnic groups are fundamental to human identity. Individuals are born into ethnic groups and they can never change this identity. They cannot be excluded, kicked out of, or excommunicated from an ethnic group; a Kurd cannot be expelled or have his Kurdish ethnicity taken away from him. However, the meaning or salience of ethnicity can change, depending on a variety of factors. Further ethnic identity is often readily evident in physical appearance and language, characteristics that guide social categorization (Turner et al., 1987). Therefore, ethnic identity always lurks as a basis for categorizing the world and building one's identity on a solid foundation. This factor may help explain why ethnic conflict is so resistant to eradication, showing patterns of increasing and decreasing but never disappearing.

The Fateful Role of History

One of the distinguishing features of ethnic groups is their history. Although ethnic groups may be distinguished along cultural, physical appearance, and language dimensions, each ethnic group has its own history that includes information about its beginnings, its heroes and heroines, and its accomplishments and conquests (Ben-Amos, 1997; Smith, 1986). On the surface, history can be described as a combination of dates, people, and events, issues over which there is little disagreement or dispute. However, these factors are only the clothes of individual; to identify the heart and soul of history, we must dig much deeper (Gershoni, 1992).

During the last five years, I have worked with the Seeds of Peace International Camp. The camp has an eerie resemblance to the Sherif camps (Sherif et al., 1961; Sherif & Sherif, 1953). The camp brings together adolescents (14–17 years of age) and their adult supervisors from ethnic and cultural groups engaged in violent and protracted conflict. Campers come from a variety of "hot" regions, including the Middle East (Israeli, Palestinian, Jordanian, Egyptian, Moroccan), the Balkans (Serb, Croat, Kosovar, Macedonian, Bosnian, Albanian), Cyprus (Greek and Turkish Cypriots), and south Asia (Indian, Pakistani, Afghani). The campers arrive at the camp in the woods of central Maine and are assigned to bunks. Campers wear green T-shirts throughout the three-week session. These shirts signify their association with the camp but do not deindividuate them because their physical differences remain easily identifiable. To the surprise of many of them, they often find themselves sleeping next to someone from the group they consider their enemy.

Time at camp is tightly scheduled to include a variety of activities. Many of these activities are common to summer camps throughout the world: swimming, playing softball and soccer, taking archery practice, and engaging in crafts. Activity groups are always ethnically mixed. Religious services for the three major religions (Islam, Jewish, Protestant) are held each weekend, and the services are interpreted for visitors. At the conclusion of camp, the campers are broken into two large groups that engage in a variety of competitive contests. A defining activity of the camp is the coexistence sessions that are held with ethnically mixed groups. During these sessions, campers discuss their feelings and perceptions of the conflict in their region, often confronting each other over the conflicts. The adult delegation leaders who accompany have their own program and participate in their coexistence groups.

A multitude of questions can be raised about the impact of the camp on ethnic conflict. But even a short visit to the coexistence sessions reveals the causes of ethnic conflict. One of the constant themes that arises in the groups involves history, or rather, *interpretations of history*. Each side attempts to legitimize its claim to land and its political position through references to history. For example, Palestinians legitimize their land claims by arguing that the Zionist movement of the 1940s displaced Palestinians who were living on the land. The Israelis respond that there were Jewish settlements in the area in the early 1900s, and Jewish immigration to the region was simply reclaiming territory. The pages of the history book are then turned back further, as each side attempts to show that their claim to the region predates that of the other side. The Old Testament becomes the history book as the tit-for-tat interpretations of history flow back and forth. The passing of a wandering band of nomads is interpreted by one side as establishing a claim to land, but the other side views this event as only leaving a disappearing footprint in the shifting sands. There is often agreement on names, dates, and events, but total disagreement on the meaning of the events. At some point in almost every session, a point of frustration is reached, several participants throw up their hands in despair, and claim that the issue is not the past, but what to do in the present. However, in the next session, history inevitably worms its way back into the discussion. The "why" of historical events replaces the "what" of these events.

Interpretations of history are not only important for establishing legitimacy of positions, but they also define present actions. A common schism between participants from the Middle East involves the labeling of terrorists. Israelis perceive the violence as acts aimed at the peace-abiding residents. The Palestinians, on the other hand, describe the actions as the examples of freedom fighters who are struggling to regain territory that has been illegally seized. Whether it is the Middle East, the Balkans, or U.S. attacks on Iraq, history is used to define the actions of each side as being defensive. One has the impression that all ethnic wars are fought between defenders; there are no aggressors.

The interpretation of history can be viewed as a group belief (Bar-Tal, 2000) that defines a group, serves as a bond between people, and legitimizes their actions. History is best perceived as a belief, rather than a compendium of data and facts, because of the critical role of interpretation and the selective recall (emphasis) of events. Ben-Amos (1997) captures this position by stating that "Like memory, history attempts to get hold of the past through a complex process that entails selection and interpretation, which are socially conditioned. Both recollection and histography are not engaged in by self-contained individuals, but by people who act according to the cultural norms of the present, and who look at the past through the lenses of their own era" (p. 130). To forsake the interpretation of history offered by one's ethnic group is viewed as an act of disloyalty. And although nations have their own histories, ethnic histories tend to have roots that go much deeper in time and spread across national boundaries.

It is unfortunate that modern social psychology tends to be ahistorical in its approach. Groups are generally created in the laboratory (Tajfel, 1970; Worchel, Axsom, Ferris, Samaha, & Schweitzer, 1978) or randomly assigned at camp (Sherif et al., 1961). These groups have no histories, and, therefore, the research must be silent on the role of history in group formation and intergroup conflict. Likewise, Turner and his colleagues (Turner et al., 1987) are mute on the role of history in developing social categories. This omission overlooks a critical feature of intergroup conflict that may help explain why some conflicts, such as ethnic conflict, are so difficult to resolve.

"The Land": The Homeland in Ethnic Identity and Conflict

Another common theme of the coexistence sessions at the Seeds of Peace camp concerns *territory*. One of the true ironies of social science explorations is that much of the research on intergroup (and interethnic conflict) is undertaken by American scientists. Land in the United States is often viewed as a commodity that has value based on what can be grown on it, what can be mined from it, or what panoramic views can be seen from it (Worchel, Lee, & Adewole, 1975). Land is bought and sold for prices dictated by the marketplace; in many states, the land surface is traded separately from the minerals and water associated with that land. This approach to land is understandable based on the history of the United States. For the most part, Americans are immigrants inhabiting a strange territory. The native inhabitants of the land were largely driven off the land; stripped of their lifestyle, language, and leadership; and the survivors warehoused on reservations. The conquerors viewed the land as a stage where they could conduct their activities such as farming, ranching, or mining. Land that could not support these activities was essentially worthless. The roots of these new Americans reaches only a few generations into the soil.

However, a characteristic of ethnic groups is the *homeland*, the land from which the group sprung. This land has historical meaning and value that is not measured by the activities that it can sustain. The land holds the spirits as well of the bones of one's ancestors and mythical figures. For example, visitors to the Big Island of Hawai'i are warned not to take away volcanic rocks, because these are the hair of Pele and contain her spiritual being. The roots of the ethnic group reach thousands of years into the land. To be buried in the land of one's ancestors is the ultimate wish of people in many ethnic groups (Scott, 2000). From this perspective, "land is an instrument of self-transcendence" (Kelman, 1997, p. 178). The spiritual importance of land is portrayed in the myths of many indigenous peoples, and it is often at the core of the reawakening of the ethnic identifies of these people. This point is clearly seen in the strivings of such people as the Hawaiians, the Maori, and the Aborigine to regain the land of their ancestors. It is the land that provides a stability and continuity to the group. The territory may be a barren mountaintop, a stretch of desert, or a rocky hillside that has no economic value, but is priceless when measured in terms of heritage and symbolism.

The role of homeland has important implications for both the causes and the processes of ethnic conflict. If land is viewed as a commodity, pieces of territory are largely interchangeable or at least compensation for lost territory is possible. If two groups are locked in a struggle over an area, the conflict can be settled or reduced by either dividing the land between the groups or finding an adequate price to "buy off" one of the parties. This is the reasoning behind some plans to find new territories or locations for the Palestinians or splitting the island of Cyprus between Greeks and Turks. However, this approach ignores the fact that the conflict is not over land, but rather over "the land." "The land" cannot be partitioned, bought, or replaced. The failure to control the homeland represents the failure of the present generation to honor its commitment to past and future generations. Viewed in this manner, it becomes readily apparent why conflict between ethnic groups that claim the same homeland is so difficult to manage.

In an effort to examine the underlying causes of ethnic conflicts, I recently asked campers at Seeds of Peace International Camp to complete a questionnaire examining several areas. One question asked them to indicate their perceptions of the cause of conflict in several regions (including the Middle East, Balkans, Cyprus, India/Pakistan). They were presented with a host of possible causes including religion, traits of the people, leaders, media, economy, history, and land. The campers in the sample came from the Middle East and India/Pakistan/Afghanistan. History and land received by far the most nominations as the main causes of ethnic conflict in each of the regions. These data supported observations made in the coexistence groups that also implicated these two factors as the leading causes of ethnic conflict.

IMPLICATIONS FOR THE REDUCTION OF ETHNIC CONFLICT

The future of relations between ethnic groups appears particularly troubling in light of present events. Even when not accompanied by headline-grabbing acts of violence and war, the pendulum of ethnic relations in many regions has swung toward creating cleavages along ethnic lines. In some cases, there is an uplifting quality to the move. In my own state of Hawai'i, there has been an increasing effort to emphasize Hawaiian culture and language among ethnic Hawaiians. Increasing numbers of Hawaiians have undertaken the study of Hawaiian language. Hawaiian immersion schools teach regular courses in Hawaiian language. Oral histories of Hawaiian people are being transcribed and preserved for future generations. The physical landscape is becoming dotted with farms practicing early Hawaiian farming techniques and early Hawaiian fishing techniques. Extensive efforts to preserve sacred cultural sites are increasingly common.

But all is not well in Paradise. The renewal of ethnic pride and ethnic identity has become the root for several conflicts between ethnic Hawaiians and non-Hawaiians. These conflicts involve such issues as ownership of land, admission to schools, and the reach of the legal system. Calls for a Hawaiian state lead to concern and fear on the parts of some. The scenario in Hawai'i is similar to that found with indigenous people in New Zealand, Canada, Australia, the United States, and Fiji.

In other parts of the world, countries are being surgically divided (or united) into new nations along ethnic lines. The unification of East and West Germany was accompanied by great celebration, but an undercurrent of uncertainty can be found in German efforts to bring back ethnic Germans who have lived in Russia for several generations. Blood ran in the rivers of Yugoslavia as the country split into several more ethnically homogeneous countries (Serbia, Croatia, Macedonia, Bosnia). The "velvet revolution" led to the division of Czechoslovakia into the Czech Republic and Slovakia. The right-wing political parties in France gained significant power on a platform to "throw out the foreigners." The Basques of northern Spain are demanding their own nation. The Soviet Union is no longer a union, and the region is now dotted by independent countries with ethnic majorities (see chap. 9, this volume). In many cases, the smaller ethnic nations may be weaker (economically and influence-wise) than the previously united nation, but the separate independent nation stands as a monument to ethnic pride.

Admittedly, the increase in ethnic identity and the formation of ethnic states is not a new phenomenon. It has occurred at other points in human history. But the present rise in ethnically defined nation-states will write a new chapter in human history. The jury is still out as to whether this chapter will be one with a happy or tragic ending.

The research efforts in social psychology and other disciplines offer some prescriptions about how these present outcomes can be nudged toward the positive side of the equation. Several of the chapters in this book (chap. 3 [Bramel]), chap. 4 [Forbes], chap. 12 [Brislin & Liu], chap. 13 [Levin & Rabrenovic], chap. 14 [McCauley & Bock]) review the research in this area; thus, there is no need for another review. The social psychological literature suggests that equal status contact between groups working toward a common goal will help stave off violent conflict between ethnic groups. Studies by Gaertner and Dovidio (Gaertner, Mann, Murrell, & Dovidio, 1989), Brewer and Miller (1984), and Worchel (1979) suggest that inviting reinterpretation or reorganization of cognitive categories to create more inclusive groupings (human beings rather than, for example, Germans, Poles, and Hawaiians) can also propel the process toward harmony. However, Jones and Morris (1993) caution that these efforts may threaten ethnic identity and the positive contributions of unique ethnic groups.

There are, however, several factors that prohibit blindly applying the results to the area of ethnic conflict. First, there are few studies of the long-term effects of interventions relying on contact, recategorization, and culture training. Second, the interventions are often one-time events that occur in a very defined time frame. Whether the approach involves a two-to-three-week session at camp, working on a school project, receiving cultural training, or meeting in a laboratory, the examination of remedies for conflict tends to focus on a single approach or theoretical perspective. Finally, there is little effort to distinguish between the types of intergroup conflict or the ultimate goals of intervention when developing theories or approaches to intergroup conflict. All conflicts between groups tend to be viewed under the same conceptual tent, "intergroup conflict," and the implication is that all of these conflicts can be managed using a similar conceptual approach, be it contact, forming friendships, or reconfiguring categories. There is little guidance as to when contact will be most effective, despite the existence of data showing that in some cases, intergroup contact may actually increase conflict and violence (Brewer, 1986; Sherif et al., 1961; Worchel et al., 1978).

To be fair, the research provides important insight into understanding the causes, processes, and "remedies" of conflict between groups. The paradigm of developing a theoretical framework and transforming concepts into controllable empirical variables deserves high respect. The research on intergroup conflict has brought us to the point where we can ask new questions and demand new answers. It has identified psychological and social processes that accompany many kinds of intergroup conflicts. And it has shown common elements of many such conflicts.

For example, there probably are common bases, such as competition for scarce resources, the search for identity, and the desire for power that ignite intergroup conflict. However, I would argue that there are also important differences in the root causes of intergroup conflicts, and the understanding of these differences is critical in developing approaches to managing the conflict. Along these lines, I suggest that the unique features of ethnic conflict such as the role of history, the importance of homeland, and the permanence of group identity present unique challenges for managing ethnic conflict. I have witnessed countless attempts during the coexistence groups at Seeds of Peace camp to invite recategorization to reduce hostility. Repeated efforts to emphasize the fact that Jews and Arabs are truly cousins from a common family do little toward fostering goodwill. Indeed, the conflicts between family members are often the most violent and resistant to change. History lessons that attempt to correct misperceptions are generally met with suspicion and anger. Indeed, the foundations on which ethnic conflict is based may require an approach that recognizes, even celebrates, group differences. The most effective approach to ethnic conflict may not be one that seeks to reduce or minimize conflict, but rather focuses on developing nonviolent and less destructive responses to this conflict. On the other hand, other types of intergroup conflict, such as those involving labor and management, developers and conservationists, and people of different religions, may best be addressed with efforts that create shared categories. Just as there is no single root cause to intergroup conflict, there is no single medicine for dealing with all types of intergroup conflicts.

A second point that should not be overlooked concerns the concept of time. Ethnic conflicts have been part of the human landscape for centuries, and in some cases, millenniums. The root causes are deeply engrained in the human psyche and in the foundation of the groups. Therefore, it is unreasonable to expect that any remedy applied today will eliminate or even have a lasting impact on the conflict of tomorrow. We live in a world of "quick fixes" and immediate remedies. The patience of people in the Western world is short. We may wish to avoid war, but we cannot tolerate a protracted war. U.S. presidents faithfully promise that armed interventions into such areas as the Balkans, Afghanistan, Iraq, and Somalia will be of short duration, often providing a withdrawal date before the invasion. We are uncomfortable with disagreement and contention in our most intimate relationships, but if these uncomfortable states persist, our solution is to dissolve the relationship. Indeed, some intergroup conflicts can be resolved in short order, but many, especially ethnic conflicts, cannot. There is no quick solution to ethnic conflicts. Like a garden that requires constant care and tending, so, too, does the approach to ethnic conflict require constant effort. No single contact, no single course on cultural training, no single effort to redefine groups, and no single war can make a lasting difference in the course of ethnic conflict. Approaches to ethnic conflict must include a long-term focus and continuing programs. Further, these approaches must not only be applied during times of obvious strife. In fact, these may be the least appropriate times to encourage contact or recategorization. The seeds of ethnic conflict are always present in the soil of the human landscape. Contact, cooperation, and understanding between ethnic groups must be emphasized in times of peace as well as during times of conflict. Ethnic Chinese and Japanese may be living in relative harmony in Hawai'i, but this does not reduce the urgency to develop greater cooperation and understanding between them. Ethnic Italians and ethnic Germans may have found a comfortable accommodation in Switzerland, but this condition should only be viewed as creating an opportunity for developing greater contact and common efforts.

Finally, the roots of ethnic conflict are not only deep, but they are broad. They extend into schools, job settings, religious institutions, political parties, and social clubs. They infect leaders, the media, and the performing arts. As a result, efforts to manage ethnic conflict should visit each of these haunts. As heartwarming as it is to see friendships develop across ethnic lines at the Seeds of Peace camp, it is distressing to see the deep-seated ethnic hatred carried to the camp by 14-year-old youth. Daniel Bar-Tal and I found ethnic stereotypes were clearly evident in kindergarten children. Although the task of developing a broad systematic approach to managing ethnic conflict is daunting, it also opens new and exciting opportunities for research and theory. For example, programs based on different theoretical foundations may be appropriate for the young but not the old, for schools but not the political arena, for the arts but not the history books.

CONCLUSION

Ethnic conflict has many common features with other types of group conflict, but it is also uniquely distinct. I stop just short of adopting the position that ethnic conflict is "incurable," but it is clear that it serves important needs that make it very resistant to change. The role of ethnicity in individual and group identity, history (and the interpretation of history), and homeland must be considered when examining ethnic conflict. Ethnic identity and ethnic conflict are not, themselves, destructive. One needs only to witness the gracious hula at a Hawaiian luau or observe "culture night" at the Seeds of Peace camp to see the richness that ethnic groups bring to the social landscape. The care given to protecting and tending significant sacred sites offers a template for approaches to conservation and environmental protection.

Ethnic violence is not an inevitable consequence of ethnic conflict. Fiske (2002) recently published a paper entitled, "What We Know Now About Bias and Intergroup Conflict, the Problem of the Century." Few would disagree with this position, but I would argue that the "problem" of the past century(ies) and of the coming century is managing the *responses* to ethnic conflict. For example, when ethnic groups have common sacred sites, as in the case of Jerusalem, the challenge for managing the inherent conflict is to develop creative approaches to sharing control of the sites while still recognizing the legitimacy of the claims of both groups. This goal is easier identified than achieved, but recognizing and respecting the foundations of ethnic identity can guide approaches to the conflict.

This chapter has identified some of the unique features of ethnic conflict and argued that these characteristics must be considered when developing approaches to managing the conflict. The literature on intergroup relations offers a starting point for addressing ethnic conflict, but it is only a starting point. Future efforts must expand the scope of research while concentrating its focus on the features that distinguish ethnic conflict from other types of conflict. One can only hope that if old Rip van Winkle were to now begin his 50-year snooze, he would awake to a more harmonious social world characterized by positive relationships and respect between ethnic groups.

ACKNOWLEDGMENTS

This chapter was prepared with support from National Science Foundation grant (BCS-0078867) and NIOSH grant. I want to thank Elise and Hannah Worchel for their help in preparing this chapter.

REFERENCES

Abrams, D., & Hogg, M. A. (Eds.). (1999). *Social identity and social cognition.* Oxford: Blackwell.

Andrews, M. (1997). Fighting for "the finest image we have of her": Patriotism and oppositional politics. In D. Bar-Tal & E. Staub (Eds.), *Patriotism in the lives of individuals and groups.* Chicago: Nelson Hall.

Bandura, A. (1999). Moral disintegration in the perpetration of inhumanities. *Personality and Social Psychology Review, 3,* 193–209.

Banton, M. (1997). *Ethnic and racial consciousness* (2nd ed.). London: Longman.

Bar-Tal, D. (1990). *Group beliefs: A conception for analyzing group structure, process and behavior.* New York. Springer-Verlag.

Bar-Tal, D. (2000). *Shared beliefs in a society.* Thousand Oaks, CA: Sage.

Ben-Amos, A. (1997). The uses of the past: Patriotism between history and memory. In D. Bar-Tal & E. Staub (Eds.), *Patriotism in lives of individuals and nations.* Chicago: Nelson Hall.

Billig, M. G., & Tajfel, H. (1973). Social categorization and similarity in intergroup behavior. *European Journal of Social Psychology, 3,* 27–52.

Bobo, L. (1988). Group conflict, prejudice, and the paradox of contemporary racial attitudes. In P. Katz & D. Taylor (Eds.), *Eliminating racism: Profiles in controversy.* New York: Plenum Press.

Bobo, L. (1999). Prejudice as group position: Microfoundations of a sociological approach to racism and race relations. *Journal of Social Issues, 55,* 445–472.

Branscombe, N., Ellemers, N., Spears, R., & Doosje, B. (1999). The context and content of social identity. In N. Ellemers, R. Spears, & B. Doosje (Eds.), *Social identity.* Oxford: Blackwell.

Brewer, M. B. (1986). The role of ethnocentrism in intergroup conflict. In S. Worchel & W. Austin (Eds.), *Psychology of intergroup conflict.* Chicago: Nelson Hall.

Brewer, M. B. (1991). The social self: On being the same and different at the same time. *Personality and Social Psychology Bulletin, 17,* 475–482.

Brewer, M. B., & Campbell, D. (1976). *Ethnocentrism and intergroup attitudes: East African research.* London: Sage.

Brewer, M. B., & Gardner, W. (1996). Who is this "we"? Levels of collective identity and self representations. *Journal of Personality and Social Psychology, 71*, 83–93.

Brewer, M. B., & Miller, N. (1984). Beyond the contact hypothesis: Theoretical perspectives on desegregation. In N. Miller & M. Brewer (Eds.), *Groups in contact: The psychology of desegregation.* New York: Academic Press.

Capozza, D., & Brown, R. (2000). *Social identity process.* London: Sage.

Durkheim, E. (1898). *The rules of sociological method.* New York: Free Press.

Fiske, S. T. (2002). What we know now about bias and intergroup conflict, the problem of the century. *Current Directions in Psychological Science, 11*, 123–128.

Gaertner, S., Mann, J., Murrell, A., & Dovidio, J. (1989). Reducing intergroup bias: The benefits of recategorization. *Journal of Personality and Social Psychology, 57*, 692–704.

Gershoni, I. (1992). Imagining and reimagining the past: The use of history by Egyptian nationalist writers. *History and Memory, 4*, 5–37.

Hogg, M. A. (2001). Social categorization, depersonalization, and group behavior. M. A. Hogg and S. Tindale (Eds.), *Group processes.* Malden, MA: Blackwell.

Horwitz, M., & Rabbie, J. (1982). Individuality and membership in the intergroup system. In H. Tajfel (Ed.), *Social identity and intergroup relations.* New York: Cambridge University Press.

Jones, J., & Morris, K. (1993). Individual versus group identification as a factor in intergroup racial contact. In S. Worchel & J. Simpson (Eds.), *Conflict between people and groups.* Chicago: Nelson Hall.

Kashti, Y. (1997). Patriotism as identity and action. In D. Bar-Tal & E. Staub (Eds.), *Patriotism in the lives of individuals and nations.* Chicago: Nelson Hall.

Kelman, H. C. (1997). Nationalism, patriotism, and national identity: Social-psychological perspectives. In D. Bar-Tal & E. Staub (Eds.), *Patriotism: In the lives of individuals and nations.* Chicago: Nelson Hall.

Kinder, D. R., & Sears, D. (1981). Prejudice and politics: Symbolic racism versus racial threats to the good life. *Journal of Personality and Social Psychology, 40*, 414–431.

Le Bon, G. (1895/1977). *The crowd.* Harmondsworth: Penguin. (Original work published 1895).

Luthanen, R., & Crocker, J. (1992). A collective self-esteem scale: Self evaluation of one's social identity. *Personality and Social Psychology Bulletin, 18*, 302–318.

Moreland, R. L., & Levine, J. (1982). Socialization in small groups: Temporal changes in individual group relations. In L. Berkowitz (Ed.), *Advances in experimental social psychology* (Vol. 15). New York: Academic Press.

Moscovici, S. (1986). The discovery of the masses. C. F. Graumann & S. Moscovici (Eds.), *Changing concepts of crowd mind and behavior.* New York: Springer-Verlag.

Reicher, S. (2001). The psychology of crowd dynamics. In M. A. Hogg & S. Tindale (Eds.), *Blackwell handbook of social psychology: Group processes.* Malden, MA: Blackwell.

Scott, J. (2000). *The lucky gourd shop.* New York: Washington Square Press.

Sherif, M., Harvey, O., White, B., Hood, W., & Sherif, C. (1961). *Intergroup conflict and cooperation: The Robber's Cave experiment.* Norman, OK: University of Oklahoma Press.

Sherif, M., & Sherif, C. (1953). *Groups in harmony and tension.* New York: Harper & Row.

Smith, A. D. (1986). *The ethnic origin of nations.* Oxford: Blackwell.

Staub, E. (1989). *The roots of evil: The psychological and cultural origins of genocide.* New York: Cambridge University Press.

Tajfel, H. (1970). Experiments in intergroup discrimination. *Science, 223,* 96–102.

Tajfel, H., & Turner, J. C. (1979). An integrative theory of intergroup conflict. In W. G. Austin & S. Worchel (Eds.), *The social psychology of intergroup relations.* Monterey, Canada: Brooks/Cole.

Tajfel, H., & Turner, J. (1986). The social identity theory of intergroup behavior. In S. Worchel & W. Austin (Eds.), *Psychology of intergroup relations.* Chicago: Nelson Hall.

Tarde, G. (1892). Les crimes de foules. *Archives de l'Anthropoligie Criminelle.*

Taylor, D. M., & Moriarty, B. (1987). In-group bias as a function of competition and race. *Journal of Conflict Resolution, 1,* 192–199.

Turner, J. C. (1985). Social categorization and the self-concept: A social cognitive theory of group behavior. In J. Lawler (Ed.), *Intergroup behavior.* Oxford: Blackwell.

Turner, J. C., Hogg, M. A., Oakes, P. J., Reicher, S. D., & Wetherell, M. S. (1987). *Rediscovering the social group: A self-categorization theory.* Oxford: Blackwell.

White, R. K. (1984). *Fearful warriors: A psychological profile of U.S.-Soviet relations.* New York: Free Press.

Worchel, S. (1979). Cooperation and the reduction of intergroup conflict: Some determining factors. In W. Austin & S. Worchel (Eds.), *The social psychology of intergroup relations.* Monterey, CA: Brooks/Cole.

Worchel, S. (1998). A developmental view of the search for group identity. In S. Worchel, J. Morales, D. Paez, & J.-C. Deschamps (Eds.), *Social identity: International perspectives.* London: Sage.

Worchel, S. (1999). *Written in blood: Ethnic identity and the struggle for human harmony.* New York: Worth.

Worchel, S. (2001). *Perspectives on ethnic conflict and the prospects for peace.* Invited address at University of Bari, Bari, Italy, December 23, 2001.

Worchel, S. (in press). Come one, come all: Toward understanding the process of collective behavior. In M. Hogg & J. Cooper (Eds.), *Sage handbook of social psychology*. Newport: CA: Sage.

Worchel, S., Axsom, D., Ferris, F., Samaha, G., & Schweitzer, S. (1978). Factors determining the effect of intergroup cooperation on intergroup attraction. *Journal of Conflict Resolution, 22*, 227–239.

Worchel, S., & Coutant, D. (1997). The tangled web of loyalty: Nationalism, patriotism, and ethnocentrism. In D. Bar-Tal & E. Staub (Eds.), *Patriotism in the life of individuals and nations*. Chicago: Nelson Hall.

Worchel, S., & Coutant, D. (2001). It takes two to tango: Relating group identity to individual identity within the framework of group development. In M. A. Hogg & R. S. Tindale (Eds.), *Blackwell handbook of social psychology: Group processes*. London: Blackwell.

Worchel, S., Coutant-Sassic, D., & Grossman, M. (1992). A developmental approach to group dynamics: A model and illustrative research. In S. Worchel, W. Wood, & J. Simpson (Eds.), *Group process and productivity*. Newbury Park, CA: Sage.

Worchel, S., Iuzzini, J., Coutant, D., & Ivaldi, M. (2000). A multidimensional model of identity: Relating individual and group identity to intergroup behavior. In D. Capozza & R. Brown (Eds.), *Recent developments in social identity research*. London: Blackwell.

Worchel, S., Lee, J., & Adewole, A. (1975). Effect of supply and demand on the ratings of object value. *Journal of Personality and Social Psychology, 32*, 906–914.

Worchel, S., Morales, J. F., Paez, D., & Deschamps, J.-C. (Eds.). (1998). *Social identity: International perspectives*. London: Sage.

PART V

Conclusion

CHAPTER 16

Contact and Identity in Intergroup Relations

Clark McCauley, Stephen Worchel, Fathali Moghaddam,
and Yueh-Ting Lee

The United States presents a fascinating paradox. On one hand, it is one of the most ethnically and culturally diverse countries in the world. In Hawai'i, for instance, there is no ethnic group comprising over half the population. And in California there are already as many Hispanic Americans as African Americans. The growing influence of migrant populations in the United States is paralleled by growing U.S. influence in foreign lands. Rulers are made (and toppled) and economies thrive (or wither) by action (or inaction) on the part of U.S. leaders.

Yet many people in the United States remain largely uninformed about such topics as ethnicity, culture, and world geography. For example, a majority of respondents could not identify the location of Japan, Croatia, or Greece. This disconnect creates awkward and often dangerous situations for the United States in areas of foreign policy or when dealing with immigration issues. The prevailing attitude in the United States is that the country is populated by one people, "Americans," who speak a common language, English. Beneath this seemingly calm surface there is another reality: the English-only movement and the fight over whether the United States should adopt English as its official language.

The terrorist attacks of September 11, 2001, and their aftermath have greatly increased recognition of the importance of developing a better grasp of ethnic identity and related issues. A common reaction to the attacks was to question what the United States had done to incite such hatred and aggression to be aimed at its citizens. It was painfully clear that there was a general lack of understanding about the type of culture that could produce an individual willing to sacrifice his life in this manner.

There was an equal bewilderment about the possibility that people could become targets of terrorism because of who they were, not what they had done. Finally, the level of fear escalated when no simple answer could be found for the question of how to answer the threat of future terrorism. Despite a terrible arsenal of weapons and clear military superiority, the United States cannot hope to destroy all present and future terrorists.

Current conflicts, then, reinforce demographic trends to highlight the critical importance of understanding the influence of ethnic identity and culture in human behavior. Equally important is the question of how tolerance, understanding, and acceptance can be promoted between people of different ethnic and cultural groups.

The chapters in this volume have begun to address these and related issues. The approaches have ranged from basic theory to specific practices, and the authors have taken us to such diverse locations as Iran, Israel, New Zealand, South Africa, China, Bulgaria, Texas, and the isolated woods of Maine. We have visited the mosque, the workplace, and a summer camp. Despite this diversity, there is considerable common ground represented in the various contributions, and group dynamics theory offers a way to see some unity in the diversity.

GROUP DYNAMICS THEORY AND THE SOURCES OF ETHNIC AND CULTURAL IDENTIFICATION

Ethnic and cultural identity are often treated as fixed at birth, but scholars see identity as something constructed in the human mind (see chap. 1). Research has only begun to illuminate how this happens, that is, how the individual comes to care about the welfare of a category of people who are mostly unknown as individuals.

Group dynamics theory provides a way of thinking about this issue, because the theory focuses directly on the sources of group cohesion, that is, attraction to the group. The theory originated in Festinger's (1950) theory of informal social influence, was amplified in Festinger's (1954) theory of social comparison, and has been modified to take account of the different effects of the different kinds of cohesion (McCauley, 1989, 1998). The foundation of the theory is the idea that attraction to a group arises from perceived interdependence related to *group goals,* and from unperceived interdependence in construction of *social reality.* Group goals include material rewards, safety in numbers, group status, and interpersonal congeniality and friendship. The social reality provided by a group is a value-laden view of the world and the individual's place in the world; it includes answers to the questions for which science has no answer. What is right and wrong? What is beautiful and ugly? What is worth living for, and dying for? Am I a worthy person, as good as others? Individuals are not usually aware of the extent to which their view of the world depends on others, although Asch's (1956) conformity experiment and others like it can show group members taking others' opinions over the evidence of their own eyes.

Both group goals and social reality depend upon group consensus. The group cannot pursue goals effectively if group members disagree about the goal or the means. Similarly, disagreement about value issues undermines the consensus that is the only antidote to uncertainty about issues of value. Group dynamics is thus a species of homeostatic theory, in which difference of opinion on group-relevant issues is controlled by communication and social pressure aimed at bringing deviates toward consensus. The greater the cohesion, the greater the force for consensus on group-relevant issues. A particularly reliable source of cohesion is the interdependence that comes from out-group threats against the in-group, including any form of group competition that threatens material, status, and social reality goals of the in-group (see Stephan & Stephan, 2000, on *realistic* versus *symbolic* group threats). When cohesion is based on out-group threat, in-group norms include hostility toward the threatening out-group.

Group dynamics theory was developed in hundreds of studies of small face-to-face groups, although it was occasionally extended to cohesion in larger groups such as religious denominations and labor unions (Converse & Campbell, 1960). More recently, the social reality power of the group has been extended to the level of cultural groups in a formulation called *terror management theory* (Pyszczynski, Greenberg, & Solomon, 1997). Dozens of experiments have shown that individuals made to think about their own mortality are more positive toward those who uphold cultural values and more negative toward those who criticize or challenge these values. According to the theory, cultural values and rituals insulate us against the fear of death because membership in a cultural or ethnic group offers a form of immortality. Group membership is a guarantee of continuity to the extent that the group has a long history and an indefinite and preferably glorious future. Identification with a cultural group is thus a particularly powerful form of group identification, and a threat to this group is particularly likely to elicit in-group cohesion and out-group hostility.

Group dynamics theory, amplified by terror management theory, can highlight and integrate many aspects of the relation between identity and ethnicity. Of course, no single perspective can do justice to the richness of the contributions to this volume, but a group dynamics perspective can illuminate some of the varied sources of identification with ethnic and cultural groups that appear in these contributions. This is the project undertaken here.

CONCEPTUAL ISSUES IN CONTACT BETWEEN ETHNIC AND CULTURAL GROUPS

The contact hypothesis is social psychology's best-known view of what to do about intergroup conflict. Contact theory is today in flux, and the chapters in this section challenge and develop the theory in several directions.

An Evolutionary and Economic Perspective

Allen and Chagnon (chap. 2) push the envelope of attempts to under-stand group identification in material terms. First, they make explicit the problem of the free rider—the rational individual who best profits his genes by letting others take risks and make sacrifices for the group wel-fare. They explain how this problem can be solved in small groups who live in the same place, interact frequently, and have family (genetic) ties. In such groups, cooperation is genetically and economically rational. For strangers, however, selfish and exploitative behavior is so obviously ra-tional that Allen and Chagnon are led to argue for a return to the kind of small-scale society that Thomas Jefferson hoped the United States would become.

From an evolutionary and economic perspective, identification with a "category" is irrational. Although exploitation of strangers should be ex-pected, sacrifice for something as large and abstract as a cultural or ethnic group should not occur. But in fact this kind of identification is the foun-dation of intercultural conflict and ethnic group violence. Categorical identification is obvious also in more beneficent behavior in which indi-viduals care about categories they are not even part of: men caring about women's rights, Americans caring about Kosovar refugees, Europeans caring about the welfare of Palestinians. The psychology of group iden-tification begins just where evolution and economics throw up their hands.

The Origins of the Classical Contact Hypothesis

Social psychology's first idea about the effect of intercultural contact is that "it all depends." The contact hypothesis predicts that more positive intergroup relations will result if and only if individuals from different groups interact in situations in which contact is personal, equal status, cooperative, and supported by institutional authorities. Absent these con-ditions, contact theorists recognize that intergroup contact may even worsen intergroup relations. As Bramel (chap. 3) points out, contact at-taining these conditions is difficult to arrange when groups have, in fact, significant cultural differences (Maoz, 2000a). Even when contact attains these conditions, there is the difficulty of generalizing positive contact with a few out-group members to the larger group they came from.

Given the practical difficulties of applying the contact hypothesis, one may wonder how this hypothesis has been so popular in and out of social psychology. In tracing the history of the contact hypothesis, Bramel offers a creative answer to this question. The crux of his answer is history. A combination of Marxist and Freudian theories responded to Nazi racism by attributing all kinds of cultural prejudice to self-interest: material or social-status superiority of the in-group justified by negative stereotyping of the out-group. In this framing, recognition of real group differences in culture was blaming the victim and rationalizing prejudice; recognition of similarity was then the antidote to prejudice.

Whether or not one accepts Bramel's assessment of the practical value of the contact hypothesis, his appeal to history must be seen as entirely consistent with social psychology's emphasis on the power of the situation in determining behavior (e.g. Asch, 1956). It is only the behavior to be explained that is unusual; here is a rare example of a social psychologist applying social psychology to explain the behavior of social psychologists. Note that Bramel's account points to the power of *negative* identification. Hostility toward Nazi Germany and its racist ideology, particularly after Germany declared war on the United States, produced increased positive identification with American values most opposed to racism. Those values included a version of *e pluribus unum* in which common humanity meant cultures dissolving in an American melting pot. Bramel leaves us with the question of whether Americans are recovering the interest in cultural differences that pluralism is supposed to celebrate, or whether 9/11 has set Americans back into a defensive view of what unity requires.

A Two-Level Contact Hypothesis

Forbes (chap. 4) offers a different kind of "it depends" about the impact of cross-cultural interaction. Forbes argues that contact at the interpersonal level may lead to more positive views of a cultural out-group, but that, at the intergroup level, contact is likely to lead to competition. He explicates his view of intergroup conflict in an economic model in which two groups compete, each trying to make the other bear the costs of the adaptation that will produce joint benefits. More generally, an encroaching culture is a threat to the status quo, including both material and status threats.

As Forbes emphasizes, and terror management theory explicates, the nature of the threat is far more than economic. Identification with a cultural group is a particularly powerful form of group identification, and a threat to this group is particularly likely to elicit in-group cohesion and out-group hostility. From an economic and evolutionary point of view, as noted earlier, it is mysterious that people should be more willing to sac-rifice and die for a "category" like ethnicity or nation than for their co-residential kin group. Political scientists since the French revolution have wondered why men are more ready to die for their nation than for their tennis club. Terror management theory suggests that ethnic and cultural conflicts are worth dying for because immortality is worth dying for.

A Mirror-Image Contact Hypothesis

Yang et al. (chap. 5) offer still another view of the impact of contact, a kind of reflection of the classical contact hypothesis. Whereas the contact hypothesis specifies conditions under which intergroup contact will have positive effects, Yang et al. specify conditions under which immigration will lead to conflict and violence. The reassuring aspect of this specifica-tion is that Yang et al. reject the pessimism that immigration always means trouble; less reassuring is the multiplication of the varieties of competition that will lead to conflict. Cultural threat is only one among the sources of conflict, which include job competition, competition for government re-sources, and ethnic biases in government policies. Yang et al. find all of these sources of immigrant-related conflict operating in every country they consider, although weaker in historically immigrant-receiving coun-tries such as the United States and Canada, and suppressed—or re-pressed—in Japan.

In terms of group dynamics, all of these forms of competition are threats to group goals, to the social reality of the group, or to both. The result of common threat is increased group cohesion and hostility toward the threatening out-group. Group dynamics theory and terror management theory suggest some differentiation among the different kinds of threat. Threat to material resources such as jobs or government entitlements should be more easily negotiated and less likely to lead to violence than threat to cultural identity and continuity.

Whether by emphasis or addition, the contact hypothesis appears able to support both optimism and pessimism about intercultural and inter-ethnic contact. Several case studies reinforce this point.

CULTURES IN CONFLICT: CASE STUDIES

Islamic Revolution in Iran

One indication of the centrality and importance of culture is that it changes only slowly, despite enormous changes in environment (see Bra-mel, chap. 3, for research that finds African cultural elements in African Americans). Moghaddam (chap. 6) focuses on two instances of cultural continuity that persevered in Iran, despite Ayatollah Khomeini's successful revolution against Shah Reza Pahlevi. The first is a centralized style of leadership in which the Ayatollah exercised a control no less authoritarian than the Shah's. This control is the more remarkable because Shi'a religious belief emphasizes individual choice of religious leadership.

The second continuity is the meaning of the veil for women in Iran. The Shah tried to discourage the veil in order to modernize the status of women in Iran, and the Ayatollah restored the veil to express the triumph of Islam over the Shah's secular state. Beneath this continuity is a remarkable fluctuation: women freed of the veil donned the veil to participate in demonstrations against the Shah. Here is another indication of the power of negative identification.

Political identification is usually thought of as positive because an individual supports a political faction or movement as good or desirable. From this perspective, negative identification is only a reflection of positive identification: an opposing faction or movement is the target of hostility because it threatens the faction the individual is attached to. But the women who donned the veil to protest the Shah are an example of how negative identification can be an independent motive that produces positive identification. Many who were opposed to the Shah identified with Islamic forces *because* they were the strongest opponents of the Shah.

Indeed the centralization of religious power in the hands of the Ayatollah is susceptible to the same analysis. Threat from a centralized out-group calls forth a cohesive and centralized in-group, despite a history of diffuse religious authority in Shi'a Islam.

Jewish-Palestinian Conflict

The conflict between Jews and Palestinians over the land they both claim has been going on since the first Zionists arrived around the beginning of the twentieth century. The conflict has had a powerful effect on political identification on both sides, and Oren et al. (chap. 7) describe some of the intragroup consequences of the conflict. These ramify in constellations of social beliefs so far-reaching that Oren et al. describe them collectively as an "ethos" of conflict. The first constellation includes beliefs about the justness of the in-group cause and an idealization of the norms and traits of the in-group. These beliefs are linked to a construction of history that gives both in-group existence and in-group claim to the land a continuity that extends indefinitely long into the past. A second constellation includes beliefs about in-group victimization and suffering at the hands of the out-group; in-group losses are played up and out-group losses minimized in comparison. The third constellation includes beliefs about the negative characteristics of the out-group, including both their immorality and their negative traits; these beliefs can be extreme enough to see the out-group as a lesser race and not quite human.

The ethos of conflict that Oren et al. describe is easily understood as the long-term effect of the in-group cohesion and out-group hostility that follows upon out-group threat. Increased cohesion is expressed in idealization of the in-group, its norms and values, and its leaders; hostility toward the out-group is expressed in a negative view of the out-group that is the mirror image of the idealized in-group. The importance of history for both Jews and Palestinians signals the threat to social reality experienced by both groups. The value of the land is more than its material value; the conflict over land is a conflict over the ethnic continuity that promises immortality. The power of this threat-cohesion dynamic is evident for leaders on both sides. Israeli Jews' support for Ariel Sharon, like Palestinians' support for Yasser Arafat, is raised by the escalation of mutual threat that began with Ariel Sharon's police-escorted tour of Temple Mount.

Ethnic Prejudice of New Zealanders and Afrikaners

In a tour de force linking individual- and group-level theories of prejudice, Duckitt (chap. 8) shows that Afrikaner students in South Africa are more negative toward minorities than white New Zealander students, and that this difference is accounted for by the higher levels of Right Wing Authoritarianism (RWA) and Belief in a Dangerous World found for the Afrikaners. The measures are all at the individual level and ask about individual feelings and perceptions, but Duckitt argues plausibly that the pattern of results should be understood at the cultural level. Historically, Afrikaners faced a threatening and uncertain frontier existence, and, more recently, their political hegemony has been threatened and lost in a revolution of the black majority in South Africa. The history of white New Zealanders has seen less out-group threat and intergroup violence. The implication is that cultures differ in reaction to minorities and immigrants, depending on their own experience of threat and conflict.

Duckitt's suggestion is entirely consistent with Bramel's appeal to history for understanding the culture of social psychologists after World War II, and with Oren et al.'s analysis of the ethos of conflict that comes with a history of conflict. The experience of out-group threat and intergroup violence can lead, as Oren et al. argue, to cultural beliefs about in-group and out-group that are adapted to the conflict. Duckitt goes still further in suggesting that the cultural adaptation may extend to what are often thought of as personality dispositions, such as RWA. RWA, in particular, may be better understood as a cultural belief about what the individual owes the group when the group is threatened. RWA items assess idealized in-group norms, willingness to sanction deviates from these norms, and unconditional support for in-group leaders. Increased hostility toward culturally different groups is thus one implication of the increased cohesion that is the response to out-group threat.

Baltic Independence and Ethnic Conflict

Ethnic and cultural conflict are usually studied in their more florid expressions. The absence of conflict where one might expect conflict, like the dog that does not bark, is less salient but no less informative for understanding conflict. Indeed it can be argued that the cases where there is surprisingly little conflict are the best hope for learning how to reduce or ameliorate conflict.

The case of the Baltic states since the fall of the Soviet Union thus deserves particular attention. Draguns (chap. 9) offers a magisterial overview of the history of three countries that had only brief experience of independence before being invaded by first the Nazis and then the Red Army. The Soviets sent Baltic elites to die in the gulags, suppressed local language and culture, and imposed Russian language and immigrants. In short, there was no lack of grievance against the Russian immigrants when the Baltic republics emerged from the fall of the USSR in 1991. In particular, economic and cultural investments in language provide a focus for competition that directly parallels Forbes's model (chap. 4).

Despite obvious tinder for ethnic violence in the Baltics, the level of violence has in fact been surprisingly low. Draguns suggests a number of explanations. One is that mutual stereotypes of Balts and Russians include many positive traits, possibly as a result of contacts of work or neighborhood that approximate the conditions of the contact hypothesis. Another is that many Russian immigrants would rather be in a Baltic state than in Russia; indeed, Draguns reports that some ethnic Russians joined in the demonstrations that preceded independence. Still another is that the Baltic states must still live in dread of the Russian bear next door, a bear that could be aroused by violence against ethnic Russians. Finally, both Balts and Russians believe they would be better off as part of the European Union, and ethnic harmony is generally understood to be a requirement for joining the European Union. The result of these considerations is a situation of perceived interdependence for Balts and Russians, with the potential of increasing cohesion embracing both sides as they work toward common goals.

Ethnicity and the State in China

The relation between ethnicity and the state is raised by Bilik et al. (chap. 10) in considering the situation of minorities in relation to the majority Han Chinese. The long history of the Chinese empire emphasizes the extent to which ethnicity was flexible and constructed; identities that look stable in the perspective of decades shift kaleidoscopically in the perspective of centuries. Tension between center and surround, between north and south, between yellow and white—all played their part until Westerners brought the anti-empire idea that each nation or *ethnie* should have its own state. This idea was contested with some success by Marxist ideology that made ethnicity a form of false consciousness blocking worker solidarity. But, as the Red Army in Russia played the nationalities card to gain support against the Whites, so the Red Army in China played the same card for support against the Kuomintang and the Japanese.

Government support for local culture and identity, even some local political autonomy, looked like a cheap price for military success in the 1930s and 1940s. But when the center collapsed in the USSR in 1991, the political power of false consciousness was revealed in an array of newly independent republics. If the center fails in Beijing, China may see a similar revelation. The great majority are Han Chinese, who are divided by many different spoken languages despite a common written language. The example of the USSR is not lost on Beijing, which is increasingly committed to building a more homogenous nation-state. This commitment is evident in attempts to replace Tibetans and Xinjiang Muslims with Han Chinese, much as the Soviets tried to Russify the Baltics, and in appeals to nationalist sentiment for regaining Taiwan.

In theoretical perspective, the history of ethnic relations in China is a transition from more fluid and constructed ethnic identities to a current hardening of Chinese identity as Han Chinese, with attendant ethnic prejudice and violence. The special political power of culture and ethnicity, consistent with terror management theory as outlined earlier, is no longer subject to Marxist counterargument in China.

9/11 in U.S., Chinese, and Arab Eyes

Lee et al. (chap. 11) provide evidence of the gulf between Americans and the rest of the world in perceptions of 9/11. For American students, the terrorist attacks were a common threat that led to increased cohesion (patriotism) and the RWA triad: idealization of in-group norms and values ("they hate us for our freedoms"); willingness to sanction deviates (attacks against Arab Muslims in the United States); and unconditional support for in-group leaders (increased poll ratings for president and Congress after 9/11). For Chinese and Muslim students, however, U.S. policies in Muslim and Arab states from Morocco to Pakistan are part of the explanation of 9/11. Theoretically, it is not surprising that the group attacked sees the attack in a different light; Americans identify more with the victims. There is a puzzle, however, in finding that Chinese and Muslim students have similar views of U.S. reactions to 9/11; group dynamics theory would suggest that Muslim students should be more negative, insofar as U.S. reactions are aimed at Muslims.

As noted several times, the response to out-group threat is one of the most reliable predictions of group dynamics theory. The same dynamic noted in discussion of the Jewish-Palestinian conflict appears for Americans in the patriotic rituals and executive authority that followed the terror attacks of 9/11. Indeed it is likely that a principal aim of the 9/11 attacks was to instigate the U.S. response that would mobilize Muslims behind al Qaeda (McCauley, 2002). The membership of al Qaeda is largely in the diaspora of Muslim Arabs who have been driven out of their native countries by authoritarian regimes. They lost the political contest at home, but hope that U.S. response in stigmatizing Muslims and attacking terrorism worldwide will threaten and kill enough Muslims to produce the jihad they seek. Group dynamics makes terrorism a strategy of jujitsu, in which the opponent's strength is used against him.

The cases considered again show both positive and negative potential for contact between groups differing in ethnicity and culture. Efforts to mobilize the potential for peace are a test of the understanding brought by these cases.

PREVENTION AND MANAGEMENT OF CULTURAL CONFLICT AND ETHNIC VIOLENCE

Contact in the Workplace

As represented by Brislin and Liu (chap. 12), multinational corporations may offer the most promising situation for attaining the requirements of the contact hypothesis. The crucial condition for positive effects of contact is that members of different groups should work together for common goals. This condition is difficult to arrange in ad hoc groups, where common goals seldom extend beyond the hours or days of a contact workshop (Maoz, 2000b; McCauley, Wright & Harris, 2000). In the workplace, however, there are important common goals associated with the production of the goods or services in a competitive market. Cooperative interdependence among the members of groups working for common goals is the "Business Case for Diversity."

Brislin and Liu also point to the potential of cross-cultural training in the form of "critical incident" explorations of cultural differences. Here, too, the workplace offers a promising forum. Each corporation has its own culture, and new hires are in the position of immigrants to a new country. The immigrant expects to learn and adapt to the new culture, thus avoiding the kind of competition Forbes describes (chap. 4) over who should pay the costs of adapting. Like any immigrant, however, the employee has the option of maintaining his native culture outside the workplace.

Learning to live and work in another country can even increase the sense of identification with home country, as Kosmitzki (1996) found for Germans and Americans working abroad in America and Germany. Again, knowledge and even affection at the individual level of cultural contact does not necessarily control the perceived relationship between cultural groups.

Examples of Peace Preserved in Bulgaria, India, Northern Ireland, and Texas

Levin and Rabrenovic (chap. 13) join Draguns in drawing our attention to examples of ethnic peace where ethnic violence might have been expected. Their first example, Bulgarians' support for Jewish Bulgarians against the Nazis, goes beyond mere absence of ethnic conflict. Rather it is a heartening example of mass support for tolerance and sympathy. Levin and Rabrenovic see this support as flowing from individual-level affective ties linking Bulgarian Jews with others in their communities; they note that Bulgarian Jews were dispersed in residence and occupation so as to offer no distinctiveness as an ethnic group. They also note, however, the organizational structures that expressed support for Jews in Bulgaria. The Union of Lawyers, the Orthodox Church, and the Writer's Union—despite being already purged of Jews—all intervened as organizations against transportation of Bulgarian Jews.

In several other examples, Levin and Rabrenovic find ethnic peace where ethnic riots might have been expected. In two Indian cities, Calicut and Surat, peace between Hindus and Muslims seems to have been preserved by a combination of individual-level affective ties and the intervention of integrated trade associations. In "Dunville," Northern Ireland, again both individual-level contacts and integrated business and civic organizations are cited. In Jasper, Texas, peace was preserved after a racially motivated murder by the intervention of racially integrated government and civic agencies. This peace is the more remarkable because Jasper was very strongly segregated by race, such as to leave few interracial friendships.

Thus the common denominator of these examples is the existence of some kind of organizational intervention against ethnic violence. The examples differ in level of personal contact or affective ties between groups, but in every case there is a strong role played by civic, business, or government organization that mediates between individual sentiment and intergroup relations. Interdependence in these organizations seems to have brought not only cohesion, but also the capacity to turn cohesion into action. Without organizational expression, individual sentiments may be helpless, as even good soldiers are helpless when broken from their combat units. The difference between a soldier and a prisoner of war

(POW) is organization, the difference made evident when hundreds of POWs can be herded along by a few inattentive guards.

Learning from Failure in Peace Education

In contrast to the optimism of other contributors, McCauley and Bock (chap. 14) begin from an experience of failure. They describe a substantial, multilevel, long-term intervention, under charismatic leadership, that was undertaken to improve relations between Hindus and Muslims living in the shanty towns of Ahmedabad, India. This intervention had its successes but could not compete with instigations to violence based on manipulation of religious symbols. Why not?

Recent research on "negativity dominance" has found a broad tendency for humans to pay more attention to loss and punishment than to gain and reward. In particular, evaluative and moral judgments seem to be dominated by negative acts, such that we judge others not at their best, or even at their average, but according to their worst behaviors. Although admitting that existing research is almost all at the level of judgments of individuals, McCauley and Bock argue that negativity dominance is very likely to infect judgments of groups as well. Thus, one attack from members of another group can undermine years of patient building of positive intergroup relations: one loss and hurt outweigh dozens of cooperations and mutual rewards.

McCauley and Bock see negativity dominance as the Achilles' heel of interventions that focus on building positive intergroup relations. They suggest that successful interventions should prepare specifically to intervene against the impact of negative intergroup events. They offer several initial suggestions in this direction, including preparing moral denunciation of perpetrators of violence by leaders of the perpetrators' group, preparing in-group and intergroup networks to quash rumors supporting violence, and, as a last resort, preparing use of force to deter or control intergroup violence. These suggestions owe much to Horowitz's (2000) analysis of "The Deadly Ethnic Riot."

"Seeds of Peace": The Special Problems of Ethnic Conflict

Worchel (chap. 15) provides a succinct review of social psychological theories of intergroup conflict, and points to the distance between these theories and the distinctive difficulties of ethnic and cultural conflict. Ethnic conflict is particularly difficult to resolve because such conflict often involves competition over land and history—resources that are not easily compromised. Homeland and history are of course the substance and symbol of continuity for a group, just as personal history and possessions are the substance and symbol of individual continuity. Terror management theory suggests that it is precisely the continuity of a group—its long history and its prospect of an indefinite future—that gives group membership power as a buffer against individual mortality.

Worchel also points to the indelible quality of ethnicity as part of what is special about ethnic identification. Although a social constructionist might note that individuals do sometimes pass successfully as members of another ethnic group, it is certainly true that ethnicity is in many societies more difficult to change than citizenship or occupation. Again, the relatively indelible quality of ethnic identification can be understood as guarantor of the group continuity that, according to terror management theory, makes a group an antidote to mortality.

For Worchel, one implication of the special power of ethnic identity is that the prescriptions of the contact hypothesis are not likely to be very helpful. In particular, the appeal to a common identity—a common humanity—is not likely to work if the larger identity is seen as undermining or competing with a powerful ethnic identity. The Seeds of Peace program that Worchel describes takes individuals from ethnic hot spots and puts ethnically integrated teams into competition. Theoretically, the competition should build increased cohesion among the ethnically diverse individuals on each team, and indeed Seeds of Peace does seem to build positive relationships at the individual level. Unfortunately, the connection between the interpersonal level and the intergroup level is far from automatic.

LESSONS FROM GROUP DYNAMICS

The question animating this volume is whether increased interethnic and intercultural contact in a globalizing world should lead to more or less conflict. The various contributions have suggested a complex array of answers, a complexity of "it depends" that ranges from considerable optimism to realistic pessimism. In broad terms, the answers depend upon the level at which contact is considered.

At the individual level, the conditions of the contact hypothesis offer the possibility of increased liking among individuals from different ethnic groups. This positive prospect is limited by the difficulties, in practice, of arranging the conditions of equal status, interpersonal contact, and common goals that can build cohesion for members of an ethnically mixed group. These conditions may be most easily and naturally attained in the workplace, with its built-in common goals in production of goods and services. But when these conditions fail, as often they may fail in integrated schools and neighborhoods, the results are likely to be conflict and hostility even at the interpersonal level.

At the group level, the powerful phenomenon of group identification comes into play in ways that go beyond what economic or evolutionary self-interest can explain. The evolutionary origins of the capacity to care about large "categorical" groups are mysterious. Also mysterious is the special power of ethnic groups for political mobilization. In this regard, it is useful to remember the many twentieth-century intellectuals, not all of them Marxist, who thought that economic and class interest would dominate politics in the modern world. Although terror management theory offers some suggestions about why ethnicity is special, there is much yet to understand. It is not obvious why ethnicity and culture are so much more important politically than family or clan, or why Allport's "common humanity" is not more easily associated with political mobilization.

Several suggestions for future research emerge from this volume. One is that group dynamics theory, developed from studies of small face-to-face groups, may have something useful to say about cohesion in ethnic and national groups—where cohesion is usually called group identification. A second is that intergroup relations may depend more on perceptions at the intergroup level, especially perception of threat to the in-group, than on the individual perceptions that are the focus of the classical contact hypothesis. A third is that political action, including intergroup violence, depends on organizations that mediate between the individual and the nation or the state. Peace interventions may be more successful to the extent that such organizations can be mobilized.

Finally, a more general suggestion is that research on ethnic and cultural contact could profit from more attention to history. History, the constructed history of the in-group, appears to be a potent source of intergroup conflict. Another kind of history is the variation over centuries in the political power of ethnicity and culture. Nationalism is the idea that an *ethnie* should have its own state. This idea goes back at least to the Jewish people of the Old Testament, but the idea was submerged in a succession of empires from Roman days until roughly the French Revolution. Social scientists and politicians alike can look to this historical variation to transcend the current view of nationalism as "natural" and ethnic conflict as inevitable.

WHERE DO WE GO FROM HERE?

Exploring the Relation of Ethnic and Cultural Identity

Throughout this volume, authors have employed the terms "culture" (or cultural group) and "ethnicity" (or ethnic group) in ways that range between an implication of stability and an implication of fluidity and flexibility. One perspective is that ethnicity deals with characteristics that are generally stable and fixed. From this perspective, there are clear limits to the way in which cultural factors can influence the definition of ethnicity. The argument is that ethnicity generally involves biological and physical factors, history, origin, and homeland. These material factors place constraints on the degrees of freedom one has for interpretation.

An alternative perspective is that individuals only know the world and give meaning to it through culture, and whether they use one criterion or another to define and give importance to ethnicity will depend on their cultural background. Thus, for example, the Tutsi and the Hutu in Rwanda have traditionally focused on height differences, whereas in the United States skin color has been more important. Anthropological research suggests there are few limits to the criteria that could be used by people in their everyday lives to manufacture ethnic heritage and ethnic differences.

The distinction between culture and ethnicity has important implications for the study of global human conflict and harmony. One issue concerns whether the process and effect of identifying with cultural groups is the same as those that result from identification with ethnic groups. A second issue concerns possible differences in the opportunities for reducing conflict between cultural and ethnic groups.

In the short term, at least, ethnic barriers often prove to be resilient. During the Vietnam War, some American advisors were effective in gaining the trust of villagers by living in the villages, speaking the language, practicing the local customs, and even marrying local villagers. Although they became part of the cultural group, they were clearly not part of the ethnic group. Similarly, in Hawai'i, non-Hawaiians can be accepted as *kama'aine* by living and adopting the culture, but they will not be viewed as native Hawaiians. Viewed in a longer perspective, however, human history involves different ethnic groups merging and dividing, as migration takes place, armies move across nations and continents, and barriers eventually break down.

What is the implication of these distinctions for reducing intergroup conflict? Will contact have different effects in situations where the group distinction has different bases, cultural or ethnic? These questions offer fertile ground for future research initiatives.

Establishing Contact

As many of our contributors have pointed out, the contact hypothesis for reducing intergroup conflict has received a great deal of attention. The research has been largely aimed at determining the effect of intergroup contact and identifying the types of contact that are most conducive to improved intergroup relations. However, all of this assumes that contact can be invited and initiated. Research on both group and individual conflict suggests that conflict often results in autistic hostility and the desire to avoid contact with the enemy. Further, leaders of radical or fundamentalist groups often go to great lengths to prohibit contact between members of their groups and out-groups. Such contact may weaken in-group identification and, consequently, weaken commitment to the group. There is a real challenge for peacemakers in recognizing that contact may reduce attraction to the in-group, rather than simply increase attraction to the out-group.

Research must examine the steps that can be taken to encourage contact between members of different groups. Specifically, how can contact between cultural groups be achieved without reducing the pride individuals have in their own groups? This issue is at the heart of the debate over creating societies in the multicultural mode as opposed to the common group or melting pot model.

A Closing Comment

The issues surrounding cultural and ethnic group harmony are complex, but critically important to the future of humankind. The chapters in this book have addressed some of these issues and raised questions about other issues. The area of study is exciting from both a theoretical and practical standpoint. If the chapters have shown anything, it is that there is no single answer or quick fix to problems of intergroup conflict. As Worchel (1999) pointed out, improving intergroup harmony is like tending a garden: the process is never completed. The plot can be cultivated and the seeds planted, but the success of the garden depends on constant care such as watering, fertilizing, weeding, and pruning. The aim of this volume has been to explicate the approach rather than provide a formula for instant success.

REFERENCES

Asch, S. E. (1956). Studies of independence and conformity: A minority of one against a unanimous majority, *Psychological Monographs, 70*(9, Whole No. 416).

Converse, P., & Campbell, A. (1960). Political standards in secondary groups. In D. Cartwright & A. Zander (Eds.), *Group dynamics* (2nd ed.). Evanston, IL: Row, Peterson.

Festinger, L. (1950). Informal social communication. *Psychological Review, 57*, 271–282.

Festinger, L. (1954). A theory of social comparison processes. *Human Relations, 7*, 114–140.

Horowitz, D. L. (2001). *The deadly ethnic riot.* Berkeley, CA: University of California Press.

Kosmitzki, C. (1966). The reaffirmation of cultural identity in cross-cultural encounters. *Personality and Social Psychology Bulletin, 22*(3), 238–248.

Maoz, I. (2000a). Multiple conflicts and competing agendas: A framework for conceptualizing structured encounters between groups in conflict: The case of a coexistence project of Jews and Palestinians in Israel. *Peace and Conflict: Journal of Peace Psychology, 6*(2), 135–156.

Maoz, I. (2000b). An experiment in peace: Processes and effects in reconciliation aimed workshops of Israeli and Palestinian youth. *Journal of Peace Research 37*(6), 721–736.

McCauley, C. (1989). The nature of social influence in groupthink: Compliance and internalization. *Journal of Personality and Social Psychology, 57*, 250–260.

McCauley, C. (1998). Group dynamics in Janis's theory of groupthink: Backward and forward. *Organizational Behavior and Human Decision Processes, 73*, 142–162.

McCauley, C. (2002). Psychological issues in understanding terrorism and the response to terrorism. In C. Stout (Ed.), *The Psychology of Terrorism, Volume III Theoretical Understandings and Perspectives*, pp. 3–30. Westport, CT: Praeger.

McCauley, C., Wright, M., & Harris, M. (2000). Diversity workshops on campus: A survey of current practice at U.S. colleges and universities. *College Student Journal, 34*, 100–114.

Pyszczynski, T., Greenberg, J., & Solomon, S. (1997). Why do we need what we need? A terror management perspective on the roots of human social motivation. *Psychological Inquiry, 8*, 1–20.

Stephan, W. S., & Stephan, C. W. (2000). An integrated threat theory of prejudice. In S. Oskamp (Ed.), *Reducing prejudice and discrimination* pp. 23–46. Mahweh, NJ: Erlbaum.

Name Index

Subject Index

About the Contributors

WAYNE E. ALLEN received his Ph.D. in anthropology in 1998 from the University of California at Santa Barbara. In 1993–94, he was a Fulbright scholar to Canada and a UCSB IHC Humanities Fellow. Dr. Allen's research in the Northwest Territories among the Déné Indians from 1991–94 focused on participatory action research, community resource management, cultural and natural resource conservation practices, and resource sustainability. Dr. Allen was the executive director of the Traverse des Sioux Treaty Site History Center, a midsized museum, and the Nicollet County Historical Society in southern Minnesota from 1996–99, during which time he was also an adjunct professor at Minnesota State University, Mankato. He is currently an assistant professor in the Department of Ethnic Studies at Minnesota State University, Mankato. Dr. Allen's research and teaching interests focus on resource colonialism, environmental racism and environmental justice, political ecology, participatory action research, and Darwinian evolution and human behavioral ecology.

DANIEL BAR-TAL is professor of psychology at the School of Education and director of the Walter Lebach Institute for Jewish-Arab Coexistence through Education, Tel Aviv University. He also is coeditor of the *Palestine-Israel Journal*. He served as the president of the International Society of Political Psychology (1999–2000). His research interest is in political and social psychology, studying the psychological foundations of intractable conflicts and peace making. Specifically, he focuses on those societal beliefs and collective emotional orientations that feed the conflicts and those that facilitate conflict resolution and reconciliation. He authored *Group Beliefs* (Springer-Verlag, 1990) and *Shared Beliefs in a Society* (Sage, 2000) and coedited *Social Psychology of Intergroup Relations* (Springer-Verlag, 1988), *Stereotyping and Prejudice* (Springer-Verlag, 1989), *Patriotism in the Lives of Individuals and Nations* (Nelson Hall, 1997) *Concerned with Security* (JAI, 1998), *How Children Understand War and Peace* (Jossey-Bass, 1999), and *Patriotism in Israel* (in press). In addition, he has published over one hundred articles and chapters in major social and political psychological journals and books.

NARAN BILIK was born in Hohhot of Inner Mongolia of China on October 30, 1957. He studied English at Inner Mongolia Normal University, and got his master's and Ph.D. degrees in ethnology at the Central University of Nationalities in Beijing between 1982 and 1989. He is interested in semiotic studies of culture and ethnicity in China and East Asia. He is a professor and chief of the Sociocultural Anthropology Department at the Institute of Ethnology and Anthropology, Chinese Academy of Social Sciences in Beijing. He is the coauthor of *Contemporary Minority Migration, Education and Ethnicity in China* (Edward Elgar, 2001) and author of *The Ethnicity of Anthropology in China* (Critique of Anthropology, Vol. 22(2): 133–148, 2002) and another five articles in English. He also published in Chinese five books and over one hundred articles.

JOSEPH G. BOCK is an adjunct professor in the Conflict Transformation Program of Eastern Mennonite University in Harrisonburg, Virginia. Previously, he was visiting professor in the International Relations Department at Hebrew University and served as country representative for Catholic Relief Services in Jerusalem, West Bank and Gaza Strip, and Islamabad. He has a Ph.D. in International Relations from the School of International Service of American University in Washington, D.C.

DANA BRAMEL did his graduate work at Harvard and Stanford, studying briefly with Gordon Allport and then with Leon Festinger. He is emeritus professor of psychology at the State University of New York at Stony Brook, where he has taught since 1965, serving for many years as director of the program in social psychology. A long-time member of the Society for the Psychological Study of Social Issues, his research has focused on intergroup perception/conflict and the political history of social psychology.

RICHARD W. BRISLIN is professor of management and industrial relations at the College of Business Administration, University of Hawaii. He has directed yearly programs for university professors planning to introduce cross-cultural studies into their courses and for cross-cultural trainers who want to increase the range of programs they can offer. He is the co-developer of materials used in cross-cultural training programs (e.g., *Intercultural Interactions: A Practical Guide*, 2nd ed., 1996) and is author of a text in cross-cultural psychology (*Understanding Culture's Influence on Behavior*, 2nd ed., 2000). He has co-edited two volumes for SAGE Publication of modules for training and educational programs: *Improving Intercultural Interactions: Modules for Cross-Cultural Training Programs*. One of his books, *The Art of Getting Things Done: A Practical Guide to the Use of Power*, was a Book-of-the-Month Club selection in 1992. He has been a G. Stanley Hall Lecturer for the American Psychological Association. He is frequently asked to give workshops for American and Asian managers working on international assignments, and the training materials he has prepared are widely used in various international organizations. His most recent coauthored book is *Turning Bricks into Jade: Critical Incidents for Mutual Understanding among Chinese and Americans* (Intercultural Press, 2000). He writes a weekly column on culture and cultural differences, focusing on their impact in the workplace, for the Sunday edition of the *Honolulu Star Bulletin*.

NAPOLEON A. CHAGNON received his Ph.D. in anthropology from the University of Michigan, Ann Arbor, in 1966. He began conducting ethnographic fieldwork among the Yanomamö Indians in the Orinoco River region of southern Venezuela in 1964 and continued his research for over 35 years. He recently retired from the Department of Anthropology at the University of California, Santa Barbara, where he is now professor emeritus. His ethnographic monograph is now the best-selling ethnography in the history of anthropology. Dr. Chagnon has made significant pioneering contributions in the areas of ethnographic field research, sociobiology, Darwinian evolutionary theory, and human behavioral ecology, especially in relation to the causes of tribal warfare. Dr. Chagnon now resides in Traverse City, Michigan.

OHAD DAVID is a doctoral student at the School of Education of Tel Aviv University. His interests focus on the nature, evolvement, and change of social identity.

JURIS G. DRAGUNS was born in Riga, Latvia. Displaced in World War II, he completed his primary education in Latvia, graduated from high school in Germany, and obtained his bachelor's and doctoral degrees in the United States. His Ph.D. in clinical psychology was awarded by the University of Rochester. He held clinical and research positions at the Rochester, New York, and Worcester, Massachusetts, state hospitals prior to accepting a faculty appointment at the Pennsylvania State University, which he held for 30 years. He is now professor emeritus of psychology.

Dr. Draguns's research and conceptual interests are focused upon the applied aspects of cross-cultural psychology, with emphasis upon psychopathology, psychotherapy, ethnic conflict and its resolution, and the effects of changes in political systems upon social behavior and personal experience. He has taught and lectured at the East-West Center in Honolulu, Hawaii; Johannes Gutenberg University in Mainz, Germany; Lund University in Sweden; Flinders University of South Australia; National Taiwan University in Taipei; University of Latvia and Baltic Russian Institute in Riga; and Interamerican University in Cholula, Mexico.

JOHN DUCKITT is an associate professor of psychology at the University of Auckland in New Zealand. He is the author of *The Social Psychology of Prejudice* (New York: Praeger, 1992/1994), the coeditor (with Stanley Renshon) of *Political Psychology: Cultural and Crosscultural Foundations* (New York: New York University Press, and London: Macmillan, 2000) and the author of more than 80 journal articles, reviews, and book chapters. His work has appeared in journals such as *Political Psychology, Journal of Personality and Social Psychology,* and the *American Psychologist,* and he has recently contributed chapters to *Advances in Experimental Social Psychology* and the new *Handbook of Political Psychology*. He serves or has served on the editorial boards of *Political Psychology,* the *Journal of Social Psychology,* and the *South African Journal of Psychology.*

H. D. FORBES teaches political science at the University of Toronto. He is the author of two books, *Nationalism, Ethnocentrism, and Personality: Social Science and Critical Theory* (University of Chicago Press, 1985) and *Ethnic Conflict: Commerce, Culture, and the Contact Hypothesis* (Yale University Press, 1997), and the editor of an anthology, *Canadian Political Thought* (Oxford University Press, 1985). He is currently working on a book-length study of multiculturalism in Canada.

YUEH-TING LEE is an immigrant from China. Yueh-Ting Lee, who received his Ph.D. from the Department of Psychology at State University of New York at Stony Brook, is currently the chairperson and professor in the Department of Ethnic Studies at Minnesota State University, Mankato. Professor Lee has published five books and numerous articles in international and national refereed journals both in Chinese and in English. Coedited with Professors Clark McCauley and Juris Draguns, Dr. Lee's recent book *Personality and Person Perceptions across Cultures* (Lawrence Erlbaum Associates, 1999) has been well received. His research focuses on ethnic and cultural conflict, stereotypes, social identity, and beliefs about justice. As a social and cross-cultural psychologist, he has also taught courses in psychology and cultural and ethnic studies for over 12 years in American higher education. In addition to teaching and research, he has been invited to do consulting and training for multinational corporations and public agencies both in the USA and in China regarding cultural competency, differences appreciation, and conflict management.

JACK LEVIN, Ph.D., is the Brudnick Professor of Sociology and Criminology and director of the Brudnick Center on Violence and Conflict at Northeastern University. He has authored or coauthored a number of books, including *Hate Crimes Revisited, Overkill: Serial Killing and Mass Murder Exposed, The Will to Kill: Making Sense of Senseless Murder,* and *The Violence of Hate,* and articles in professional journals including *Criminology, Justice Quarterly, Journal of Interpersonal Violence, Journal of Social Issues,* and *Youth and Society.* Dr. Levin has spoken to college, community, and professional groups around the world including those at the White House Conference on Hate Crimes.

JOYCE F. LIU earned her master's degree in clinical psychology at the University of Wisconsin, Madison. She pursued doctoral studies at the University of Hawaii at Manoa, focusing on cross-cultural, intercultural, and ethnic minority psychology. Joyce is translating her academic training into application at E*Trade Financial by developing their diversity recruitment and retention initiatives. Recent publications include coauthored articles in *Culture, Diversity, and Ethnic Minority Psychology.*

CLARK MCCAULEY is professor of psychology at Bryn Mawr College, and a director of the Solomon Asch Center for Study of Ethnopolitical Conflict at the University of Pennsylvania. He received his Ph.D. in social psychology from the University of Pennsylvania in 1970. His research interests include stereotypes and the psychology of group identification, group dynamics and intergroup conflict, and the psychological foundations of ethnic conflict and genocide. His recent work includes a new measure of intergroup contact, "the exposure index."

FATHALI M. MOGHADDAM is professor of psychology at Georgetown University. Born in Iran, educated in England, and presently in the United States via work in various Western and non-Western countries, his main research focus is on justice and culture. His most recent books are *The Individual and Society* (2002), *Understanding Terrorism* (with T. Marsella, 2003), and *The Psychology of Human Rights and Duties* (with N. Finkel, forthcoming).

NETA OREN is a doctoral student at the Political Science Department of Tel Aviv University. Her interest focuses on the changes of public opinion through intractable conflicts.

VICTOR OTTATI completed his undergraduate degree at the University of Michigan (Ann Arbor). He earned his Ph.D. in social psychology from the University of Illinois (Urbana–Champaign). He is currently an associate professor within the Department of Psychology at Loyola University Chicago. His basic research interests fall within the areas of attitudes and social cognition. His applied research interests include political psychology, cross-cultural psychology, mental illness stigma, and consumer psychology.

HANH HUY PHAN was born and raised in South Vietnam, where she received a baccalaureate in both French and Vietnamese prior to coming to the United States to pursue her graduate education. She received a B.S. and M.S. in sociology and completed her Ph.D. course work in the same field. She is currently a professor of ethnic studies at Minnesota State University, Mankato. Her teaching interests deal with multiculturalism, interracial/interethnic relations (dating, family, adoption), sexism, racism, women of color, and Asian American studies.

LUIS POSAS is currently an assistant professor in the Department of Sociology as well as in the Department of Ethnic Studies at Minnesota State University, Mankato. As a sociologist he has a strong interest in the study of structural inequalities, especially along the lines of ethnicity in the United States and abroad. From this perspective, he has taught several courses that include cultural pluralism, Latino studies, urban minority problems, and others. He has also carried out research on the social dynamics involved in the early stages of the settlement process of ethnically distinct groups in specific areas of southern Illinois and southern Minnesota.

STEPHANIE POWER is a Ph.D. student in the Department of Sociology and Social Work at Texas Woman's University, and a native of Canada. Her main area of interest is social inequality.

GORDANA RABRENOVIC, Ph.D., is associate professor of sociology and education, and associate director of the Brudnick Center on Violence and Conflict at Northeastern University. Her substantive specialties include community studies, urban education, and intergroup conflict and violence. She is the author of the book *Community Builders: A Tale of Neighborhood Mobilization in Two Cities* (1996), and coeditor of the book *Community Politics and Policy* (1999) and the *American Behavioral Scientist* special issue on hate crimes and ethnic conflict (2001). Dr. Rabrenovic is currently studying racial disparities in suspensions and expulsions from public schools.

KAN SHI, Ph.D., is a professor of industrial and organizational psychology, and Human Resources management director of the Center for Social, Economic & Behavior Research, Institute of Psychology, Chinese Academy of Sciences.

SEIJI TAKAKU is a professor of psychology at Soka University of America, Aliso Viejo, California. His research interests focus on cross-cultural examinations of people's apology (and excuse)-giving behavior, interpersonal forgiveness, and various strategies involved in interpersonal/intergroup conflict resolutions. His recent publications include articles in the *Journal of Applied Social Psychology* (2000), *the Journal of Social Psychology* (2001), and *the Journal of Language and Social Psychology* (2001).

STEPHEN WORCHEL is dean of the College of Arts and Sciences at the University of Hawaii at Hilo and professor of psychology. He has previously held academic positions at the University of Southern Maine, Texas A&M University, University of Virginia, and the University of North Carolina. Dr. Worchel has been a visiting scholar at Fudan University, University of the Basque Country, University of Waikato, and University of Padua. For the past three years, Dr. Worchel has worked with the Seeds of Peace International Camp, a camp that brings together adolescents from cultures in conflict including the Middle East, Cyprus, and the Baltic countries. Dr. Worchel has published numerous research articles on intergroup relations, conflict and violence, group dynamics, and social identity. His most recent book, *Written in Blood: Ethnic Identity and the Struggle for Human Harmony* (Worth, 1999), explored the importance of ethnic identity and its role in violent conflict. Dr. Worchel is presently working on a National Science Foundation grant to examine approaches for reducing hostility and negative stereotyping between ethnic groups engaged in violent conflict.

GONGGU YAN, Ph.D., is an associate professor at the school of psychology at Beijing Normal University, China. He was a visiting scholar at the University of South Florida and Old Dominion University in the USA. Dr. Yan is actively involved in applications of psychological theory and technology in human resource management, especially in personnel selection, performance assessment, and development. He is also interested in cross-cultural comparison between Chinese and Western personalities. His most recent work focuses on developing a competence model and corresponding assessment tools for an international pharmaceutical corporation.

PHILIP Q. YANG is associate professor of sociology at Texas Woman's University. His current research interests include immigration, racial and ethnic studies, Asian Americans, and transnationalism. Yang is the author of *Ethnic Studies: Issues and Approaches* (State University of New York Press, 2000) and *Post-1965 Immigration to the United States: Structural Determinants* (Praeger, 1995) and the editor of *Introduction to Ethnic Studies: A Reader* (Kendall/Hunt, 1999). His recent articles have appeared in such journals as *International Migration Review, Ethnic and Racial Studies, Diaspora, Journal of Asian American Studies, Population and Environment,* and *Journal of Ethnicity in Substance Abuse,* and in edited volumes such as *Ethnic Los Angeles* (Russell Sage Foundation, 1996).